The *Assoluta*
Voice in Opera,
1797–1847

Gemma

(nell' Opera Gemma di Vergy)

The *Assoluta* Voice in Opera, 1797–1847

by Geoffrey S. Riggs

McFarland & Company, Inc., Publishers

Jefferson, North Carolina, and London

Frontispiece: Giuseppina Ronzi–De Begnis in the title role of Donizetti's *Gemma di Vergy*. Photograph courtesy *Opera Quarterly*, Oxford University Press.

Library of Congress Cataloguing-in-Publication Data

Riggs, Geoffrey S.
    The assoluta voice in opera, 1797–1847 / by Geoffrey S. Riggs.
        p.   cm.
    Includes bibliographical references and index.

    ISBN 0-7864-1401-4 (library binding : 50# alkaline paper)

    1. Singing — History and criticism.   2. Opera — 19th century.
3. Style, Musical.   I. Title.
ML1460.R54   2003
782.6'6 — dc21   2002152266

British Library cataloguing data are available

©2003 Geoffrey S. Riggs. All rights reserved

No part of this book may be reproduced or transmitted in any form or by any means, electronic or mechanical, including photocopying or recording, or by any information storage and retrieval system, without permission in writing from the publisher.

Manufactured in the United States of America

McFarland & Company, Inc., Publishers
  Box 611, Jefferson, North Carolina 28640
  www.mcfarlandpub.com

To the memory of Wendy Hilton (1931–2002),
whose staunch confidence
and enthusiasm in a prolonged project
helped make this book a reality.

Acknowledgments

This book marks the culmination of a journey of twenty-five years.

Completion might not have been possible without the timely assistance of Robert Gutman. To him I offer appreciation and thanks. Likewise, I can never repay the generosity of those artists who took the time to provide their insights to me while I was in the throes of preparing this project: Martina Arroyo, Grace Bumbry, Katherine Ciesinski, Lauren Flanigan, Christa Ludwig, Olivia Stapp, and Frederica von Stade.

Helpful collectors have included Constantine Cassolas, Anthony Coggi, Bill DePeter, Enrique Eskenazi, Regina Fiorito, Henry Fogel, Douglas Fox, John Hagen, Paul Jaretzki, George Jellinek, Tom Kaufman, Brian Kellow, Mark D. Lew, Eugene Moon, Ed Rosen, Mal Ross, and Joost Van Berge.

Others also generous with their time have been Jill Bahcall, Sandy Carland, John De Gaetani, Jenny Rose, and Nathalie Wagner. The feisty world of opera fora on the Internet also introduced me to unlikely-sounding but helpful contributors like "Brian," "Evans 9899," John "sills," and "REG."

For assistance in obtaining important materials, I thank Harold Bruder, E. Thomas Glasow, Fiona Willis and the staff of Oxford University Press.

I also owe gratitude to Don McCormick, Seth Winner, Jacqueline Davis, Sara Velez, and the Rodgers & Hammerstein Archives staff at the New York Public Library for their assistance during prolonged research analyzing many recordings of the past and present.

Any writer would be lucky to have an editor as alert to consistency of style as Barbara Griggs. Given the complex descriptive challenges in a retrospective like this, I hope I have still honored her high standards for lucid and effective writing. I am deeply in her debt.

Last, for physical layout in the book, I must thank my wife Liz, who has had to coax, cajole, and sometimes drag me, kicking and screaming, into the twenty-first century and the wonders of computer technology. Special features like the charts I owe entirely to her continuing patience and good humor.

Contents

Preface

In the wake of the *bel canto* revival inspired by Maria Callas, a whole repertoire of heroic coloratura roles, composed from circa 1800 to 1850, was reintroduced for the first time in nearly a century.

Unlike the Mimis, the Aidas, the Carmens, these heroic parts have had no continuing performance tradition. One can talk of the heirs to the *verismo* tradition for Mimi, of the high mezzos who maintain *Carmen* as a staple of the lyric stage, and so on, but present-day interpreters of the heroic *bel canto* cannot be considered the true heirs to an authentic tradition. With all of her imposing musicianship, Callas was fundamentally a twentieth-century phenomenon.

The Assoluta *Voice in Opera, 1797–1847*, traces the available contemporary descriptions of some of the divas who created heroic roles from the Cherubini Médée (1797) to the Verdi Lady Macbeth (1847): Giuditta Pasta, Maria Malibran, Giuseppina Ronzi–De Begnis. These extraordinary singers helped shape an operatic tradition that emerged briefly during a time of transition. While the coloratura style typical of the eighteenth-century *opera seria* had not yet gone out of fashion, the newer, more forceful orchestral style of Beethoven and Weber was by this time exerting enough influence on vocal writing to require from a diva an unprecedented power of vocal projection. The combination of this new vocal forcefulness with the traditional *bel canto* agility makes this the most taxing music ever composed for the female voice. Bellini summed it up when he wrote triumphantly to Giuditta Pasta that he had finally fashioned a role for her "encyclopedic" talents.

Contemporary descriptions of the original superstars for whom these transitional roles were written and remarks by singers who have sung some of them (including Martina Arroyo, Grace Bumbry, Lauren Flanigan, Christa Ludwig, and Olivia Stapp) are used to illustrate the technical and musical challenges that these roles present to today's singers. Such parts should be sung only by those artists who exceed the narrow boundaries of the traditionally understood vocal categories.

1

To understand the extent to which these boundaries have been breached in our own time, retrospectives are provided on the history of these roles on disc, showing how much the composers' intentions have either been honored or ignored.

❧ 1 ❧

Earliest *Virtuosi*

Many of the connotations of vocal category have nothing to do with the purely musical uses to which a voice type may be put. The harsh, rough bass voice is freighted with connotations of rusticity, crudity, and low class, and was for decades confined to comedy. Or the high soprano voice would suggest, if used in the nonmusical context, youth first of all. The modern tenor would suggest a noble, high-strung impetuosity, and the baritone a mature, more settled quality, and so on. These vocal connotations are extra-musical and therefore primarily of dramatic value. They work their effect through nonmusical means.

The castrato voice, lacking such connections to the stereotypes of real life, derived its drama from its music and its musical feats. Some people prefer the vibrato-less voice of the falsetto or male alto to the natural voice of the true countertenor because they prefer the voice to be deprived of its human associations and to have a disembodied quality. In my opinion, this is not all that the human voice is about. But that is a matter of taste. Other people believe that the beauty of musical instruments increases as they approximate the qualities of the human voice. Of course, the castrato sound was a naturally produced one (unlike the falsetto) that remained an abstraction in its timbre, not its vocal production.

In reading the glowing contemporary descriptions of the effect that the greatest castrati (Farinelli, Caffarelli, Pacchierotti) made in performance, one can only imagine an expressive excitement combining compassionate sympathy, overwhelming authority, haunting melancholy, and poetic, rhapsodic trance. Apparently, all of this was conveyed through a spontaneous musicianship demonstrating the mastery of a three-octave range projected with clarion vocal resonance, powerful and brilliant, easy stamina, and incredibly long breath control. This resulted in a sweeping line, coloristic variety, impeccable agility, and a relaxed, smooth top. Small wonder that these castrati *virtuosi* could create such a furor.

It is true that the early twentieth-century recordings of Alessandro Moreschi (the last of the castrato line) hardly suggest such vocal completeness, yet, as Henry Pleasants reminds us:

> Moreschi was not a brilliant performer, and he was past his prime when these records were made. ... It is important ... when listening to them, to remember that it is a man in his mid-forties that we are hearing, not a Farinelli or a Caffarelli in his early twenties, and that in the age of bel canto Moreschi, even in his prime, would probably not have been numbered among the great singers.[1]

The attraction and influence that the castrati had at the peak of their own era, and the curiosity and awe they occasionally attracted during succeeding generations cannot be exaggerated. That influence was due to a vocal gift that, brilliantly and artistically developed, could yield the listener an experience roughly equivalent to the most startling combination of power and agility imaginable from either the female register or the male sound. We can perhaps understand why every other kind of voice was considered secondary to this unique phenomenon for so long.

In the *opera seria*, the female voice — a "natural," "human" sound — would sometimes be used with similar pyrotechnics when portraying a supernatural figure. Even here, when the woman's voice would be used in this way, the actual vocal range was never as wide as the castrato's. Though the sorceress's singing might be as heroic as the castrato's, only the latter might counterbalance heroic sentiments with more touchingly human ones. Thus, even in these instances, the patterns of expression given the castrato were drawn from a wider palette than those given the female singer. The application of multi-colored vocal writing to the mortal woman of strong character emerged only at the very end of the eighteenth century.

Indeed, it would not be going too far to say that opera made the castrato and the castrato made opera. The chief critical reason for this craze for both may have lain not just in the exotic symbolism of speech expressed through song or in the remarkable qualities of the mere sound of a Farinelli or a Caffarelli in his prime. It lay also in the fact that this androgynous sound appealed to something universal in us: the actual feats it accomplished in the exploitation of such an unusual sound. Thus, whether the fictional character being represented was either male or female (castrati portrayed both sexes on stage), the music in the traditional *opere serie* used to portray such characters might exploit both aspects of such a voice simultaneously. For instance, a young castrato portraying a damsel in distress might display heroic, powerful tones one evening (gender bending) while the same castrato portraying an obscure prince out of the classics in the next evening's opera might dazzle the audience with the lightness and ease of his pyrotechnics and crystal-clear top (again, gender bending). Most important, to those accustomed to the form, nothing in all of this would seem ludicrous in any way.

One could argue that the theatrical effectiveness of a heroic character's moment of intense crisis did not just spring from the mere presence of an actor on stage giving a visual image of that character. Rather, it sprang out of the artistic transformation of the character's personal crisis into a universal one through the probing exploration embodied in dramatic song. Thus, the operatic spectacle drew its chief dramatic strength from the dazzling accomplishments of the singer rather than the strictly functional words of the libretto. A voice was judged properly theatrical and musically effective not just because of intrinsic sound but because of what that sound could do. This subtracted any naturalistic associations from the performer's actual voice, which was only one step away from subtracting the gender associations that went along with it.

The metaphor worked purely through what the voice was doing rather than through its intrinsic sound. Only with a musical and powerful voice, and one capable of the myriad shifts of color and weight already suggested at the beginning of this chapter, could so wide a musical and emotional range be expressed that the audience, swept off its feet, would feel they had witnessed a complete image of human experience.

That image became doubly exciting in its reconciling of vocal opposites within one and the same performer. Many of the roles written for the greatest castrati encompassed not merely a blurring of gender but also a blurring of the distinctions usually applied to the equivalent female vocal categories (soprano, mezzo, etc.). Farinelli, for instance, would make a practice of singing both a soprano aria and a mezzo aria in the same evening,[2] and Pacchierotti was variously described as both a soprano and an alto castrato by contemporaries.[3]

The development of the use of a large range as a metaphor for the complete human experience later became the woman's domain in the sixty or so years from ca. 1790 to ca. 1850. It is at the end of the eighteenth century, in a generation that includes the more natural characterizations of Gluck and Mozart, that some critics perceive a greater realism in opera because of an increased demand for a one-to-one correspondence with physical and sonic reality. (True, the development of the trouser role for the female voice may not quite fit this notion; still, the travesty tradition is really a remnant of the castrato tradition.)

At any rate, for these next sixty years, we finally see and hear from a woman's voice, while in the act of portraying an actual flesh-and-blood character, the transfer of the castrato-exploiting metaphor of a large range onto the "mere mortal" portrayed more "realistically" by the female singer. That metaphor, as the woman takes over this kind of singing, still consists of the particular becoming the universal through the breaching of standard vocal categories. The rest of this book will be concerned with the nature of such vocal writing and of that rare breed of singer, whom I shall term the *assoluta*, intended for such music.

❧ 2 ❧

Women's Voices

Most female voices tend to fall naturally into four principal categories: coloratura/lyric soprano, dramatic soprano, mezzo-soprano, and contralto. The light soprano usually sings high, florid music; the dramatic soprano sings high, stentorian phrases; the mezzo sings mostly in the middle register; the contralto, mostly in the lower register. Occasionally, a phenomenal singer comes along who can encompass every aspect of vocal writing for the female voice. Giuseppina Ronzi-De Begnis, Giuditta Pasta, Isabella Colbran, Mary Anne Paton, and other very special divas of this sort who thrived during the first half of the nineteenth century had specific roles written for them that exploited this phenomenal ability. I would guess that at least nine operas featured exactly such roles during the fifty years starting with the premiere of Cherubini's *Médée* in 1797. Some of these operas, such as *Norma*, maintain a tenuous currency in today's opera houses.

These roles all require the highest degree of agility for their floridly intricate passages, together with the heroic weight necessary to sing over an emotionally charged orchestra. As a rule, the light soprano will lack the lower register, as the contralto will lack the upper, and the true dramatic soprano, whose upper register is frequently the most sensuous part of her range, will lack both the flexibility on top and, occasionally, the strength in the low notes. The mezzo will have both her strength and her flexibility in the mid-range, whereas all the roles we are dealing with have bifurcated tessituras, about half above and half below the middle register itself where comparatively little time is spent.

It is the fundamental variety of *fach* (category) that the creators of these roles must have shared that has determined, for the purposes of this study, my designation of both the roles and their interpreters as simply *assoluta*. The term *prima donna* has historically been used for the first lady of an opera house, and the term *assoluta* has been understood to be merely an intensive of that august position. But the first lady of an opera company could sometimes be a straight soprano with nothing mezzo-ish in her at all, or she could be (as Madame Stolz at the Paris Opera of the 1830s and 1840s was) a straight mezzo who rarely sings anything soprano-ish. Obviously, therefore, a term with more stringent connotations of specific vocal category is what is needed. As for the term *soprano assoluta*, it has come to suggest something very specific — perhaps, too specific: the perfect soprano who is capable of taking on roles only within the soprano range. *Soprano assoluta* has been occasionally used to refer to the role of Norma and to some of the other roles we are examining. In my use of the term *assoluta* by itself to suggest a distinct category, I am expanding these connotations even further beyond soprano limits, thus using *assoluta* both for a kind of singer and a kind of role. I have chosen this somewhat *ad hoc* term because, as we shall see, roles like Médée, Lady Macbeth, Norma, and so on, transcend traditional bounds of mezzo, dramatic, and coloratura. There are enough of these unusual roles to point to the inevitable conclusion that here we have an already defined *fach*. Hence, my designation of *assoluta* pure and simple, both for the roles themselves and for those special singers who can truly do them justice.

It is necessary to reevaluate these roles and their meaning, because it is obvious they are not now generally understood. Possibly because there has been a fitful history of performance, we have lost track of the composers' intentions and have forgotten the original creators of these roles. This special kind of heroine is absent from the more familiar works of Mozart, Verdi, Wagner, or Puccini, which have held the stage during the last hundred years. Except for certain performances of *Norma* or *Nabucco* and the occasional *Macbeth*, the *assoluta* was almost completely forgotten until the Callas revivals of the late '40s and '50s.

The *assoluta*'s heyday was the first four or five decades of the nineteenth century, the period which coincides with the flourishing of Romanticism all over Europe, and she represents the artistic emancipation from the neo-Aristotelian proprieties of character: consistency, suitability to station, trueness to type, appropriateness of behavior, and so forth, along with the Romantic interest in human heroism, the defiance of the gods, the extremes of human character, of situation and behavior, and a total unpredictability. Whereas in the *opera seria* we have already drawn attention to the fact that the sorceress might show a kind of wildness, it was not until the advent of the music drama of character that the mature woman was finally portrayed in her infinite variety and heroism.

What more natural metaphor could there be for such a character than a voice of infinite variety with both heroic weight and flexibility? In opera, the expressive medium of character is the singing voice — it is the voice that is the persona of the music drama, not the face and figure as in the prose theatre. The voice in the *assoluta* repertoire is capable of daredevil feats with a chameleon's ability to change color, and she is therefore given the most difficult music to sing, high, low, trills, roulades, sustained notes. She must have the flexibility of the trapeze artist and the strength of the weight lifter. And this bewildering capability, these feats of vocal derring-do, are a metaphor for her heroism, and the breadth and variety of her character is measured by her astonishing range.

The various dualities in these *assoluta* roles have not gone unnoticed by musicologists and performers. Reference is made to their histrionic demands that go hand in hand with their technical vocal requirements; the point could also be made that these roles often require that both a public figure's demeanor and a private woman's introspective air be dramatically conveyed by the artist — all in the same evening. The most frequently mentioned duality in Norma, in the *Devereux* Elizabetta, or in any of these other roles, is their crucial juxtaposition of both coloratura and dramatic writing.

But, strangely, too little attention has been paid to the juxtaposition of vocal writing for both soprano and mezzo in one role. As we examine not just the music for these roles but the careers of the divas of the *ottocento* who created them, we find that this taxing repertoire seems as clearly linked to mezzo roles like the Bellini Romeo as to the standard soprano repertoire. At any rate, Ronzi–De Begnis, the first *Devereux* Elisabetta, also performed roles like Romeo along with Norma and Anna Bolena.[4] Giuditta Pasta, as well as creating Bolena and Norma, sang Cherubino, Romeo, and Cenerentola.[5] Isabella Colbran, the first Rossini Armida, created his Desdemona in 1816,[6] and there were other equally versatile divas conspicuous for singing these *assoluta* roles. This double soprano/mezzo ability would give an extra dimension to Norma's low-lying confrontation with Pollione in the last act, to Gemma's long monologue in her last scene, to Elisabetta's "Alma infida" in the second act of *Roberto Devereux*, or to any number of other passages where the lower extremes of the female voice are used in these nine roles. Ideally, for our own time, if we wish to reproduce the kind of experience that the composers themselves appear to have expected from the divas they wrote for, we shall have to insist on a sound that is not the hollow, contrived one we have grown used to for the lowest sequences, but rather a genuinely deep and mezzo-ish timbre that is a completely relaxed sound.

A prima donna who can sound like the most fleet-footed coloratura in Norma's first-act cabaletta and then turn right around and deliver her fourth-act ultimatum to Pollione in the tones of a superb contralto is extremely rare. But that is exactly the point. The very rarity of such a singer is the law of an *assoluta* role's performance. The necessity that is the mother of any production of these operas should not be simply the fact that Donizetti's *Devereux*, Cherubini's *Médée*, and Bellini's *Norma* are superb examples of musical theatre, but also the occasional presence of the fabulous vocalists for whom such operas are specifically revived. One does not announce, as part of a regular circus program, a trapeze act with a multiple somersault in it unless one is sure that the artist will do it right every time without falling into the net. In this case, doing it right means treating the operagoer to an Elisabetta or a Norma whose vocal type will definitely not be soprano but rather an extraordinary kind tending, perhaps, toward mezzo. In other words, one does not choose an opera of this kind for production and then cast about for singers to perform it. Rather, the extraordinary singer becomes the reason for these operas to be produced. The full potential of a beautiful human voice is meant to be demonstrated by affording her an occasion to express musically the beauty and variety in a composition that describes the soul of an operatic heroine.

The fascination that these roles hold for both the spectator and the performer lies in the fact that they also go against the concept of neo-classicism in characterization that reached its most moving operatic heights in, ironically, Richard Wagner, a figure too often regarded as the quintessential Romantic composer. Instead, the audience, in an opera such as *Norma* or *Anna Bolena*, becomes stirred by a bewildering variety of vocal, musical, and technical effects. To make a moving evening of dramatic song out of an arbitrary use of every aspect of a supreme diva's capacities seems, on the face of it, a hopeless proposition, but the purpose of this study is to show the successes as well as the failures of both the composers and their interpreters in attempting just that. Although the transparency of the most deeply moving Wagner roles may not be paralleled in the *assoluta* repertoire, it is a misconception to assume that the varieties of vocal sound and style in the *assoluta* tradition cannot be used as a springboard for an evening of genuinely stirring music.

What is required for the dramatic Wagner, Strauss, late Verdi, and *verismo* heroines is a natural vocal amplitude on top to cope with the orchestral fabric. Despite the greater technical and stylistic complexities of the *assoluta* roles, some divas might find Isolde, or the *Götterdämmerung* Brünnhilde, more taxing than certain *assoluta* roles precisely because of the more demanding requirements in the high register. This is not to suggest that these standard dramatic roles exploit the high to a greater extent than the *assoluta* roles. It is merely that when the high is used in Wagner, Giordano, and so on, the tone must be more naturally full and rich on top than the penetrating but more flexible high required in the *assoluta* role.

A diva with a rich high such as Helen Traubel's will meet the Wagnerian requirements with legitimately musical results, whereas a diva with a thin high, however penetrating, may have to force in Wagner, yielding totally unmusical results. It is thus possible that the diva with a thinner high may find the straight dramatic roles in *verismo* more taxing than the *assoluta* roles in which she may have quite a proficiency. On the other hand, a Diva with a naturally thick high would find an *assoluta* role, with its demands for upper-range flexibility, infinitely more taxing than the standard Wagnerian or *verismo* dramatic soprano role. In fact, and this is the crucial point, the greater difficulties that the straight dramatic soprano finds in an *assoluta* role may be more daunting than any difficulties that the versatile *assoluta* finds in the heavy, but less agile, writing of later decades.

Usually, the lesser likelihood of a superb Isolde turning into a superb Norma as opposed to a superb Norma turning into a superb Isolde serves to underline the degree to which an *assoluta* must be regarded as the supreme technician, and the degree to which her vocal feats within the repertoire constitutes the ultimate technical challenge.

Under such circumstances, only a voice that is truly phenomenal, extraordinarily beautiful, and capable of encompassing the difficulties successfully is worth casting as an *assoluta*. Otherwise, the point of the one-to-one correspondence between the musical line and the heroism of the character would be lost. The likelihood is that when an extraordinary voice presented itself to a composer, he began to look for a libretto that would be heroic enough to do justice to the music he wanted to write for her.

To master any of the *assoluta* roles, a diva must have an instrument that projects with ease over an energetic orchestra. It must have the innate capacity to move grandly into its tones and to swell or diminish those tones at will. She must have a technique that encompasses all *bel canto* ornamentation and the skill of combining this facility with her most heroic vocal quality. She must have an instrument with an easy and flexible high encompassing at least the notes around high D flat, and an equally flexible low capable of reaching down to the low A or the low G. Within this range, there must be an ability to sustain with ease a protracted passage using her lowest notes combined with as great an ease in sequences using an unusually high tessitura. Of necessity, all these abilities must be tied to a technical facility that enables her to vocalize with no apparent fatigue no matter how prolonged the scene or how extreme the requirements.

❧ 3 ❧

Luigi Cherubini (1760–1842): *Médée*

On March 13, 1797, Cherubini's *Médée*, with Mme. Julie-Angélique Scio in the title role, was first performed at the Théâtre Feydeau in Paris, astounding its audience and launching a new operatic genre. More than anything else, the opera was a psychological study in music of a woman of character, a heroine who could plumb life's depths and celebrate its heights, who combined the strength and courage usually ascribed to heroes and the flexibility of mind proverbially ascribed to women. She could be fierce and firm as well as tender and yielding, and her mood could turn on a dime. All this and more, which was merely suggested in François Benoit Hoffman's words, was fully expressed and exhibited in Cherubini's music.

The variety and richness of the dramatic turns were underlined in the orchestra, as the heroism of the lead part was expressed through the complexity of her vocal line. The strength and virtuosity of the performer thus became the musical metaphor for the character.

Never before had a composer been known to combine so many disparate elements into one opera and one role. The character's emotional range had to be matched by the performer's vocal range from low B flat to high B natural, three notes higher than the usual mezzo role and three notes lower than the usual soprano role. There were many extended passages with what would then have been considered a mezzo tessitura and many with a soprano tessitura. Coloratura singing was required both high and low, often in the same sequence.

Particularly striking for that time was the combination of a forceful orchestra with an agile vocal line.

The dramatic structure of Médée's character development is worth examining in some detail, if only in an attempt to appreciate the effect of one astonishment after another that the first-night audience must have experienced. We cannot begin to see her role as they did by merely going to the opera house for one thing, because she is not usually sung today as the composer intended. For another, we cannot hear her without the diluting effect of her many vocal descendants, both great and small.

The element of surprise is central to the representation of Médée's vocal character in each one of the seven numbers or vignettes that she sings. A new aspect of her being is presented in each vignette.

Before her first appearance, the other characters have given a description of Médée so forbidding that one is actually surprised by how human and simple she is when she comes on. She assures the people of Créon's kingdom they have nothing to fear (Créon is the father of Dircé, Jason's new intended), and only after Créon threatens her with imprisonment does she lash out. As the King storms off with his entourage, he warns her not to sojourn at his court. Médée responds by pleading for some direct acknowledgement from Jason who has lingered behind.

After this, the effect of Médée's address to Jason in her first musical vignette, after she has been on stage for nearly a quarter of an hour, cannot be overestimated and must have surprised its first audience. Here, in "Vous voyez de vos fils," Médée is shown as expansive, understanding, loving. Her humanity and simplicity are movingly shown. She delivers a warm, womanly supplication to Jason that he return to her.

In projecting these feelings, the aria features a broad sweeping line of architectural grandeur requiring an easy *passaggio* (that tricky part of the voice commonly regarded among singers as the "bridge" between the middle and upper register) interspersed with occasional startling exclamations that contrast strikingly with the more majestic flow of the main melody. In addition to all that is unusual in this piece, the element of surprise is further enhanced by the subtle hints of greater vocal difficulty than we have yet heard from any of the other characters. Obviously a vocal picture of a character under tremendous stress, the aria is calculated to make a remarkable impression when sung by a phenomenal artist. The innate grandeur of its phrases necessarily implies the expectation on Cherubini's part of vocal tones of heroic amplitude. With her voice at its freshest and richest, Maria Callas garnered ten minutes of applause after singing this aria at La Scala in 1953, albeit in her habitual Italian as "Dei tuoi figli."[7]

Yet perhaps the most remarkable thing about this aria is that, in addition to its inherent theatrical value, it is placed immediately before the Act I finale, where the very nature of Médée undergoes a disconcerting change and the vocalism correspondingly becomes more arduous.

In the second vignette, "Perfides ennemis," a duet with Jason that consti-tutes the finale to Act I, Cherubini emphasizes an altogether different aspect of Médée's character. Featuring a counterpoint of her and Jason's soliloquies of regret at past mistakes, the duet shows Médée much more accusatory in her remarks to Jason, more self-hating as well. She unnerves the spectator by becom-ing suddenly threatening and judgmental, more earthy, even practical in an off-putting way; Jason hasn't appreciated all she has done for him, she has been a fool. All of a sudden, instead of reaching out for understanding and reconcili-ation, she is showing she can brusquely defend herself, even bridle, if need be.

As a result, in this entire exchange, the musical phrases suddenly become more clipped, much fiercer, with a pronounced use of a heavy lower register. The sound of her singing line becomes wilder with a suggestion of something dangerous. The orchestra too becomes more assertive for her deeper phrases than it has been so far. This unnerving change in emphasis and vocal style from Médée's first "Vous voyez" seems designed as a dramatic ploy to highlight the technical versatility of the kind of diva capable of taking these abrupt charac-terizational reversals in stride. As Henry F. Chorley commented, "The close of this first act of *Médée* is one of the marvels of music; almost in opera what one of Lear's great scenes is in tragedy."[8]

Obviously, the abrupt shifts in Médée's role do not end with the first act. However, just to take stock of what has been featured so far, we have heard strik-ing changes in tessitura, with shifts in vocal color and dramatic persona, together with clear instances of heroic requirements in the lower register, betokening a woman with perhaps unsuspected and dangerous powers.

Nothing in all of these taxing ingredients is one whit lessened in Acts II and III. In both acts, Médée is onstage practically throughout, and her fireworks only let up about a third of the way through the second act. Tremendous sta-mina is required above and beyond that needed for her first scene in Act I.

At the beginning of Act II, again after a sequence of spoken dialogue, comes Médée's crucial confrontation scene with Créon. A significant number of the requirements expected of the performer are exploited in this third vignette, "Ah! Du moins à Médée." Despite Créon's extreme reluctance, Médée successfully per-suades him in this ensemble to let her stay in his realm one more day. Here, for the first time, Médée's wily determination is fully exhibited as she succeeds in gaining that extra day. She at first reaches out for understanding in much the same way she had done with Jason in her opening aria — the suppliant being cruelly resisted. When that doesn't work, she projects resignation and quiet sor-row, thus immediately vanquishing Créon. Finally, grim brooding comes to the fore at the conclusion of the ensemble as soon as Créon has granted her her wish.

In projecting all of these machinations, she once again surprises us by revealing something still more uncanny and threatening in singing lower, for the second half of this scene, than she has yet done anywhere in the opera. A lot happens, though, before she reaches that point. To begin with, we have the sweep-ing line in her initially well-controlled solo plea to Créon. Though the turmoil within her is hinted at in her brief agitated assurance that she will forget Jason and his cruelty, it is only a momentary lapse, and most of the solo is remarkable for its comparative equilibrium. However, in her subsequent responses to Créon's reluctance to allow her to stay, the tessitura becomes wilder and the vocal line more and more troubled. When she senses total obstinacy, she somberly addresses Jove as the all-seeing knower of all cruelty. It is here that the use of the low is at least as pronounced and as heroic as in the Act I finale. From the dusky tones of this passage, one senses the tense renewal of her strength for the final verbal assault on Créon. After this moment, the rigidly patterned quality of her solos no longer exists. Volatility characterizes the remainder of this scene: within individual solos or even lines, one can hear her singing protracted phrases that can lie quite high one moment or dip quite low the next. For the first time, her vocal line reaches beyond the two-octave boundaries of low B and high B to as low as B flat, the lowest that the role is ever required to go. This volatility even characterizes the close of this sequence, including Médée's final reaction to Créon's ultimate decision to let her stay one more day, "ce jour," after all. And in addition, the orchestra for this ensemble is as prominent as in the finale to Act I, again necessitating a truly heroic vocal tone.

Clearly, Créon's decision is the fateful action that facilitates Médée's eventual (and gruesome) revenge on Jason, their two children, and Dircé. As such it marks a pivotal moment of the central act of Cherubini's work. In affording the listener an experience as uncanny as Médée's suddenly descending to her very lowest note, Cherubini seems, perhaps, to be giving us a subtle intimation of the gravity of Créon's decision as a point of no return.

In fact, the sudden use at such a juncture of the character's lowest note in all these *assoluta* roles constitutes a pattern readily observable throughout the decades when this style of vocal characterization flourished. As we shall see, the dramatic use of an extraordinary singer's lowest note immediately before the peripeteia of the drama is also in Bellini's and in some of Donizetti's operas.

When it comes time to persuade Jason to let her meet the children for a "tender farewell," Médée's pleading, in the fourth vignette, has a more overt undertone of menace than has yet been perceptible. She is wily here in much the same way she had been with Créon, but, for the first time, the sense of menace, which so far has been attached only to her more bitter remarks now spills over into her attempts to gain pity. Where before something only too human and painfully honest had seemed to shine through her more "womanly" and searing pleas, here the plain dissembling is readily apparent even when she acts tearfully.

Médée's vocal assault on Jason begins this vignette with among the highest-lying moments of the entire opera. In pleading to see her children one last time, she feigns innocence through the use of a suppleness scarcely suggested till now and which produces a truly spine-chilling effect. Here, that chilling, wily manner has finally overtaken an altered top register as well. Only after Jason accedes to her request does Médée's music settle down to something roughly approximating the character of her music at the end of Act I.

For the last moments of Act II, Médée's fierce arietta finale, sung against the counterpoint of Jason's wedding procession and the combined forces of chorus and orchestra, rings down the curtain. Her vituperation is, once again, in startling contrast to the music last heard from her, the duet featuring her wily overtures to Jason and her absent children. Here, as Act II closes, we have an overpowering, withering invocation to Hymen, the god of marriage, to assist her in her vengeance — her first invocation to higher powers for the express purpose of wreaking general misery. Nowhere in the opera, as yet, has she been shown in so unvarnished a light, and this startling finale gives us a clearer hint of just how dangerous she truly is. Nothing is hidden from us in this raw fifth vignette lasting scarcely two minutes. The hearer is now given an idea of what Créon's over-generous "ce jour" holds for those around him.

For these two acts, the audience has been treated to extended heroic passages that exploit both the high and the low register in abrupt shifts in tessitura, an energetic orchestration, and some long scenes, with the prima donna dominating the stage and displaying vocal endurance.

However, the myriad ingredients of the role do not stop there. In the last act, we are finally treated to a scene of daunting pyrotechnics suggestive of the agile vocal writing of the *opere serie* as exploited by Handel. In this final scene, we hear all the technical and vocal hurdles intrinsic to an *assoluta* role. By encapsulating these requirements, Cherubini establishes a pattern further developed by Donizetti during the 1830s, the heyday of the *assoluta*, of brilliantly exploiting all dramatic effects inherent in *assoluta* writing through the severe test of a single dramatic scene.

In "Du trouble affreux," her first two-part aria of Act III and her sixth vignette, she experiences a moment of remorse as she is reunited with her innocent children. Médée is thanking the supreme powers for staying her hand and for having given her a moment of agony while staring at her children as she was on the verge of slaying them.

"Du trouble affreux" seems to parallel the cavatina/cabaletta form perfected by later *bel canto* composers. The second section, an *allegro*, features supple vocal writing of an agility barely hinted at up to now. Vulnerability, motherly love and self-horror are all reflected in this almost unhinged music. She is still murderous, but skittish, afraid, and only too self-aware of a desperate conflict within her. Thus, a suggestion of very slight hysteria typifies the music of this passage, though a hint of a new resolve develops in the final phrases as she senses her fury at Jason returning. Now, in contrast to the agile high vocalism, and as a way of expressing her effort to regain some degree of self-control, the diva is required, suddenly, to dip down, for the final time in the role, below middle C to low B flat. Still, these last phrases do not alter the generally high tessitura of the *allegro* by that much.

The agility typical of the music for most of this aria has rarely been heard in the first two acts and, amusingly, this vocal style seemed so incongruous to Leonard Bernstein in 1953 that he made the decision to omit the second half of this aria altogether. He saw, in the glittering agility of Médée's music for this passage, an unexpected contrast with the rest of her vocal part, but he failed to see that this was deliberate, and therefore chose to make the omission.

In a way we can be grateful to Bernstein's short-sightedness, for the incongruity he imagined serves, once again, to highlight two interrelated laws behind every role conceived in the mold of the *assoluta*. The first law is total unpredictability, which is clearly manifested in the passage that Bernstein found so disturbing. The second is technical comprehensiveness, the inclusion of every technical and vocal accomplishment ever expected of an operatic diva, no matter how incongruous the effect might seem. Cherubini's music can make this dramatically gripping, given an artist who can combine a mercurial vocalism with a sense of dramatic persona. The completeness of such an accomplishment is compromised if shock and surprise are eliminated in the name of misguided believability. "Believability" or consistency is a standard that goes against the grain for a character who, like Médée, is an outsized figure in her emotional depth. The heroism of the performer in encompassing the vocal and technical contradictions of such a part matches the heroism of the character. Roles like Médée probe the depths and heights of both the vocal range and diverse musical styles, reflecting the character's odyssey through varying states of mind.

In order to express the complex reality behind such a figure, it is essential that the diva display its full emotional gamut through every aspect of her technical ability. The diva must be willing to give all her care and attention to every facet of that expression, no matter how seemingly arbitrary its volatility. Fortunately, Maria Callas made other recordings with this aria intact.

After the two-part aria comes the seventh and final vignette for Médée, a full-fledged *scena* and her longest sequence in the opera. She is left all alone on the stage. For the first time, she intones an imposing, declamatory recitative, not characteristic of any of the set pieces associated with her up to now. This passage expresses a resurgence of her pride, her dignity and her determination as she berates herself for her moment of human weakness. It is a somber section with a tessitura that is fairly low, though there are some declamatory phrases that lie rather high and are detached from the rest.

She then calls on the fury Thisiphone for strength against her maternal instincts in a solo encompassing roughly three fourths of Médée's range at its climactic flourish. Bloodlust and compelling majesty are combined here, and the traditional humaneness of "the mother" and, more crucially, of "the woman" are abandoned (shades of Lady Macbeth's "Unsex me here"). The agility here extends down into the lower register.

Cries of horror offstage launch the second half of this *scena*, as the chorus exclaims on the after-effects of the cruel and murderous gift sent by Médée to Dircé. The desperate cries spur Médée on to a final brisk solo that lies amazingly high as she resolves to slay the children after all. Here is the rawest expression of danger and evil in Médée's entire role. As she invokes all the Furies, the frenzy of the music is hair-raising with a heroically agile style, propulsive phrases, weighty declamation, and the recurrent high B-natural. It is with this passage, in fusing the agile and vocally heroic, that Cherubini places the role beyond the reach of all but the most phenomenally gifted artists. Médée now becomes an *assoluta* role.

Ester Mazzoleni, the Médée at La Scala in 1909, stated that, for her,

> ... every time I reached, at the end, the [invocation to the Furies] I was almost in a state of hypnotic trance. It is in my opinion one of the greatest dramatic scenes ever written.[9]

At the conclusion of the final scene, Médée has one completely exposed series of harsh, fierce recitative phrases, with minimal orchestral accompaniment, once she has completed her infanticide. She then leaves the scene. This final minute shows her in triumph, attended by all three Furies and self-transformed into a veritable goddess. These phrases can make quite an effect, but the full gamut of the role's technical variety has already been traversed by the end of the frenzied solo described so vividly by Mazzoleni.

In bringing the vital aspects of a defining *assoluta* role into place in this last act, not only has the *assoluta*'s agility been called upon, but we have heard her sing well below middle C, often considered the lower limit of the straight soprano, and, in her final solo, turn right around and hit high B-natural, not as part of a single climactic phrase but as a note used for dramatic repetition.

Since, in singing below middle C at the opening of the third act, Médée hits low B flat and, in her final solo, encompasses the iteration of high B-natural, one is therefore dealing with a range surpassing two octaves. To sing throughout this range is, in itself, not an impossible feat, but it is compounded by the requirements throughout the role for total ease and technical proficiency at both extremes. Certainly, such a combined vocal and stylistic range requires, at the very least, an unusual voice and an unusual technique.

Some bewilderment accompanied the opera's premiere, though it was generally recognized that the achievement of the starring French diva, Mme. Julie-Angélique Scio (actually regarded in Paris as "prima donna assoluta"),[10] had been extraordinary. In an appraisal of her performance by Arthur Pougin, he remarked on her having been "in turn touching and impassioned, harrowing and arrogant, wild and timid to a degree that baffles description."[11] Indeed, Scio's surprising versatility in every respect is further attested to by her creation of Constance, sometimes termed a mezzo, in Cherubini's *Deux Journées* (1800). *Médée* had a checkered performing history during the nineteenth century. Neither Angelica Catalani, the reigning diva of the early 1800s, nor Giuditta Pasta, who created one of the most familiar *assoluta* roles, Norma, in 1831, appear to have sung this role. The exceptional nature of Médée, though, was generally recognized in the nineteenth century. Henry F. Chorley wrote that the role needs

> a voice ... like a clarion, and a frame of adamant and gold, capable of undergoing the strain and fatigue of such a long display of unmeasured

emotion ... after the compass and lungs of a Catalani are found, we must then ask for Pasta's grandeur of expression ... and withering scorn, and fearful vengeance, and maternal remorse ...[12]

Wilhelmine Schröder-Devrient and Thérèse Tietjens did sing the role along with other German and Austrian luminaries such as Mme. Schick, Clara Stoeckl-Heinefetter, and Mme. Milder-Hauptmann, the creator of Leonore in *Fidelio* (to whom Franz Josef Haydn once said, "Dear child, you have a voice like a house").[13] But, in France, the land of *Médée*'s birth, it was unusual for divas to take on this work, Mme. Cruvelli, in the time of Verdi, being a conspicuous exception,[14] but even she was of German extraction. The German/Austrian monopoly of truly proficient Médées (sung mostly in German) led to a general smattering of less conscientious performances throughout this period, finally yielding, in 1855, a Frankfurt production that epitomized the ambivalent attitudes prevalent during the 1800s towards *Médée*, and that had a negative impact on the opera that reverberates down to the present day.

The nature of these attitudes was reflected in special, fully accompanied recitatives composed in German for Frankfurt by Franz Lachner in place of the work's original spoken dialogue in French. During the nineteenth century, spoken dialogues became less and less acceptable for serious opera. As a result of this change, it was merely a matter of time till some adaptor's recitatives for *Médée* caught on. The negative impact of this Frankfurt production lay in precisely that happening with Lachner's meddlesome handiwork. For a long time, only Lachner's version was available on discs and only in an Italian translation. This became the Ricordi version and was used in most productions.

Above all, the structure of the role in Cherubini's original conception consists of a beautifully crafted series of musical vignettes, each one of which stands on its own as a self-sufficient dramatic cantata of impeccable proportions, and which, at the same time, introduces a specific technical facet of Médée's vocal persona with unerring dramatic instinct. This design is sadly gutted by declamatory phrases of musical fustian throughout, such as those Lachner cobbled together in what he presumably regarded as the Cherubinian style. Possibly, no other version was viable for Lachner's time. Again, Chorley noted in 1851 that "[*Médée*] is inaccessible. There is a time for everything," and goes on to say how improbable the erecting of a new Parthenon would be.[15]

However, today, when authentic-style renditions of pre-nineteenth-century works are so eagerly promoted, Cherubini's own original may finally start being accepted, even with the indifferent libretto by François Benoit Hoffmann. Olivia Stapp performed both the Lachner version in the usual Italian and the original version in French, and she stated that, while Cherubini's music is fascinating in its original language, the French dialogue is incredibly drawn out and stilted and plays on stage like second-rate Corneille.[16] Stapp's warning is well taken. A suitably abridged prose version of the dialogue in the vernacular ought to remedy the problems. Perhaps, adapted sections from a modern Euripides translation, where applicable, would be viable. All of Cherubini's original music should, of course, always be performed complete and always in the original French with carefully synchronized supertitles. Other more recent artists who have performed the French original are Susan von Reichenbach, Christine Ciesinski, Iano Tamar and Phyllis Treigle. These performances have helped vindicate Cherubini's original feeling for the French language as reflected in his music.

It is true that Callas's interpretation of the Lachner version was almost universally praised and rightly so. Lachner's hectoring recitatives were delivered by her with a variety and an aplomb that they emphatically do not deserve, while Cherubini's music was revealed with devastating clarity and insight as one of the truly superb vocal and dramatic characterizations in opera. Cherubini's creation was given its due with a thorough musical understanding by an outstanding artist.

However, if one can ignore for a moment Callas's dazzling accomplishment, what we are really being treated to in any tape of Callas as Médée is a string of unsubtle recitatives sung in the wrong language — Italian — and foisted onto a group of exquisitely fashioned French pieces whose character is diluted by the Italian and whose prominence is destroyed by a sea of orchestral recitative not of Cherubini's writing.

In the composer's original structure of having the transitional passages spoken and not set to music, the voice and the technique of the singer are not being swamped by the dialogue interspersed throughout. Rather, the voice and technique are being highlighted through this sharp dramatic relief. This is because the musical vignettes then stand with more startling clarity and underline Cherubini's intention. This intention is that the singer and what she is singing be made bold through the diva's display of new talents at every stage of Médée's seven vignettes.

Let's review the sequence of those vignettes in the light of this intention always to surprise. In the first act, having only seen Médée stand musically mute on stage during Créon's aria, she is then heard singing an aria of her own that matches any technical effects Créon may have displayed earlier. She has not sung here in any strikingly threatening manner, yet she proceeds to do just that in the act's final duet with Jason (vignette two). When the second act opens, we still have not heard her sing outside of a perfectly unexceptionable soprano's range, but once again she surprises us in the first sung sequence of this act (her third vignette) by revealing something more uncanny and threatening in plunging down to a startling low B flat before the end of the sequence. She has not yet sounded piteous, innocent, supple, or soothing anywhere, but she sings in precisely that way in the upper two thirds of her range for her second encounter with Jason, her fourth musical vignette. In her fifth one, the second-act arietta, she sings, for the first time, against an energetic choral accompaniment. In the sixth, the first sung sequence of the third and final act, limpid, airy, supple agility of an intricacy barely hinted at previously is heard from the diva, and, in her final and longest *scena* (the seventh), we have her very first accompanied recitative of the whole opera, which is of a highly nervous and abrupt character, after

MÉDÉE

ACT	SELECTION	1 FLEXIBLE LOW	2 INTRICATE COLORATURA	3A ABOVE HIGH B	3B OR BELOW LOW B	4 LONG SEQUENCES	5 FLEXIBLE HIGH	6 HEROIC COLORATURA	7 HEROIC TONE	8 HEAVY LOW
I	Vous voyez								X	
	Perfides ennemis								X	X
II	Ah! Du moins à Médée				X	X			X	X
	Chers enfants					X	X			X
	Je viens aussi					X			X	
III	Du trouble affreux	X	X		X	X	X		X	
	Eh quoi?					X				
	O Tisiphone!	X	X			X	X		X	
	Tu pleures...Arrête!	X	X			X	X	X	X	X

■ Sequence where all assoluta elements are concentrated

which her meditations are brought to an end with a display, this time, of a heroic agility in which she also gives us three high B-naturals.

Never once does Cherubini allow Médée to sing without something new and unexpected coming from her voice. It is almost as if, in Cherubini's mind, the very act of singing necessitated for Médée a musical and vocal discovery, implying a revelation of something new of which her character is capable, a *coup de théâtre*. If such was his intention, how devastating to this are Lachner's accompanied recitatives that feebly imitate the idiom of the recitative opening Médée's final *scena*— the sole one that Cherubini himself wrote for her. Not only is the element of vocal and technical surprise at the opening of Médée's most important moment ruined by this previous use of such an idiom, but the prosaic quality of Médée's pronouncements in Lachner's hands lacks the interplay of vocal light and shade that is the hallmark of Cherubini's writing. The harsh nature of the new recitatives takes away from the shock of Cherubini's own recitative for Médée's eventual atrocities in the final act. It seems likely that it was both unpredictability and variety that Julie Angélique Scio was expected to capture in the expressive contrasts so admired by Arthur Pougin in his description.

The solution of the New York City Opera when reviving the work for Grace Bumbry worked fairly well: relatively few cuts in Cherubini's music for the title role, but only a skeleton left for Lachner's recitatives, allowing the musical and dramatic development of Cherubini's own writing a better chance at proper appreciation. Still, there is no perfect substitute for strictly confining Médée's singing to Cherubini's music alone.

Médée on disc

In 1797, Cherubini created a new kind of operatic role for a female singer, designed to represent the character of a woman as she had never before been conceived for the operatic stage. Both her persona and dramatic function were for the first time released from their neo-classical bonds, and we have a woman here who is an effective character in the Aristotelian sense, one who makes things happen, and yet has none of Aristotle's other attributes. She exemplifies neither consistency of persona, nor appropriateness of behavior. In fact, she is completely unpredictable, for she contains within her more than one character. She is a compound of the natural woman of Gluckian drama and the virtuosity and range of the unnatural castrato of *opera seria*.

This kind of role was introduced by a new heroic-sounding breed, a diva *assoluta*, who, like Julie-Angélique Scio, occasionally performed mezzo repertoire, but who also had the capability of doing full justice to the pyrotechnics exclusive to a high soprano. The latter always remained a requirement for the true *assoluta*, but Médée and the later *assoluta* roles entailed much more than that. A vocal persona at once bright and broodingly cavernous seems implicit both in the scores of these operas and in the vocal tradition for these roles subsequent to Scio. One is reminded, in analyzing the vocal and dramatic propensities of these primarily nineteenth-century singers, of the heroic but supple vocal practices of the castrati of the previous century. A sense of continuity with this prior tradition is necessary if we are to understand the nature of the voices that the composers of the *assoluta* roles had in mind.

It is perhaps possible that, given the similarity in Médée's music to later *assoluta* roles, Scio's talents in combining soprano and mezzo (together with the expressive volatility that Pougin refers to) were not all that different from those of the diva *assoluta* of the next generation, typified by Isabella Colbran (the first Rossini Armida, 1817), Giuditta Pasta (the first Norma, 1831) or Giuseppina Ronzi-De Begnis (the first Elisabetta in *Roberto Devereux*). Unfortunately, Scio's ascertainable repertoire, other than Cherubini's *Médée* and Constance in *Deux Journées*, is made up, to a large extent, of music that has been either lost or ignored, so a sense of the vocal center in Scio's instrument is possible only by extrapolation.

This last consideration concerning "centers" leads us into a fundamental question regarding those theatrical and musical reasons that led to the writing of such variety in one and the same role for the diva with a large dramatic/heroic range and a florid ability. That question is whether or not these phenomenal singers had only one vocal center or several, meant to be exploited through contrasts in tessitura carefully tailored for the prodigy — be that prodigy Scio, Colbran, Pasta, or someone else equally amazing. Not merely musical but theatrical history as well appears to have been made by these singers, if one can trust some of the contemporary comments. An important component of the theatrical quality intrinsic to their music-making was apparently the split nature of the sound they had at their disposal. This will become apparent as the hybrid attributes of the later *assoluta* creators are examined. Clearly, the homogeneous style favored by many singers of both today and not so long ago goes very much against the vocal aesthetic invoked by the original composers and their interpreters of the time, if the nineteenth-century critics can be taken at their word. Greater vocal longevity might very well be achieved, in certain cases, if today's method (or the method generally regarded today as being ideal) rather than that of Pasta, Colbran, etc., is applied. However, this need not be kept in mind if the instrument is innately varied in tonal color to begin with, and if the sound is consistently musical throughout an enormous range, however "encyclopedic" (Bellini's own term for Pasta) the vocal palette.[17] Granted, such a rich but flexible instrument could only be expected once or twice within a generation at most. The rarity of this kind of prismatic vocal persona helps define the startling qualities with which the composers of an *assoluta* role meant to invest their scores. The occasional vocal homogeneity of singers like Rosa Ponselle, Frida Leider or Eileen Farrell stamps them as full-fledged phenomena, but possibly not the kind intended as instruments for the contrasts that the original *assoluta* composers had in mind. Nor are such homogeneous singers necessarily the kind of vocal phenomena who, like Colbran or Pasta, are always as much at ease in the coloratura writing of the mezzo repertoire as in that of the soprano. Differences within the instrument are the key.

The original *assoluta* tradition can boast a tiny handful of direct vocal inheritors who have left us audible examples of versatility in contrasting excerpts from non-*assoluta* repertoire, affording us a glimpse of their comprehensive inheritance. We will take a look at them in Chapter Fifteen, "Voices from the Past." But, for reasons made clear there, such inheritors have not left us any mementos of their artistry in true *assoluta* excerpts, let alone entire *assoluta* roles.

Those who have left complete interpretations of these roles rarely equal either the technical assurance heard in the homogeneous vocalism of a Leider or the prismatic spectrum of the earliest divas in Chapter Fifteen. In terms of sheer vocal abundance, Zinka Milanov, Birgit Nilsson, Anita Cerquetti, Joan Sutherland, or Montserrat Caballé may astound in occasionally recalling the ease of a homogeneous Leider type. But their range of color can be correspondingly limited, however sincere they are as performers. Consequently, both as musicians and actresses, the more perceptive and varied are artists like Magda Olivero, Leyla Gencer, Beverly Sills, Renata Scotto, or Elena Souliotis. Gencer and Souliotis may even display unusual vocal gifts as well, perhaps closer to those in the original models in Chapter Fifteen. But with all five in this latter group, it is the interpretive impression that dominates, thanks to the greater variety of vocal inflection. They rarely match the technical assurance of the "abundant" group, although there's no good reason why that need be the case.

Meanwhile, the various attributes of *assoluta* singing are not consistently honored in the *Médée* discography.

For most music lovers of the past century, *Médée* was merely a musty reference in some old encyclopedia until Maria Callas revived it at the Maggio Musicale Fiorentino in 1953. True, Ester Mazzoleni had revived it in 1909, but that somehow did not put *Médée* back on the map the way the pioneering revival at Florence did. Fortunately, this latter performance survives, and, although nips and tucks abound, it still preserves a more faithful performing edition than any later Callas broadcast or recording. Its conductor, Vittorio Gui, did not abandon the notorious Ricordi score, with its Italian translation and Lachner recitatives, but it's probably inconceivable that Florence would ever have considered giving the work in French, let alone retaining the spoken dialogue. So we should be grateful for what we have. Callas's colleagues are not ideal in every case, but she herself is in her element here, making it doubly fortunate that Florence presented her in her least heavily cut *Médée*. Carlo Guichandut's Jason is no match for La Scala's Gino Penno six months later, let alone Jon Vickers, who was to be Callas's most distinguished Jason. Her other colleagues at Florence are at a much higher level than Guichandut: Fedora Barbieri as Neris, Mario Petri as Créon and the fine Gabriella Tucci as Dircé, called "Glauce" in the Italian version that Callas always sang.

Most such recordings taken "live" from the stage, rather than made in a fully equipped recording studio, are not available on any mainstream labels, such as Decca/London, EMI or RCA. This rare Florence broadcast is no exception: like all of its kind, it has only been issued on a variety of smaller labels, all quite obscure and of limited distribution. At least one or two of these labels will not keep their pressings in print for long, primarily due to lack of proper resources. The sound quality of these pressings is highly variable. On the one hand, variations in sound quality can be attributed to, perhaps, different original sources for a performance. On the other, variable sound quality can also be attributable to different second-generation transfers of identical material. In the case of most issues of this Florence *Médée*, the sound is not all that distorted, even though it's obviously not a high-fidelity recording. However, the mike placement of the original renders some of the singing fairly distant, and one has to make an adjustment when listening through the echo. This or other similar problems plague many of these rare dubs from "live" performances. It comes with the territory. What is so marvelous in such cases is the rescue for posterity of historic and unforgettable moments that we would otherwise never be able to experience for ourselves, moments that past generations have lionized, but which we can now verify through rare documents like these.

To fully judge Callas's achievement in *Médée* means tackling directly the precise degree to which she did or didn't have proper title to the whole *assoluta* repertoire. Ideally, true mastery of this repertoire requires a perfect singer. Is Callas a perfect singer? No. However, there were things that made her exciting and apt in *assoluta* roles. Above all, the sheer voice she started with was ideal. At its best, her sounds gave off intimations of that prismatic quality that we will be observing among the original creators of all these parts. This quality was something that not even Rosa Ponselle — or Giannina Russ or Lilli Lehmann, for that matter — shared. Musically, she understood what was required, but, in honoring that technically, she only attained ideal mastery for a few years. That, in itself, was still a significant accomplishment above and beyond most of her contemporaries, but those contemporaries, however less versatile, usually lasted a bit longer. Granted, one can point to similarly brief primes in the nineteenth century like Giuditta Pasta's or Pauline Viardot's, but there were also divas of that same period, like Teresa De Giuli Borsi or Giuseppina Ronzi–De Begnis, who were apparently tremendously resilient. They show that the disturbing brevity of a Callas career need not be a given. The general course of Callas's career hardly suggests that of a perfect singer.

Callas's essential odyssey went from having:

a) a quite powerful, highly expressive, instrument with an astounding top and distinctly colored registers, marked by great flexibility and occasional, but not acute, uncertainties in pitch, highly eccentric diction, together with a musicality and an inspired musicianship well beyond most of her colleagues. Also a respectable legato, not altogether flawless in the most wide-ranging phrases (1947 — season of 1952/53).

Subsequently:

b) a strong, highly expressive, but not overwhelmingly powerful, instrument with an intermittently astounding top and distinctly colored registers, marked also by great flexibility and a securer sense of pitch, clearer diction, together with the same musicality and inspired musicianship. And an even finer legato, especially in the most wide-ranging phrases (season of 1953/54 — season of 1955/56).

Later:

c) a hardly remarkable, though highly expressive, instrument with an unpredictable top and distinct registers, showing good flexibility, strong musicianship, occasional uncertainties in pitch, cloudier diction, unpredictable, but occasionally captivating, musicality, with a respectable, but not superb, legato showing intermittent flaws in wide-ranging phrases reminiscent of the merely rough sufficiency of her earliest years (season of 1956/57 — 1960).

And finally:

d) a considerably darker, less malleable, though still expressive, instrument with a tenuous top and more disturbed registers than ever, cloudy diction, showing imaginative musicianship, but precarious technical control throughout, impaired flexibility, unsure sense of pitch, spotty musicality. And a respectable, but not superb, legato showing, again, some flaws in wide-ranging phrases (1961–1965).

Of the half dozen extant recordings of Callas as Médée, the first Florence performance is one of the three finest and most representative examples of her interpretation, the other two being a La Scala broadcast of December 1953 and the famed Dallas production opposite Jon Vickers from the fall of 1958. Luckily, all these three showcase the best that she was capable of at each stage of her career, save her fourth and poorest phase. As with most such broadcasts, each of these is available on a number of different labels, all of limited distribution.

The studio recording made in 1957 for Mercury with Tullio Serafin could have competed. But Callas was suffering from exhaustion at the time. Since she had just garnered negative publicity for having declined a last-minute appearance that was forced on her at the conclusion of a backbreaking tour in Edinburgh, she did not feel free to ask that the Serafin recording be postponed, so the recording sessions proceeded as scheduled. Her interpretation in this set is, sadly, typical of her poorest singing during this third phase. An important opportunity was thus badly mishandled by everyone.

In the Florence opening, Médée's first aria, "Dei tuoi figli," exerts an immediate effect: Callas makes palpable the helplessness that Médée feels, giving Cherubini's phrases an unforgettable chill of desolation. However, her vocalism at the outset is actually rather unsettled, even though the voice itself sounds secure and ample. The registers don't quite yield an easy legato, and at one point, at the words "le orrende passioni," there is the hint of an uncomfortable loosening in the vibrato as the phrase surges upward. Gui does not maintain full tension in this aria either, and he allows too much time to occur before the final cry of "Pietà," resulting in premature applause. The climax has been breached, and there is thus no applause at all when the aria proper ends. This unevenness in tension is a recurring problem at odd moments throughout the broadcast. On the one hand, when Gui is engaged, everything becomes electrifying and he lives up to his reputation. On the other, moments like that alternate with too many where Gui seems to be content with a more formal musical rhetoric. John Ardoin has rightly pointed out that Gui and Serafin appear to take the most Classical approach to this work of all the conductors whom we hear with Callas in this role.[18] That is not doing Callas—or Cherubini—any favors.

Things look up in Act II with the strongest reading Callas ever gave of the plea to Créon. All the danger in her, all the sorrow, all the manipulativeness is there in full. This may also be a tribute to the fact that here she sang her least cut version of the scene, leaving her the needed room to develop it properly. Mario Petri is an excellent colleague as Créon. The tension and pathos between the two are maintained brilliantly through to the final chords and the audience erupts in applause at the end, utterly swept up by it all. Callas's voice is now thoroughly warmed up. However, neither in Act II nor in the first act are her scenes with Jason up to what she would achieve in later productions. Her own occasional fussing with the legato and Guichandut's inadequacies prevent the Médée/Jason relationship from being the totality it could be. Callas and Gui are both to be commended for a true head of steam in the wedding finale that closes Act II. This is pulverizing, climaxing with a massive high C that seems to engulf everything around it. Is it just one's imagination, or is Callas's slashing attack on this note calculated to parallel the sudden snatching up of a torch as the curtain falls? Whatever, this is rip-roaring theatre, and one begins to see why the seal on Callas's international fame dates from this evening.

Much of Act III is not on the same level. Tension occasionally lags, and Callas herself is sometimes too deliberate. She is certainly energized enough throughout by anybody else's standards, but, compared to what she herself achieves with Bernstein and Rescigno at La Scala and Dallas, this reading with Gui doesn't quite sustain the same flow or tension. The happy exception is one sequence, and that a critical one: a version of "Del fiero duol" with the fullest version she ever sang of the quicker section beginning "Fu per voi." This is one of the clearest transcriptions we have of Callas in her earliest phase performing a "live" rendition of a heroic coloratura aria. It occupies a deserved niche for that reason, but also because it's arguably the most satisfying reading of this aria we have from her. Everything is impeccably placed, with none of the imbalances of her opening "Dei tuoi figli," and the emotions flow from one extreme to the other with utter naturalness. Here, Callas wins herself the ovation she just missed in the first act. This and the second-act plea with Créon are the finest moments of her first *Médée*.

Later, in December of the same year, there is the "live" performance at La Scala under Leonard Bernstein, featuring Maria Callas and Gino Penno. Bernstein's reading of the score is a pleasant surprise. It is, in fact, masterly. Nominally a Classical work (1797), *Médée* still foreshadows Romanticism strongly enough to play to Bernstein's strengths. With the singing here just as good as the conducting, it could be an ideal performance, were it not for some really odd cuts. Still, this broadcast remains a stirring experience. Callas, if anything, is even more authoritative than in Florence. Her voice is not as ample as it had been the previous spring, but the control, if anything, is even more startling, while the interpretation has developed considerably for the final moments. In addition to Gino Penno's Jason, Callas's other colleagues here are Fedora Barbieri as Neris, Giuseppe Modesti as Créon and Maria Luisa Nache as Glauce.

Weighed against the various advantages in the Bernstein reading is Callas's slight dilution of that combination of helpless desolateness captured in her opening aria in Florence. Now it is more an urgent plea with a clearer sense of purpose — almost with an aura of command thrown in. The ovation it receives is certainly not hard to understand, since this time Bernstein is careful to maintain the tension right on through to the end. He does sacrifice the final "Pietà" in so doing, which may be a cheat in a way. A conductor of Bernstein's genius could probably have maintained enough sweep to hold premature applause at bay until the "Pietà." This is but one instance of strange omission unique to this performance.

Throughout the evening, ferocity now is more the norm under Bernstein. Callas thrives in the driving fury of Bernstein's approach. While the second act becomes tremendously exciting this way, the balance of feelings in the plea with Créon are now weighted a bit more toward resentment rather than the lament-plus-resentment that had made the scene in Florence so special. The advantage here is that the Act II wedding finale hits with even greater force than at Florence. Callas does not hold the high C as long, but it sounds just as secure, and Bernstein's sweep toward the final chords complements her savagery.

Unfortunately, for reasons discussed above, Bernstein cut out the "Fu per voi" section of "Del fiero duol." But the final *scena* is as complete as it ever was with Callas, given that she never performed it uncut. This, fittingly, is the climax of the Bernstein performance. Never before and never again would Callas be in such sovereign command of this terrifying sequence. The passagework is immaculate, the vitriol in her sounds takes one's breath away, the ease of her broad phrasing suggests infinite reserves. There is no question of fatigue here. This is still pretty much a heroic voice sailing through Cherubini's quintessential heroic scene. It rings down the curtain on a Callas evening that also signaled a remarkable artistic partnership little discussed in most studies of her career: the collaboration of Maria Callas and director Margherita Wallmann. Wallmann may have had the knack of sparking in Callas a long view when it comes to acting; thus, an entire scene becomes one long arc with one or two dominant emotions around which others figure as variations on a basic theme. It's hard to say whether other observers have sensed this, but, when listening to some of the broadcasts of her Visconti collaborations, one is struck by the continual play of specific emotional gestures in a virtuosic whirl. However, in this Bernstein *Médée*, and also in Callas's finest *Norma*, a Wallmann production broadcast from La Scala in 1955, there seem to be parallels in the fusion of certain emotions, however varied, around a basic mood or feeling. The result works wonders with Callas and is just as interesting, in my view, as the whirl of insights we get from her with Visconti or Zeffirelli. Whether this effect is consciously Wallmann's or merely coincidence, the result is haunting. Granted, we are not dealing with any visual elements here, which could arguably make the effect much different. But I would suggest that the aural effect, at least, does hold true for most of the Wallmann broadcasts. Callas is very relaxed and confident in all these broadcasts. One would like to know as much about the Wallmann directing style as most buffs do today about Visconti or Zeffirelli. She has been unjustly neglected.

The Dallas production in November 1958, conducted by Nicola Rescigno, also has a fine director, one intimately acquainted with the traditions of the original Greek drama on which Cherubini's opera is partly based. Alexis Minotis knows his Euripides, an inestimable value in this production. Compelling as Callas is in the Wallmann broadcast, this Minotis reading is, dramatically, her most detailed reading. Her colleagues, aside from Vickers, include Elisabeth Carron as Glauce, Nicola Zaccaria as Créon and the young Teresa Berganza as Neris.

A real boon is Jon Vickers' Jason. Here, finally, the pain and resentment and the dying but still present feelings of love between Médée and Jason are fully revealed. Their first-act argument is searingly bitter. For the first time, we fully understand what Henry F. Chorley meant when he compared the first-act finale to *King Lear*. Their duet in Act II is just as painful. Jason's feelings for the children are as agonizing as Médée's. Callas here may possibly be giving a hint that her feelings for her children are still too strong to consider killing them. This feeling isn't underlined, but the vague suggestion certainly fits with what happens in "Del fiero duol" in Act III. The tension between the two principals does not let up even in the final lines of recitative at the conclusion of the opera when in utter disbelief Vickers cries out to Médée to give reasons for her infanticide. When Callas coldly responds "Eran figli tuoi," Vickers lets out a hideous moan of pain that is ruthlessly interrupted by Callas's final lines.

While so much in Callas's performance here is justly celebrated, the last act catches up with her — somewhat. (Apparently, she had spent much of that day talking on the phone, due to Sir Rudolf Bing's having just fired her from the 1958/59 season at the Metropolitan Opera.) In absolute terms, she is still in reasonably good control of this last scene, but the abandon of 1953 is just not there. There is now a manufactured quality, particularly on top, although the interpretation continues strong.

For quite a while, all the interpretations that followed in Callas's wake used the Italian edition with recitatives from Lachner. Each of these singers has something unusual to offer. None of them is worthless. They each provide some useful window on just what kind of woman Médée is.

Magda Olivero's interpretation, best heard "live" from Dallas in 1967, is the most unstrung there is. This is not a plush sound. It doesn't even have the amplitude of the Callas of 1958. There are also distinct gaps in her voice in its lower half, which plays havoc with some of the legato lines. But she is an imaginative musician who knows how to phrase a Cherubini utterance well. Despite certain intonation problems, she sings through some of these with surprising aplomb, and, in fact, they are not as severe in the later scenes. Her colleagues are Bruno Prevedi, who practically had a copyright on Jason for the next few years, Bianca Maria Casoni as Neris, Nicola Zaccaria as Créon and Graziella Sciutti as Glauce. Nicola Rescigno conducts. This has been fitfully available during both the LP and the CD era. One of its earliest releases is an HRE LP.

In the first act, Olivero's "Dei tuoi figli" is plagued by uncertainties in pitch at the outset. Her fight with Jason is more effective, although "Io lo giuro a gli Dei" gets lost since it lies too uncomfortably low for her. She has the instinct to know where the turning point in this duet is: her vivid "Fuggir" becomes a spoken growl!

It may be that no Médée is more extreme than Olivero in the sequence with Créon in Act II: she is practically weeping in the opening phrases. She is consistent in rendering "preghiera" as a haunting *pianissimo* both times, while the second one is followed by a near sob. The vividness of this approach continues in her second duet with Jason. Here, the quiet venom of "Vedervi posso ancor" makes one's skin crawl; throughout this number it's clear she is feigning. Olivero leaves no doubt that here is a woman completely set on vengeance by the conclusion of the duet. She leaves nothing ambiguous in the impression that she means the children no good. She and Rescigno are not together at the start of "Questa promessa." She comes in late and has to scramble a bit. What is surprising is how accurate she is in picking out Cherubini's tricky intervals here. Moreover, despite a less than tractable instrument, it's equally surprising to hear an interpolated high C at the close of the curtain that is on pitch and steady.

In the more agile vocal writing of the last act, Olivero's singing may not always be beautiful, or powerful, but one has to acknowledge its mastery of interpretive nuance. Unfortunately, "Del fiero duol" finds her having to scramble back and forth across some of the most conspicuous gaps in her voice. It's a wonder her occasional hoarseness doesn't leave the entire voice wheezy and gravelly. Particularly uncomfortable are the repetitions of "che il cor mi frange" and "Io sento ancora." After interpolating a respectable high B flat at the end, she loses the pitch in attempting to find the tonic. Her closing *scena* is more effective. There is a sense of quiet danger in "E che?" Great sadness then enters the voice at "la voce arcana," and the "Vo' fuggir" is spoken, harking back to her way with this word in the Act I duet. One must then acknowledge a well-disciplined flexibility in the upper half for the closing measures of this solo. The transitional utterances following this opening solo are marked by the performance's last uncertainties in pitch. In fact, "Oh voce dolce al cor" strays badly. But everything is secure again in the "Atre Furie," where the most taxing passagework is adroitly tossed off. She nails every note precisely, and Rescigno's headlong tempo does not make that easy. This is a triumph of grit, nerve, and technique. But her pitiless lines of recitative closing the opera are not as effective. Particularly acute is the way "vo'" of "Al sacro fiume io vo'" becomes lost in her non-existent low.

One magnificently sung rendition of the title role comes from the young Gwyneth Jones. It's regrettable that some vocal problems overtook her later, because, like Callas, she started out with a fine instrument. Her voice conforms more to the familiar map of the dramatic soprano, the low register being not as strong as the top. Jones is not a true *assoluta*; but what she does well she does very well, and she's a fine actress. But is she good with the text? That may seem an odd question in light of her superior dramatic commitment, but Jones has one odd quirk: a problem with consonants. It's not that her general delivery is bland. Far from it! But consonants sometimes blur, leaving an impression of a series of vowels morphing into each other. The vigor of her dramatic reading is definitely at a high level, so this elocution problem is strictly mechanical.

Jones's interpretation is oriented more to the suffering than to the fury, but fury is still there, and the whole is fleshed out quite plausibly. The first-time use of a fuller edition (albeit still the bastardized Italian one) plays a positive role here. Though one suspects the downplaying of Médée's savagery is partly due to Jones's weaker low, at least there are no vocal shortcuts.

As a nearly complete reading featuring a beautiful voice used with dramatic intensity, we would be the poorer without this set. It is from Decca/London in 1967. Jones' broad phrasing is prodigious, and, while she sometimes rushes ahead of the conductor, Lamberto Gardelli, she is rarely unmusical. Her colleagues are Bruno Prevedi once again singing Jason, Fiorenza Cossotto as Neris, Justino Diaz as Créon and Pilar Lorengar as Glauce.

Jones begins her entrance aria in a measured way, contrasting a soaring "passioni" with a stinging "Crudel!" There is great longing in her closing "Pietà!" The duet is charged with grandeur, and that word "Crudel!" again stands out. With all this, she manages to impart an uneasy hint of our not having met the entire person — yet.

As her second scene opens, we are faced with a helpless woman in the "Date almen," particularly at the words "tutta sola." "Preghiera" is given a luminous piano, while her words snap at "Re degli Dei," and there is a slight sob on "Ancora un solo dì." In her duet with Jason, she captivates with a murmured "Figli miei" and a tender "Mai più vi rivedrò." "Posso" of "posso ancor" is delivered almost with a gasp, and "Amor" becomes a plaintive cry. Even as she can taste the victory of seeing her children, her "Come gioir potrò?" is still heartbreaking in its painful honesty. In the act's closing arietta, unflappable vocalism on high rings down the curtain.

In the final act, she is unstrung as she recoils at first from striking her children. In "Del fiero duol," she makes an affecting soft attack at "Ah, miei tesor," then a *crescendo* as the phrase builds. "O Dei del Ciel" is given a haunting piano. In the "Fu per voi," we hear smooth negotiation of the wide-ranging passagework, even though the low B flat is weak. The aria ends with a strong interpolated high B flat. The "E che" has a fateful-sounding opening, despite a gravelly moment at "lascio." In the "Oh fosca Erinni," the low-lying "Distruggi il mio sen" and "Rendi il pugnal" may not be sufficiently strong, but Jones compensates with admirable fervor and fine precision in picking out the awkward intervals. She gains more bite in the low for the solo's closing measures. We then have an inspired "Oh voce dolce al cor," easy, fluent and implacable. The way she hurls out "Spietato" lingers long afterward, though there's a hint of more gravel in a rushed "vendetta." A fluently launched "Non più dubbiezze" heralds a perfect delivery of its passagework hurtling downward. Jones has managed to suggest the invincible without subtracting the feminine. A splendid paradox. It's frustrating that Jones does not provide a full surge for "T'arresta" at her final appearance. More electrifying, though, is her lingering "t'aspetta" followed by a rousing conclusion from Gardelli.

Claque has released a "live" 1968 broadcast of the traditional Italian version, with most of the usual cuts. It was beamed from the Teatro la Fenice and featured Leyla Gencer. Aldo Bottion sings Jason, the young Ruggero Raimondi is Créon, Daniela Mazzucato is Glauce, and Giovanna Fioroni the Neris. Carlo Franci leads an incisive reading.

It is unfortunate to have to introduce Gencer in this book with this performance. In 1968, the glottal attack has completely overtaken her, and even the instrument is frayed. Here is a keenly insightful and heartfelt artist capable of true greatness in this repertoire, but the fractured vocalism in her opening aria is painful to hear. Her imagination, though, has not yet deserted her, and she gives a haunting delivery to a soft "Se mai mi fossi apparso"—immediately offset by a "passioni" that is a real trial. One must still acknowledge the artistry that can project a suffering human being here, and her "Pietà" is an unforgettable cry of desperation. In fact, Gencer's way with words is so often magical that it seems churlish not to be grateful for this reading. When one encounters her further along in this book, her mastery of words is matched by affecting vocalism, and one can realize how much musical greatness she was capable of. Here, in the duet, she bites down strongly on "Questo Imen non sarà," "detesto" is bloodcurdling, and she finds a good collaborator in Franci. But there is a tremolo at "O fatal vello d'or," she rasps "Fuggir" (although the effect is dramatically plausible), and she is seriously hoarse in the closing section.

The seesaw pattern continues in the second act. There is admirable indignation in the "Vo' scordare Giasone," but the "udir vogliate" is uncomfortably produced. There is admirable desperation in "tal pietà," and a spectral "Re degli Dei!" But Gencer loses hold of the music entirely on the repeated "Mio Re." Fortunately, her low is rich and biting throughout, and the scene ends with a manic "scrutator." In her duet with Jason, she emits an incredulous "Vedervi posso ancor" and a swift about-face in a revolted "ripudio esecrato." Surprisingly, we have our first example of a limpid delivery in a pleading "Da te divisa," but control slips after that. Act II's arietta finale, "Questa promessa," has a strong start, but the tremolo on top catches up with her.

The start to "Del fiero duol" is solemn, and poignancy pervades "che il cor mi frange." This artist, with such an assured piano, cannot sustain it at "O figli miei" and "Ah, miei tesor." Tenderness returns at "santa," which carries over into the opening of the "Fu per voi." There is a heartbreaking "O miei tesor" here, and Gencer shows respectable flexibility throughout the (abridged) passagework that Franci allows her. He snips out the phrases with the low B flat, and the singer's unsteady high B flat ends the aria. In the grand *scena*, "E che," Gencer is peremptory with herself. "Come mai puoi sentir" is as spectral as her "Re degli Dei" in the second act, but acute gravelliness follows. Similarly, in "O fosca Erinni," a successful "Rendi il pugnal," with its terrifying low, is offset by an off-pitch "giammai." We have a fine frenzy in this solo's tricky closing measures, but "l'amor" founders on a bad rasp. After the solo, there is fluency in the "Oh voce dolce al cor," and the "Atre Furie" shows good control of the top. Fluency continues in the passagework, only the very final phrase betraying fatigue. "Al sacro fiume io vo'" is as strong and assured as "t'aspetta l'ombra mia" is erratic. Franci and the chorus drive to a strong finish.

Like Gencer's immediate predecessor, Gwyneth Jones, Leonie Rysanek too would reap much of her fame in the German repertoire. But, also like Jones, she would attempt the occasional foray into *bel canto* repertoire as well. Rysanek also shared with Jones a genuinely sumptuous instrument under uneven control, though Rysanek stayed the course better. She is said to have remarked that she would watch Gwyneth Jones on stage in amazement at so much sound coming from so small a frame. But if there is anyone who matches Jones in abundance of sound, it is Leonie Rysanek herself. We have her *Médée* complete in a broadcast from Vienna. It comes from her peak year, 1972, and, in many respects, she outshines her petite colleague. There is more variety of shading from Rysanek and words come through more clearly. The demonic in her impersonation is more driven and seems more dangerous. But, as we trace our way through her performance, we realize that's not the whole story.

Jason is the inevitable Bruno Prevedi, Créon is sung by Nicola Ghiuselev, Neris by Margarita Lilowa and the Glauce is Lucia Popp. Horst Stein conducts. This 1972 performance has been made available on Melodram.

In Act I, Rysanek cannot sustain an even line at too low a tessitura, but the radiance and security in higher-lying words like "passioni" seem like bolts of lightning. On the one hand, there is a softening of tone for "Torna sposo per me," but the smudged "per tanto amor che volli a te" detracts. Her wrenching "Pietà" gives a gleam to the end of the aria. In the duet, no one makes "l'Orco" sound so demonic, and this is complemented by the surges for "Questo Imen traditor." In repeating her shocked "Fuggir" softly, she conveys deep hurt, and the final electrifying high note provides a stunning curtain.

Unfortunately, Maestro Stein adopts cuts in the scene with Créon, but its cumulative effect remains strong. Rysanek's voice is now completely warmed up, and her vivid presentation is both moving and terrifying. She is persuasive at the start, and we can easily believe "tal dolore." Her low, now capable of better line, is still inadequate for something like "date" of "Un asil date a me." However, her customary plaintive quality is so right for "Come mai rifiutar," and her closing phrases are towering. With Jason, we hear shivers of anticipation at his capitulation, and her sinuous cooing weaves a spell, as she softly rides the high tessitura with insolent ease. Both the taxing tessitura and Jason are wrapped around her little finger as she first lingers in triumph on "favor," then almost sobs with joy at "sovvenir." Her finest moment is a staggering "Questa promessa," every word making its effect, capped with the written high B flat instead of the interpolated high C of some others. But it is a glorious and richly expressive high B flat all the same!

It is frustrating that, despite Rysanek's vocal health, she cannot master the daunting vocal writing in the final scene. There is no question of fatigue. She still sounds indomitable. But the frequent dips down into chest and the intricacy of certain phrases highlight her shortcomings. In any case, by 1972, she is even less of a *bel canto* stylist than thirteen years earlier at the time of her 1959 Metropolitan debut as Verdi's Lady Macbeth. Her voice may be at its richest in 1972, but Rysanek isn't able to muster the musical discipline needed for Médée's last act. Her control of line in the low may be improved from the first act, but it still falls short here. Nevertheless, there are spine-tingling moments: a "No, non mai" that seems to extend in an eternal agony; a heartbreaking "vincerà"; a *messa di voce* on "O" of "O figli miei"; a shudder of remorse on "v'amo tanto," and a compelling high B flat at the close. But the intricate passagework in the (abridged) "Fu per voi" remains clumsy. At the outset of the final *scena*, Rysanek is in a daze, slowly coming back to reality with a quiet "Son ciechi gli occhi miei" that makes the skin crawl. "Rendi il pugnal" starts almost whispered until we reach "d'incertezza." A dramatically effective finish to the solo is partially offset by shortness of breath and wild scoops up and down for Cherubini's huge intervals. "Oh grido di dolor," however, is almost perfect, though she is clumsy again for the turn on "cor." The "Atre Furie" boasts incredible high Bs and surprisingly competent downward passagework. But there is the inevitable caveat, as Rysanek flings herself rather sloppily at the final phrase with its last high B. Here she shows further shortness of breath and abbreviates her chance for another good high B, which she clearly still has in her. At her final appearance, she almost loses the low-lying "vo'," but overall grandeur does not desert her, and her epic "t'aspetta" suggests a long time indeed!

In 1977, Hungaroton released a studio recording of Cherubini's *Médée* starring Sylvia Sass. The Prevedi era is now over and Veriano Luchetti performs Jason. Klara Takács sings Neris and Créon is Kolos Kováts. Lamberto Gardelli once again conducts.

Sass's is not a sumptuous sound, but it boasts genuine power. Her tone has a sour whine that breaks through from time to time, and perhaps this functions as a legitimate component of her interpretation. Her vowels are not the cleanest, although she counterbalances that through more varied delivery than most other interpreters. Sass seems calculated to a degree, and this makes her presentation less heartfelt than more straightforward readings. However, there are moments of real excitement.

In Act I, her "Pietà" at the conclusion of "Dei tuoi figli" terrifies the listener as more of a peremptory command than a plea. The duet, "Nemici senza cor," works better for her, with an easier tessitura than the aria. One of her better excursions into the top register is here when she unleashes a fine "Ah!" introducing her extended "Fuggir" solo. In fact, her entire delivery of the lines taking off from "Fuggir" mark the most effective stretch in this act.

In Act II, the most intriguing moment in the sequence with Créon is her treatment of the solo, "Ebben! Tutto mi manca!" Here, she manages to evoke both exasperation and sorrow. However, it's hard to tell how much feigning there is here, since she still lacks the specificity needed in this kind of passage. Granted, others have made this moment straightforward, so one can assume that Sass is doing the same. However, the degree of ambiguity nags. How much of it is deliberate? Vocally, her top remains particularly shrill through much of the act, although the duet with Jason is marginally better. She opens by wheedling him, as if butter wouldn't melt in her mouth. But she also conveys a quiet watchfulness of Jason, carefully measuring his response. It's then disorienting to have her suddenly project *anger* at him as she thanks him for granting her some time with the children! More authentic is her intimation of a deep and private sorrow at "cari miei tesor," as is her disgust with "falsi sospir" and her towering rage over "Così mi lasci tu." Nothing much distinguishes or detracts from her "Questa promessa."

The final act seems labored in places, an exception being her deft handling of the passagework in "Del fiero duol." She also has enough low here to make her crucial low B flat effective. There is no interpolated high B flat at the end. Her great *scena* goes well in the first half. She is marvelously indignant with herself every time she repeats the words "Come puoi" and critical words in the low like "incertezza" and "delitto" register quite well. But the transitional moments preceding her final heroic coloratura solo falter badly at the second "voce dolce al cor" flourish: the sour whine that disfigures so much of her singing returns to no apparent dramatic purpose. The final breakneck passagework as she resolves on slaying her children is accurate enough, but she has to cool down the temperature in order to get all the notes in. Thus, the hallmark of this moment, its fusion of the heroic and the florid, is compromised, since evidently Sass does not trust herself to maintain the musical accuracy in a passage this intricate while her voice is at full throttle. So the imperative to open up the voice all the way gets sacrificed.

It was gratifying when Nuova Era finally issued every note of Cherubini's score and in its original French. The spoken dialogue is somewhat trimmed, but not excessively. Patrick Fournillier's conducting has a true sense of drive, offset by occasional lapses of ensemble that are more acute in the earlier scenes. Luca Lombardo's Jason and Patrizia Ciofi's Dircé are overshadowed by Jean-Philippe Courtis's Créon and Magali Damonte's Néris. The recording is taken "live" from a 1995 production at Martina Franca in Italy with Iano Tamar as Médée.

Tamar's Médée is marked by an abundance of dramatic energy, some gleaming tones and effective word painting, but a shortness of breath and a hollow low make her less than ideal for the title role. In her opening aria, "Vous voyez de vos fils," Tamar sounds husky with an unruly top that is not warmed up. Her vocal shading fails to match the sorrow implicit in Cherubini's orchestral colors. The duet "Perfides ennemis" fits her better, even if one wishes there were more of a contrast with her preceding aria.

Act II shows a distinct improvement. At last we hear a true line in her singing, giving us, in her plea to Créon, our first window on the genuine sorrow that eluded her in Act I. Her low, however, fails to satisfy here, with a B flat that gets lost in the various sounds of colleagues, chorus and orchestra. The opening of her Act II duet with Jason is given a straightforward, uncomplicated rendering: there is little that strikes us as potentially underhanded. One imaginative touch, though, is the suggestion of a dying fall for a repeated "loin de vous." There is also vivid anger at "Tu paîras chers les pleurs que je feins de verser." Some of Tamar's finest singing is heard in the Act II finale: it boasts the cleanest line so far. She does not opt for a high C at its climax, but everything is fluent and richly expressive, with a musicality far more consistent than earlier.

Act III shows both her best and all her limitations. Her voice is now cleanly focused, but she is stretched to her limits—and beyond—by the pyrotechnics. There are still things to admire, but they are not much in evidence in "Du trouble affreux." Somehow Tamar misses the resurgence of humanity in this aria. "Chers" of "chers enfants" goes a bit wild, making her cut off the note too quickly. The passagework in the aria's second half, "Vous avez," goes sharp, and there is a weak low B flat on "courroux." At the conclusion, there is shortness of breath and some slurred passagework. Mirroring a pattern of hers in the earlier acts, Tamar improves somewhat as the scene progresses: her final *scena* is impressive in many ways. It is also a thrill to be experiencing for the first time the magnificent structure of Cherubini's Act III finale uncut, with its telling highlighting of the original French text. Tamar turns "Est-ce à toi de vouloir être mère?" into a single grand utterance broadly phrased. In "O Tisiphone!" there is, again, occasional shortness of breath, but she rallies for its concluding phrases, even though resorting to some hollow tones for its final low notes. "O cris plus doux pour moi que les chants d'allégresse" is grandly done and the "Plus de faiblesse" boasts easy, if over-exclamatory, high Bs, and she executes the downward run coming off the second B superbly. She has plotted her breathing more carefully here, and better musical authority is the result.

Tamar may not be the Médée of one's dreams, but she gives us some idea of how this music can sound in its original form. Fournillier's conducting is also far from polished, but, ensemble gaps and all, it allows a sufficient enough framework for the performers to give us a glimpse of Cherubini's conception.

Even a fleeting glimpse is considerably more than one is given in the Newport Classic recording featuring the inadequate Phyllis Treigle. Bart Folse conducts an Opera Quotannis production of the original French version at the Mannes College of Music in New York City. This set was recorded in 1997. It is clearly inferior to its predecessor on Nuova Era. Since the latter has already given us Cherubini's original with an effective, if uneven, protagonist, it's hard to see the point of the former. Treigle's inadequacies in the title role extend to a recurrent tremolo, unfocused tones, and a gray, monotonous tone color. She is obviously working too hard and sounds it throughout. Folse's conducting is perfunctory, and the Jason and the Dircé are best left unnamed. The few attractions this set can offer include an effective Créon in David Arnold and a truly accomplished Néris in D'Anna Fortunato. (An odd coincidence that, both here and in the Nuova Era, the Créon and the Néris come out the strongest.) Arguably, another point in Folse's favor may be a more tightly prepared ensemble of period-instrument players than we hear in the sloppier sounds of the Fournillier reading. But that is offset by the casual manner in which Folse skims the surface of Cherubini's masterpiece. Newport Classic's packaging makes much ado over this being the first complete recording of the original French version — a confusing claim. Yet reading inside reveals that this sorry set actually is the first to retain every word of the spoken dialogue. Hence the offensive packaging. The one positive result here is that the accompanying booklet is a worthwhile product, with a thoughtful and conscientious introduction by the conductor and a literally complete French/English libretto. This contrasts with a French-only libretto in the Nuova Era, which also provides bizarre introductory material that spends more time on Mercadante's Medea opera than on Cherubini's! If one wants a good text and introduction for the original work, Newport Classic is preferable, but if one wants a more-adequate-than-not rendering of Cherubini's original design, only the Fournillier, with all its faults, will do.

◁ 4 ▷

Gioacchino Rossini (1792–1868): *Armida*

The first nineteenth-century role to combine all the characteristics in Cherubini's *Médée* is the title role in Rossini's *Armida*, created by Isabella Colbran in 1817 at Naples. Though it is an extraordinary experience to hear the way Callas, during her vocal prime, so easily overcame the many difficulties of Rossini's heroine, it is unfortunate that the part itself has none of the emotional depth of Médée's music. Rossini was rarely able to rise above the level of the *opera seria* libretto that he was setting. This score is historically important, since Rossini himself had arrived at a turning point in the development of his musical style. For the first time, he experimented with a more elaborate orchestration than hitherto, or than Italians were accustomed to.

The role of Armida is clearly designed for a diva whose characteristics one can easily glean, and Colbran's repertoire is better known than Julie-Angélique Scio's, most of which has been abandoned. One significant aspect of Rossini's accomplishment is the location of the *Armida* premiere: Naples, the heart of southern Italy. For an opera with vocal pyrotechnics to be premiered in Italy at this time was, of course, the norm, but there is a lot more than just fioritura in Armida's music. Those characteristics that distinguished not just *Armida* but *Médée* were a new kind of package for Italian audiences. *Médée* had its premiere outside of Italy; and, though Cherubini was Italian, he had composed his masterpiece in a style that found favor with French audiences, and more so with Austrian and German ones. *Armida* may be the first time that any Italian, in his

native land, dared to produce a work that showed traces of an unwelcome North-
ern "pedanticism." Certainly, *Armida* ended up being labeled too Teutonic by
several local observers.[19] Sure enough, *Armida*, along with *Médée* (both sung in
German), enjoyed quite a vogue in Austria and Germany. What Rossini was
developing in the work was a continuation of what Cherubini had done before
him and what Donizetti would develop to its highest level when Italy would at
last be sympathetic to more dramatic musical effects. It was only during the
Donizetti era that Italian divas such as Tadolini (at La Scala in 1836) would perform *Armida* once more in its native land and language.

Isabella Colbran, whom Rossini was later to marry, was termed a mezzo
by her contemporaries. Actually, her repertoire was more varied than such a
term would suggest. After having made her debut in 1801, Colbran, by 1817,
had sung with success roles such as the mezzo part of Paisiello's *Nina* in 1811
along with the soprano roles of Donna Anna in *Don Giovanni* in 1812 and the
Countess in *Figaro* in 1814. She had also created Rossini's *Elisabetta* in 1815 and
the role of Desdemona in his *Otello* in 1816,[20] a role mezzos have sung as often
as sopranos, and which is regarded as a straight mezzo role by its well-known
interpreter of recent decades, Frederica von Stade.[21] Colbran's apparent versatility was made possible by the fact that, during her prime, she had an enormous
range extending down to the low G — hence her proficiency in the mezzo repertoire — and up to the E above high C — thus combining the technical resources
required for practically all roles written for the female voice.[22] One gets the
impression that, though capable of surprising agility in the extreme high, her
voice was essentially a dark instrument, powerful in the middle and lower range,
with an innately portentous, highly theatrical timbre. Colbran's may not be an
isolated case, merely one of the earliest in a line of divas who, in their technical versatility, typify what the composers clearly had in mind in fashioning
music like Armida's. Colbran's discernible abilities give us the clearest notion
yet of the kind of vocal persona expected, of the diva who would perform such
roles.

Armida (like Médée) balances scenes calculated to exploit the deeper
recesses of a mezzo (her lament at the end of the opera for Rinaldo's desertion,
"Lasciarmi, oíme") with happy, radiant phrases for the higher reaches of a
soprano. Elsewhere, weighty fioritura exploits both extremes of the voice. An
example of this is Armida's final scene when she denounces Rinaldo in the fiery
passagework culminating with "E l'alma tua nutrita Fù ognor di crudeltà."
Therefore, a straight mezzo could not begin to do any of these roles justice. But
the similarity in *Armida* to the hybrid style of vocal writing in the contrasted
scenes in *Médée* falls into place when one realizes what Isabella Colbran, nominally a mezzo, had in common with the greatest castrati, viz., an ability to perform roles highly disparate in tessitura: the mezzo roles of Nina and the Rossini
Desdemona on the one hand, and Mozart's soprano heroines on the other.

By 1817, Colbran's tantalizing gifts had sustained this varied kind of repertoire for sixteen successful years, demonstrating the genuine resilience of her

instrument during that time. It was unfortunate, therefore, that, just a few months before the November 1817 premiere of *Armida*, she showed the first signs of vocal decline. Rossini obviously composed *Armida* with the Colbran sound at its zenith still in his imagination.

Rossini did not abandon the more dramatic musical path he had taken for the first time in *Armida*. This style reached its culmination in *Semiramide* (1823), an opera that was a true masterpiece in the depth of its expression and the variety of its musicodramatic effects. Such variety seemed infinitely more meaningful in *Semiramide* than in the more two-dimensional theatrical effects in the music of *Armida*.

However, *Semiramide*, which was also fashioned for Colbran, though six years after her decline, did not match up a heroic vocal style with fioritura to the same extent as *Armida*. There were only a few dramatic phrases in Semiramide's music, and they were well within the capacities of Nellie Melba, a soprano who never touched an *assoluta* role in her life and whose sole excursion into the dramatic repertoire (a *Siegfried* Brünnhilde opposite Jean de Reszke) was an unmitigated disaster. The intricacy of Armida's fioritura was, however, fully duplicated in Semiramide's music.

This being the case, unfortunately, the upshot was that only once did Rossini have the opportunity to compose for Colbran an opera that combined all the contrasted features of what it is now possible to recognize as a true *assoluta* part. (His *Elisabetta, Regina d'Inghilterra* was premiered as a vehicle for the still vocally hale Colbran in 1815, but this opera did not have the orchestral energy of *Armida*.) These features, which are consistently present in all the remaining *assoluta* scores that follow in the wake of Cherubini's *Médée* and Rossini's *Armida*, are:

    1) fioritura singing in the most intricate *bel canto* tradition;

    2) florid singing combined with heroic weight;

    3) a heavy or dense sound in the lower range;

    4) vocal power over an energetic orchestral accompaniment;

    5) widely varying tessitura: the alternation of extended sequences whose tessitura lies quite low with those lying quite high;

    6) at least one lengthy scene during which the character dominates the stage;

    7) a range extending down to at least low B-natural and up to at least high B-natural with at least one further semitone required at either end.

Taking as a guide the vocal histories of the women who created the *assoluta* roles following Médée and Armida, most of whom had mezzo as well as soprano roles in their repertoires, it is possible to deduce the kind of voice the *assoluta* roles were designed for.

Only a role that clearly conforms to every one of these seven features can be said to involve the full talents of a complete dramatic coloratura singer or, rather, an *assoluta*. Armida belongs in this group. The performer of this role must, through a sensitive and moving instrument, do full justice to Rossini's

expressiveness along with mastering the seven vocal and technical difficulties that
the part entails.

Armida on disc

This is no doubt a truism, but it still bears repeating: the currency of
Rossini's *Armida* would not be what it is today had not Maria Callas performed
this opera at Florence in 1952. True, she never tackled any of the other *seria*
Rossini heroines, but her example in bringing Armida to life helped spark
renewed interest in many of them. In reviving it, her conductor, Tullio Serafin,
does not deal kindly with the six tenor roles in this opera that surround the
heroine like planets around a star. Their music is severely truncated at Florence,
and poorly sung at that. Francesco Albanese's Rinaldo is like a fly stuck in amber:
his portrayal is an anachronism, neither tied to a living tradition that preceded
him, nor alert enough to the example of his distinguished partner to revive one.
Serafin's conducting, with all his cuts, still gives the singers superb support. He
molds Rossini's music into a genuine singing line, and he gives Callas the scope
she needs to animate Rossini's heroine through rigorously musical means. This
'52 revival has been available in fair sound on a number of obscure LP and CD
labels, including one LP issue on MDP that is the basis of this current review.
(Certain passages missing in the original Callas tape are supplied here from a
Cristina Deutekom performance — see below.)

In Callas's opening scene, she sounds on the verge of tears at Goffredo's
initial reluctance to assist her, portraying astonishment at "No" for an answer.
She then proceeds to convey slyness in the aside, "Per me ognun sospira e geme,"
while displaying the "string-of-pearls" effect for which her passagework was
famous. This is topped by spectacular runs in "Per me propizio il fato." Her first
duet scene with Rinaldo gives us a tender "E me qui trasse amore." Throughout their moments together, Callas maintains languishing tones in the midst of
sparkling fioritura. One spine-chilling effect is at the repeated "Fuggirmi," where
the word emerges wrathful at first, turning cooing the second time. At the same
time, her "Vacilla a' questi accenti" proves, in its fusing of the devious and the
hopeful, that her longing for Rinado is still deep and real. Vocally, we then have
a flawless run down the scale heralding their duet, "Cara/caro, per te." Callas
sustains a lightness here despite the rich feeling, successfully rendering the quick
notes fully integrated into the larger expression. In the final moments of Act I,
there is a somber opening for "Che terribile momento," affording rich colors in
the low, and her contrasting "Amica la sorte" in the closing ensemble is redo-
lent of hope and the dreams of love, climaxing on an electrifying high C.

In the Act II duet, Callas strokes Rinaldo gently with her roulades on "Mio
bel tesor," and we have a hypnotic trill on "Caro, se m'ami." "D'Amor al dolce
impero" achieves perfect line down to her lowest note (low G) in roulade after
roulade. Moreover, she manages to make the whole genuinely enticing. Pande-
monium breaks out in the audience after a final triumphant top note.

None of Armida's music in Act III, Scene I is available with Callas, so MDP merely uses the Deutekom/Botazzo reading of the lovers' last duet. (We will assess their rendering later.) Act III, Scene 2 is overwhelming: Callas is by turns reproachful ("infido"), urgent, accusatory ("tradir"), tearful, vitriolic, scornful (for one flourish), and wheedling (for the next). In her "Se al mio crudel tormento," sorrow and wrath are in perfect balance and there is spectacular passagework, clarion highs and rich lows. In "Dove son io?" she recalls the contrast between the two "Fuggirmi"'s of the first Act duet by repeating a similar effect here: "Fuggì" sounds angry the first time, tearful the second. "Potè l'ingrato" turns into a cry of anguish and "stato" is a musical whimper. Her final imprecations, "E' ver … gode quest' anima," are marked by the sternest inflections in the lower half of the instrument: "involati," "t'affretta," "empio," "resti," her second devastating "tutto" all show how pitiless she has become in her conscious choice of vengeance over love. The darkest powers are summoned up in the listener's imagination by her utterance of "Furie" and "Averno" in the same dark colors. Finally, the way she peals out a closing high E flat sums up her destructive urges at the end.

Like the Callas performance, Cristina Deutekom's "live" reading from 1970 has only been made available on a variety of smaller labels, including Mondo Musica. Her partner is Pietro Botazzo as Rinaldo, and Carlo Franci conducts.

The touchstone to Deutekom's interpretation is its regal stance. Even in the plaintive "Sventurata" at the opening, she sounds stern, and there is little change of mood at "E sarà ver?" She adopts an eccentric method of handling the fioritura; it is not necessarily off-putting, but it is disorienting. Most of the passagework is articulated in a peculiarly segmented way that is distinct from either nickel-and-dime aspirating or knee-jerk glottal attacks, but, at the same time, is not phrased with a true legato. It suggests the bells of a music box or the presence of a human marimba in her throat! It is precise enough, but is it musical? Personally, I find it more intriguing than unmusical, and it certainly is tied to an excellent technique in other respects. She is capable of the broadest phrasing for moments like "Speme non ho," and she knows how to integrate excellent *pianissimi* into a phrase. Her first duet with Rinaldo may betray a basic hardness in the voice that mitigates true tenderness, but she is in good control here and always strikes one as musical. She successfully communicates the feelings in "Non espor sì bella vita" through tearfully syllabic accentuation. There is, however, little feeling of an aside at "Vanne … i passi precedi d'Armida." "Amica la sorte" conveys excitement at fulfilled hopes, but, again, little sense of her tenderness for Rinaldo. There is a good high C as the curtain falls.

The Act II duet is delivered with clear, limpid tones, but certain lines of recitative are impassive. "D'Amor al dolce impero" snips out the first choral interjection, and some of the passagework is altered to avoid the low G. There is spectacular aplomb, though, shown in everything she *does* sing here, which is by no means negligible. The "marimba" effect may be fairly pronounced here, but everything still remains effective.

The final act is more persuasive. Its opening duet is not particularly convincing, with its lack of shading and real tenderness, but once past that, Deutekom's reading becomes stronger. Maestro Franci cuts out the passage closing Scene I, so the next time we hear her is the last confrontation with Rinaldo and the ultimate resolve on vengeance. The predominant impression at the outset of this closing scene is merely a sense of insult at Rinaldo's betrayal rather than an additional feeling of deep and personal loss, though her fioritura is always energetic and incisive. She sports a physically strong low here as well, while its coloring may be nondescript. She succeeds in infusing it with proper desolation in her "Dove son io," and the "E' ver ... gode quest' anima" boasts a highly effective "resti." A strong high E flat crowns this scene.

A release from 1992 on Arts marks the first commercially made *Armida*. Led by Rossini specialist, Claudio Scimone, it features Cecilia Gasdia in the title role and Chris Merritt as Rinaldo.

In Act I, Gasdia at first alternates between perkiness and impassiveness. Her control of Rossini's passagework is certainly fluent, but there is little differentiation between coloratura passages uttered for others and those intended as wily asides, a critical consideration in Armida's first scene, which is primarily scheming. Given Gasdia's coloratura ability, she can sometimes make a telling effect with a flourish on a word like "crudel." But she still lacks needed presence to make something like the tricky "Per me propizio il fato" a true expression of triumph. A pleasant surprise it is to hear this Armida suddenly showing more snap once she's alone with her uncle Idraote, as she spits out words like "dispetto." Once alone with Rinaldo, though, there is another surprise, not so pleasant: Gasdia goes flat on a repeated "amor" in "E in me fia spento amor." In addition, she loses authority in descending to "piagò." There may be a new tenderness in the way she attacks "dolce" of "dolce mia speranza," but she drifts back to impassivity on "speranza." As one might expect, her "Caro, per te" is efficiently rippled through. More imagination then takes over in a hushed "Che terribile momento," climaxing with an assured *crescendo*. Equally assured is a deft trill on "son" of "son io" and a conspiratorial "Vanne: i passi precedi d'Armida" partly achieved by transposing the line down. She ends the scene with her first hint of glee in "Amica la sorte" and joins Chris Merritt on a final high C.

The second act shows Gasdia trilling expertly on "Caro" and lofting easily through the delicate passagework of the opening duet. She has a go at being the grand hostess in her "Mio ben," although a studied quality detracts from a sense of easy authority. At the opening of "D'Amore al dolce impero," the middle-register phrases expose problems in diction. The passagework as the aria develops is happier.

In Act III, Gasdia's spirited delivery in the opening exchange with Rinaldo registers immediately. Her recitative of desperation, "Dov'è? ... dove si cela," is equally spirited with an affecting "Senti/Perfido! non m'ascolta" and a stricken "fier tormento!" Her last scene shows genuine hurt for "Ed è pur vero?" She negotiates the flourish on "vigor" splendidly, and there is a touching "E asciutto il ciglio." While much of the fioritura in "Se al mio crudel tormento" is sure, it lacks crispness lower down for turns like "Segno di duol." In general, her delivery lacks any threat of the supernatural. Accomplished, though, is her passagework on "Dà fine al mio penar." Going from that to the transition for the "Dove son io," Claudio Scimone shows himself a master, and Gasdia is clued in immediately. There may be a gravelly moment on "palpiti," but "Del mio trovar" is her most convincing moment. One regrets an overlong scoop on "Amor," where she almost doesn't reach the pitch, but the mood is successfully sustained to the end of the solo. The final moments are not as successful. "E' ver ... gode quest' anima" has her fading away on the ... "tta" of both "Vendetta" and "t'affretta," and the entire delivery lacks proper breadth, "suo furor" flatting badly in the closing phrases.

A more recent release from Sony presents a 1993 production at the Teatro Comunale in Bologna under Daniele Gatti. Renée Fleming and Gregory Kunde star as Armida and Rinaldo. Fleming has an exquisitely beautiful voice. Hers is the most communicative instrument of all in conveying Armida's excessive longing for Rinaldo. This makes her especially effective in the duets. But it also makes her final-act choice of vengeance over love a surprise. Her Armida has seemed such a generous person up to that point.

Fleming is irresistible in the first scene where we are greeted with an opulent shower of pear-shaped tones. How could Goffredo ever deny her plea for help, especially after that affecting sob at "per me" of "E' la vita omai per me"? Yet there doesn't appear too much of a difference for the aside that follows, "Per me ognun sospira e geme." One hankers here for a clearer sense of the danger in this woman. What we get further on are fine runs for "Per me propizio il fato," even though there is an occasional slight aspirate. More ginger appears in her next scene, alone with Rinaldo. She accuses him of neglect, spitting out "Un marcato disprezzo," letting the word "marcato" lose tone but gain vehemence in the process. Her vocal effectiveness in this scene is formidable: a precise trill on "natura," tender accents for "La dolce mia speranza," a spectacular flourish across all three registers at "Oh istante," and adept phrasing for the tricky passagework in "Caro, per te quest' anima." Again, there is her continued obsession with Rinaldo, which Fleming never lets us forget. Weighed against her vocal authority here, there is surprising shortness of breath in the coloratura climaxing "Sì, amor ... /Se un' alma fiera." In her next scene with Rinaldo, "Deh! se cara a te son io" becomes a virtual anatomy of the trill! Her solo in the ensemble ringing down Act I, "Amica la sorte," is dazzling, although "d'amor" lies so low that it sounds guttural. She does not opt for the high C at the end.

The duet in Act II is melting. Especially notable is a prolonged trill in "Caro, se m'ami" and a thrilling climax to "Ecco il centro del piacer." Fleming then captures the enticing beauty of "D'Amor al dolce impero." Her singing shows remarkable smoothness across the scale, and the passagework is trippingly done. This is the finest sequence in her portrayal.

It is Act III that poses daunting challenges. There are some individual touches in Fleming's entrance duet. She sounds as if Rinaldo has hit a raw nerve when she snaps at him: "Che! Dubiteresti ..." The same happens with "E ciò non basta?" But when we reach Armida's invocation of the Furies, Fleming's low register fails to achieve the desired effect on key words like "traditor" and "tormento." Her final scene, encapsulating Armida's attempt to restrain her beloved from leaving, allows her tender regard for Rinaldo to surface once more. There is a haunting softness to her "la fè." She is in sure control of the fioritura at "Segno di duol non dai." However, one flourish trips on an ungainly register break in the lower mid-range. At another point, the word "pietà" lands in the same gap. She runs short of breath at "E l'alma tua nutrita," making the final ... "ta" lose power; her voice is also lost in the low notes of the coloratura on "Da' fine al mio penar." Her lamenting soliloquy, "Dove son io?" is superior, opening with glistening tones; minimum pressure is maintained throughout her range, making her lower register fit with the musical statement. The clarity of her diction, the authentic sound of heartbreak in her voice, and her unfailing legato throughout, make nothing in her hushed lower tones stand out uncomfortably. She increases the tension effectively on "Che fo?" and "Di voi che udir dovrò?" is expressively delivered. This is followed by fine passagework on "Del mio trovar si può Più atroce stato!" The downward scales at "Cinta benchè d'orror" are likewise beautifully shaped. For the closing "E' ver ... gode quest' anima," "t'affretta" is brought up to avoid a weakness lower down. She ends up being quite effective in the way she hurls out, at score pitch, her incensed "tutto!" There is no high E flat at the end, but the brio in her singing brings these final measures to an exciting conclusion.

One has to regret that Fleming's Armida at Carnegie Hall, three years later with Eve Queler, has not been released on CD. There was more variety to her reading on that occasion, and the danger her character posed to all the other principals became considerably clearer.

ॐ 5 ॐ

Assoluta Manquée (I)

At the Théâtre Feydeau in Paris in March 1797, Médée's first-act aria in Cherubini's opera opened the sung portion of the first *assoluta* role that defines the species. This opening of *Médée* in Paris initiated the tradition of the florid yet heroic heroine whose range of over two octaves required the talents of an *assoluta*.

The sound of Cherubini's opera was certainly new and unusual at the time, not just because of the difficulties of the title role but because of Cherubini's orchestration. Though the orchestral size is not unusual, and Verdi, Donizetti, and others of the Italian school ended up with a greater number of instruments than Cherubini, there is a kind of emotive energy to Cherubini's orchestra that is not present in the sound of a Pergolesi, a Handel, or even a Mozart orchestra. Certainly, the vocal line for these eighteenth-century masters never requires an outpouring of energy similar to that required by Cherubini and the later *bel canto* composers. Gluck, in *Alceste*, had achieved in his orchestra something like what Cherubini had done, but without such an intricate vocal line to match it. It was Cherubini who forged the unusual juxtaposition of the extravagant vocal tendencies of the eighteenth-century *opera seria* and the newly developing dramatic tendencies of Gluck. There was no precedent for the degree to which Cherubini had wedded an orchestra to everything that was going on in the pyrotechnics for the character.

That Médée and Armida were both fashioned in this way is extraordinary enough, but there are at least seven other parts that define every aspect of the *assoluta* role as fully as these two. Using them as a model, one can easily match up their technical characteristics with one or more sequences in these seven other *assoluta* roles: Reiza in Weber's *Oberon* (1826), Anna in Donizetti's *Anna Bolena* (1830), Norma in Bellini's *Norma* (1831), Gemma in Donizetti's *Gemma di Vergy* (1834), Elisabetta in Donizetti's *Roberto Devereux* (1837), Abigaille in

Verdi's *Nabucco* (1842), and Lady Macbeth in Verdi's *Macbeth* (1847). For convenience, all nine defining *assoluta* parts will be referred to as the **A,i** group.

These specially conceived parts for the *assoluta* did not emerge out of a vacuum. For the performer capable of interpreting them, there are a number of related roles that fit such a vocal persona as well. Some of these earlier parts opened the way for the composition of the nine grand vehicles central to this book, and related roles continued to be composed both during and after the heyday of the *assoluta* repertoire itself.

This chapter is intended as an overview of the earliest models that appeared prior to Médée. One might call such roles *assoluta manquée*. By using the word *manquée* I mean that these trailblazers lack one or two attributes associated with the nine operas that make up the **A,i** group.

Frequently, there are compelling stylistic reasons for the lack of various *assoluta* requirements in other parts. The earliest models for *assoluta manquée* are parceled out here in categories **B,iii** (pioneered in 1767), **A,ii** (pioneered in 1781), and **B,i** (pioneered in 1782).

My numbering for all such sub-groups is keyed to their descending order of casting difficulty. Thus, on the one hand, categories **A,ii** through **A,vii** (see Chapter Fourteen) still benefit most from a genuine *assoluta*'s performing them despite their lack of one or two defining *assoluta* attributes. On the other hand, categories **B,i** through **B,iii** do not necessarily require a diva *assoluta* but have, as a group, some stylistic attributes in common with **A,i** through **A,vii** and might therefore benefit from *assoluta* casting.

Since the *assoluta* role is essentially a conglomeration of the intricate fioritura of the *opera seria* and the later instrumental effects of Gluck, followed by Mozart, it comes as no surprise that it is these pioneers in the so-called Classic style who laid the groundwork for the breakthroughs of Cherubini and Rossini.

Three sub-groups preceded the introduction of the **A,i** roles pioneered by Cherubini and Rossini:

The first, with Gluck's *Alceste* in 1767 at Vienna, paved the way for the use of the instrumental accompaniment to convey the emotional moments in the heroine's character development. As a result of the greater development in the orchestra and the more ambitious use of characterizational color, the singing voice in turn was given less intricate, but more simple and bold, musical expression through less florid but direct and passionate vocal writing.

Of course, using nineteenth and twentieth century *verismo* as the yardstick, the sheer flexibility required of a diva singing the role of Alceste is by no means negligible, but compared with the florid music Handel had composed for his characters, at the zenith of the *opera seria* roughly twenty-five years before *Alceste*, Gluck's vocalism is very restrained.

Some of the vocal exuberance Handel and other practitioners of the *opera seria* invest their characters with is more directly recalled in Mozart's operas. However, while the requirements in Mozart for extreme vocal flexibility are in marked contrast to Gluck, the ideal of tracing the intricacies of character development as far as they can be traced in music is pursued as eagerly in *Così fan tutte*, in *La Clemenza di Tito*, or in *Zauberflöte* as in *Alceste*. It is, rather, the extremest reaches of instrumental commentary, to the point where the orchestra becomes as emphatic as the singing voice itself, which are explored only in *Alceste* and not, to such an extent, in Mozart. One cannot help wondering what the leading diva of the early nineteenth century, Angelica Catalani (who actually found the orchestra too conspicuous in *Clemenza di Tito*),[23] must have thought of *Alceste*.

In sum, the prevailing characteristics of Gluck's heroine are the requirements for weighty tone and for only moderate vocal flexibility compared with Mozart's heroines. Thus, *Alceste* clearly requires a heavy, powerful vocal persona, one capable of the grand, long line. Together with such vigorousness and flexibility as it does require, the role also demands an easy high B flat. Alceste is the kind of heroic part that belongs with the **B,iii** category in which seven other operas are also listed. In the wake of Gluck, roles patterned after the *Alceste*/**B,iii** model began to be composed years later in the wane of the *assoluta* era, starting with Senta in Wagner's *Der Fliegende Holländer* (1843) and ending with Renata in Prokofiev's *The Fiery Angel* (1927).

B,iii Group

1767   Gluck: *Alceste*
1843   Wagner: *Der Fliegende Holländer* (Senta)
1845   Wagner: *Tannhäuser* ("Dresden Venus")
1859   Verdi: *Un Ballo in maschera* (Amelia)
1870   Wagner: *Die Walküre* (Brünnhilde)
1876   Wagner: *Götterdämmerung* (Brünnhilde)
1876   Ponchielli: *La Gioconda*
1927   Prokofiev: *The Fiery Angel* (Renata)

Sub-group two is illustrated by Mozart's *Idomeneo* presented in 1781 at Munich. The role of Elettra is a demanding portrait, full of roulades, fury, dementia, a foil to the lighter role of Ilia. Elettra is much closer to what can be defined as the *assoluta* part than is Alceste. Elettra's instrumental accompaniment is not quite as formidable as Alceste's, but her roulades are extremely intricate, and some of her other outbursts are just as vehement as in Gluck. In a sense, Elettra constitutes one long Mad Scene from beginning to end. The tessitura varies much more sharply than does Alceste's, and it is suggestive that Rudolf Kloiber in his guide to operatic vocal *fach*, *Handbuch der Oper* (1966), seems to regard Elettra as a *zwischenfach* role; at any rate, he calls her both a "Dramatischer Sopran" and a "Dramatischer Mezzosopran." The full extent to which Elettra is a truly heroic role is thrown into some doubt, however, when one looks at the more consistently heavy instrumentation of *Alceste*.

Elisabeth Grümmer, a performer of both Elettra and Ilia, said of Elettra in her interview with Lanfranco Rasponi:

... Elettra in *Idomeneo* is in the lyric range. Certainly, it requires more volume than Ilia, and dramatic expression, but if you look at the score well, there is no demand for a dark-colored or heavy voice.[24]

What Grümmer obviously achieved, in performing the role with her silvery voice and immaculate technique and musicianship, was an entirely successful musical presentation of Elettra's actual notes, a presentation that eschewed the contrasts of vocal color that the writing requires. Grümmer's successful mastery of the music in this manner does not necessarily prove that an occasionally dark vocal color is not needed for Elettra or unintended by Mozart. Only the clear fact that Grümmer successfully performed the part anyway (without trying to make her voice unduly heavy) can be offered as a kind of proof that the heaviest, most powerful sound is not always an absolute necessity for this role. While it is overstating it to maintain that Elettra is "in the lyric range," as Grümmer puts it, a fully heroic instrument is likewise less essential for the part.

Lanfranco Rasponi regards Elettra as a dramatic with agility, while soprano Claire Watson describes the role as one "which needs a real spinto." To resolve all these seeming contradictions, a look at the score shows that Elettra combines the requirement for an occasionally heavy instrument with as much ease in the highest register (it reaches up to high C) as in the lowest (it reaches down to low B), and with the need for a dramatically expressive coloratura. She is the trailblazer in the **A,ii** *manquée* group, the one group closest in quality to the defining *assoluta* model of **A,i**. The reason for her restriction to the **A,ii** group lies in something Martina Arroyo drew to my attention when discussing this category and the **A,ii** role of Valentine in Meyerbeer's *Les Huguenots* (1836) in particular. There is a difference in the **A,ii** parts between the generally heroic vocal weight required for those passages not needing agility and the more lyric vocal weight usually expected of the singer in agile passages.[25] Therefore, only the defining *assoluta* characteristic of combining in one and the same sequence a diva's fullest tone with the maximum in agility is missing to make Elettra, Valentine, or any of the **A,ii** parts defining **A,i** roles. They are still taxing enough to benefit, musically and dramatically, from the talents of a true *assoluta*. There are twelve roles in the **A,ii** group. Musically and stylistically, the *Idomeneo*/**A,ii** group contains an astonishing variety of operatic idioms, but the critical combination of wide tessitura and range, heroic declamation, and generally lighter agility remains constant. At the same time, its astonishing variety embraces everything from Mozart to a number of challenging star vehicles from the *assoluta* heyday of the 1830s to middle Verdi to Offenbach to Berg's *Lulu* in 1937.

A,ii Group

1781 Mozart: *Idomeneo* (Elettra)
1791 Mozart: *La Clemenza di Tito* (Vitellia)
1833 Donizetti: *Lucrezia Borgia*
1835 Halévy: *La Juive* (Rachel)

1836 Meyerbeer: *Les Huguenots* (Valentine)
1844 Verdi: *Ernani* (Elvira) (described, *Macbeth* section)
1850 Verdi: *Stiffelio* (Lina) (described, Time of Transition)
1853 Verdi: *Il Trovatore* (Leonora)
1855 Verdi: *Les Vêpres siciliennes* (Hélène)
1857 Verdi: *Aroldo* (Mina)
1880 Offenbach: *Les Contes d'Hoffmann* ("maîtresses")
1937 Berg: *Lulu*

The third sub-group, preceding the **A,i** revolution of Cherubini and Rossini, was also introduced by Mozart in the role of Konstanze in *Die Entführung aus dem Serail* (1782). Extravagant intervals reminiscent of the Mozart Elettra characterize Konstanze, written for Caterina Cavalieri, a singer with a generous range. The role includes most of the technical hurdles in Elettra, with dramatically expressive, though not fully heroic, coloratura and with swings in tessitura. What distinguishes the Konstanze type from the **A,ii** group introduced in *Idomeneo* is Konstanze's consistent spinto level throughout, with no increase in weight for the declamatory sections. She is the first **B,i** role, a category that has sixteen parts in all. The *Entführung*/**B,i** model comes to an end in 1853 with the role of Violetta in *La Traviata*.

B,i Group

1782 Mozart: *Die Entführung aus dem Serail* (Konstanze)
1787 Mozart: *Don Giovanni* (Donna Elvira)
1790 Mozart: *Così fan tutte* (Fiordiligi)
1791 Mozart: *Die Zauberflöte* (Königen)
1808 Haydn: *L'Anima del filosofo* (Euridice) & (Genio)
1815 Rossini: *Elisabetta, Regina d'Inghilterra* (referred to, *Armida* section)
1823 Rossini: *Semiramide* (described, *Armida* section)
1831 Meyerbeer: *Robert le Diable* (Alice) (referred to, *Oberon* section)
1833 Bellini: *Beatrice di Tenda*
1835 Halévy: *La Juive* (Eudoxie)
1835 Donizetti: *Lucia di Lammermoor* (referred to, *Norma* section)
1835 Donizetti: *Maria Stuarda* (described, *Gemma* section)
1836 Meyerbeer: *Les Huguenots* (Marguerite)
1851 Verdi: *Rigoletto* (Gilda)
1853 Verdi: *La Traviata* (Violetta)

Alceste in 1767, Elettra in 1781, and Konstanze in 1782 typify the three important ur-currents of *assoluta manquée* vocal writing inaugurated prior to the time of Cherubini's *Médée*.

✣ 6 ✣

Carl Maria von Weber (1786–1826): *Oberon*

In London in 1826, Weber's operatic swansong was his *Oberon*, composed to an English text by James Robinson Planché and featuring the vocal talents of John Braham, James Bland, and Mary Anne Paton. The last-named was at the start of a distinguished career. Weber composed for her, in this opera, the third of the defining *assoluta* roles central to this study — the role of Reiza. Reiza was the first of a number of *assoluta* roles to require what became a customary voice span from low B flat to high C.

Since the whole form of the opera consists of extended, highly Romantic musical episodes alternating with spoken dialogue, it bears a certain resemblance, both in its energetic orchestration and in its theatrical idiom, to *Médée*. However, with a less effective libretto, it is not as compelling throughout. There are still awesome moments, dramatically as well as musically, in Reiza's role. Her greatest and longest *scena*, "Ocean, thou mighty monster," has become a justly admired concert staple for artists capable of singing with agility against a pervasive orchestral accompaniment. In this extended scene, as Reiza lies hopeless, stranded on an island, we have the weighty, low-lying opening phrases, further requirements for technical versatility as the aria proceeds, and heroic fioritura in the high-lying coda. At one point, there is even an exposed trill thrown in for good measure.

During Mary Anne Paton's operatic career of twenty-two years (1822–44), some of the other roles she sang were the soprano roles of Agathe in *Der*

Freischütz, Susanna in *Le Nozze di Figaro*, and Polly in *The Beggar's Opera*, and, in true *assoluta* fashion, the mezzo roles of Rossini's *La Cenerentola* and Pippo in *La Gazza ladra*. She also sang the role of Alice in Meyerbeer's *Robert le Diable* in 1832, occasionally called a mezzo in some librettos of the nineteenth century, together with the high soprano role of Isabelle in the same opera in 1834. Her tones were described as brilliant, sweet-toned, and powerful. She had a two-and-a-half-octave range from low A to high E.[26] Aside from Mary Anne Paton in creating the role, Wilhelmine Schröder-Devrient, Anna Barthe-Hasselt, Thérèse Tietjens and Lilli Lehmann also tackled this music, during the fifty-plus years following *Oberon*'s premiere, in German, as Reiza.

Though "Ocean" is unquestionably Reiza's finest moment, similarly wide-ranging requirements are not lacking throughout the rest of her music, clearly demanding a first-rate artist. In a role of this kind, conceived by a musical genius like Weber, the presence of such a variety of vocal requirements is an index to its depth and complexity and should not be regarded as mere mechanical baggage. The potential of the supersinger who can master these technical pitfalls is fulfilled in such precise vocal writing, thus matching the fireworks to the feelings of the character. Of course, a perfect fit of this kind is always bound to be rare. In Reiza's case, however, Weber succeeds, although his success can only be appreciated through an artist whose technique is up to the many changes in Reiza's mercurial vocal line.

Reiza's expressive music teaches a lesson critical to understanding the *assoluta* phenomenon: the dramatic effectiveness of successful vocal writing can lie exclusively in the genuine feelings in the music; it need not also depend on the context of a decent text and plot. A great composer can convey the essence of human feelings no matter what.

The peculiar excitement unique to a spectator's attending a strong *assoluta* performance is multi-layered. First there is the librettist who may or may not craft a compelling text. Then there is the composer who charges that text with many different feelings and translates those feelings into dots on a page. Then there is the performer who translates those dots into sounds. Finally there is the spectator who translates those sounds back into feelings.

The great imponderable is how well all these feelings travel. At each stage, the reality behind them is a little different because they are being transmitted through variable human agents. If the essence of these feelings remains tangible despite the many layers, then the spectator is suitably enthralled. At the same time, while their essence may remain intact, it is virtually impossible that all the feelings will remain precisely the same throughout the process.

First, the librettist may write little more than a bald vignette depicting someone like Reiza lost at sea. So the task may be conceived of as merely depicting a woman who is alternately forlorn or hopeful in her longings for rescue. Whatever feelings a librettist conveys can sometimes be perfunctory, depending on the depth of his or her own comprehension of human nature.

Then the inspired composer may relate the baldness of the verses to a dazzling variety of universal feelings encompassing everything from nostalgia, to regret, to horror, and finally to triumph, and so on. Frequently, the librettist hasn't had an inkling of these feelings, for they are all in the composer's head. The composer may think they are implicit in the text, to the point of being fooled, or may consciously be bringing his greater sensitivity to all human feeling onto a text whose blatant shallowness is clearly seen. Whichever it is, the composer's ultimate task is the same: translate the myriad feelings projected onto Reiza into notes on a page. The feelings translated are no more Reiza's than the shallower feelings the librettist has. Reiza does not have true feelings of her own because she is fictitious. As with the librettist, the reality behind any composer's feelings is merely whatever reality lies behind the composer's own understanding of human nature. Therefore, the feelings the composer entrusts to the little "dots" are strictly the composer's, and, in so entrusting them, the dots are used as a "courier."

Then the dots travel by way of the performer. The performer connects the dots through the use of individual feelings, as individual and apart as the composer's. Then the dots become sounds. By now, the sounds, not the dots, are a courier for genuine feelings, but they no more hold the composer's feelings than the dots hold the librettist's—much less the fictitious Reiza's. Only the performer's feelings are carried in the sounds, which are then picked up by the spectator. The performer's feelings may bear a resemblance to the composer's, but they can never be identical. Thus, the sounds can never carry precisely what the composer feels.

Finally, at the end of this process, feelings are retrieved from the performer's sounds. But the feelings retrieved are, by then, no more the performer's than they are the composer's or the librettist's. They are now the spectator's. While it is essential that the performer's feelings be genuine in order for the spectator to retrieve anything, the only feelings, in reality, that function as raw feelings without any intermediate courier whatsoever are the spectator's.

All along, there is a game played squaring a fiction against reality: a pretense that the fictitious Reiza has any feelings at all. The reality is that three different artists, the poet, the composer, the performer, contribute different sets of feelings to the three couriers: the verses, the dots, the sounds. My own feelings as a spectator may be as intense as anyone's, since no courier is needed to drive the feelings home. Here the experience of the feelings comes directly from the feelings themselves.

There is also my gratitude in this experience. For the essence of any feelings to survive the "game," there must be recognizable points of contact among the three creators. Consequently, when these points of contact reach to the listener's ear, I am grateful because the humanity of the feelings uncovered in a great *assoluta* performance makes me appreciate the common feelings shared on both sides of the footlights. Ultimately, my gratitude comes from the accomplishment of the performer. While my response to the fictitious character is a game much like an actress feigning a character, the feeling of the performer is real, and a phenomenal *assoluta*'s understanding of the essence of a composer's insight is real. Therefore, my feeling toward the performer is also real. I admire, love, and am grateful to her because she reminds me of our shared humanity. The performer is devoted to representing reality to us—not just a fictitious reality of a feigned character in a faded libretto, but the true reality of all human experience. So when a beautiful voice has the plangency of a Calvé, a Leider, a Ponselle, a Farrell, or a Ludwig, it is as though it says, "We know, we know, it's a vale of tears, and the lovelier it is in its complexity, the sadder is mortality." This consciousness of mortality in the vocal line is what opera's vocal music really is, and anything less is beside the point.

Bluntly put, the function of the great artist is to break your heart and to blow your mind, and the true function of the operatic spectacle is to enhance rather than compromise that experience. Beyond any compelling truth in some fictional character, the tragic hero or heroine is actually emblematic of our own heroism — and that of all the artists, for both artist and spectator are heroes of the human condition. Recognition of this makes us privy to the emotional illusion in the vocal line itself. Full awareness of that illusion makes the finest works in the *assoluta* style critical to the history of the lyric stage.

Reiza on disc

It was March 1922 and a genial young giant of a man in his early thirties stepped into her studio. She indicated she was ready to hear him. He sang two Wagner excerpts for tenor. His voice was *immense*. His musicianship was middling. His German left a lot to be desired. His temperament seemed instantly endearing. "You need at least a year of work," she said. "We can study some Wagner roles during that time. When we are finished, I expect the world to be at your feet."

The tenor's name was Lauritz Melchior. The rest is history.

His imposing teacher knew a thing or two about enormous voices. She had one herself. Anna Bahr-Mildenburg had sung Kundry and Ortrud at Bayreuth. She had won Gustav Mahler's unstinting admiration. No less an eminence than Lilli Lehmann had deigned to substitute for her when she was indisposed. Bahr-Mildenburg was the artist who was one of the first to record a snippet from Reiza's "Ocean, thou mighty monster." It was an acoustic containing only the opening recitative.

Reiza's "Ocean" aria and Norma's "Casta Diva" are the two *assoluta* arias that were recorded most often before 1937, the banner year when we have our first complete renderings of *assoluta* repertoire: the Metropolitan opera broadcast of Cigna's *Norma* from February of that year, the studio *Norma* also with Cigna from later that spring, and a German radio broadcast in August of *Oberon* featuring Teschemacher and Rosvaenge.

Here we will just take a look at various divas' recordings of the "Ocean" aria, and later we will assess complete recordings of *Oberon*.

Since most of the distinguished records of Reiza's "Ocean" are in German translation, we will be using that in this limited retrospective. Bahr-Mildenburg's piano-accompanied acoustic is no exception. Her opening word "Ozean" immediately conveys all the expanse of the world's waters in its oceanic size. Entrusted with the task of stretching Reiza's recitative across an entire 78-rpm record, this singer adopts the slowest tempo ever heard in this passage. Almost every note is milked, while glorious sound pours forth. Her reading defines grandeur. Awesome as are her top notes, the sonorousness of her low on "Welt" is just as crushing. This deliberate reading is topped by an optional high B flat of epic proportions on the word "du," to be followed by Weber's own low B flat two octaves down at "ein" of "ein Schreckbild dar," sung with equal authority. The high option on "du" is adopted by a number of other interpreters across the century. It, and the imposing "ein Schreckbild dar," serve as an effective close to this 78. It would be hard to imagine a more overwhelming way of opening our retrospective on this piece.

Another early acoustic, this time with Lucie Weidt, gives us somewhat more of the piece. The accompaniment is now an orchestra. Like Bahr-Mildenburg, Weidt has an imposing low. She also interpolates an impressive high B flat on "du," following it with a fine low B flat two octaves down. Unlike Bahr-Mildenburg, Weidt is given a chance to test her flexibility. It proves less sure on downward passagework than in going up. She has some sense of style, however, rendering "scheitern" with the appropriate appoggiatura. She imparts surpassing grandeur to "die Sonn' geht ab" and finishes the line by giving us the crucial "lispeln" with a fine trill as in the score. The excerpt ends on the words "im Wellenkreis."

In many ways, the most surprising 78 may well be Lotte Lehmann's two-sided Polydor from 1919. The conventional wisdom on her is that here was a highly expressive singer with a moving instrument used with more fire than care, unsuited for *bel canto* discipline. Not in 1919. Her "Ozean" is a revelation. It's not just that she has the full range required. It's her sheer ease at both extremes that's staggering. The low register on "Welt" and on the low B flat further on sounds just as sure as her easy high, although she does not go for the optional high B flat. Moreover, all this technical discipline does not diminish her immediacy as a born communicator. The character stands before us, deeply stirring. Like Weidt, she has the stylistic sensitivity to adopt an appoggiatura for "scheitern." Maybe more astonishing, she finishes out "lispeln" with a deft turn coming off an impeccable trill. This is not the only example of her facility. When it comes time for the make-or-break roulade on "Rettung," every note stands out clear and articulated, with no aspirate. One can only regret that these amazing gifts are not more widely preserved in her discography. Presumably she lost this kind of facility fairly early in her career, yet certain taxing dramatic soprano roles were already behind her by 1919, including the role of the Dyer's Wife in Richard Strauss's *Die Frau ohne Schatten*. If this role, arguably her heaviest, did not affect her adeptness at *bel canto*, one wonders whether anything could have.

Apparently, she never performed the role of Reiza, but, going by this souvenir of 1919, one can't see why. The only concession she makes to the staggering requirements of this piece are in the concluding measures: like many another, she takes an extra breath in the closing repetitions of "Rettung naht," dropping one "Rettung." This gives her the needed breath to deliver a stunning high C and the ringing conclusion following it. One can regret the subterfuge, but what she does here is still so compelling, and the rest is so utterly satisfying that this record must be judged a triumph.

Judging from Frida Leider's few recordings of florid material, her mastery was far from negligible, despite her greater fame as a Wagnerian. Her coloratura seems to have been not only more fluent than Flagstad's, Nilsson's, or any other Wagnerian soprano of the last eighty years, it also stacks up well against many a soprano who concentrated on the traditional *bel canto* repertoire. Items like her mid-Twenties *Trovatore* excerpts, or the Countess's "Dove sono" from *Nozze di Figaro* recorded in 1921 during her first recording session for Polydor, clearly show this.[27]

We may not have Leider's "Casta Diva," but her "Ozean" is an extraordinary souvenir. Coming from that first session, this shows a stunning facility on top, a delicate trill done piano, excellent articulation in the florid coda and a conviction that surely would have paid off handsomely if we had the whole opera.

Were there a caveat, it would be an ordinary lower register that doesn't match the richness of color throughout the rest of the instrument. The paradox is that, though the upper third of Leider's voice boasts a brightness that is striking, much of the middle is rather dusky, even while all three registers are flawlessly knit. To have such a splash of color combined with a homogeneous technical placement is remarkable. The irony is that such homogeneity may not have been what Weber expected or received out of Paton. It is rather hard, for instance, to imagine Frida Leider alternating the light soprano role of Polly in *Beggar's Opera* and the sultry mezzo role of Pippo in *Gazza ladra* as Paton did.

That said, for sheer fluency and vocal ease, Leider's "Ozean" is at the same exalted level as Ponselle's "Casta Diva." They both share the deceptive characteristic of making the aria sound easy! As Leider begins, it is evident that, even though her low is not as distinctive as Lotte Lehmann's, it is still musical. Like the latter, she does not go for the optional high B flat. More important, she also shares with Lehmann an overall line that helps her unfold each stage of this grand *scena*. Certain details here may be astonishing, but it is the seamless way in which she integrates the disparate elements that stays with one. Although she does eschew the interpolated high B flat, she still has enough stylistic understanding not to be literal. Thus, she adopts a handsome appoggiatura for "scheitern." Like Lehmann, she obeys Weber's trill, giving a delicate one, at "lispeln."

This is a voice whose greatest strength does not lie as much in the low as Lehmann's. Leider's richness is in the mid-range. There is simply more amplitude and surge here and up on top. Nobody else makes the taxing coda seem so easy. The roulade on "Rettung" is perfect, and she wings her way through the final phrases, complete with a flawless high C and descent, like some mighty eagle. Everything is shaped with scrupulous attention to the words, with no extra breath before or after the soaring notes capping the climactic phrase.

Frida Leider's self-evident assurance in Mozart, Beethoven, Weber, Verdi, and so on, suggests she would easily have equalled Caballé, Sutherland, and quite a few others in the heroic *bel canto* works.

Yes, but would she have equalled Ponselle in this repertoire? Based on the "Ozean," I have a hunch she might have. And, similarly, with her striking command of the stage (if we go by the grateful critics of her time) she might perhaps have equalled Callas in encompassing not just *Parsifal*, *Tristan*, and *Walkuere*, but also the *Trovatore*s (sung in the original Italian), the *Don Carlos* (both Leider and Callas recorded Eboli's "O don fatale"), the *Fidelio*s (Callas's first great success, in Greece), the Mozart heroines, and so on. Along with *Norma* (from early in her career), Leider possibly could have triumphed in *Nabucco* and *Macbeth* as well.

As it was, Leider was coming up just when Franz Werfel was spearheading the great Verdi revivals in pre-Nazi Germany, often featuring Meta Seinemeyer, whose superb Verdi cuts from the same period can't be overlooked. However, one cannot help wondering what might have been, had Leider moved in on Seinemeyer's Verdi territory just a bit more.

Maybe Frida Leider does not share, any more than Rosa Ponselle does, the prismatic qualities of those who created these roles. But in her *Oberon* record, Leider does share the ease of vocal movement, together with the amplitude of tone, that was required from those who earned the original composers' approval in essaying this repertoire. Leider's lack of a rich low comparable to Ponselle's and Ponselle's lack of Leider's fantastic ease on top do not preclude their both having sufficient control at the extremes of their range. In Leider's "Ozean" and Ponselle's "Casta Diva," the artists defer to each other in specific ways, but not in fundamentals. Perhaps these amazing vocalists fall short of the full package intrinsic to the true *assoluta* voice in these two arias, but both are so extraordinary in their insouciant ease that one can only marvel how rare the genuine article must be if even these two phenomena don't quite have it all! We can still be grateful that they remain unique in showing us how natural these fearsome arias can sound in the throats of singers who somehow don't seem human.

With Leider's rendition before us, some of the compromises adopted by others tend to stick out more. There are moments where some of her successors may make a more telling effect in the lower voice, or where still others may apply a touch more color. But nobody can quite match Leider's approach, turning the music into an inevitable expression of character. Above all, she is unique in how she manages to make the technical hurdles seem both incidental and indispensable to Reiza's expression of her true feelings. Even Lotte Lehmann presents these hurdles more as exclamation points, however genuine, than as intrinsic features of a psychological road map.

The greatest vocal opulence is brought to this aria by Leider's successor, Kirsten Flagstad, with perhaps the most perfect voice of its kind. In her 1937 RCA 78 with Eugene Ormandy, she delivers a *decrescendo* on the opening "Ozean." But when it's time to reach for "Welt" in the low, she takes a while finding it. One senses she may have recorded this somewhat too soon. Her low comes more easily to her a few years later. Thus, it seems plausible to assume that Flagstad's finest moment with Reiza may have been when she performed the role complete in Zurich in 1942. Unfortunately, nothing of this seems to have survived.

In the Ormandy 78, there is an occasional sign of lack of familiarity with the music. One example is her changing "friedlich" to two notes of the same pitch rather than going down for ... "lich." She does not take the option of the high B flat, and the low B flat is not attacked cleanly. One must salute her poignant appoggiatura on "scheitern" while regretting her less than clean attack at "er erwacht." Still, the general fluency shown is striking, considering the awesome power of her instrument. She also has Leider's and Lehmann's gifts for making music a natural medium of expression. It's what she expresses with that instinct that needs some qualification. No, it's not inexpressive; it doesn't lack engagement. It's just that it doesn't seem to have the degree of variety needed. Words, strangely, may not have overriding importance for her. While they are not unclear, she simply does not allow them to govern the shape of her phrasing. However, it is still a thing of wonder to hear this august organ conquer certain vocal hurdles, like a precise trill on "lispeln," shown in Weber's tricky passagework. Her sense of communication remains less crisp than that of her distinguished forebears. Thus, one is more keenly aware of a lack of projection in words further down the scale. These necessitated certain awkward shifts from Leider too, but the expression of the word didn't get lost there as they seem to here. Flagstad's weakish low is also evident in the roulade at "Rettung," even though every note is impeccably placed. Like Leider, she finishes the final repetitions of "Rettung naht" in grand fashion, without breaking the phrase or dropping any of the notes. However, rather than following the word "naht" and carrying the vowel up to the high C as a single vocal gesture, Flagstad introduces an aspirate, distorting the word and making it "na-haht" instead. Need it be emphasized that the high note itself is altogether glorious!

Eileen Farrell's "Ozean" is the only rendition comparable to Leider's in its combination of opulent tone, alert execution, natural feeling and dynamic variety. Her dynamic variety may not be tied to so specific a projection of character, but it does reflect a sovereign ease with this vocal style comparable to a Leider or a Ponselle. Farrell brings more variety to this piece than Flagstad, while having the same continuous column of an instrument. This "Ozean" was recorded in 1955 with Thomas Schippers and made available on EMI. Farrell's voice is at its freshest with an easy top and a rich low. Both the optional high B flat and the low B flat immediately following are equally stunning. "Scheitern," too, is given a lovely appoggiatura. Her arsenal includes a lightening of the voice, indicating vulnerability, apt for someone overwhelmed at being stranded. Thus, we have a limpid "fliehet" and a delicate soft trill on "lispeln," again reminiscent of Leider. The flexibility of her instrument is astonishing. However, she is not always in sync with Maestro Schippers, coming in slightly late, for instance, on "Heil! Es ist ein Boot, ein Schiff!"

There is a wonderful touch at the start of the final surge of melody, "Mein Hüon! Mein Gatte": Farrell sings at less than full voice, giving herself room to build the passage in a grand manner. There is thus limitless expansion of the dynamics here, climaxing in a good roulade at "Rettung," and all seems set for a fine finish. Here, though, she falls short of Leider: she adopts the Lehmann ruse of dropping a note or so at the end, still delivering a smashing high C. One should be grateful for such an exciting coda. Nevertheless, the wonder is whether, with better coordination from podium and vocalist, Farrell couldn't have phrased the ending without dropping out. Granted, she's in good company in choosing to recoup this way for the sake of a solid top note. But Farrell's resources are limitless, and it's a shame to hear her take a detour of this kind. Of course, what remains is still one of the most affecting interpretations we have.

We conclude this retrospective with a rare rendition in English. Although Maria Callas and Nicola Rescigno recorded "Ocean" commercially in EMI's Paris studios in 1963/64, the best example of Callas in this piece was not released until over twenty years later: Melodram gave us a "live" rendition under Georges Prêtre from Royal Festival Hall in London. Dated February 27, 1962, this is not much earlier than the studio effort. But rarely does Callas achieve such a high standard so late in her career. This recording has historical value beyond her surprising vocal control, since Reiza's "Ocean" was Callas's audition piece for her teacher, Elvira De Hidalgo, when she was first starting out. One can see why De Hidalgo accepted this feisty pupil on the strength of this aria. The desperation of the stranded castaway, the overwhelming expanse of water, the volatile switches in Reiza's mood — all are vividly intuited in Callas's reading. This diva was nothing if not a born communicator, and her plunge into Reiza's storm-tossed world leaves one almost sensing the bite of the keen salt winds. Callas's vocal fettle in 1962 may not be comparable to her Armida or her finest Médée, but she still has her moments. The full enormity of Reiza's plight is impressed on the listener immediately, despite the tape's distant miking. Her voice appears to have all the amplitude needed for this music. One would ordinarily expect such miking to minimize the impact of even the biggest voice, rather than the reverse. So it seems that Callas still had reasonable vocal heft left at this time. Nevertheless, it is not surprising that she forgoes the optional high B flat, for there are still signs of that typical "puckered" quality. Since this is one flaw that distant miking should de-emphasize rather than heighten, one can only conclude that it was still a predominant characteristic. More regrettable here is her cloudy diction. What remains imposing is Callas's low, which is firm and expressive. Disappointing, however, that a musician of all the attainments of a Callas would not opt for the appoggiatura at the word "ringing" some moments later, but so it is. She delivers a precise enough trill on "lulling," however hurriedly she moves off it. In most respects, her flexibility and accuracy remain sure. Even the roulade comes off well, although its "launch note" emerges a bit wild. She recovers immediately and proceeds effectively to the final measures of the coda. Like so many others, she too drops out for a few notes before attacking the high C. In addition, after coming back on track, she still takes an extra breath right before the high C itself. It proves a precaution well taken, for Callas produces what may be the last good high C of her career!

The legacy of complete *Oberon*s is uneven. In addition, while most full recordings are in German translation, and one is even in Italian, none is in the original English. Hearing the entire opera performed in the original could well be a revelation. While a few complete renditions may have their moments, it's arguable that no singer of the entire role has ever given Reiza her due. One can be grateful that some have come awfully close, but the degree to which even the finest still fall short is the strongest indicator of how elusive this part is. Also, Reiza clearly comes closest to combining quasi-Wagnerian characteristics with the full *assoluta* package. Three essential scenes define her character: the finale of Act I ("Haste, gallant knight"), her grand aria after being shipwrecked ("Ocean! thou mighty monster") and her lament in the last act ("Mourn thou, poor heart"). We will concentrate on these sequences in assessing the various complete recordings.

The earliest of these serves as a useful object-lesson in highlighting the pitfalls in this role. Margarete Teschemacher possesses an instrument that glows on top with a radiance curiously at odds with a craggy quality further down. Her attack often seems unstable, even though the core of her tone usually remains steady. She appears in a German Radio broadcast under Joseph Keilberth. Walther Ludwig and Helge Rosvaenge sing Oberon and Hüon. The performance dates from August 15, 1937, and is somewhat cut. It has been put out by Koch.

We are not far into the Act I finale when we become aware of the embarrassment that Reiza's intricate agility gives Teschemacher. A "cackly" quality emerges whenever she has to move the voice beyond a certain speed. Hers is a voice that needs time to "grow" into a note, better suited to Wagner or Strauss. She is, however, a good communicator, she understands and conveys the idealist in Reiza, her indomitable courage, even a slightly mischievous zest too often neglected by others. To her credit, she does the finale's coda, the mind-boggling coloratura of the "Seele, froh in Jubelklängen," uncut. It doesn't come off too well, but one salutes her understanding of why Weber put it there. It is clear that she cannot contain her excitement, precisely the effect Weber intended.

Far better is her gorgeous opening for "Ozean." Here the voice is given more time to come into its own. Its shining youthful quality toward the top is an asset. Only "Welt" in the low brings her up short, causing an unmistakable wobble. This is disconcerting, considering that she was only 34 at the time. One thrills to her vibrant projection of Reiza's predicament, and her high B flat on "du" is nothing short of fantastic. The two-octave drop to the low B flat, though, leaves her almost inaudible. Her comfort with the style is not too reassuring: she forgoes any appoggiatura for "scheitern," and there is no trill for "lispeln." A single word "wieder" displays her best and her worst: her loveliest quality shines out for "wie" ... while ... "der" further down the scale is completely unfocused. Similarly, there is also a hole where "naht" should be. The climactic roulade on "Rettung" is blurred, and she drops out on a few notes before attacking the high C. Her unsurpassed glory in this note almost compensates for the many compromises along the way. It seems to come from the very middle of her voice. It has undeniable power, a width that is heroic, not the top note of a lyric soprano.

Is it perhaps the narrowness of Teschemacher's low that dictates the omission of "Trauere, mein Herz" in the last act? This sequence certainly has the lowest tessitura of all, and one suspects it's the sequence that would have found her the most wanting. Either Maestro Keilberth was simply doing her a favor, or the exigencies of radio time may have dictated the cut. Since the lament is one of the most haunting melodies Weber ever wrote, the omission seems regrettable.

The first studio *Oberon*, made around 1950 under Hans Mueller-Kray and with Franz Fehringer in the title role, has a few points of interest, including Karl Liebl's Hüon and Friederike Sailer in the cameo part of the Mermaid. Helene Bader's Reiza is nowhere near this level. Hers is a sour sound with a pronounced wobble throughout. It is also far too thin for this role, and she flounders badly in the coloratura. She seems trapped in this daunting music like a poor creature inside a spider's web. The recording was a mere stopgap in the record catalogue for years. But one wonders if Bader's Reiza is even that. This set was released on Period.

Far more fitting for Weber's final masterpiece is Vittorio Gui's reading in a "live" broadcast from October 24, 1957, over Radio Italiana. It features the ubiquitous Mirto Picchi in the title role, Petre Munteanu as Hüon, and Anita Cerquetti as Reiza. This has been issued on the On Stage label, and is sung in Italian translation. Since none of the other sets is in the original English either, this performance is not really at a disadvantage.

Anita Cerquetti's sound is a cathedral. It is both effortless and tender. She shows a surprising ease in Weber's intricate passagework, considering the staggering size of the instrument. What we get to hear of the florid coda to the Act I finale is astounding, although Gui snips out its single most tricky flourish. All the same, one is grateful for her agility and ease. For the first time, shortened or not, this passage makes musical sense.

For Reiza's "Ocean," Cerquetti adopts Flagstad's grand *decrescendo* in the opening word, "Mare." This typifies her approach to the entire *scena*. She, and Gui, establish a timeless, suspended feeling here, suggestive of the way a castaway might lose all track of time through sheer loneliness. Cerquetti does not adopt the high B flat, but her low B flat is superb, vividly communicating the essence of the pitiless seas. Unfortunately, there is no appoggiatura or trill. But her stylistic sense is far from lacking: she evokes the majestic movement of the wings of a condor when going up and down the scale describing the setting sun. All this is achieved without breaking the mood of suspended time. In the coda, every note of the critical roulade is in place. Again, though, like too many others, she drops a few notes leading up to the high C. But once there, the effect is exhilarating, encapsulating her joy and relief at being rescued.

Cerquetti's Act III lament is appropriately haunting, and so beautiful in the piece's low tessitura that Ponselle is brought to mind, an artist who did perform this on stage and in the original English but who sadly left no recordings. Cerquetti's delivery also reminds us that Reiza is a musical image of growing up. We have gone from the eager young girl scarcely able to contain her excitement in her Act I closing to this lament from a woman who has learned suffering and fear. The very plot of this opera concerns a rite of passage for two young lovers who seem to have come of age once their trials are over. This is mirrored brilliantly by Cerquetti's conquest of vocal trials.

In the early seventies, DG released the first studio recording to attempt to present the uncut score with artists of international caliber. This set features Donald Grobe in the title role, Placido Domingo as Hüon and Birgit Nilsson as Reiza. Rafael Kubelik's conducting offers arguably the finest interpretation on disc. The strengths of Weber's opera come through more clearly here than in any other performance.

The magnificence of Nilsson's instrument must be squared against occasional spotty fluency in the lower half of certain florid passages. In Act I, her "Eil, edler Held" easily establishes the resilience of Reiza's character, with its broad phrasing and bright tones. Her "Seele, froh in Jubelklängen," however, has some aspirates, but credit must still be given for her singing this passage uncut.

Clearly, her voice is best suited for "Ozean" in Act II. At its opening, the voice is given a chance to expand in a way it hasn't in Act I. One moment of uncertainty in a somewhat hollow low B flat at "ein" takes away slightly from a grandeur to her overall reading and to the gloriously measured tempo that Kubelik provides. She does not adopt the optional high B flat. We do have some aspirating again, but it's not as conspicuous as in Act I. She takes an appoggiatura at "scheitern." Oddly enough, her broad phrasing seems to desert her at times: "Heller nun empor es gluhet" finds her snatching an extra breath after "empor." She also doesn't possess a true trill, but offers a contradiction of sorts for "lispeln": there is what seems to be a vague shake in her initial attack for the trill, while the trill itself is not sustained. The DG recording evidently plays havoc with her splendid top in the coda, making it lose some color. From the fearless attacks, however, one can guess that it must have rung out thrillingly in the studio. She seems to sustain the taxing tessitura effortlessly, even though — without losing a note — she does snatch an extra breath immediately before an easy high C. All told, this is the most compelling sequence in her interpretation, but it doesn't necessarily dominate the field of Reiza interpretations.

Spotty legato in the low brings her up short for the Act III lament. This must be the least convincing moment in her Reiza. She has trouble sustaining a moment like "die Woge euch droh'n," where "euch droh'n" not only dips down to the low register but comes at the end of a long phrase, making extra demands on her breath. The crucial words "Dunkel und Grau'n" also find her uncomfortable.

The nineties have yielded two new recordings, one conducted by James Conlon and the other by Marek Janowski. With Conlon's principals, the emphasis is on richness of voice. Two aspirants to *heldentenor*, Gary Lakes and Ben Heppner, perform Oberon and Hüon. Reiza is sung by an opulent spinto with touches of the dramatic, Deborah Voigt. This is the only set that uses an adaptation by Gustav Mahler, and the German translation is somewhat different from the customary one. It was released by EMI.

Not surprisingly, Voigt's Reiza boasts a warmer persona than Nilsson's. What is surprising is that, despite a less ample instrument, her low sounds richer than Nilsson's. In addition, while the coloratura may be ungainly, it's free of aspirates. The extended Act I finale does show her snatching a breath at one or two awkward spots, but Voigt, like Nilsson, performs the intricate coda uncut.

Her "Ozean" in Act II displays a fresh, eager sound. An over-deliberate approach tames what could have been a vibrant reading, but there are still uncommonly vivid moments. She may not opt for the high B flat, but there is still a clean quality to her singing on top. Surprisingly, her secure low B flat suggests a young Marilyn Horne. Stylistically, she does not offer an appoggiatura at "Grabe," nor does she offer a trill for the dying winds. Unfortunately, Maestro Conlon — or the sound engineer — obliterates her simile of the setting sun as a returning hero. Her greatest moment is the way she launches the concluding "Mein Hüon, mein Gatte": she adopts magnificently broad phrasing, and she and Conlon are completely together. Unfortunately, the roulade at "Rettung," while not downright slurred, is not fluent either, and a clumsy splice on the last note doesn't help. No notes are dropped on the way to the fine high C, even though she does snatch an extra breath immediately before delivering it.

The feelings in her lament in the last act seem generalized, but the easy flow of her line in this essentially mezzo aria is striking. Haunted descents to the low, like the words "Dunkel und Grau'n," emerge effectively.

The recording studio does not suggest as much opulence in Inga Nielsen's Reiza with Marek Janowski. In fact, this may be the slimmest instrument we have heard in the role outside of Helene Bader, but there's no question that she is a polished musician with a fine voice and one capable of taking in stride the daunting hurdles in Reiza's music. Unfortunately, whether because of Nielsen herself or Janowski, her interpretation doesn't seem to have much individuality. Her colleagues are Deon van der Walt in the title role and Peter Seiffert as Hüon. This is an RCA Victor release.

Nielsen's "Eil, edler Held" in Act I shows her without the verbal clarity of others, but her coloratura in the uncut coda may be the most impeccable of anyone's. She has complete control. Her instrument does not have the ease of Voigt's in the low, and the concluding "fort" reveals a somewhat hollow tone.

The opening of her "Ozean" in Act II lacks grandeur, a tentative "Welt" down in the low register even more so. There is no optional high B flat, and she almost speaks the low B flat. Other similarly sustained words in the lower half of the voice, such as "erwacht," also find her straying slightly from pitch. But her fine schooling is apparent elsewhere: "scheitern" has a deft appoggiatura, and "lispeln" is given an exquisite trill. There are still apparent moments of unease with Maestro Janowski. It's odd to hear her snatch an extra breath before "wieder." Janowski's uncommonly slow tempo may be to blame. Once the concluding section begins, though, Nielsen's musical authority is welcome. She rips through the tricky intervals and all of Weber's passagework with astonishing ease. The roulade at "Rettung" is flawless, as is the high C. She snatches an extra breath before the high note, but she sings every note leading up to it, and the C itself is quite secure.

For the Act III lament, her brains are at work to diffuse the disparities in her instrument. She carefully adopts a quiet, almost whispered, interpretive stance for the entire piece, thus trying to make logic out of the smothered low notes: on repeated hearings, though, the sketched-in quality of her "Dunkel und Grau'n" is too conspicuous.

In surveying the field of Reizas, Cerquetti and Voigt have come closest to encompassing the many gradations in this role. The fact that even these two make the occasional compromise shows how a complete assumption is still wanting.

❧ 7 ❧

Gaetano Donizetti (1797–1848): *Anna Bolena*

With all of the shifting back and forth from repertoire to repertoire on the part of certain great singers of the early 1800s, some present-day critics have concluded that what was true of these extraordinary voices was true in general; they mistakenly argue that distinctions among vocal categories were less precise than in our own day, that singers sang any role they pleased, and that composers were therefore more cavalier in writing for the voice than they should have been. This needs considerable qualification.

As a matter of fact, fifty years before the heyday of the *assoluta* role, in the eighteenth century, operatic composers were as steeped in vocal differentiations and recognized as many types as the playwright did stock characters. In Handel's *Alcina*, for example, there is a different vocal category for every character — seven to be exact. And this matching of vocal categories with stock characters was well entrenched in operatic history, both in *opera seria* and in *buffa*. But stock expectations coming out of the familiar designations of soprano, mezzo, and so on, become blurred at the height of the *assoluta* era. In a manner reminiscent of the bygone versatility of a Farinelli or a Pacchierotti, recalled in Chapter One, divas now take similar advantage of the ambitious extravagance of *assoluta* composers ready to ignore the customary pigeon-holing. Such composers can now make capital of the rare bird who flouts familiar categories. Contemporary writings attest to a recognition of such pigeon-holing and to how unusual it was, even then, to go beyond it.

Stendhal's comments on Mary Anne Paton's contemporary, Giuditta Pasta, for example, highlight this understanding:

> ... [Pasta] possesses the rare ability to sing contralto as easily as she can sing soprano. I would suggest that the true designation of her voice is mezzo-soprano, and any composer who writes for her should use the mezzo-soprano range for the thematic material of his music, while exploiting, as it were, incidentally, and from time to time, notes which lie within the more peripheral areas of this remarkably rich voice.[28]

It is obvious that he took for granted the existence of specific vocal categories and that he relied on his reader to understand their characteristics. He also showed in his description of Pasta that, above all, he appreciated how unusual the transcendence of such categories was, and that, most emphatically, he expected a nineteenth-century observer to share in this appreciation.

While this awareness of vocal categories consequently seems apparent in operatic audiences of the time, it must have been all the more keen in the minds and ears of the composers who had worked with these voices. Today, when the distinction between mezzo and contralto has actually become blurred, it is instructive to read Donizetti's painfully aware letter to Ricordi in 1833 in which he shows a consciousness of vocal categories easily comparable to that of our own time. He had been obliged to use Adelina Spech for the premiere of his *Torquato Tasso*, and he complains about the fact that "La Spech, a contralto who has pulled herself up by the teeth to mezzo-soprano, has caused me to turn half my opera inside out."[29] Clearly, anyone who was actually deemed successful in breaching these vocal divisions during such a musically conscientious era must have been fully as extraordinary as the contemporary commentators suggest.

Madame Pasta, the remarkable diva who so excited Stendhal's admiration, created the next two significant *assoluta* roles to follow Reiza: the title role in Donizetti's *Anna Bolena* (Milan, 1830) and the title role in Bellini's *Norma* (1831). Threading its way like a motif through the repertoires of many of these divas from now on is the mezzo role of Romeo in Bellini's *I Capuleti e i Montecchi* (premiered in 1830). Pasta was no exception. She may not have been the first diva *assoluta* to sing this trouser role, but she was certainly one of the earliest, and she also sang a number of other mezzo roles in addition to many soprano parts. Her mezzo roles included the Rossini Desdemona, which Colbran had created, Cherubino, Tancredi, and Cenerentola. Her soprano roles included Donna Elvira, Servilia in *La Clemenza di Tito*, Donna Anna, and Ninetta in *La Gazza ladra*. In addition to the *assoluta* roles of Bolena and Norma, she created Amina in Bellini's *La Sonnambula* (1831) and the title role in Bellini's *Beatrice di Tenda* (1833). At the time that she created Corinna in Rossini's *Viaggio a Rheims* (1825), she was being called a contralto.[30]

At her peak, she had a range from low A to high D sharp. Besides her ability to sing both contralto and soprano, tenor Giacomo Lauri-Volpi has surmised from the available evidence that she had three definite sounds: chest, head, and a kind of falsetto.[31] It may be possible that, without this special falsetto, her vocal capacities would merely have embraced that of mezzo-soprano and contralto. In fact, a certain P. Scudo agrees with Stendhal that her instrument was fundamentally a mezzo-soprano.[32] Bellini simply regarded her singing as "encyclopedic" and let it go at that. That hers was not a homogeneous instrument seems certain. Again, Stendhal:

> One of the most uncommon features of Madame Pasta's voice: it is not all moulded of the same *metallo*, as they would say in Italy; and this fundamental variety of tone produced by a single voice affords one of the richest veins of musical expression which the artistry of a great singer is able to exploit.... In fact, the history of the art might tend to suggest that it is not the perfectly pure, silvery voice, impeccably accurate in tone throughout every note of its compass, which lends itself to the greatest achievements of impassioned singing. No voice whose timbre is incapable of variation can produce that kind of opaque or, as it were, suffocated tone, which is at once so moving and so natural in the portrayal of certain instants of violent emotion and passionate anguish.[33]

Anna Bolena is certainly one of the most moving of these *assoluta* roles to be fashioned for such an instrument. It inaugurates the 1830s Golden Age of *assoluta* writing. This opera signaled the appearance of a role whose music was finally as expressive as Médée's had been. Bolena's music has a compelling sweep that shows the sure signs of a profound musical understanding — the fusing of vivid drama with the ultimate in difficult song. Moreover, unlike *Médée* and Weber's *Oberon*, *Bolena*'s libretto, by Felice Romani, helps in making this opera unusually strong dramatically. It is, in fact, the strongest drama yet conceived around an *assoluta* heroine. Romani was the most successful of the librettists in this idiom and dominated the field during the 1830s. In fact, Romani's steady connection with some of the remarkable achievements in this genre is uncanny. Not only did he create the texts for *Bolena* and *Norma*, his libretto for Mercadante's *Conte d'Essex* is thought to have strongly influenced Cammarano's libretto for Donizetti's *Roberto Devereux*. *Anna Bolena* constitutes the only instance of a direct collaboration on the part of the most prolific composer of *assoluta* roles, Donizetti, with the most prolific writer of dramas built around this kind of character, Romani.

In the operas so far examined, and this includes the bulk of *Anna Bolena*, an *assoluta*'s music usually consists of sequences that exploit discrete vocal and technical characteristics — one scene might be high, one might use a heroic low, one a flexible low, one might be slow, one fast, and so on. But we have had the isolated case, here or there, of a single scene bringing together all the facets of *assoluta* vocalism exploited throughout the rest of a role. While Reiza's "Ocean" scene and Médée's final act have already done this, the concentration of such an effect in Anna's final *scena* establishes a new plateau for vocal endurance and technical resilience. It is *Anna Bolena*'s Mad Scene inside her prison cell that sets this opera apart from every previous work of its kind and may have contributed to *Anna Bolena*'s longtime obscurity.

Now perhaps it's nothing new to ascribe the all-too-rare production of an *assoluta* opera to forbidding vocal demands. But these were surmounted in the continuing popularity of a work like *Norma*. So maybe it was different problems that figured in the relative obscurity of the others. On one hand, *Norma* thrived because of Bellini's musical genius. On the other, rare scores of equal worth, like Cherubini's *Médée* and Weber's *Oberon*, appear to have foundered. Could this have been because *Médée* posed the uncomfortable choice between stilted dialogue or spurious recitative?

Only Donizetti's *Anna Bolena* (and *Roberto Devereux*) constitute exceptions to all this. Here, failure to survive for so long seems solely due to monstrous vocal demands and to nothing else.

Bolena's final sequence is almost without parallel in the annals of *bel canto*. If its musical supremacy were not so linked to its vocal extravagance, Donizetti's opera (with Romani's superb libretto) would not have had to wait till the 1950s and Maria Callas to come out of obscurity.

The role of Bolena traces quite an odyssey before culminating in her final moments. In her first appearance on stage, concerning a spiritless evening's vigil of regret and loneliness marked by the King's neglect, a resilient middle and lower range is required for her opening aria, "Come, innocente giovane." In fact, suppleness throughout the upper middle of her instrument is required as well if the reflective, nostalgic mood of this piece is to be successfully conveyed. Still, lyrical yet low-lying phrases, such as "Son calde ancor le ceneri" with its low B, constitute one of this aria's most striking characteristics. In her ensuing cabaletta, "Non v'ha sguardo," with its high tessitura, in which Bolena declares her helplessness at the empty glitter of the throne and the cheerful mien she must assume, her range reaches high B and three high Cs, the high C being, in fact, the highest this role ever goes. The intricacy of the coloratura here and its *lirico* weight clearly require a pliancy that is only possible if the diva can give her tones a transparency that will contrast to the more dramatic utterances lying ahead.

In Bolena's next scene, when she is startled to see that a former love of hers, Percy, to whom she was once betrothed, has been recalled from banishment by Henry VIII, a command of the middle and lower middle of the voice is needed, but no additional requirements.

It is in her third scene following this one that unusual demands are finally made of the singer's vocal stamina. This scene consists of Bolena's private, ill-fated session with the newly-returned Percy and her consequent apprehension and arrest by Henry on the grounds of adultery. Here, she is not merely on stage for a considerable time but is required to exhibit the kind of resilient low mandated in her first aria, and then a truly heroic tone and the capacity to combine that tone with coloratura flexibility. At the opening of this scene, against her better judgment and at her brother Rochefort's urging, Bolena finds herself face to face with Percy again after many years. She entreats him not to play with fire and to have some thought of her own delicate political situation. Among other things, she reminds him of the dangers surrounding her with a quick downward scale to a low B flat on the words "il terror." Throughout, in fact, the low B flat is the lowest she ever goes, so this intimation of the worst that could betide her assumes critical dramatic importance through using her lowest note. Bolena's fears are realized only too soon, and the second she senses the King's wrath, as he discovers her with Percy in her private apartments, she pleads with him for a moment to collect herself. But he is obdurate and announces his decision to appoint judges for a trial of adultery. For the first time, realizing she is trapped unjustly, Bolena's vocal line, in response, now flashes with a strength and an energy barely hinted at previously. The singer performing Bolena is now given an opportunity to show the full power of a *drammatico* sound in the concluding *stretta*, "Ah, segnata e la mia sorte." Not only is the full heroic strength of an *assoluta* called for here, but the actual music Bolena sings to launch this *stretta* requires the performer to show coloratura flexibility hand in hand with her heroic strength. This energetic ensemble rings down the curtain on Act I.

A considerable number of the vocal and technical aspects that make up this role have been highlighted in Act I, but it is only in the second and last act that the true intensity of the part is fully realized. In the opening scene of Act II, Bolena discovers that she has a rival for Henry's affections who has unwittingly caused her entrapment by the King. The rival is Jane Seymour (Giovanna), who has been one of her closest friends until now and who shocks Bolena by confessing her part in the intrigue. Though Bolena is at first incensed, she soon realizes that Giovanna is as much a victim as herself and excuses her.

This scene requires nearly as much vocal stamina and staying power as the last scene of Act I; in addition, the singer performing Bolena now needs to display a portentous lower range when responding to Seymour's suggestion that she, Bolena, save her life by confessing adultery, renouncing the throne, and thus foregoing any trial altogether. In outrage at such a humiliating idea coming from a friend, Bolena comes out with a hurt, declamatory line, "tu consigliar mel puoi," which dips down to low B on "mel." The greatest contrast is shown when, learning of the existence of a rival, Bolena bursts forth with a series of heroic coloratura flourishes lying quite high as she calls down a curse. After this demonstration of vocal strength, Seymour's confession that she herself was Bolena's rival has left Bolena almost speechless; her brief, shocked interjections at Giovanna's confession offer a contrast this time to the latter's heartbroken, soaring vocal line. When she finds her voice again, Bolena spins out a silken line of forgiveness. The simplicity of what she is singing is the overriding impression here, leading into their closing duo.

In scaling down her phrases for the reassurance of Giovanna, Bolena shares with her an intimation of common human frailty and vulnerability. Giovanna is certainly weaker and less mature, and there is a strong feeling throughout the opera that it is Giovanna's unworldliness that has endeared her to the King. The role of Seymour was created by Elisa Orlandi, a singer who, unlike Pasta, was a straight soprano with none of the ambiguities of *fach* that Pasta had. Orlandi was nineteen years old when *Anna Bolena* was premiered, and, in fact, she died when she was only twenty-three. As a straight soprano, it is quite obvious that she was expected to present a lighter, less dusky foil to Pasta's deeper characterization of Bolena. This duet scene is therefore a confrontation between a voice of darker hues, Bolena's, and a brighter soprano, Seymour's. The imposing woman and the younger, more helpless girl are thus juxtaposed. In the final coda that closes this duet, "Ah! m'attende," Giovanna sings her opening phrases a semitone higher than Bolena's responses, thus reinforcing the sense of Giovanna as the lighter, brighter sound. Because of certain performing traditions that have been built up around similar duets, the assignment of Bolena to sopranos has led almost inevitably to Giovanna being given to mezzos. This seriously alters the original impression that Pasta and Orlandi must have conveyed of magnanimous maturity versus terrified innocence. Above all, this reversal no longer makes Bolena's simple melody a gentle attempt to approach Giovanna on her own level.

In her next scene, at the trial, Bolena sounds completely heroic once more. Percy, on trial as well, refutes the charge of adultery by claiming Bolena as his lawful bride before she married King Henry. At his declaration of willingness to take her back and away from the court and Henry, Bolena expresses regret in haunting, pathetic phrases at having ever given him up. A somber but understated use of the lower middle, as in her Act I aria, marks this passage. The voices of Percy and Anna then join in counterpoint to Henry's expressions of amazement at the "discovery" of Anna's former attachment. Anna's joint phrases with Percy require now a very flexible low, as in the midst of moderately intricate passagework she expresses her own sense of regret by singing a low B on the word "tradita" when referring to her betrayal of Percy. This moment of self-effacement soon passes when Bolena is told by Henry that nothing in her situation has changed by this revelation; infamy and condemnation will still be her lot. At that, both Bolena and Percy call down imprecations on Henry's cruelty while the King expresses self-righteousness in a trio. This section is strongly reminiscent of the trio that closes the first act of Verdi's *Il Trovatore*, except that even more heroic agility is required of the diva in this scene's concluding measures.

For Anna's last scene, a panorama of her emotional existence is displayed in the vocal line. Donizetti, in depicting Anna awaiting her execution, exploits the *assoluta*'s vocal resiliency and stamina to an even greater extent than in the final scene of Act I. As she enters the stage and begins her opening recitative, it becomes apparent that her hold on reality is slipping. She imagines it is the day of her appointed wedding to Henry, and, in reliving that day, so bound with memories of a happier youth, Bolena's phrases take on a bright, high texture that call for resiliency in the upper range. In a headlong vocal flourish extending up to high C for the first time since her opening Act I *scena*, she imagines the altar decorated with roses. But the vision soon turns sour. She cries out in desperation, fancying she can spot Percy in a rage disrupting the nuptial.

ANNA BOLENA

ACT	SELECTION	1 FLEXIBLE LOW	2 INTRICATE COLORATURA	3A ABOVE HIGH B	3B BELOW LOW B	4 LONG SEQUENCES	5 FLEXIBLE HIGH	6 HEROIC COLORATURA	7 HEROIC TONE	8 HEAVY LOW
I	Come, innocente giovane	X								
	Non v'ha sguardo		X	X			X			
	Voi, Regina!	X								
	Io sentii	X								
	Questo di	X								
	Cessa					X				
	S'ei t'abbore	X			X	X				
	Alcun potria					X				
	Ove sono?					X				
	In separato carcere					X				
	Ahi segnata					X		X	X	
II	O mie fedeli					X				
	Dio, che mi vedi					X			X	X
	Sul suo capo					X	X	X	X	
	Dal mio cor					X				
	Sorgi					X				
	Arresta	X								
	Fin dall'età più tenera								X	
	Salirà d'Inghilterra sul trono							X	X	
	Piangete voi?			X			X			
	Al dolce guidami	X			X	X				
	Qual mesto suon?					X				
	Cielo, a' miei lunghi spasimi				X	X				
	Chi mi sveglia?		X	X	X	X	X	X	X	X
	Coppia iniqua	X	X			X	X	X	X	X

Feebly, regretfully, she prays for just one serene day at her first home with Percy. In this poignant cavatina, "Al dolce guidami," a sad, somber use is made of the *lirico* sound in the *assoluta*'s middle and lower-middle range recalling Bolena's opening aria. This valedictory cavatina, though, is considerably more melancholy than her first-act aria. It closes with a cadenza extending up to high B flat and two octaves down to her second low B flat of the role, followed by shocked, piano cadences from her ladies in attendance. When, after "Al dolce guidami," the rest of the condemned prisoners pass by in review, Bolena is now abstracted, in a reverie. Between fleeting returns to sanity, she prays for eventual surcease of her trials in a brief solo, "Cielo, a miei lunghi spasimi." The surprise of those hearing this score for the first time in our modern age and recognizing "Cielo" as a veritable transcription of the "Home, sweet home" melody has been commented on *ad nauseum*. Of course, the main point of this melody is to stress the naive aspects of Bolena's character, or, perhaps, her desperate attempts at normalcy in the midst of an emotional storm. At any rate, the touchstone of this melody's simplicity is the relative ease of its technical requirements. There are practically no extraordinary vocal feats required. The result of this is that the recitative and cabaletta which follow and conclude the opera are all the more startling.

This final upcoming sequence epitomizes the art of the *assoluta* in a brilliant way no other composer had yet achieved. It is here that Donizetti brought together within one sequence all of those extreme vocal and technical elements that most distinguish an *assoluta* role. By successfully combining these elements within a single *coup de théâtre*, he effectively set himself apart from every other composer in the genre.

In this extraordinary sequence, Bolena is hearing the sound of the royal festivities for Henry's wedding to Jane Seymour as the court commences preparations for their nuptials. Then, on learning from the attendants what is the source of the rejoicing, Anna declares with scorn that the crime is not yet completed — her blood has yet to be shed — and she descends, in a declamatory line of recitative, to her third low B flat of the role, at the end of the phrase "e versato sarà," which is held on "… rà" for two counts. Then, in "Coppia iniqua," the "guilty pair" (Henry and Jane) are not worth Bolena's vengeance or her curses, intimating that she wishes to die in a loftier state of forgiveness without yielding either to anguish or resentment. Dramatic coloratura is virtually defined in this cabaletta: not only are these sentiments expressed in an energetic manner by both the singer and the orchestral (and occasionally choral) accompaniment; the intricacy of the heroic phrases that the diva is called upon to sing make this a passage of extreme difficulty as well. The most remarkable feat here is a series of trills launched at the B squarely in the middle register and ascending up to the F sharp in the *passaggio*. Considerable resiliency, flexibility, and power are required, in addition, at the extremes of the vocal range, as phrase after phrase exploits the highest and lowest registers in the midst of already difficult *fioritura*. Thus, this aria contains two more high Cs, each coming at the crest of a *crescendo*; and, at the same time, when Anna reaches the word "vendetta" in the *da capo*, she sings a roulade at full strength that descends down from a high B flat to a full-count middle E flat. Bolena's final high B flat, marked *f* in the score and with a fermata over it, and some brief *f* phrases for the remaining principals on stage ring down the curtain on this last overwhelming scene of Donizetti's opera.

Bolena on disc

With *Anna Bolena*, there was inaugurated a more active performing tradition for a defining *assoluta* role than had ever been the case before. Starting almost immediately after the Pasta premiere, Ronzi–De Begnis, Schröder-Devrient, Grisi, Tadolini, Strepponi, Barbieri-Nini, and Tietjens all eventually sang Bolena on stage. In this work, Donizetti was to score his first significant operatic triumph.

One of Maria Callas's greatest recordings is the 1957 Visconti production of *Anna Bolena* broadcast live from La Scala. It helped spark the post-war revival of forgotten Donizetti operas and consolidate growing interest in *bel canto*. Callas's colleagues were Giulietta Simionato as Giovanna Seymour, Gianni Raimondi as Riccardo Percy and Nicola Rossi-Lemeni as Henry VIII. Gianandrea Gavazzeni was at the podium. Callas repeated her riveting performance the next spring, reaping an unqualified triumph despite an initially hostile audience angered by her withdrawal from a Rome *Norma* the previous winter. It was this 1958 revival that served to inspire Herbert Weinstock's biography of Donizetti. The only cast change here was the magnificent Cesare Siepi as Henry VIII.

As cannot be stressed enough, Callas shared the startling quality of prismatic vocal color that Pasta had. In addition, as we hear in the numerous tapes and records of her artistry, Callas shared with Pasta the ability to tap into a mezzo-ish timbre for her lowest notes. For instance, from the same year as her first Bolena, we have recordings showing Callas's dusky tones throughout the mezzo roles of the *Tauride* Iphigénie (in Italian translation) and Rosina (*Il Barbiere*), even though the latter finds her adopting certain traditional soprano options. The fact that she possessed with Pasta this combination of mezzo-ish quality with the bifurcated nature of her voice is what made Callas the logical choice to reintroduce the *assoluta* heritage to modern ears. It was right and fitting that her *Anna Bolena*, the most challenging of the *assoluta* roles that she assumed, solidified a *bel canto* revival that Callas, more than anyone else, helped initiate, having previously sung the Rossini *Armida* (1952) and the Cherubini *Médée* (1953) — both introduced in Florence.

The one recording that survives of Callas's Bolena is taken "live" from the opening of the Visconti production on April 14, 1957. By rights, the best CD edition of this Callas performance should be on the Verona label, since their sources for all this material are usually the superb transfers of the old BJR editions on LP. However, a Verona *Bolena* has proved elusive, while the more easily available, commercially released, EMI edition appears to be a rush job, done without half the care of the old BJR LP. This is a shame. In fact, the entire Callas "live" series on EMI has proved uneven, although one should be grateful that such material is being made more generally available. On the other hand, if an old limited-edition series on LP, such as the BJR, was occasionally able to make a silk purse out of a sow's ear, it seems rather mingy of EMI not to make the same effort, given the vaster resources at its disposal.

The '57 performance enshrines easily the most captivating Anna on disc. No singer rips through this monster of a role with such panache. It may sound like a cliché, but Callas absorbed this music in her very bones. Gavazzeni's cuts may be hair-raising, and Rossi-Lemeni hardly sings Henry VIII's music at all, but with the energized Gavazzeni in the pit and with Simionato's Seymour blazing alongside Callas, this adds up to quite a show.

If compelled to select just one performance of this work, it would remain the Callas for me, warts and all. Arguably Callas's most challenging role, Bolena seems to inspire tremendous authority from her, rather than caution or "hedging." This is particularly remarkable since, by 1957, there had been a fair number of unpleasant encounters with her growing vocal problems.

Striking is the simplicity of her opening scene, despite how vividly it lodges in the memory. This is true of much of her performance. Its virtue lies as much in a directness of utterance as in an accumulation of detail. While there is true inspiration in that detail, the insight in its simplicity is harder to describe. The reserve of Callas's first appearance becomes an asset through her sincerity. Ideal control is lacking in the opening scenes. One regrets Gavazzeni's severe cut in the middle of the page boy Smeton's opening song, but Callas's abrupt interruption does not lose effectiveness; it alters the mood significantly, however reticent her reading of "Come, innocente giovane." At "core," we have a textbook example of Callas's string-of-pearls effect in her passagework, even though, surprisingly, she does not match this with respect for the miniature *decrescendo* markings that mine Bolena's music throughout. The impression left by a wobbly high B flat is offset by an enticing "seduce" in "Non v'ha sguardo." A cut of the *da capo* brings us to a coda marred by a flawed high C flat, enharmonic high B, at the flourish on "lusingar." Things look up vocally in the succeeding scenes. There Callas expresses hopelessness at "non tradirmi, o core," and in "Io sentii" she practically murmurs "Si diffonde sul mio cor." The trills in this ensemble are lovely, as is the flourish at its conclusion. A shudder goes through "Ohimè" signaling the final *allegro vivace*, which is somewhat trimmed and ends with an unsteady high C. The trauma in this scene of greeting Riccardo Percy, home from exile, makes us realize that she is still deeply in love with him. In the final scene of the act, Callas imparts a sad resignation in agreeing to an audience with Percy. We have the same sense of hopelessness as before when she delivers a pained "vano di mia ragion consiglio." From the hopeless woman, we are suddenly confronted with the true Queen when Percy's impetuous declaration of Bolena as his lodestar elicits her "Misero!" But Queen or not, this is still a vulnerable woman with her soft "è vero" as prescribed in the score. The few extra cuts that Gavazzeni takes here are startling and regrettable, for Callas's voice is finally warmed up in "Ah! mai più" and in her desperation for the "Ah! ... per pietà," culminating with tender regard for Percy in the closing phrases. Her astounded "Giusto Cielo," at the page boy Smeton's sudden emergence from hiding in her chambers, and the pure terror in her second "son perduta" are merely signposts of a character losing consciousness; her entire existence is unhinged in a matter of moments. After reviving, Callas opens the ensemble "In quegli sguardi" addressing the furious King Henry, honoring the score's *decrescendo* markings on "impresso" and "oppresso." She gains an even more effective contrast, softening for the repeated "condannarmi" as the quintet draws to a close. Then Henry's official pronouncement of imprisonment provokes Callas's sharply delivered "ad Anna." In the closing *allegro vivace*, she is now all outrage, urgency and anxiety, spitting out the intricate turns of the "Ah! segnata." Her fine high D rings down the curtain.

Gavazzeni again indulges in some trimming for the opening exchanges of Act II, but he retains the prayer, of which Callas delivers a properly grave reading. Joined by Jane Seymour, she treats us to an immaculate legato on "Non mi obbliasti tu." Seymour's assurance that Bolena's false confession to adultery would save her life is met with Callas's proud low B, "mel" of "Tu consigliar mel puoi!" She is peremptory in asking who the other woman might be who has engaged the King's affections, and there is towering outrage in wishing the worst on her rival. She climaxes her curse with a fine G on "scure" leading into the closing passagework. When she finally understands that Seymour herself is her rival, she turns dangerous, ugly even, in her iteration of "mia rivale," interjecting accents of incredulousness, disgust, and anger. Callas's tones tower over Simionato's Seymour as she bids her rival rise, declaring the King the only guilty party. But she softens on "te" at the close of the declaration, signaling her willingness to relent for an old friend. Her tender "Va, infelice" is suffused with magnanimity and climaxes with a haunting *diminuendo* on a high A. The artistic rapport between her and Simionato is an asset throughout the broadcast, but particularly in this scene. One may regret that, after such superb singing, Callas's closing high C with Simionato veers slightly sharp, but that cannot detract from the musicality and sheer heart conveyed in this duet. In the trial scene, Gavazzeni's cuts really seem abrupt. Perhaps the reasons for his trimming may be due to a wish to keep the dramatic temperature high. But so much of King Henry's music is cut that it seems apparent that much of the evisceration is because of the difficulty Rossi-Lemeni had in tackling such intricate vocalism. This second scene of Act II is the King's great moment, and the failure of the singer to capitalize on this dooms the whole sequence. One can't help wondering how Cesare Siepi might have coped with this scene in the 1958 revival. When Weinstock writes of how inspirational the '58 performances were, one gains the impression of a totality, making it doubly frustrating that not a note survives of the '58 run. In this extant '57 performance, Callas copes as best she can, but even she cannot escape the impression of sketchiness, given so many gaps. Perhaps there were fewer of them in '58, although we do know that Gavazzeni retained his cuts in other performances. In '57, one is struck by the way that Callas's opening "A' piedi tuoi" bespeaks the Queen incarnate and of how her vitriol jumps out when accusing Henry of tricking Smeton through torture. She has only scorn for the King when comparing happiness with Percy to life as a royal "consorte." One of the more startling of many cuts here omits Henry's tricky "Ambo morrete" and his "Ella a tacersi apprese," making Percy's declaration of a prior claim to Anna abrupt indeed. However, Bolena's transformation here from desperation to despair is skillfully charted, culminating in a telling "Ahimè." In "Ah! del tuo cor," she is sincerely touched by Percy's readiness to have her back, but the flow of the scene is stemmed by yet another omission: some development material in the ensuing ensemble is left out to spare Rossi-Lemeni, and this breaks up the arc of Callas's characterization as well. This is compounded by yet another gap which skips to the concluding *presto* as soon as Percy insists on the "Consiglio" giving him a hearing. The unsettled reading of this scene concludes with an unsteady high C from Callas. Gavazzeni's questionable choices in this performing edition come to a head when Percy's great prison scene with its superb "Vivi tu" is omitted altogether. Thus, we go right from Jane Seymour's closing *scena* pleading with the King at the conclusion of the trial to Anna's final Mad Scene — two scenes for the female voice in a row! That said, one must give credit to the brilliance of Gavazzeni's actual conducting, particularly in the final scene. A touchstone to Callas's fine interpretation was her remarkable rapport with her conductor, making this one of the finest collaborations of her career. Gavazzeni was indeed a genius, however wayward in some respects, and his sure dramatic handling of scene after scene is a boon, especially when this particular leading lady is treading the boards. In the opening "Piangete voi," Callas is abstracted as she imagines herself on her wedding day, shortly to become queen. Her hushed reading is somewhat marred on the tape by radio interference. Her high C on "infiorato" is respectable but not of optimum ease, although her G is of remarkable beauty at "del mio serto." She then switches to alarm at Percy's possible jealousy, "Ch'io non lo vegga." This becomes relief and happiness as she imagines him smiling, launching a downward scale with a *diminuendo* on "gioia." The cavatina, "Al dolce guidami," is ideally rapt in all its passagework: there are excellent *pianissimo* trills, good *decrescendi*, and a haunting treatment of the spiralling turns on "nostro amor" leading into the final "un giorno rendimi." This is offset somewhat by a cracked release on the top A. She restores the mood effectively, though, and offers a telling alternation of dynamics for the figurations on "un giorno sol," concluding with an elaborate cadenza done piano. In the *materia di mezzo*, Callas is back to regal outrage for "le guardie," and her darker tones are used to thrilling effect in her appalled recognition of Percy among the condemned, descending to a strong E flat on ... "cy" of "Percy." But she is in a daze when catching sight of Smeton. Surprisingly, she does not follow all the miniature *decrescendi* in the concluding moments. In "Un suon sommesso," she restricts them to "tramandan" and "tronco." In the setting of "Home, Sweet Home," "Cielo, a' miei lunghi spasimi," she does observe the *decrescendo* at "palpiti." Her reading of the entire "Cielo" is haunting, but there is then yet another cut taken by Gavazzeni, bringing us straight to "Suon festivo?" In her declaration that her blood must now be shed, she eventually finds the low B flat for "sarà," but the attack is oddly uncertain. It is surprising that, thrilling as her final cabaletta, "Coppia iniqua," becomes in her hands, there are none of Donizetti's deft *decrescendi* observed. This takes away from the image of her blocking out anything that might prevent her from facing her doom with dignity and forbearance. There is a true haughtiness at its climax, Callas's assurance converting the technical difficulties into brilliant expressions of character. Even the notoriously difficult ascending trills in the cabaletta seem to convey her wish to escape from the nightmare. She progresses through all six trills on "scenda" on a single breath, pauses and then re-attacks for the following phrase, starting at "Ei." At the conclusion of the first statement, she avoids the high C at "favor," saving it for the *da capo*, where it rings out strongly. Her climactic high B flat, like her high C on "infiorato" at the start of the scene, is not ideally free, but it's a strong tone, effectively making a commendable curtain.

An inspired coda to our documentation of her mastery in this role is a rare rehearsal document from a concert under Nicola Rescigno given in Dallas, November of '57. There is an early LP release of this rehearsal on HRE, and it has enjoyed a regular currency on a number of smaller CD labels since. She offers a fascinating, well-voiced reading of the Mad Scene. The recorded evidence of her Dallas Medea already suggests how congenial she found the Dallas company, so it's not surprising that this rehearsal of a Bolena extract finds her in such glowing form. In fact, her high C on "infiorato" here is both cleanly taken and truly evocative in its coloring, and there is an extra edge of sadness in her "È vano." She inadvertently repeats "Percy" instead of rendering her first "gioia" and she does not do her patented *diminuendo* on the downward scale for the second "gioia." There is occasional gravel at one or two points here, and the close of her spiralling turns on "nostro amor" seems unsure, while the turns themselves are as assured as ever. Here, reality returns for Bolena on "che vedo," but as in the Gavazzeni broadcast, she is vividly back in dreamland before her "Cielo" solo, which is marked by a lovely final cadenza. The strongest possible contrast is drawn in her subsequent commands to those around her upon hearing the festivities outside. Her final "Tacete" may be a more refulgent sound than anything we hear at La Scala. There is also an excellent low B flat on "sarà," and there is an attempt at some of the *decrescendi* in the cabaletta. The trills appear to be fine, but she is clearly "marking" the first time around. The repeated "Tacete" introducing the *da capo* again makes a grander effect than at La Scala, and while she again avoids the high C in the first statement, the one in the *da capo* is quite good. This rehearsal affords a rare glimpse of the very moment when Callas reworked a passage, evidently for good: after the first run through of the cabaletta, where the trills are phrased as at La Scala, there is a hushed conference, and a newer grander reading is offered to end the rehearsal. Instead of maintaining the word "scenda" through all six trills, she finishes the word on the fourth one, re-attacks for the last two trills on "Ah" and then delivers a majestic *rallentando* linking the final trill to the word "Ei" on the next line, making a single long-breathed phrase. The effect is spellbinding, and is the way she always sang it from then on, whether in the EMI studios in 1958 (also with Nicola Rescigno), or in a 1962 concert in London under Georges Prêtre.

Leyla Gencer, Callas's immediate successor in this role, is available in two "live" broadcasts, one from 1958 and one from 1965. Since her singing is fresher in the 1958 performance, we concentrate on that one. As with the Callas revival, Gavazzeni conducts, using the same heavily cut edition. Aldo Bertocci sings Riccardo Percy, Giulietta Simionato repeats her fine Giovanna Seymour and Plinio Clabassi offers a Henry VIII infinitely superior to the inadequate Rossi-Lemeni. As an overall performance of the opera, this may be less uneven than the Callas broadcast, but it does not offer the same peaks, even from its identical Giovanna Seymour. The recording is now available on an Opera D'Oro CD.

In Bolena's opening cavatina, "Come, innocente giovane," Gencer offers nice articulation at moments like "ceneri," but there is occasional flatness. The cabaletta, "Non v'ha sguardo," features some excellent passagework, but she cuts off the final note prematurely, again ending under pitch. In Scene 2, Bolena's protestations to Percy founder once more on a flat note, this time "fe" of "difese." Throughout this scene, deft softening of the tone helps in awkward scoops up to proper pitch, so she is evidently aware of the problem. But when she attacks full voice, the problem re-asserts itself. Gencer's facility in coloratura rarely abandons her, and we hear a fine trill at "in mezzo al cor." The high C closing the scene is also fine. In the next scene, Gencer registers brilliantly her anxiety at meeting Percy. Vocally, she dispatches a strong low B flat at "ed il terror" and the superb phrasing seems endless. Her "Giusto Cielo" at discovering Smeton in her chambers suggests someone on the verge of fainting, making her eventual collapse suitably persuasive. Her "In quegli sguardi" emerges as an affecting plea, although the "Ah! segnata" is marred by gravelly attacks and shortness of breath. Nevertheless, it is an individual reading, highlighting her alarm more than her regal outrage, and climaxing in an excellent high D, which she nails at the final curtain. The absence of pitch problems in this scene is notable.

Act II starts on an exquisite diminuendo at "Ah" during the opening chorus. In the prayer, Gencer makes "tu, giudica tu, o Dio" a striking utterance of a lost human being, delivered as a single downcast phrase. At Giovanna's warning that only Bolena's affirmation of adultery will save her life, Gencer's rejection emphasizes hurt at a friend's thoughtlessness rather than the outrage of a queen. Her pitch problems recur with a flat "Seymour." She can still deliver a good low B, at "mel puoi," and, finally, at "una viltà" we hear the outraged queen for the first time. Gencer's flexibility is exemplary in the "Sul guancial," although there is a long scoop at "scure." She conveys disbelief at her discovery that Seymour is her rival. When finally ready to face this painful truth, her "Sorgi" projects determination, but no forgiveness. That we hear in a tender "Va, infelice." Unfortunately, her "sarà" here crests quite flat. But "la mia pietà" closing the solo is deeply expressive, and one is left overwhelmed at Bolena's generosity. The duet ends with good passagework and an excellent joint top note from her and Simionato. In the next scene with the King, she is spirited without being forbidding. This is no *grande dame* attempting to cow everyone, but a deeply susceptible human being of great courage. Her realization of the importance of Percy in her life is marked by a piano on "Ahimè!" In "Ah! del tuo cor," she imparts regret at "qual prova a me tu dai" through deft *portamenti*. This is the heart of her reading, and the scene ends with a creditable high C. She is even more haunting in the final scene, whispering her entrance phrases to her waiting women. "Infiorato" is sung with a magical *pianissimo* on the high C. The flourish on "gioia" crests on yet another *pianissimo*. There are some lovely trills in her cavatina, "Al dolce guidami," although lower down, at "de' scorsi affanni" and "de' miei prim'anni," she seems to produce only a vague shake. But her control of piano singing is so sure in other ways, particularly in the chain of rising turns leading into her final "un giorno rendimi." The closing cadenza is sung on a *pianissimo*. In the *materia di mezzo*, Gencer's control seems to falter somewhat: there is a crack on "esse" and the miniature *decrescendo* markings at "come il gemer tronco" are not observed. There is good passagework in the "Cielo, a' miei lunghi spasimi." When the reality of the day of execution finally hits home, so do the pitch problems: a prolonged "cessate" goes flat, although there is a good low B flat on "sarà." With all the assurance of her extreme low, it is disconcerting to hear the middle low tripping her up in the cabaletta, "Coppia iniqua": "ta" of "vendetta" is lost in both statements and the chain of would-be trills on "scenda" only become true trills higher up. In fact, the second time around, not only do the lower trills fail to register, the topmost trill also deteriorates into a blur, going flat in the process. As in the *materia di mezzo*, none of the miniature *decrescendo* markings is observed here either, but she delivers assured passagework both times on "pietà, favor, pietà" with its top C. She ends the scene climaxing on a strong high B flat.

The first studio recording of the complete opera released commercially stars Elena Souliotis and was completed in 1969 for Decca/London. Silvio Varviso presides over a well-sung performance. Souliotis's colleagues include John Alexander as Percy, Marilyn Horne as Jane Seymour and Nicolai Ghiaurov as King Henry. When it comes to Souliotis's Bolena, one must conclude that she was somewhat past her brief prime, having been one of the more notorious cases of premature vocal burnout during the heady Sixties. Nevertheless, there are moments where the stature of her artistry can claim respect.

Souliotis does not put her best foot forward in the opening *scena*: closing flourishes on "nel vano mio splendor" find her straying from pitch, although the cabaletta has a number of lovely touches. Here we can savor her soft opening for the *da capo*, even as a slight unsteadiness becomes apparent in the climactic phrases. Her second scene is not much of an improvement, with an "Io sentii" that lacks trills, and a wailed top note at the end. Her control of piano singing, though, has its appeal, with an affecting treatment of the cadenza. She comes alive more in the third scene, portraying anger at herself on "Debole io fui," and there is true bitterness at "ammenda ne feci." She is already outraged with Percy for "Misero" and doesn't let up entirely until "è vero," with a beautiful piano, richly expressed. In "Ah! non sai," she dispatches a secure run down to an excellent low B flat. This is followed immediately by another beautiful piano on "Ah! mai più." Varviso takes a small cut in this scene, but such nips and tucks are hardly comparable to the wholesale pruning from Gavazzeni. For "Ah! per pietà," Souliotis comes off determined in ordering Percy to leave the court. There are no compunctions and no doubts in her voice. She sounds secure in the conviction that Percy would accede to her command. We still hear some sadness at the vanished dream of true love. We have a regretful harking back to their past love when Bolena tells Percy it's time for him to find another truer love. Souliotis goes for a high B flat in their last note together. But the urgency of her words to Percy seems too much like the urgency of "Giusto Cielo" at the page's sudden appearance. Fear doesn't register properly, not even when she faints at the King's entrance. She is, however, tearful and harrowed in reviving: another expert use of her piano, and the word "sospetto" virtually whispered. Few Bolenas give such a vivid effect of living a nightmare at "Deh! Sire…" and a repeated "Giudici" is almost sobbed, but Souliotis loses pitch for a moment on "Ad Anna!" She also loses breath at "tiranna," although the act closes strongly with her high D.

In Act II, a quietly affecting prayer opens Souliotis's duet with Marilyn Horne's Jane Seymour. Such a moving start is offset by Souliotis anticipating her outrage at Seymour's dishonorable proposition, inquiring "Tremi?" with the tones of an angry queen rather than a worried prisoner. This telegraphs too much the astounded response of "E consigliar mel puoi? Tu, mia Seymour!" Souliotis projects a full sense of the insult to royalty here, but it is too late. This is compounded by a wobbly "Seymour" further on, although her low B on a repeated "tu consigliar mel puoi" is as strong as ever. She broadly phrases "Sul guancial del regio letto," making a magnificent effect until her vocalism becomes undisciplined at the climax. This lapse is redeemed by her genuinely hurt interjections on knowing it is Seymour who has alienated the King's affections. Her "Va, infelice" may display real forgiveness, but the spell has been broken by an insensitive "Sorgi." In addition, her final high C becomes an attenuated wail. The trial scene also suffers from undue emphasis on royal indignation. There is too much would-be haughtiness in the voice, and certain notes betray a wobble. By the time that Bolena makes her sally against the absence of justice "d'Enrico in corte," Souliotis is sounding baleful, as if seeking to terrify the King rather than redeem her reputation. But when confronted by the direct question on her previous attachment to Percy, she finally sounds scared with a terrified "Io?" She seems touched by Percy's generosity in "Ah! del tuo cor magnanimo," even though she loses the line a bit on an unmusical "Perisca." She dispatches a good run on "orror," but offers a curtailed shriek for a high C at her exit.

Bolena's final Mad Scene finds Souliotis at her most imaginative. It is true that Callas had already laid much of the groundwork for this scene, but credit must be given Souliotis for her sensitive response to the traditions that Callas had revived. There is a strong high C for "infiorato," and Souliotis conveys well the wildness of an hallucinating patient in her desperate vision of the enraged Percy. In "Al dolce guidami," there is a shimmer used in place of the absent trills, musically telling at least. A striking effect is the *crescendo/decrescendo* on a moving flourish leading into the "Ah! Colà, dimentico." There is her excellent piano for the closing measures. Souliotis uses the Callas cadenza, the final note going a bit flat. A highlight is her trance-like "Smeton! T'apressa" as her delirium returns. Also notable is her sensitivity to Donizetti's many markings for a miniature *decrescendo* on single notes. We have a string of these at "come il gemer tronco" where she responds beautifully: poignant accents accord perfectly with the image in Romani's words of a broken groan. The setting of "Home Sweet Home" in "Cielo, a' miei lunghi spasimi" is also perfection. We then have the keenest possible contrast in her indignant "Suon festivo?" Unfortunately, a repeated "Tacete" wobbles, although there is a good low B flat on "sarà." "Coppia iniqua" is transformed by Souliotis's further attentiveness to the miniature *decrescendo* markings. Sung this way, we understand that Bolena is refraining from curses in order to escape her own anguish. There are some vocal compromises here: the all-important trills become straightforward steps up to a G below high C, and Souliotis adopts the Callas/Gavazzeni sleight of avoiding the high C in the first statement, saving it for the *da capo* only. She ends the opera on a strong high B flat.

An illuminating point of comparison is Souliotis's rendition of the Mad Scene on her 1966 Decca/London LP under Oliviero de Fabritiis. It is clear from this excerpt that Souliotis could have been an even greater Bolena than she was. While her rendition on the complete 1969 recording can be riveting, sometimes beautiful, her Mad Scene on this recital is always beautiful. The simple ease and freedom of her high C at "infiorato" is fully matched by the plush coloring of the actual note. She becomes especially appealing on "il crin," and there is a spellbinding *diminuendo* on "gioia" at the crest of the opening recitative. She comes closer here to giving us soft trills in the "Al dolce guidami" than in '69. Her phrasing is broader: unlike '69, she now executes the entire chain of turns leading to the final iteration of "un giorno rendimi" in a single breath. Again, we have the Callas cadenza at the conclusion of the cavatina, and this time she ends on pitch. Once the cavatina is over, her imagination does not seem as engaged as in the later recording: "per me morite" is less expressive and her "Smeton" is more the imposing monarch than the dreamer. There are not the same poignant accents on Donizetti's miniature *decrescendi* at "come il gemer tronco." Instead, the phrase emerges generally tearful. But the "Cielo, a' miei lunghi spasimi" setting of "Home Sweet Home" is even finer than in '69. It is impossible to imagine this being better done. One unpleasing inheritance from Callas's Bolena is the Gavazzeni cut, adopted by de Fabritiis here, of some measures following the "Home Sweet Home" setting. But Souliotis is left with more than enough to dazzle us. Here, every "tacete" is rock steady, and her top peals forth in "Coppia iniqua." Once again, however, there are no real trills— so critical here — and this is compounded by her ignoring the miniature *decrescendo* markings that she sings with such poetry in her later recording. This entire rendition of the scene must be judged an intimation of greatness rather than a perfect whole. One keenly regrets the absence of any reading that combines the full understanding of '69 and the vocal ease of '66. Perhaps Souliotis's voice began to lose consistency too soon for her ever to be able to combine the two. At least, her complete '69 recording leaves future generations with some inspired flashes of insight, and some of that insight is already there in her excellent vocalism of '66.

The Beverly Sills *Anna Bolena* boasts a literally complete reading of the score. A tiny handful of interpreters of these *assoluta* scores claim direct contact with mentors for whom these vocal traditions stand as a living, breathing idiom. Beverly Sills thoroughly understands Donizetti as musical speech, thanks to her teacher Estelle Liebling, a Marchesi pupil and an inheritor of the García tradition. Sills' affinity with this language of dots is evident on every page. Like Callas, she has absorbed the style in her very bones. The resulting wealth of detail in her reading is staggering. So is the extent to which her voice is unsuited for this role! All her colleagues in the recording are more comfortable vocally. However, only her Giovanna Seymour, Shirley Verrett, is as conversant with the Donizetti style. Stuart Burrows offers a bland Riccardo Percy and the young Paul Plishka sings a nondescript King Henry. Fortunately, Julius Rudel's conducting is nearly equal to Gavazzeni's in getting inside the drama. The set was made in 1972 and was first released on ABC. It is now available on DG.

In the first scene, Sills is vividly upset when she interrupts Smeton's disturbing song. She then delivers a fetching cavatina, "Come, innocente giovane," with shapely phrasing and the right feeling for Romani's poetry. The final cadenza offers a telling *pianissimo* and a *crescendo* at its crest, plus an exquisite interpolated top note on the final "splendor." She is so into the character that it's too bad when she raises "Re" in "che omai più giunga il Re," rather than ending it down. The emphasis on "Re" at score pitch would most likely have been inadequate in Sills' slender low. The cabaletta, "Non v'ha sguardo," points out the paradox of hearing an impeccable stylist perform such a role with a limited instrument. She can apply an exquisite trill at a moment like "condanna" (in the first statement only); a grace note at "sospirar" becomes a haunting, musical whimper; a downward scale introducing the *da capo* is of surpassing beauty, and the *da capo* itself is imaginatively embellished. However, here is where we are first aware that she's stretching her voice beyond its natural bounds. Throughout, she shows a recurrent wobble and some flat top notes. In the next scene, her encounter with Riccardo Percy, she vividly conveys the still young girl who fell in love with him many years before. "In mezzo al cor" is strengthened by delicate trills. Shades of her raised "Re" in the previous scene, she also raises the second "Son fuor di me," after singing the first at score pitch. Donizetti is making both a visual and a musical point here. Bolena is quietly curtseying, uttering a downward phrase of *inner* unease. Thus to go back up the scale on "di me" is to utter these words too outwardly. Arguably, this adjustment is less serious than "Re" since Sills has first let us hear this phrase through at score pitch. She employs a few embellishments in "Questo dì" and ends the scene with the traditional high C. In the long final scene of Act I, Sills inserts a note of warning in "mel guida," as if intimating to her brother that any consequences from her granting an audience to Percy will be on his head, seeming to say "Well, you asked for this!" Her solo "Debole io fui" exhibits real fear, but vocal stretch marks from the effort of this role begin to appear. After Percy joins her, the futility of her loveless marriage with the King is registered full force. Her disgust is conveyed in "sono orrendi," sung with a flourish that plunges into baleful chest voice on … "di." Although her low register remains uncomfortable, she can manage, as here, to integrate it with her phrasing in a telling way — the mark of a sure musician. Her "Che con me" is then expressively embellished, making her avoidance of the low B flat on "il terror" regrettable. In a role of this kind, a singer like Sills is clearly on the horns of a dilemma: either avoid moments like this or apply a sound that is unconvincing. She does raise the words "terra e mar." The great actress comes to the fore in her treatment of the crisis precipitating her discovery by the King. She may be the only Bolena whose awareness of Smeton elicits a properly hushed "Giusto Cielo." She is still aghast, but without the conventional exclamation. Both hushed terror and growing hysteria are played off brilliantly. Sills' plea to the King, "In quegli sguardi," becomes acutely painful, and, following the score but rarely heard, "o Re … Lascia che il core opresso" is spun out on a single breath. Getting set for the moments leading up to the final *allegro vivace* discloses more vocal strain, but nobody else sings the *vivace* itself with such pinpoint accuracy. A flourish leading into the *da capo* is embellished with a climactic top note. Then the actual *da capo* is launched on the verge of tears. The finale is capped with a high D.

Sills' opening scene in Act II when she must learn the truth of the King's infatuation with Jane Seymour shows her at her most overwhelming. She has a colleague fully worthy of her in Shirley Verrett as Giovanna, and the chemistry between these two is easily on a par with the Callas/Simionato partnership. Sills may have her vocal flaws, but the emotional impact here is indelible. She opens her words to her waiting women in a withdrawn "O mie fedeli," and there is a lovely piano flourish on "Cielo." While the prayer that opens the great duet has problems, we then have an encapsulation of her best and worst in the keen bitterness of "E consigliar mel puoi?" alongside subsequent vocal shortcomings. We hear a break in the voice as she reaches down to the low B on "mel puoi." The effort involved also occasions a clumsy aspirate or two. Things improve when her quick, flashing "O! chi è costei?" conveys Bolena on the scent for blood as she seeks the truth of who the other woman is. Once again, there is an adjustment as she sings "Vill-tah" instead of "Viltà" to transit easily into her low. The

Italian "i" is apparently too uncomfortable so low down. Too bad in view of her generally fine Italian. "Sul guancial" marks an upturn. The precision of her passagework is phenomenal, and she is suitably beside herself with fury, using the shape of Donizetti's phrasing with pure genius. She indulges in a fleeting *parlando* effect on ... "so" of "sposo," but it hardly detracts from the overwhelming surge of authentic musical fury. As she realizes the other woman is Seymour, there is an uncanny use of vocal face. A faint gasp right before a spoken "Tu" and "Che ascolto" convey a visual image of Bolena averting her gaze. It may be impossible to define exactly how she manages to convey this, but convey it she does, purely in her dramatic shading. One doesn't have to see this, one plainly hears it. How is a mystery. It is unique: the aural image of a deeply hurt woman shutting out the world. As Verrett sings her "Dal mio cor," Sills' interjections are gut-wrenching, culminating with a "Sorgi" in tears. The "E reo soltanto" is given a very specific reading: there is anger and disgust aimed directly at the King. Her tearful solo of forgiveness is crowned by a lovely moment: an expressive portamento of deep regret on "pena." In the coda, there is expert passagework from both artists, and they bring the scene to an end with an assured high C. The next scene is not as fully inspired, even though it has its moments. Sills' entrance, and its recurrent problems, reminds one of the dangerous game she is playing with her voice. At the same time, certain words emerge with admirable strength — a vivid "infamia," a spoken "Ah! che di' tu?" It's hard to forget an almost whispered "Ahimè," and the words "tu dai" become a musical whimper of profound loss. One brilliant touch in the "Ah! del tuo cor" is her treatment of "perfida," where her piano on this word vividly suggests her shame at having chosen royalty over love. At the end of this scene, Sills delivers the traditional high C. For the Mad Scene, she surprises by adopting a lively delivery in her opening words. We are reminded that Bolena truly believes it to be her wedding day, not her execution. So she is in a festive mood. There is a fleeting moment of thoughtfulness as she gives a withdrawn reading of "infiorato" with a *diminuendo* on the high C. But her mood does not seriously alter until "Oh! chi si duole?" There is a perfect transition from terror to weeping at "infelice son io," and she then withdraws back into herself at the crest of the cadenza on "gioia." Perfection is reached in the *pianissimo* trills in the cavatina, "Al dolce guidami," and in the evocative embellishment at "colà, dimentico." The chain of rising turns leading to the last "un giorno rendimi" brings us additional trills. After the cavatina, Sills fudges the lower note in "suon" of "Qual mesto suon?" by merely sounding it on the "n" consonant, but she effectively conveys the line's rapt terror. "O!" in "O! in quale istante" is separated from the rest of the phrase as a sudden exclamation, and the entire solo is vivid in projecting pure horror. She sobs at encountering Percy among the condemned — and makes the phrase a bit easier on her low by changing "Percy" to "Riccardo" to avoid the "i" vowel on a middle E flat. Unlike other interpreters, she is clearly back at her wedding day for "t'appressa," making it almost as vivacious as her opening lines. She does not deliver the miniature *decrescendi* in "come il gemer tronco" as marked in the

score, but oddly enough she delivers one at "esse." She becomes spellbinding in
the "Cielo, a' miei lunghi spasimi." In the approach to Anna's final cabaletta,
Sills does not surmount the many hurdles all that well. The voice is too small
and is overtaxed. "Cessate" climaxes on a wobbly high note, but though she
barely touches the low B flat on "sarà," the effect of the word itself is strong. With
this, there is an elaborate flourish on "versato." Once she launches the taxing
"Coppia iniqua," the listener is made aware of strain throughout. One wonders
why, having such musical sensitivity, Sills chooses to ignore, like other Bolenas,
the numerous *decrescendo* markings. Naturally, the ascending trills are good,
and she even amplifies these with additional alternating trills in the *da capo*, but
there is a wobbly ascent to an added top note on the last "Sì" leading into the
da capo. An interpolated high E flat ends this uneven reading of the final aria.

      An interesting point of comparison with Sills' last scene is the equally lyric
Renata Scotto's rendition of the same sequence from a "live" Bolena of 1975,
available only on a few pressings of limited distribution. An early LP edition is
on HRE. Featured are Umberto Grilli as Riccardo Percy, Tatiana Troyanos as Giovanna Seymour, and Ezio Flagello as Henry VIII. Fernando Previtali conducts.

      Bolena's Mad Scene remains the acid test for any Bolena. Scotto opens it
with a touching delivery of Bolena's bewildered phrases to her grief-stricken
ladies-in-waiting. There is a good high C at "infiorato," and Scotto gives us an
effective *pianissimo* at "serto di rose." There is also an equally effective pause,
hair-raising in its impact, before "infelice son io," although the crest of her
"gioia" sounds uncomfortable. Haunting *pianissimo* trills grace her cavatina, "Al
dolce guidami," while the crest of the turns leading to the final "un giorno
rendimi" becomes unsteady. The diminuendo on the aria's final note takes its
time reaching true pitch. Once the cavatina comes to a close, Scotto is beside
herself with hysteria at "O! in quale istante" and turns strident. One can salute
a perceptive communicative flair at key points in her delirium: an indelibly
trance-like "Smeton! T'apressa"; a perfectly accented reading of the miniature
decrescendo markings at "come il gemer tronco," and a "Cielo, a' miei lunghi
spasimi" that is deeply absorbed. When sanity returns, and she knows she must
face execution, she resorts to *parlando* on "sangue" and delivers an embellished
"versato" capping it with a "sarà" whose low B flat comes out hollow, but strong.
Unfortunately, there is no pulling back at any of the *decrescendo* markings in
"Coppia iniqua," and there are pronounced glottal attacks for certain words like
"no" and "non impreco." In addition, the passagework on "pietà, favor, pietà"
with its high C gets lost the first time, becoming more cautious, but more accurate, in the repeat. The ascending trills start out as real in both statements, but dete-
riorate in a blur as Scotto goes up the scale. She is plainly exhausted at the end.

      A "live" concert reading at Lincoln Center in 1985 of Joan Sutherland's
Bolena, opposite Jerry Hadley's Percy, and with Richard Bonynge conducting,
gave me the impression, soon confirmed in her studio recording of 1987 for
Decca/London, that, with the fearsome assignment of Bolena, Sutherland had
finally hit her Waterloo. The Lincoln Center concert was never made generally

available, so there may seem little point in bringing it up here. However, just to listen to this formidable vocalist performing a work "live" and comparing it to a studio recording was instructive. This was because, while the instrument itself may clearly have been affected by the march of time, Sutherland's ways of coping were remarkably similar in the hall and in the studio. The sounds may have had many problems at this point, but the consistency in quality, from good to indifferent, had to be respected. Everything was so carefully worked out by the Bonynges that one could be sure that the discipline involved would stand the singer in good stead.

The reason why Bolena may still be Sutherland's Waterloo, despite the discipline, lies in her deliberate adoption of certain vocal shortcuts. As was the case at Lincoln Center, her recorded studio version avoids too much heavy going in the lower half of the voice, significantly rewriting Donizetti's music at times. It's one thing retooling a line of recitative that's marked *a piacere*, or similarly to embellish a *da capo*, but quite another to take a strong skein of melody that is not even repeated, and change that. The Bonynges appear to be rewriting passages for the purpose of confining them to a higher tessitura. This is done again and again, virtually transforming their character. One has the feeling they would not have made so many alterations had the singer tackled the role earlier in her career. The irony is that two of her colleagues, Jerry Hadley as Percy and Samuel Ramey as King Henry, provide some of the most accurate renderings of this music on disc. In a way, this set is distinguished more by Hadley and Ramey than by Sutherland, even though one thing she does have over her colleagues is a superb stylishness of phrasing. Hadley, for one, shows very little style, but he attempts to sing the role more accurately than anyone else. He makes an honest stab at the trills in the Act I cabaletta, even following a difficult *decrescendo* marking on one of them. However, Ramey not only articulates precisely every note of the King's intricate passagework, he makes it all sound positively easy. The remaining principal, Susanne Mentzer as Jane Seymour, is not at the same level, although her musicianship is adequate.

In Sutherland's opening scene, we already encounter tendencies typical in her portrayal: deft passagework offset by a hollow low B and a wobble from D on the treble stave up to the A below high C. After an accomplished cavatina, she dilutes the command of Bolena's character by bringing "congedo" up in pitch. In the cabaletta "Non v'ha sguardo," Sutherland simplifies the climactic flourishes of the first statement, only to embellish the second statement and add on a high E flat at the end. In the next scene, Bolena's tight-lipped insistence that the whole kingdom believed Percy innocent, "Innocente il Regno intero," is launched at higher than score pitch, changing Donizetti's projection of initial reserve. Sutherland's grasp of Bolena's mood is surer in a perplexed "Io sentii," opening the first part of the scene's closing ensemble. Her trills are as expert as ever on "in mezzo al cor," but a high B flat in the cadenza sounds frayed. In the *materia di mezzo*, she alters the first "Son fuor di me," going up, even though this is an aside.

It's not hard to figure out why Sutherland takes this dodge and only follows the original downward phrase when it's repeated: the first iteration appears against orchestral agitation, while the singer's weakened E above middle C can be more effective against a softer orchestra in the second. Astoundingly, even the second line of the concluding ensemble, "con si lieti e fausti auspici," is also brought up in its entirety, thus offsetting the contrasts that Donizetti set up in alternating phrases high and low. This is a first statement of a melody where there are no *a piacere* markings. However, Sutherland builds up a good head of steam in the coda, climaxing on a fine high C. The final scene of Act I surprises with a rich variety of dramatic inflection: "e un serto ebb'io di spine" twists the knife on a powerfully bitter "spine," and "sospetto" later on has a nice taut quality. She is still lifting crucial words and phrases up, changing the emphasis no less than five times in less than thirty minutes of music! However, her low is not always unsure. While "ed il terror" ends on almost a *parlando* delivery, an astonishing lapse for Sutherland, her "terra e mar" is a perfectly exciting plunge. It is too bad that the *da capo* of her "Per pietà" lacks the urgency of much else in this scene, but she heightens the excitement of the duet's coda with a more galvanized delivery and ends with a good high B flat. The "In quegli sguardi" ensemble is deeply moving in its opening, the very image of a lost soul. There is also great excitement in the *da capo* of the closing *vivace*, "Ah! segnata," with its dazzling embellishments and climactic high D ringing down the curtain.

The opening of Act II presents an imprisoned Bolena even more dejected than most interpreters make her. There is a tearful delivery of "In terra non v'ha riparo per la mia ruina." Set against this despondent persona is an odd reading of "Andate," where the pitch is suddenly brought up (as so frequently in this recording), altering the sad affection of Bolena's parting word. Even more disconcerting is a similarly transposed treatment of the closing words, "o Dio," of her prayer, detracting from the hushed privacy of this moment. When Giovanna suggests a way of avoiding execution, Bolena's troubled question "Tu consigliar mel puoi?" becomes a moment of hurt withdrawal from an erstwhile friend with a fine low B flat. When first learning of a rival, Sutherland, before knowing it's Seymour, delivers a ferocious and intricate vocal flourish on "Favella," and the word "Viltade" carries immense strength. Once again, though, an important effect of Donizetti's is blunted when "suo cuore" is changed from a snarl down to the E above middle C to an exclamation further up the scale. "Sul guancial" is rendered strong, although the growling effect on the middle Cs' "letto"/ "sospetto" is jettisoned through yet another upward transposition. After realizing the woman is Seymour, Sutherland is tearful in her wish for disbelief on the interjections like "Ella," "mia rivale?" and "Dio!" She clearly wants to move beyond the pain in her "Sorgi" solo with its elaborately decorated reading of the "È reo soltanto" and a tender "Va, infelice." Brilliant passagework and a high C climax the scene. In Bolena's trial scene, it is confusing to hear her attempt at dignity compromised by robbing "mia dignità riprendo" of its *gravitas* through eschewing the E flat above middle C. The core of Sutherland's characterization at this point is clear when "un nobil core" tells us she finally regrets abandoning Percy and now recognizes too late that she still loves him. It is that lost love more than any queenly propriety that now guides the Sutherland Bolena. She fades away memorably in a wilting "Io," but her downward scale on "orror" is not impeccable, descending almost to *parlando* at its close. In "Quanto, quanto," we have yet another phrase raised upward, only this time her tenor joins her: "l'empio strazio che d'Anna si fa!" There is a *de rigeur* high C with Hadley at her scene's conclusion, capping this sequence. Lots of thought has evidently gone into the Mad Scene. Words are sometimes highlighted, and there is an uncommon sense of progression through much of it. We also have one of Sutherland's most exquisite trills for the "serto di rose." "Toglimi a questa miseria estrema" becomes a single, intensely beautiful phrase, and there is an excellent, deeply joyful flourish on "gioia." All her trills are as beautiful as ever in "Al dolce guidami," and the chain of upward turns leading into "un giorno rendimi" are effectively elongated. Once the cavatina is over, we return to some of the vocal compromises with her low: "Le guardie" turns up rather than down to A flat on the stave, and, astoundingly, when Bolena sees Percy joining her on the block, Sutherland simply omits the E flat above middle C altogether with no substitution. Another odd change may or may not have been deliberate: Sutherland does not follow all of Donizetti's musical setting of "Home Sweet Home," reverting, for instance, to the original song in eschewing Donizetti's ornamentation on "Ciel, riposo." The few flourishes Donizetti adds are clearly within Sutherland's capacities— it is excursions into the low that she has avoided, not modest ornaments in the middle of the stave as here. Very odd. After this moment, Sutherland's atypical vividness flickers somewhat: there is little outrage in her final preparations for the block against the backdrop of the festivities outside. Rather, she seems to be holding back from emotional upheaval in a heavily ornamented "Manca solo" statement. The stance in "Coppia iniqua" is left ambivalent: it is not clear whether it is an expression of scorn, of turning away from further bitter thoughts, of forgiveness, or of wrath disguised. Sung transposed, Sutherland's ambivalence may be deliberate: a decision to let the music speak individually to each listener. No apparent effort is made to follow the miniature *decrescendo* markings, though there are some modest embellishments in the first statement. It is a delight to hear genuine ascending trills leading into "ei" both times, and the second statement is spectacularly embellished, climaxing with yet another trill and an interpolated top note to close the *scena*.

In an uncanny way, some of Sutherland's traits, like her approach to the softer top notes, are mirrored in Edita Gruberova's singing, even though Gruberova does not have such an imposing instrument. She has made a specialty of Donizetti's three queens, Anne Boleyn, Mary Stuart, and Elizabeth Tudor, and is always conscientious in projecting a vivid "story" in each of these parts. Gruberova's Bolena may not match the incandescent imagination of a Sills, but she doesn't simply give a *pro forma* reading. She is commendably earnest, albeit not distinctive. The comparison with her senior colleague remains apt, since she is constrained to make adjustments for an instrument that is essentially a lyric coloratura with its center of gravity much higher than that of the true *assoluta*. Her recording comes from a "live" occasion in 1994. Elio Boncompagni conducts a variable cast, consisting of Delores Ziegler's Jane Seymour and Stefano Palatchi's King Henry alongside José Bros's superior Riccardo Percy. This set was released on Nightingale. Many of the Gavazzeni cuts are adopted. However, Riccardo's "Vivi, tu" in the last act is restored, giving Bros an opportunity to contribute some of the better singing in this recording.

Bolena's plight seems all too real in the cavatina of the opening *scena*. Gruberova's effective *pianissimi* contrast with an occasional sour note at full voice. She conveys a sense of suffocation at court with an effective "non sarei si misera." As with some other Bolenas, critical words like "congedo" are transposed up for a more telling delivery by a limited voice. The tripping passagework in the cabaletta, typical of much of her reading, is an asset, despite the same sour sound. The *da capo* is deftly embellished, and she caps the whole with a high E flat at the close. In Gruberova's next scene, there are sleights reminiscent of both Sills and Sutherland on the lower phrases, but she launches the "Io sentii" properly rapt throughout; "si diffonde sul mio cor" is nicely shaped and there are good trills at "in mezzo al cor." The scene ends with the traditional high C. Her declamatory recitative with her brother opening the next scene betrays pressure and a wobble. At full voice, her would-be shading consists more of verbal explosives than vocal nuance. The latter is more apparent at moments like her withdrawn delivery of a thoughtful "e vero." Moments like this are offset by avoidance of key vocal gestures like the low B flat at "il terror." She is best at conveying her sense of being a trapped woman at court. Her helplessness here is shown by the way she conveys her momentary loss of consciousness and, then, "In quegli sguardi," her weakened state after she has revived in King Henry's presence. In sharp contrast, the combative words, like "ad Anna," betray a wobble, and the final *vivace* itself shows her avoiding the middle D altogether, fundamentally changing the melody in its first statement. The *da capo* is further changed with some striking embellishments, and a high D is interpolated at the close.

For the opening of Act II, the "Andate" is brought up as in the Sutherland, but the prayer is unchanged, with a faithful rendering of the concluding phrase and a harrowed delivery of "o Dio." At Seymour's revealing the King's degrading terms for mercy, Gruberova suggests speechlessness and wonderment at a friend suggesting this, a reading offset by a weak low B. Like other moments of outrage, her curse on an unknown rival, "Sul suo capo," emerges pressured and tremulous. In addition, the middle C is barely audible on "sospetto," however dazzling the balance of the passagework. Once she realizes the other woman is her own friend Seymour, her interjections are done quietly, utterly crushed. When she regains composure, we hear a quiet "Sorgi" and a big flourish for the "E reo soltanto." Her solo of forgiveness, "Va, infelice," is soft and breathless, as if abashed at her earlier vehemence, becoming tenderly forgiving. She joins

Delores Ziegler on a joint high C at the curtain. In the trial scene, Gruberova starts with a pleading tone — nothing that is either commanding or regal until the "Il regio nome." This is then heightened by a vehement reading of her defiance of the King, where her wobble flares up badly. A number of the Gavazzeni cuts are adopted in this sequence. Gruberova's charting of this scene does not cohere until confronted by Percy with the truth of her former attachment. A sad daze overcomes her for the "Ah del tuo cor," a highlight of her interpretation. Here, we have a simple woman singing softly a melody of regret. The obligatory high C closes this penultimate sequence. Bolena's final sequence finds her again in a daze: much of the opening recitative of the Mad Scene turns into vagueness. There is an accomplished *diminuendo* on the high C for the "decorated altar." In the cavatina, there are crisp trills, and the studied *ritardando* for the spiralling chain of upward turns on "nostro amor" demonstrates Gruberova's outstanding breath control. She adopts Callas's cadenza to close the cavatina. In recognizing Smeton among the prisoners, her voice is all eery smiles as she inquires after his "silent harp," and all the miniature *decrescendo* accents are scrupulously followed in "come il gemer tronco."

Returning to reality, her declaration that only "Bolena's blood" remains to be shed finds the voice somewhat guttural, and her flourish on this line sidesteps the low B flat. She still shows astounding breath control in the final cabaletta: all six trills on "scenda" are linked to the following "Ei" as a single grand phrase! She also manages to suggest certain of the cabaletta's *decrescendo* markings, although not carrying them through consistently. The *da capo* has the dubious distinction of a flat "iniqua," but it is embellished with flair and, despite some suggestion of a whine, climaxes effectively on a high E flat.

❦ 8 ❧

Vincenzo Bellini (1801–1835): *Norma*

Giuditta Pasta's other *tour de force*, the title role in Bellini's *Norma* (La Scala, 1831), was set, like *Anna Bolena*, to a text by Felice Romani. Bellini expressed great satisfaction with the way he had musically and dramatically shaped the *assoluta* role of Norma to match what he heard in the "encyclopedic" character of Pasta's singing.

Unlike Bolena's music, no specific sequence in Norma's music seems to confront an interpreter with every vocal and technical difficulty posed throughout the rest of the work. The fine level of Romani's text, and Bellini's expressive music for all the principals, not just Norma, have made his opera succeed — where *Anna Bolena* failed — in being one of the few *assoluta* vehicles to gain a foothold in today's operatic repertoire. Moreover, each one of Norma's scenes successfully makes its desired effect in terms of imparting dramatic structure to a precise development in Norma's characterization. As I have already suggested, the reason why *Norma* survived and *Anna Bolena* did not may have been the feasibility of finding just enough divas across the decades able to handle each of Norma's individual scenes creditably and so establish a regular performing tradition, whereas the rarity of a diva who could tackle Bolena's final scene rendered any continuous performing tradition well-nigh impossible. Also, the reason certain heroic divas continued to sing Norma into the twentieth century was, possibly, Wagner's great admiration of Bellini. The attractiveness of this role tempted some singers at the turn of the century, like the Wagner disciple Lilli

Lehmann, who felt they had the training and the musical predisposition for it. Wagner's particular admiration for Bellini and Rossini among the *bel canto* composers did not, of course, prevent Donizetti vehicles like *Lucia* from surviving in the same way, but Lucia is not really a true *drammatico* coloratura role. As a **B,i** part, it is easier to cast. Happily, since the advent of Maria Callas, the notion that Bellini is the only true Romantic composer for the dramatic coloratura singer and that Donizetti is somehow a vapid twitterer is fast disappearing.

What does distinguish Bellini from Donizetti is his greater concentration on the individual subtleties and flavor of Romani's verses, to the detriment of the dramatic flow as a whole. Still, what emerged was something where, as Wagner remarked, there was "real passion and feeling." "The right singer has only to get up and sing it for it to win all hearts. I have learned things from [it] which Messrs. Brahms & Co. have never learned."[34] On the one hand, Norma's music was less compelling dramatically than Bolena's, but, on the other, it was more poetic. Bellini had absorbed in his music the very texture of Romani's verses. It is Bellini's responsiveness to Romani's words that makes vivid diction a hallmark of a great Norma.

Bellini's musical poetry is immediately apparent in Norma's first sequence, "Sediziose voci ... Casta Diva ... Fine al rito ... Ah! bello a me." The harmonic translation of Romani's ritualistic verses into Bellini's particular idiom render the music for this sequence riveting enough for a prevailing misconception to have arisen: the full heroic dimensions of the title role are summed up here. This is hardly true. Again, unlike Bolena, Norma really has no such scene. Rather, it is in the discrete differences from scene to scene that the inherent fascination in Norma's music arises.

When we first hear her in this unusually extensive opening *scena*, the impression formed of her from her opening lines in the recitative, "Sediziose voci," is of immense strength. She rebukes the Druids and her father Oroveso for their impatience, and, as their High Priestess, she warns them that disaster will be theirs if they rebel against the Romans before the appointed time. The phrases are formal, measured. They work their effect through deliberateness, rather than through an overt display of energy. They require a deep-seated vocal production with a powerful lower range, and when Norma assures the Druids that a day of reckoning is at hand for the Romans, she foretells the imminent destruction of Rome from within, "Morrà pei vizi suoi, Qual consunta morrà," with a descent to the low B on the final "morrà."

In true *assoluta* style, the following cavatina is markedly different from the previous recitative. Instead of requiring the heroic tone associated with proud, imposing pronouncements, "Casta Diva" needs prodigiously long breath to sustain its expansive phrases. And, where a strong low is required in the recitative, a very resilient high is needed for the syncopated high Bs in the first verse leading to a high C, for the *crescendo* on the high B in the second verse also climaxing in a high C, and for the generally high tessitura of the entire aria. Even with the traditional downward transposition of this aria from G to F, initiated by Pasta and approved by Bellini, and with the occasional omission of the second verse, an unusually responsive high is still needed. Actually, in those cases where the second verse is retained, hardly anyone has performed the *crescendo* in the second verse that replaces the first-verse syncopation. Most instead repeat the first-verse syncopation, Marian Anderson in concert being one of the few who observes the distinction in the second verse — but of course even she transposes. On the other hand, Joan Sutherland, who is one of the very few to perform both verses in the original key, does not sing the original *crescendo* in the second verse but instead repeats the syncopated notes. Even Maria Callas, while singing both verses, repeats the syncopation in the second verse and also transposes down. Obviously, singing, in the first verse, a series of high Bs (or high As in the transposition in F) demands greater flexibility, while singing, in the second verse, a long *crescendo* on a single high B demands greater strength and breath control. Evidently, all these attributes were intended to be displayed in Bellini's original conception for the aria, and, while the technical comprehensiveness of "Casta Diva" may not be as thoroughgoing as Bolena's final cabaletta, the contrast being drawn here between flexibility in the first verse and strength in the second is musically and dramatically crucial in showing something of Norma's mercurial character; this contrast ought to be respected.

Where a smoothness of tone suggesting infallibility seems implicit in "Casta Diva," the *materia di mezzo* beginning "Fine al rito" displays the first hints of that all-too-human dynamism and recklessness that is Norma. The orchestral accompaniment is more assertive here than previously. Though, in her opening recitative, we felt Norma's strength, it is here where we first sense a power in her that is not stately or imposing but electric, volatile. She warns all unbelievers to leave the ceremony, singing this in biting heroic phrases that, though not as florid as the concluding cabaletta of this sequence, nevertheless have a scintillation and brilliance difficult to sustain against such a forceful accompaniment.

After declaring to the assemblage that, for them, moral vindication against the Romans is inevitable, she then privately admits, in a florid, bright cabaletta, "Ah! bello a me ritorna," that she and the Roman Proconsul, Pollione, were once deeply in love, and, could they but recapture the magic of those days, she would be willing to live a simple private life with none of the heavy responsibilities she now bears. Since Norma is anticipating a more carefree and happy future, the tessitura becomes high once more, but, instead of long phrases expressing infinite assurance, as in "Casta Diva," the high phrases here are slightly shorter and considerably more agitated. The more sprightly quality of this aria is turned to expressive advantage by Bellini as Norma remembers her youthful feelings of falling in love, and she uses the high C to convey what seems to be reckless abandonment in trying to wish her present troubles with Pollione out of existence. In this cabaletta, her wistful desperation calls forth the first thoroughly intricate coloratura singing of the role.

Norma's next scene is a more extended sequence than the opening one. Here, we see her first in private with Pollione's two children as she confesses to her confidante, Clotilde, that Pollione's offspring are hers as well. John Ardoin has remarked how, in singing this role, Callas was able to draw the proper timbral distinction that must be made (if the full range of this *assoluta* role is to be realized) between the coloring of Norma's public statements and her private ones. The contrast of public and private is shown in the slightly different way that the lower register is used here. The lowest phrases seem subdued, uncertain and shadowed by insecurity. As she dares to contemplate the possibility that Pollione might desert her, she shudders at the very notion, describing "un tal dubbio" with her first, and only, descent below the low B — two low B flats— on "dubbio." The shrinking, harrowed quality of this phrase is a far cry from her bold and public prophecy of the destruction of Rome in the first scene where she intoned a low B, even though her very lowest register is also being used here — and used in conjunction with an attempt, like her prophecy of Rome's destruction, to look into the future. Most singers adopt the standard practice of singing "dubbio" with an apoggiatura, thus only singing the low B flat on "...bio" and thereby, perhaps, altering the introverted quality of this phrase. What this use of Norma's lowest note achieves dramatically is similar to the intimation of disaster in Bolena's use of the low B flat when warning Percy of the perils that surround her.

When Adalgisa, one of the youngest Druid priestesses, unexpectedly appears at this point filled with remorse for having considered renunciation of her calling for the sake of a lover, Norma reassures her of her freedom to desert the order for a man if she so chooses. Here, unlike the opening recitative to this scene, Norma's phrases become airy, brighter. The tessitura of Norma's vocal line becomes much higher, as Norma, in letting up on some of the weight of texture of her vocalism elsewhere, is now allowing herself to emerge as more simple, more of this world, in showing Adalgisa that she has nothing to fear. For Adalgisa is certainly a musical and vocal cousin to Giovanna in Donizetti's opera. The character of Adalgisa was created in 1831 by Giulia Grisi, the straight soprano whom Bellini had already rehearsed the year before in the high soprano role of Giulietta in his *I Capuleti e i Montecchi* opposite the Romeo of her sister, Giuditta Grisi, a mezzo-soprano. Giulia Grisi had never sung anything other than straight soprano roles when she created Adalgisa, and, in fact, throughout her career, there is no indication that her range ever went below middle C.[35] As in the case of the Bolena/Giovanna scene, Norma's vocal maturity is deliberately juxtaposed to Adalgisa's innocence in all these Norma/Adalgisa duets. The intricate coloratura we heard in Norma's first-scene cabaletta is now displayed as, in recollection of her own seduction by Pollione, Norma completely releases Adalgisa from her vows. Still, the kind of unbridled desperation that was expressed in her previous cabaletta is not present here. Rather, in a joyful, untroubled gesture of congratulation for Adalgisa's good fortune, "Ah sì, fa core," Norma spins out a radiant, extended cadenza ascending to high C. A sterner stance returns to the role in the following recitative with Norma's declamatory phrases of outrage on discovering, when Pollione enters, that Adalgisa's suitor is none other than he himself. Norma then bursts out with "Oh non tremare," full of weighty agility as intricate as her lyric "Ah bello a me" and "Ah sì fa core," and unlike the less florid but just as heroic *materia di mezzo* of her first *scena*. She declares to Pollione that he, rather than Adalgisa, is in far more danger from her. The high is used here as taxingly as in "Ah bello a me" and "Ah sì, fa core," culminating in another iteration of the high C. After this use of the high, the stately "Oh di qual sei tu vittima" trio uses a portentous, powerful middle register. Norma solemnly tells Adalgisa here that death for her would have been preferable to Pollione's ruthless deception. In the rousing finale to this scene, "Vanne sì," Norma, beside herself with fury, orders Pollione out of her home and her life. This finale marks a partial return to the use of the upper register in "Oh non tremare," though here she does not go up to high C, and the phrases requiring both heroic strength and flexibility are not quite as florid as in "Oh non tremare" and are more like "Fine al rito" in the first scene. The orchestral accompaniment for "Vanne sì," though, is even more energetic than anything we have heard so far. Many interpreters cap this finale with an added high D at the end.

In the first scene of Act II, Norma's third scene, she at first contemplates killing her children, but then decides to give them to Adalgisa and Pollione and, on their union, to end her own life. Adalgisa dissuades Norma from such a path and, telling her that she no longer loves Pollione, plans to demand of him that he return to his children and to Norma. This scene is not quite as long for Norma as her first two, and vocally it depicts a somewhat weaker, more broken character than we have yet seen. Something of her heroic quality is heard as she opens the scene holding a knife poised over her sleeping children. But such phrases are fitful, and the tender, *lirico* line she spins out in addressing the children before raising the knife indicates her true character and lets us know in advance that she will not have the heart to go through with the murder. In telling Adalgisa of her desire to end it all and to entrust the children to Pollione, Norma implores her, in florid, high-lying phrases reaching up to high C, not to be too neglectful a stepmother. Adalgisa replies in the same strains, telling her she would willingly persuade Pollione to return to Norma before she would ever take the children and Pollione away from her. Though a small handful of twentieth-century Normas have been well cast, the prevailing allocation of Adalgisa's music to a mezzo has necessarily resulted in this entire exchange being transposed downward from C to B flat.[36] This merely compounds the crucial error of making Adalgisa sound more rather than less mature than Norma. In the following duet, "Mira, o Norma … Cedi … Sì, fino all'ore," Adalgisa's plea to Norma for her to keep her children is met with a bewildered confession from Norma of her own human weakness. What both women sing here is quietly moving in the way that Bolena's forgiveness of Giovanna was and is marked by relative vocal and technical simplicity. Again, a downward transposition, this time from F to E flat, is customary. Though this is undoubtedly Adalgisa's most commanding dramatic moment, such a transposition takes away from her trusting, youthful character. In the *materia di mezzo* ("Cedi"), her successful persuasion of Norma to refrain from suicide in expectation of Pollione's return evokes Norma's awe-struck "O giovinetta." The two of them now sing their cabaletta, "Sì, fino all'ore," a *tour de force* of *bel canto* pyrotechnics expressing defiance of the outside world and a sense of united purpose that, in the voices of the right interpreters, can prove overwhelming. The tessitura of this cabaletta is even more high-lying than the opening florid exchange of their scene.

Norma's final scene, the third of Act II, is by far her longest. Here, in addition, the weight of the vocal line is at its heaviest. It is in this scene that Norma, on learning of Adalgisa's failure to bring Pollione back to his children and to her, resolves on revenge. As soon as she tells the Druids that the time is now at hand for them to rebel against Rome, Pollione is caught trying to abduct Adalgisa. Left alone with him, Norma tells him she is going to allow the Druids to start their campaign against Pollione's countrymen by first sacrificing both him and Adalgisa. But when it comes time to tell her brethren of Adalgisa's betrayal of her vows, Norma cannot bring herself to accuse her. She considers herself at least as guilty and suddenly names herself as the priestess who has committed the betrayal. Thus, she and Pollione are led to their deaths, leaving Oroveso to fulfill his promise to care for the children.

When this scene opens, Norma is still in the same lyrical mood as at the end of the previous scene — another cadenza with a high C, another series of limpid phrases. But, when she learns from Clotilde of Adalgisa's failure, the phrases in the upper register suddenly become declamatory, abrupt. She spins out another vocal flourish with the high C, but the weight and the instrumental coloring are now threatening as she calls out for Roman blood. As she exhorts the Druids to feats of war and pillage, her unlovely cries of recitative are accompanied by as energetic an orchestral texture as in the finale to Act I. When left alone with Pollione, their duet limns a spirit at its most threatening and most troubled. Imposing, portentous phrases in the lower register open "In mia man" when Norma demands that, as a price for his life, Pollione forget Adalgisa and leave her home and her country forever. The implicit vocal darkness and sheer weight of her Act I prophecy of the fall of Rome is recalled in this ultimatum. When Pollione has finally convinced Norma that he would willingly die rather than submit to such a demand, Norma, in a burst of heroic coloratura, replies that, in that case, not only Pollione will die but hundreds of Romans as well, and even Adalgisa will share his fate. At the very point where she tells Pollione of the flames that await Adalgisa, we hear Norma, for the first time, use not just a heavy lower range but a resilient and flexible one as well, including a series of ascending trills starting down at middle E flat to launch her vengeful promise of Adalgisa's fate. This is a crucial moment in the role, for it is here that the one remaining technical and vocal accomplishment not yet encompassed in Norma's music is finally displayed. Here, Norma becomes one of the defining *assoluta* roles. Pollione's expressions of grief at the thought of Adalgisa also being a victim call forth from Norma a final burst of heroic fioritura lying quite high and containing her last use of high C. A vocal color of vengeful triumph still seems

NORMA

ACT	SELECTION	1 FLEXIBLE LOW	2 INTRICATE COLORATURA	3A AT OR ABOVE HIGH B	3B AT OR BELOW LOW B	4 LONG SEQUENCES	5 FLEXIBLE HIGH	6 HEROIC COLORATURA	7 HEROIC TONE	8 HEAVY LOW
I	Sediziose voci				X				X	X
	Casta Diva			X		X	X			
	Fine al rito					X	X	X	X	
	Ah! bello a me ritorna		X	X		X				
	Vanne, e li cela				X	X				
	Oh, rimembranza!		X	X		X	X			
	Ma di' ...					X				
	Oh non tremare		X	X		X	X	X	X	
	Oh di qual sei tu vittima					X			X	
	Vanne, si					X	X	X	X	
II	Dormono entrambi!								X	
	Deh! con te		X	X			X			
	Mira, o Norma		X	X			X			
	Ei tornerà!			X						
	In mia man	X	X	X		X	X	X		X
	Dammi quel ferro!					X			X	
	Qual cor tradisti					X			X	
	Deh! Non volerli vittime					X			X	

implicit at the opening of the following recitative as Norma summons the Druids for the double sacrifice of Adalgisa and Pollione. Then, when no further technical *assoluta* accomplishments remain for Norma, her sudden confession that it is she alone who is to be sacrificed alongside Pollione leaves her music bereft of everything but a requirement for long breath and poignant regret. In "Qual cor tradisti," both Pollione (his love for Norma now reawakened by her self-sacrifice) and Norma sing a solemn duet that soon becomes an ensemble for everyone on stage. Though Norma's phrases are long here, they are not quite *drammatico*, and they lie more in the middle register than any previous music in this scene. Following this ensemble, a plea to her father, Oroveso, to care for the children introduces the finale, starting with a slow solo of Norma's, "Deh! Non volerli vittime." This lies mostly in the middle and culminates in a full ensemble similar to "Qual cor tradisti" in which Norma expresses her sense of release.

Though, at first, reaction to this somber score was somewhat mixed, growing appreciation of Pasta's remarkable achievement in it turned the tide within the year, and, by the following season, not just in Italy but throughout the rest of Europe, *Norma* was as firmly established as *Anna Bolena* had been. Stellar artists both within and outside Italy took it on: Maria Malibran, Giuseppina Ronzi–De Begnis and Giulia Grisi were but a few of the luminaries who tackled the opera in its first decade. In addition, so did a star of Central Europe, Wilhelmine Schroeder-Devrient. She may have been a bit unlike other divas when it came to her singing style, but evidently not so unlike in her vocal type and roles. She first sang Norma in 1835. Like Pasta, as well as Paton and Colbran before her, Schroeder-Devrient took on both mezzo and soprano roles with equal success. Her mezzo Romeo in Bellini's *I Capuleti* was thought by some her finest role, while her *Fidelio* Leonore greatly impressed both Wagner and Berlioz. Another admirer was Beethoven himself who saw her in *Fidelio* only a year or so after her operatic debut as Pamina in 1821. Among the *assoluta* roles she sang, there was not only Norma, but also Bolena, Médée, and Reiza. It is unfortunate that, due to his untimely death soon after the *Oberon* premiere, Weber was never able to hear Schroeder-Devrient in his last opera. Certainly, when Weber heard her as Agathe in his *Der Freischuetz*, he avowed his undying admiration, stating that he had not merely found her an excellent artist but had been particularly thrilled by her execution because "it went beyond anything I could have conceived for the role."[37]

Whether or not Schroeder-Devrient's singing style was comparable to her *assoluta* contemporaries is uncertain due to some unflattering comments made by Henry Fothergill Chorley when judging her singing in the Italian repertoire.[38] These comments were made late in the 1830s, during which her vocal decline had already begun. Before that, she had earned herself the soubriquet, "Queen of Tears." Berlioz himself, who had so admired her in *Fidelio* in 1830 at the outset of this peak *assoluta* decade, was quite distressed by a *Les Huguenots* he saw in 1842, when her singing in the role of Valentine seemed to him completely unmusical.[39] Evidently, whatever happened to her artistry during the 1830s must have been quite severe. So it was only in the 1840s, at the end of her career, that Schroeder-Devrient came the closest to actually creating an *assoluta* role. Completely smitten with her artistry, Wagner eagerly took her for the premiere of his *Rienzi* in the trouser role of Adriano. An impulsive, head-strong young man, Adriano is a character in a situation similar to that of Romeo in Bellini's opera. Joan Sutherland, who has recorded some of Adriano's music, has remarked on its Bellinian flavor. With its alternations in tessitura, and its combined requirements for great vocal strength and flexibility, Adriano would be a defining *assoluta* role were it not that, while the part does go down to the low A flat, it does not require as extensive a use of the high as the true *assoluta* part, reaching only up to high B flat. Schroeder-Devrient, at this stage of her career, must have felt relieved that, with all of Adriano's requirements for flexibility, they did not extend much into the extreme upper register. It seems relevant that Adriano, a Bellinian role sung occasionally by mezzo-contraltos, was realized by a diva proficient in four different *assoluta* roles; probable, therefore, that, for a singer this capable to assume the creation of a mezzo-ish role, she must have had a mezzo-ish center to begin with. If so, we are again confronted with an *assoluta* specialist and interpreter of Norma with a dark vocal quality.

Norma on disc

Long before the entire opera became a staple of the record catalogue, the aria "Casta Diva" always had a life of its own on disc. Although I would sub-scribe to the supremacy of Rosa Ponselle's Electrical 78 in terms of its sheer fluidity, there are one or two other fine renditions in the era B.P. (before Ponselle).

If I had to pick just one of them, it would be the excellent "Casta Diva" made in the acoustic era by Giannina Russ—a superb souvenir demonstrating that impeccable *bel canto* standards did not languish altogether during the interreg-num of *verismo* in the first quarter of the twentieth century.

There is also a "sleeper" acoustic that Andrew Porter, in his article in *Opera on Record*, dismisses as "a failure."[40] True, this acoustic doesn't have the secure musicianship of a Ponselle or a Callas, but Norma's character is there, making this "Casta Diva" more of a command than the traditional reverie.

The acoustic referred to was made by an artist who had just turned 61 years old: Emma Calvé. Like Giuditta Pasta, Bellini's hand-picked creator for this for-midable part, Calvé too alternated mezzo and soprano roles at will. And at one point, Calvé "ornaments" into the chest register like a true alto. She may not give us the usual otherworldly trance and I would not recommend this as one's introduction to the piece, but I can't help feeling that our full knowledge of Norma's character would somehow be diminished without this brave attempt by a semi-retired diva in 1919.

We will examine further central readings of the acoustic era when we sum up the characteristics of the true *assoluta* voice at the end of the book.

From the advent of Rosa Ponselle on, few dominate this role the way she did. Only Ponselle herself seriously threatens the supremacy of her famed electrical "Casta Diva": among her earlier acoustics, there is one "Casta Diva" in which the cabaletta, though transposed, may surpass the electrical in sheer fluency. It features expert divisions on "diedi" and shows slightly less reliance on portamento, resulting in a cleaner, more classical, reading that many might prefer. To cap it off, she climaxes on a high note that is fearlessly attacked with no apparent preparation and effortlessly sustained, in contrast both to the elaborate portamento leading up to the climax on the electrical and also the tightened tempo pulling her swiftly down from that high note. Unlike the cabaletta, "Casta Diva" itself is less expressive on the acoustic than the electrical and also less beautiful vocally. Her top is unquestionably gorgeous throughout, but the rich sonority of her low register, and its innate expressiveness, is not completely there. For one thing, it is disappointing to be expecting the rapt somberness of her familiar "Senza nube e senza vel" and be greeted instead by a "senza" that is always brought up in pitch, the way Pasta apparently did in the repeat. Furthermore, instead of ending on the familiar "Ciel" sung piano, her younger self simply takes the lower alternate without shading of any kind.

Her more familiar electrical remains unique in its reading of "Casta Diva" itself. While she does not show the characteristic shifts of color inferred from contemporary accounts of Pasta, Ponselle uses her ample tones to strong effect in communicating Norma's aria as a sincere prayer by a troubled human being. The balance struck is exactly right. We are introduced to this character as both a leader of her community and a compelling woman right away. Ponselle paints who she is vividly in her opening recitative, "Sediziose voci." Her supremacy in sheer line sheds a welcome aura on the aria, making the phrases seem as inevitable and as soothing as moonlight itself. All the slow divisions serve to convey both ceremony and inwardness, surely exactly what Bellini intended. It is hard to know whether, on stage, there may not have been greater variety of color in her delivery. But for all that, this electrical suffers from no lack of feeling and easily accounts for the veneration in which Ponselle was held for this role. It is a shame that her complete interpretation of Norma has not survived, her "Mira, o Norma" opposite Marion Telva's Adalgisa being the only other souvenir of her interpretation. Rumors continue of an extant broadcast of two scenes from a Metropolitan *Norma* during the Thirties, but they remain only that: rumors. If this were to surface, it might also occasion surprise at some of the transpositions Ponselle took. Her command of intricate flexibility and the *bel canto* style, however, was consistent throughout her career, as shown in a contemporaneous *Traviata* and Zerlina's "Batti, batti."

Especially as a recording voice, Ponselle has a distinctive persona. Could it be that charisma came to be attached to this music partly due to her? Of course, vocal aptitude was a given when it came to artists like Frieda Leider or Ester

Mazzoleni, both of whom still sang this opera in the Twenties. Yet we have no recorded "Casta Diva" from them, while personalities like Vera Amerighi-Rutili and Grace Moore are on record. In fact, Moore's "Casta Diva" is startling and serves as a reminder of just how popular this piece became. Unlike Ponselle, there is not a suggestion of anything other than high soprano from Moore's performance. Surprisingly, however, there is some real authority brought to the recitative, even though the opening of "Casta Diva" itself is not so sure, and there is a moment of flatness. Further disappointments include occasional aspirates in the slow divisions and the absence of the cabaletta. What remains pleasing here is an intrinsically expressive voice, as well as a lovely one. Moore might not have made a great impression in the part as a whole, but lovely tone and sincerity still count for a lot.

A random sampling of "Casta Diva" from the vinyl era discloses other compromises. This aria has frequently been included on various recital discs, performed by the likes of Montserrat Caballé, Anita Cerquetti, Sylvia Sass, Antonietta Stella, and Ilona Tokody.

Although Montserrat Caballé was capable of bringing true conviction to this part in performance, that is not immediately apparent in her recital reading of "Casta Diva." It is certainly not unfeeling, and there is a much surer sense of style than we hear in someone like Moore, but it lacks individuality. Another surprise is an occasional unsteadiness of tone. Beyond that, this rendition reflects another development that is troubling, even though Caballé is far from being alone in that: Although I can understand why earlier recordings simply reflect contemporary traditions, I am troubled when textually conscientious periods, like the vinyl era, sanction readings that don't reflect Bellini's original intent. I have already drawn attention to the distinction that Bellini made between the syncopated high Bs in the first statement of "Casta Diva" and the single long *crescendo* in the second. This progression gives a heartfelt indication as to where Norma's thoughts are leading her. One might almost say that there's not much point in performing the "Tempra, o Diva" at all unless the *crescendo* is adopted, since this transformation is a crucial indication of character. Yet most singers of the twentieth century simply repeat the syncopations. Caballé joins her colleagues in this.

Anita Cerquetti's performance, on a London recital record released in 1957, is marked by an acute imagination in the use of varied dynamics. The results are magical. In addition, certain words like "Tempra ancora" are melting. She takes the higher ending on "Ciel." There is no cabaletta. In many ways, this may be the most beautiful voice on any of these recital discs. In fact, there are moments when the directness of Cerquetti's rendition reminds one of Ponselle herself. However, we hear no trill from her, and, once again, while choosing to sing the "Tempra, o Diva" as well, she does not give us Bellini's original *crescendo* along with it.

Sylvia Sass's recording on her recital disc opens with an odd-sounding recitative in which her strange diction emerges as something of a handicap. She is, though, clearly committed and into the part. Her divisions are not as clean as they could be, but some emerge effectively, thanks to an evocative *mezzo piano*. There is no trill, and she takes the high ending on "Ciel." In the cabaletta, we hear another *mezzo piano* as she makes the words "Difesa a te sarò" intensely intimate, conveying how precious Pollione still is to her. It's hard to say whether her full-voiced top was really as glary as it seems here. One suspects that faulty engineering could be the reason. Even so, Sass whisks by the last high note with an even more pronounced portamento both up and down than Ponselle does on her electrical. So perhaps there is some wear here on Sass's top after all. Although she still repeats that confounded syncopation just as all the others do, Sass adopts an interesting compromise of sorts: She sings the repeated syncopation with a genuine *crescendo*, thus suggesting something at least of what Bellini had in mind here.

Like Cerquetti, Antonietta Stella has a rich, beautiful voice. Even her divisions are, for the most part, respectable. We have no trill from her, she ends with "Ciel" going up and, in the cabaletta, while there is a hint of some aspirated divisions, "diedi" comes out quite well. Unusually, she performs the *materia di mezzo* linking the "Casta Diva" and the cabaletta. Unfortunately, here is where she starts sounding tentative. The authority and fluency needed for this section are just not present. Her rendition lacks bite and augurs some of the imprecision in the cabaletta, even though, in certain respects, the latter shows a slight improvement. Throughout the *scena*, she remains musical. All things considered, the "Casta Diva" itself is probably the most creditable stretch in her performance, although, once again, we have those syncopations repeated in an otherwise acceptable second statement.

Finally, Ilona Tokody in a "live" reading is richly expressive. She shows an unsteady top, but the rest of her instrument does seem to approach the right color and weight for the part. There is some extra echo in the sonics, but not enough to cast doubt on the heroic proportions of Tokody's voice. She displays a fine low B when predicting the fall of Rome. It's in the aria where she starts having problems. She goes sharp on the syncopations (and simply repeats them a second time with, again, no *crescendo*), her *pianissimi* are quite breathy and her divisions are ungainly. (She performs the aria with no chorus.) In general, there is strain. It is useful, however, to listen to a reading like this, for despite the authentic amplitude of a voice like Tokody's, she is still struggling with the daunting demands of this music!

The earliest studio recording of the entire opera is on Fonit-Cetra and on a few other spin-off labels as well: featured is Gina Cigna in the title role, Giovanni Breviario as Pollione and Ebe Stignani as Adalgisa. Vittorio Gui conducts. Recorded in 1937, it took five months to complete—from March to July of that year.

A pupil of Emma Calvé, Cigna is a rare Norma on disc who can claim direct inheritance of the original Marchesi-García tradition traceable back to Bellini's own day. Her fine dramatic interpretation and dark vocal persona certainly reflect this heritage in a compelling reading, however modest her facility in coloratura may be. Stignani is a more than worthy colleague. One problem here is Breviario, whose Pollione does not hold a candle to many of the later Polliones in the discography.

Although the sound, naturally, is dated monaural, the voices still come through vividly, and there is a strong sense of acted drama.

Even so, the full impact of Cigna's interpretation comes through more vividly in her Metropolitan Opera broadcast of 1937, first made available on the privately issued EJS label. It was made February 20, 1937, only a month earlier than the studio recording, yet Cigna's voice sounds remarkably fresher. In addition, she allows herself the luxury of pulling back from the intensity of her studio reading, making the broadcast far more inward. Illogically, the later studio recording sounds less thought-out, while, at the same time, its worn vocal quality embraces pitch problems in the mid-range and a throaty sound in the low. These flaws are less conspicuous in the broadcast, which features Giovanni Martinelli as Pollione, Bruna Castagna as Adalgisa and Ezio Pinza as Oroveso. Ettore Panizza conducts. This is the earliest complete recording of any *assoluta* work.

To say that Cigna sounds more vocally assured and more interpretively mature in this Panizza performance is not to call her Norma flawless. One may sometimes be haunted by certain inflections that recall her Met predecessor, Rosa Ponselle, but some of Cigna's recitatives, powerful as they are, tend to be a bit explosive. Certainly, the opening "Sediziose voci" is more *parlando* than Ponselle's. Also, while Cigna's low register may be effective, it does not have as much control as the rest of the voice. Surprising in light of her generally dark vocal coloring. In her prophecy of the fall of Rome, she almost speaks the low B on "morrà," though managing to touch the correct pitch. The contrast with a not very musical low startles when a beautifully shaped "Pace v'intimo" in the upper register melts the listener. She chooses not to end the recitative by going up on "mieto" as Ponselle does. The passagework in the "Casta Diva" is uneven. There is some aspirating in the coloratura, though the syncopated phrase is done elegantly. The divisions bridging the two statements give an occasional hint of flatting. In the second statement, "Tempra, o Diva," she repeats the syncopations as most do, and then ends the aria with a lovely softening of tone for "regnar tu fai" and a *messa di voce* on "ciel." There is a sense of reverie at certain moments of the aria, but it's hard to tell whether the occasional vehemence breaking that mood is interpretation or a vocal lapse. The piece still exerts a powerful enough spell in her hands. Unfortunately, the ensuing fireworks are fairly gusty, and she has to snatch a few awkward breaths in breakneck measures like "Dal druidico delubro La mia voce tuonerà." This scrambled reading is partly redeemed by a genuine *dolce* quality on "cor" for the line introducing "Ah! bello a me ritorna." There may well be a neatly managed *decrescendo* at the crest of one flourish, and the passagework at "diedi" may well pass muster, but elsewhere the cabaletta is marred by shortness of breath. There is no *da capo*.

Cigna injects the opening recitative of the next scene with too much verismo. There is also a peculiar self-importance to certain inflections that undermines the character's essential dignity. She shows better control higher up: a masterly *crescendo/decrescendo* for "Oh, rimembranza." Maintaining the magic, she continues in her memories with a tellingly abstracted "Segui" and beyond. We have a prolonged *crescendo* on the "Ah sì" launching the "Ah sì, fa' core." A shortness of breath in her solo is followed by a lack of unity from Cigna and Castagna. Despite the applause, Panizza follows the score by going right into the subsequent recitative without stopping. Cigna's shock on realizing that Adalgisa has been singing of Pollione is expressed partly through raising the exclamation "Costui" to a high-pitched cry. Unfortunately, this is followed by a clumsy "Oh non tremare." Granted, Norma herself is unstrung here, but note that the sentiments do not show her indiscriminately lashing out. She tells Pollione she understands that Adalgisa is blameless, reserving her fury strictly for him. This is wound-up anger, not undisciplined rage. The latter is suggested in Cigna's reading. The unevenness is typified in one scale on "Trema per te, fellon" emerging clearly and the other going awry. Things improve for the opening of "Oh di qual sei tu vittima." Here, her dignity is restored. There is even more sorrow than anger in the coda. Unaccountably, there is a laugh from the audience at "Lo compi." Cigna presents "Vanne, sì" as tense, private snapping at Pollione. It's only when the others join in that she pulls out all the stops. Panizza shapes a growing musical storm as Cigna builds up to a solid high D, greeted with a roar as the curtain closes.

There is always a risk that showing too much unmitigated fury in the preceding scene will leave the singer with nowhere to go for the opening scene of Act II. Norma's mere contemplation of infanticide is her nadir. Cigna eventually suggests this, but at first we hear the repetitive hectoring of the previous scene. ..."e in fronte Mi si solleva il crin" develops into yet another big cry. But there are few explosive phrases once "Teneri figli" begins. In fact, this becomes truly poignant. Cigna is careful not to break the spell. Only when the melody itself comes to an abrupt halt does she cry out again: speaking, rather than singing, "son i miei figli," blurting it out with a shudder of horror. The description "All passion spent" suggests itself for much of what follows. Instead of attempting to top the desperation of the scene closing Act I, Norma is now presented as dejected, remorseful at what she nearly did and more demoralized than purposeful. With Adalgisa, her phrase "Questi infelici" is a moment for Cigna to sweeten the tone, as if assuring herself that she still loves her children. Then, for the devastating words "io gli perdono, e moro," Cigna makes it clear, by draining the tone, that she is already dead inside. There is no stern resolution here, no energetic declaration. This is further brought out by Panizza's very slow tempo for "Deh! con te." Cigna can scarcely get the words out, she has sustained such a shock. The impression is of overwhelming exhaustion. Not much emerges above a *mezzo piano*. Her most striking effect (and Panizza's) is reserved for "Basti a te che disprezzata." Here, each syllable is gasped out weakly on a separate breath. There are faint sobs at the end of the solo. She is still crying right through Castagna's opening solo for the "Mira, o Norma." Then Norma's "Ah! perchè" response emerges as a hurt rebuke to Adalgisa. Cigna shows a *fear* of being dissuaded, and when she finally is at "Hai vinto," she projects this as a tremendous leap of courage. Her tone is sweetened for "Trovo un' amica ancor," and the "Sì, fine all' ore" cabaletta is handled with imagination and feeling. Cigna, Castagna and Panizza handle the *ritardando* in the *da capo* with real tenderness, and we hear an affecting grace note on "ricovrarci."

The final scene opens uncertainly with a rushed and wild cadenza. In fact, the high C is a bit of a scramble. Cigna follows this flubbed phrase by nailing the high C in her call for Roman blood. She maintains her fury by becoming incensed during her initial exchange with the arrested Pollione. Her hysteria abruptly stops when she finds she cannot stab him, at which point she becomes exasperated with herself on "Poss'io sentir pietà." She flounders around in explaining to the multitude that Pollione must be "questioned." Then, her fateful duet with Pollione opens with quiet excitement on "In mia man." Rather than being hysterical, she is exhausted, at the end of her rope when she sings "Consumar potrei l'eccesso." "È tardi" becomes gloomy, weary. She barely breathes out "Nel suo cor ti vo' ferire" only to round viciously on him for "Sì." This duet becomes an image of a woman who has little purpose left in life. Unfortunately, Cigna herself seems to have given up on certain vocal hurdles as well: there are no trills at "Adalgisa fia punita" and the flourish at "Nelle fiamme perirà" is jettisoned entirely, replaced by starkly syllabic delivery. A further sign of the musical uncertainties in Cigna's low is the loss of tone at "Infelice al par di me," where the lowest notes on "di me" are inaudible. She rallies after the duet to produce a spellbinding *crescendo/decrescendo* for the all-important "Son io." She is abstracted, in another world for a soft "Il rogo ergete." The affecting moments showing Cigna with her father, together with the final "Deh! Non volerli vittime," climax Cigna's reading, and Panizza's. Cigna's deeply reflective, inward "Oltre ogni umana idea" is indelible. Both she and Martinelli convey their exchange over the children as an intensely private moment, not for the ears of those around them. This stance continues when Pinza as Oroveso inadvertently explodes on "Madre," making Cigna's "Acquètati" her reflexive way of reminding Pinza that this must be kept within the family. She continues the exchange as a private one. Pinza's lacerating "Lasciami" induces Cigna to bracket her second "Ah! padre" with special significance. "Prego" is delivered with a moving *decrescendo*, followed by an extra breath before a sobbed "ancor." Her contained "Deh! non volerli vittime" haunts one with its understated pathos. A heartbreaking *crescendo* on the final "lor" and then a moving "pietà" cap a thrilling interpretation of Norma's final moments. Cigna's level of inspiration here doesn't necessarily redeem the parts that are unmusical, but she gets at the heart of something truly genuine at the end. It is a rare accomplishment. Panizza's conducting, moreover, leaves one in no doubt of the stature of this work.

The next recorded Norma has less interpretive flair but finer vocal gifts: Zinka Milanov. She is heard at her vocally strongest in the published broadcast of December 1944, even though a 1954 broadcast shows a finer interpreter and stylist for the role. One wishes she had been given a chance to record the role some time around 1951, when she was at her apex. That would have been a formidable entry in the *Norma* discography. As it is, while the '44 outing may be effective, one needs the '54 set to complete the picture. The '54 may make a number of compromises through adopting the Ponselle transpositions, and through Milanov's own deteriorated mastery of *bel canto* intricacy, so unlike Ponselle's continued resilience. Thus, even Milanov's inherent resources, lovely as they are in places, may no longer add up to a Norma. But she is more a Norma *temperamentally*, particularly in the final scene.

Since her physical capacities better matched the role in the earlier outing, we concentrate on that reading as her primary Norma. It also features Jennie Tourel as Adalgisa. Others in the cast are Frederick Jagel and Norman Cordon, business-like colleagues as Pollione and Oroveso. Cesare Sodero conducts. This rare performance has been issued on CD by Grand Tier.

Milanov opens with a full-throated pronouncement to the restless Druids. The sound is truly powerful, but a somewhat explosive delivery, recalling Cigna, similarly undermines the priestess's dignity. We still haven't equalled Ponselle. Naturally, when faced with an instrument of such opulence as Milanov's, one is grateful: the ringing top matches a rich low, whether savoring an imposing "morrà" for her prediction of the fall of Rome on a solid low B or a shimmering "mieto" on top. The "Casta Diva" features broad, easy phrasing, with the intricate passagework well integrated. She doesn't quite catch the mood of the aria until the repeat: the "Tempra, o Diva" statement has more of a "moonlight" feel to it. Like everyone, she repeats the syncopation here rather than adopting Bellini's contrasting *crescendo*. In repeating, she, surprisingly, starts pressing on the tone a bit. Another moment of clumsy vocalism comes at the end of the aria, where there is an ungainly release at the end of the concluding "ciel." Her control in the flourish on "sa" leading into the cabaletta is more elegant, but some headlong divisions in the actual cabaletta come out overblown and blurred. Still, the supremacy of her voice amazes. Her climactic top note at the conclusion seems miraculously of a piece with the rich tones lower down, making a vocal impact possibly superior at this point to Ponselle's.

We are back to an explosive delivery for the opening of the second scene. One must still credit her with an evocative, dreamy delivery of "Nol fossi!" There is also another reminder of the awe that this imposing instrument can render: Milanov's somber reading of Norma's fears at the prospect of Pollione's abandoning her in "un tal dubbio" and its haunted low B flat resonate long after. Her Norma is not always comforting or consoling with Adalgisa's confession. The "Ahi! sventurata" emerges urgent and deeply shocked, not understanding at all. There remains nothing reflective in her stance as she peremptorily demands that Adalgisa tell her everything. Only in her private reflection do we have a dreamy

"Oh, rimembranza" of exquisite beauty. Then, in turning back to Adalgisa, she is more agitated than ever, reiterating "Ah! tergi il pianto," which only seems to get her more and more upset rather than calming Adalgisa. The seesaw pattern continues with a captivating *pianissimo* for the vocal flourish at the beginning of "Ah sì, fa' core, abbracciami." As so often, the passagework is ungainly here. Jennie Tourel's polished response comes off as a reproachful lesson in *bel canto* fluency. After their duet, Milanov seems to anticipate her betrayal in questioning "Roma?" before she even knows the identity of Adalgisa's lover. When she really knows who it is, she practically screams "Pollion!" In the "Oh non tremare," she furiously attacks the scales on "Trema per te, fellon!" They emerge pretty much a scramble. One must say that her high Cs here are nothing short of glorious. Then, her "Oh di qual sei tu vittima" finally shows us incomparable song. Here is sweeping phrasing whose expanse suggests polished marble. The beauty in her voice and the anguish in Bellini's melody are a heady brew, effacing all that has gone before. She seems to be singing from the heart. Milanov's fury returns for the "Vanne, sì," delivered with greater fluency than the "Oh non tremare." There is no high D à la Cigna.

The opening of the scene of Norma alone with her sleeping children displays Milanov holding back tears as an especially poignant "e in fronte/Mi si solleva il crin" suggests sorrow more than mute terror. In delivering the opening words this way, she prepares the listener better than Cigna does for the heartbreaking melody at "Teneri figli." But "Teneri figli" itself has uneven tonal focus and even more disquieting sounds when she prepares to strike her children. Her reading is not specific enough to determine whether the ugliness is deliberate or a sign of uneven vocal discipline. One thing seems apparent: this moment, so crucial to Norma's character development, becomes fairly two-dimensional here. We may be prepared, through Milanov's growing vocal agitation, for her horror at the thought of killing her children, but somehow the moment doesn't engage our sympathies. Milanov is more stirring when, having just ordered Clotilde to fetch Adalgisa, her lonely "e poi" is marked by a lovely piano. Still, the inward stance is not maintained. The crucial "io gli perdono, e moro" becomes precipitate, entirely extrovert. Only when Milanov sings "Pei figli suoi t'imploro" does her inner feeling seem to return at "t'imploro." From that, her "Deh! con te, con te" is once again resolute and commanding. She has made up her mind and is following it without a sense of trauma. Again, her passagework is not too fluent, and Tourel once more gives a lesson in precision. But Milanov's "Ah! perchè" registers well. She expresses the traditional musing regret, and there are long incomparable phrases, in the luminous way we would expect from her. She eagerly embraces Adalgisa's idea at "Hai vinto," and she then rips into the duet's cabaletta with relish. In the repeat, the opening "Ah, sì" extends forever from both Milanov and Tourel before they launch into the reprise. Waves of energy propel them to the conclusion of this scene and to a deserved ovation.

The opening of Norma's last scene shows occasional signs of fatigue. Both cadenzas, the lyrical one expressing hope for a reunion and the heroic one readying herself for battle, rush the top note. Milanov doesn't seem to settle down until her hushed reading of "Son vendicata adesso." Unfortunately, she is surprisingly squawky in the middle high for her vengeful phrases to Pollione. Norma's startling inability to kill Pollione is followed by a resolute delivery of her words to the multitude explaining why he must not yet be killed.

When left alone with Pollione, Milanov's vehement opening phrases in the duet verge on the petulant. From here to the end is where the 1944 performance proves especially uneven. Up to now, sheer instinct and abundant vocal health have carried her through. But in this last scene a noble poise is needed above and beyond everything else. Milanov does not always deliver. "Questo ferro" is brought way up and shouted, while her singing becomes a bit wild at "potrei l'eccesso." True, the emotions at this point are extreme, but, as with her grow-ing agitation before raising the dagger over her children in Act II, Scene 1, the effect here seems two-dimensional. A saving grace is "Adalgisa fia punita," where Bellini's trills are in place, and Milanov finishes with a rousing delivery of "perirà" that seems limitless. She supplements this by going deadly quiet at "è tardi" before launching "Già mi pasco." Unfortunately, there are a few unfocused tones toward the climax. Despite a clumsy extra breath before "io" at "Son io," the transitional moments before the final two-part ensemble ring with authority. Her majestic "Il rogo ergete" seems to sum up the whole character. "Qual cor tradisti" boasts a fine control of dynamics, including a *decrescendo* at "morte" of "In vita e in morte," and a beautiful tapering off on the final word. Her control of dynam-ics is also there in the way she maintains a perfect piano on the cadenza for "Un prego ancor" before the "Deh! Non volerli vittime." Once again, though, there is some unfocused tone as she winds up the reiterations of "pietà." After the momentary fall from grace here, she gets stronger and stronger. By the final phrases against the entire ensemble, she has dwarfed everyone else, and one mighty surging top note closes the afternoon. The effect is fitfully impressive, but a totality is not achieved in the final scene of this '44 broadcast.

She comes closer to achieving that in the otherwise poorer 1954 perfor-mance. Here is where the '54 draws a favorable contrast with the '44. Though there are questionable vocal shifts here, these final moments have much more to them than those of a decade earlier. Her Pollione in '54 is Gino Penno, the Oroveso, Cesare Siepi, and Adalgisa, Blanche Thebom. Fausto Cleva conducts. This performance was first put out on LP by Melodram. There may still be some undue agitation at the outset of the fateful duet for Norma and Pollione, but the word "l'eccesso" emerges with greater tautness that convinces more and is mar-ginally more musical. The trills may no longer be present in '54, but "perirà" still makes a grand effect. In addition, the "Già mi pasco" comes out much more disciplined and incisive. The transitional moments before the two-part finale are even more evocative than in 1944, with a whole world of inner sadness barely hinted at previously: not only is "Son io" made a single unbroken phrase, it is now softened magically, seeming to suspend time. In the "Qual cor tradisti," her tapering off at "Sarò con te" is more magical as well, while the ending has a luminous quality that surpasses the earlier performance. The closing "Deh! Non volerli vittime" also shows greater musicality, with the reiterations of "pietà" more carefully integrated into Bellini's melody. The expression seems more genuinely heartfelt and direct. Perhaps the closing measures of the '54 can't quite match the vocal outpouring of '44, but there is more poignancy and humanity in these final moments.

The next great Norma is Maria Callas. Some will single out the June '55 *Norma* from the Radio Italiana studios as Maria Callas's finest, while for others it's La Scala's Opening Night from that December. I find that both 1955 *Norma*s surpass anything Callas achieves elsewhere in the role. The Opening Night of December 7 preserves an extraordinary evening at La Scala. In addition, even though Ebe Stignani's Adalgisa is admirable in the June performance, Giulietta Simionato's at La Scala is altogether incandescent. Mario Del Monaco's Pollione is heard on both sets. As for Callas herself, the Scala broadcast is one of those rare occasions when she comes on thoroughly warmed up — and then just gets better. The June radio performance, on the other hand, shows Callas hitting her full stride only in the second scene.

As the Scala broadcast proceeds, Callas's volatility dazzles more and more. Even the recitatives are mesmerizing. Her unerring instinct with this role calibrates exquisitely Norma's alternating feelings of pride, helplessness, outrage, vulnerability, resignation — all the myriad moods that make this role so demanding, both dramatically and vocally. The climax comes when Callas gives a heartbreaking inflection to her confession in the last scene that she, Norma, is the priestess who has broken her vows and fallen in love: "Son io." When she sings this simply and very softly, the audience lets out an audible gasp. There is even a smattering of clapped hands — and it's only a line of recitative! Apparently, it was on these words that Norma slowly removed her priestess's crown of laurels. It may be more than coincidence that this production, like Callas's triumphant *Médée* with Bernstein, was directed by Margherita Wallmann.

Taking the two 1955 broadcasts as overall performances of Bellini's masterpiece, there are trade-offs in both. While Callas herself is even more dazzling in December than in June, and Simionato's December Adalgisa is at a higher level than Stignani's, Tullio Serafin's conducting in June is superior to Antonino Votto's in December. Unfortunately, Votto makes a few small cuts that show less sympathy and understanding of Bellini than does Serafin's more complete, more loving treatment. Strangely, editions of the December broadcast take the opening twenty minutes or so from the Radio Italiana performance. There does not seem to be any explanation for the missing twenty minutes in this La Scala performance. Did Milan radio simply miss the boat that evening and start transmitting late? Fortunately, all editions switch over to the genuine Opening Night before Callas's first entrance.

Though the virtues of both broadcasts are evenly matched, I seriously believe that, for Callas herself, the December one is not just her finest extant interpretation of Norma, it may be just the finest extant example of her artistry anywhere. It seems proper that we assess this amazing evening in detail, since, even though her voice no longer has the full amplitude of the ideal *assoluta*, its variety of colors and shadings recall the encyclopedic vocalism that Bellini valued in Pasta. Callas's instrument is still a fairly strong one and, at this point in her career, retains an apt *assoluta* sound. Along with Del Monaco's Pollione and Simionato's Adalgisa, this performance also features Nicola Zaccaria's Oroveso. It has been made available on a number of smaller CD labels, including Hunt, HRE, Legato, Melodram and Gala, among others. Once past the substitution from Radio Italiana for the opening twenty minutes, the sound quality on most of these is reasonably adequate. There is, however, one conspicuous moment of radio static that intrudes right after Norma has broken off the tender melody to her sleeping children, steeling herself to kill them. There is no question that here the Gala pressing has substituted the same phrases from another Callas performance without static. Some may prefer Gala's ruse, but ultimately one regrets the loss of Callas's most telling singing at La Scala. Static or no, this moment still makes an indelible impact, and we would be the poorer without it.

Callas and Wallmann have forged a reading of the role that manages to make Norma's abrupt shifts cohere into a multi-dimensional character. That this is possible is ultimately due to Bellini's own genius, but it took implicit faith in that genius to make the Callas/Wallmann collaboration so superior. Fortunately, Callas's colleagues here responded almost as positively to Wallmann's inspiration, and the sheer luck that finds Del Monaco and Simionato at their vocal freshest as well makes this broadcast a triumph of ensemble, arguably the finest overall performance available.

Callas's opening "Sediziose voci" has all the imposing dignity of Ponselle, albeit with a somewhat slimmer sound. It is the richness of coloring that makes the comparison valid. In addition, through Callas's restraint, it is still possible to feel Norma's disapproval of the impatient Druids. She reminds them of the inexorable fate that condemns Rome to its eventual destruction with an air of calm finality. A gloomy low B on "morrà" caps her prophecy. An appropriate ray of hope floods her tone for "Pace v'intimo," and a haunting *diminuendo* is applied on "mieto." Hers must be one of the simplest deliveries of "Casta Diva," like a prayer. "Senza vel" is uttered softly, and the passagework before the "Tempra, o Diva" is light and dreamy. Oddly, when she follows all the other singers by merely repeating the syncopation instead of following Bellini's *crescendo*, the second time emerges blurry, but the rapt interpretation is scrupulously maintained throughout. Not until "regnar tu fai" toward the conclusion does Callas permit herself the first hint of urgency in the tone. But she seems to step back again in the closing cadenza, going soft at its crest and applying a *diminuendo*. After the aria, she delivers "Dal druidico delubro/La mia voce tuonerà" as real vocal thunder. Then the vulnerability returns for the intimate flourish at "il cor non sa" introducing the cabaletta. "Ah! bello a me ritorna" is marked by both tenderness and defiance against the world. Her top here is in reasonably good control, but is definitely thinner than the rest of the voice.

For the second scene, Callas draws a contrast between the dignity of her recitative as a public figure in the first scene, and her slight sense of agitation here in disclosing her private fears. There is a hint of anger at the thought of Pollione leaving her, followed by an expression of sorrow for her children. She easily descends to a haunted low B flat in disclosing her doubts over Pollione to Clotilde. Subsequently, with Adalgisa, her "parla" and her "Che t'affligge" maintain a ceremonial quality; this is an audience, not a mere visit. Norma's tender side is not dominant until a soft "Oh, rimembranza" to herself. But in ordering "Segui" to Adalgisa, she returns to her imperial persona. During Adalgisa's narrative, she recalls more private memories at "cari accenti," where we have a *diminuendo* on "trovava." Again, she maintains a careful distance here between her memories and her words to Adalgisa: "Ah sì, fa core" is reassuring, as if telling Adalgisa firmly it's time to start a new life outside the order, not merely permitting her to. Another *diminuendo*, this time on a high C, elicits a gasp from the audience, and the concluding cadenza for Callas and Simionato renders a lovely trill. In following the score, Votto properly steps on the applause with the chords under the duet's final note launching the transition to the trio. Callas continues impersonally in questioning Adalgisa. The transformation into outrage on Pollione's entrance is instantaneous and unexpected at "Ei." She turns into vitriol at "Ben io compresi?" In the incensed "Oh non tremare," Callas is careful to maintain grave accents for "lei," reserving her full fury for "tu sei." At the reference to "figli tuoi," everything starts tenderly, then is superseded by a threatening *crescendo* into the dipthong on "tuoi." She is emphatic for "Oh di qual sei tu vittima," not lamenting like some. But she continues to keep her fury in check after the trio: "Ebben! Lo compi" is at first restrained until she lashes out at "parti. Seguilo." Then the opening solo of the "Vanne" ensemble is pulled back again, this time through clenched teeth, only "sì" giving us a momentary window on her real feelings. Finally, they explode into towering indignation at the word "indegno." From that point, there is unbridled wrath in her delivery climaxing in a clean high D, eliciting an ovation from the audience as the curtain falls.

Act II opens with Callas's voice portraying a palpable feeling of having gone through a long weary night. A sense of pride in her sons appears when she sings that death at least would prevent them from suffering "slavery" under a stepmother. Her "Teneri figli" may be the most beautiful vocalism of the evening: an almost disembodied thread of tone winds its way through her poignant melody of love for them. Then panic becomes dominant when she suddenly recoils from killing them. Panic at herself continues to motivate her in abruptly summoning Clotilde. Later, with Adalgisa, Norma's single word "risoluto" seems to fuse both energy and resignation. A shaft of tenderness then lights up the tone when she offers Adalgisa custody of the children. This changes to resolve at "io gli perdono, e moro." At first, quiet assurance dominates the "Deh! con te," yielding to greater urgency toward the end of the solo. When Adalgisa starts their duet by trying to dissuade Norma, Callas's "Ah perchè" communicates rueful reflection. But there are no uncertainties in her voice when she suddenly accepts Adalgisa's advice after all. Determination and confidence put their stamp on a rousing cabaletta closing the scene.

The final scene opens with a radiant delivery of her opening solo. She is serene and contented, singing the cadenza of hope in an evocative piano. Her "Favella" to Clotilde is urgent, but still emotionally contained. No menace is felt until "Ed io fidarmi," coming from the voice at "Ella tramava." Her cadenza of wrath is superb, with an excellent high C. Then, when Pollione is caught, her aside "(Son vendicato adesso!)" is a moment of quiet triumph. A slight smile seems to play around the vocal face at "Sì, Norma," but her inability to kill Pollione leaves her seeming not to know where she is. She projects bewilderment, almost a sense of mental wandering, before resolution returns in her pronouncement to the multitude that Pollione must first be "questioned." The fateful duet for Norma and Pollione opens with Callas thoughtful and incisive for "In mia man." She seems to be scrutinizing Pollione closely when recalling his children. Then the ultimatum that he abandon Adalgisa to save his life is delivered in even tones, until a vehement "Giura!" When he declines, she reveals what she nearly did to the children, in tones of utmost sorrow. When vengeance returns as she threatens to have Adalgisa condemned to the pyre, good musical manners keep her on an even keel through a series of impeccable trills that highlight her deadly determination. When she says she will wound him through Adalgisa's death, her equally deadly "Sì" stays just as even and poised.

With the return of the Druids, her change of heart may be the highlight of Callas's interpretation. In confessing that she herself is the priestess who has forsaken her vows, there is a rapt finality to her "Son io": this is sung piano with an ever so slight *crescendo* on the concluding "o" vowel. A gesture of appreciation from La Scala's audience startles. Callas's "Qual cor tradisti" features imaginative shading of dynamics, including a *diminuendo* on "con te" and a beautiful piano ending. When she discloses that she and Pollione have offspring, she delivers "Oltre ogni umana idea" defiantly, making it clear that this is a public declaration. Intimacy returns on the flourish at "Un prego ancor" addressed to Oroveso, beginning this moment full voice and then softening the tone completely. "Deh! Non volerli vittime" starts as a murmur. Later into the solo, "padre" is lovingly softened, yielding to a growing urgency in "abbi di lor," where an effect like musical tears transfigures "abbi" as she moves down the scale and then expands her tone for "lor." Both the austere and the vulnerable seem fused in these final moments.

After surveying the Callas legacy in this role, good and bad, I have concluded that this La Scala opening night remains the most satisfying example of the diva's artistry, in which she surmounted all of the following in that one performance:

  a) both lyric and heroic coloratura;

  b) bridging the gulf between the vulnerable woman and the vengeful fury;

  c) incredible stamina during a long and wearing role;

    d) heroic declamation as convincingly voiced as intricate fioritura;

    e) vocal excellence even in her opening phrases of the evening;

    f) intricate ensemble work performed alongside as consistently sympathetic a colleague as Giulietta Simionato;

    g) surprisingly clean and forward diction;

    h) singing with well-equalized registers and still capitalizing on the contrasts between them.

There are some virtues like these in earlier Callas broadcasts. But can one go down this list and check off quite so many accomplishments for any single occasion? That December Norma is such a staggering anthology of the things that made Callas properly "encyclopedic" in the Pasta tradition.

Callas's two commercial sets for EMI are less multidimensional than either 1955 performance. Her first recording is in 1954 where the late John Ardoin hears her more the warrior/leader and less the troubled woman.[41] Conducted by the ever-supportive Tullio Serafin, Adalgisa is the fine Ebe Stignani and Pollione is the strident Mario Filippeschi. This is not as well cast as the later set (1960), which deserves closer examination because of that. At the same time, I have to demur on aspects of this set as well. Ardoin's more positive assessment of Callas's dramatic stance in the 1960 recording (with Serafin again at the podium and Christa Ludwig and Franco Corelli as Adalgisa and Pollione) seems to claim that the tension between the leader and the troubled woman is in perfect balance.[42] However, I find that vocal caution rather than further refinement has dictated too many of Callas's choices. As it is, there are some dire vocal lapses, despite her circumspect approach. She cannot tackle Norma's fury without a recurrent tremolo throughout the upper half of her voice, and even her pitch is prone to stray. At the same time, Serafin's conducting is, if anything, even finer than in '54, while Ludwig's Adalgisa is unbearably poignant. Curiously enough, Corelli suffers from some pitch problems, but for the most part he is in fine voice. Ludwig is the main reason for valuing this set. I would agree with John B. Steane that, ultimately, Callas herself makes a more vivid impression on the '54 set.[43] I might find her more satisfying in this recording were I not so cognizant of how much she accomplished "live" the next year.

An important addendum among Callas's earlier extant *Norma*s (available on a few obscure labels) is her Covent Garden debut (November '52) opposite Mirto Picchi's Pollione, who may be Callas's most musical partner. Her Adalgisa is a younger Stignani, Giacomo Vaghi sings Oroveso, and the conductor is Vittorio Gui.

There are some differences here from the inspired interpretation Callas offers later with Wallmann. Although there is no lack of insight, one feels there is less cohesion to the many threads in this character. Individual moments stand out more than the whole, despite Callas's voice being at its plushest. Unfortunately, the opening "Casta Diva" falls prey to some imprecision, although there are some lovely grace notes. Exceptional also is the time she takes coming down from the top note climaxing the cabaletta — an exhilarating effect!

In Scene 2, the voice is far stronger, though we do have an occasional over-theatrical gasp in the recitatives. Her initial approach to Adalgisa is different from what we hear with Wallmann: here, she is less careful in maintaining her distance, bringing her private self more forward. Words like "parla" and "t'afflige" emerge more gently as a result. She is still wreathed in memories at "Segui," rather than delivering a command. Vocally, she surprisingly opens the all-important "O rimembranza" with an aspirate and indulges in an almost *verismo* scoop on … "bran" … of "rimembranza." The climactic top note of "Ah sì, fa core" is sung full voice without the mesmerizing *diminuendo* at the Scala performance. That said, the breadth of her younger instrument pays rich dividends in the trio and the fiery conclusion to the act. Her anger knows no bounds, and neither does her voice. Her fury is less disciplined than at La Scala, even to the point of not holding back at "Lo compi": indeed, she spits this out vehemently. She caps an incensed tirade by ending the act with one of the finest High Ds we have from her.

The full poignancy of her more developed interpretation in '55 is not quite there in Act II. There are still moments of stellar vocalism, like a beautiful reading of "si solleva il crin," where she's only describing her hair standing on end! Granted, the pity of it all, so tellingly communicated later at La Scala, may emerge at certain moments here, like a delivery of "I figli uccido" that seems choked with grief. But this is then followed by a reading of "Teneri figli" that seems less tender than three years later. Once this melody evaporates into bitter recitative, she even loses pitch for a moment. With Adalgisa later, she sounds less guarded in the lines starting "Una preghiera sola." Again, a theatrical gasp intrudes in the recitative, but the longest Bellinian phrases are already being delivered with the heightened sense of style we will hear in '55. One nice touch is a grave reminder to Adalgisa of her promise, "Tu giurasti." The scene closes with superb vocalism from both Callas and Stignani, climaxing on a joint high note that defines sumptuous.

The opening for Norma's final scene is not as evocative as it was later on. The cadenza of hope is sung full voice with no softening. Her relationship with Pollione for this closing scene is less overtly vindictive. Her "(Son vendicato adesso!)" comes out reflectively, and even her "Sì, Norma" seems a private statement for Pollione alone. She is also more unhinged than in '55 when she finds she cannot kill him, "pietà" suggesting a stifled sob. She even softens the tone for the second line of "In mia man," at "niun potria spezzar tuoi nodi." Sadly, she loses the pitch at "Pel tuo Dio," and "Mi poss'io" is trapped in an unstylish scoop. There is enough dramatic momentum to carry both Callas and Picchi past the end of the duet and into the ensuing exchange without interruption by applause. The capstone of her lauded La Scala interpretation, its "Son io," is not quite mirrored at Covent Garden: the utterance is sung beautifully enough, but the effect is offset by yet another indulgent gasp at the close. With "Norma non mente," attention is diverted away from the drama when Callas goes off pitch on "mente." The final two-part ensemble, however, is spectacular both vocally and dramatically. Here she is in total control of her faculties and gloriously reaches the final moments of Bellini's opera.

All things considered, this broadcast is still a vocal feast, and, with Gui's sympathetic conducting and Picchi's all-too-rare musicianship, it adds up to quite an event. Like the earliest *Norma* extant, that of Gina Cigna's at the Metropolitan in '37, a piece of history has been preserved with this Covent Garden set.

A less fortunate piece of history is Callas's aborted debut as Norma at the Rome Opera, January 2, 1958. She had to sing that night under painful circumstances. It was a gala opening, the president of Italy was attending, and Callas was extremely ill. Her depleted energy gave out during the opening scene, and she had to withdraw. Incredibly, the Rome Opera had not planned ahead for an understudy! Since it is practically axiomatic that substitutes for Norma don't grow on trees (shades of a classic *New Yorker* cartoon showing a hapless impresario sticking his head out from behind the curtain, asking "Is there a Siegfried in the house?"), the performance had to be cancelled. The whole incident was considered a scandal, certainly the worst of Callas's career. What came out of it was not all bad, however. Perhaps the Rome Opera had learned its lesson. At any rate, a day or so later, it re-opened with a performance featuring the next important Norma, one with a more refulgent sound than either Cigna or Callas: Anita Cerquetti.

This January 4 broadcast is more satisfying than the excruciating lone scene of Callas's '58 broadcast. Gabriele Santini's conducting here may not exactly be inspirational, Miriam Pirazzini's Adalgisa may lack the requisite poetry and Giulio Neri's Oroveso its wonted strength, but the combination of Cerquetti's Norma and Franco Corelli's Pollione is exciting. Corelli does not show any more sympathy with the *bel canto* style than he does with Callas on her second studio *Norma* with Ludwig, but he finds more variety in the role than Del Monaco in '55. In any case, the high voltage of Corelli's Pollione makes sense when paired with as sumptuous a voice as Cerquetti's. This performance has been released on GOP.

Cerquetti's opening recitative glows with strength. Her prophecy of the fall of Rome boasts a strong low B. Unfortunately, there is no piano on "mieto." There is, however, a reasonably rapt quality to certain words in the aria like "sacre," and "volgi" is nicely softened. The vocal impression, though, still dominates. The extremes of Cerquetti's voice somehow evoke Ponselle's, although her middle register is not as expressive. She does not maintain absorption in the aria quite as successfully as Ponselle, or as successfully as she herself had in her recital record. One wishes the prayerful downward scales were softer. In addition, it's unsettling to hear a singer with this easy flow of tone snatch an extra breath for "lo zelo audace." Perhaps she can't be blamed for repeating the syncopation in "Tempra, o Diva" like so many others, but it still rankles when one realizes the effect she might have made on Bellini's original *crescendo*. She again misses the mood in a full-voice cadenza toward the end, but softens nicely at "fai." There is no trill, but the final "nel ciel" is also soft like "fai," even though at first the pitch sags until a scoop pulls her up to the note. The *materia di mezzo* is delivered in a slow, deliberate way. When it comes time for Cerquetti to deliver the flourish on "sa" before the cabaletta, she does so softly, setting the scene for a deeply felt cabaletta. The passagework at "diede" is also good. There is no *da capo,* but we are grateful for such a strong finish.

Norma's confession to Clotilde that the children are indeed hers opens Scene 2 and is rendered more in sorrow than in agitation. ..."un tal dubbio" starts with some aspirates but ends with a fine low B flat. "O rimembranza" gets a *decrescendo,* and there is an effective fading quality to the ensuing phrases. Squareness returns in some of the interjections like "Io stessa/Arsi così" during Adalgisa's narrative. There is also too much distance elsewhere: a word like "trovava," for instance, doesn't seem personal enough for such a poignant aside. The opening of "Ah sì, fa core" also seems relatively uninflected. Here, she "whisks" the high C, but the passagework as a whole is fluent. There is curt phrasing in the *insieme* cadenza with Adalgisa. But an imaginative "Quale fra noi si noma?" shows her still remembering her first days with Pollione, and, continuing at this inspired level, she utters "Ben io compresi?" on the verge of tears.[44] In a strong "Oh non tremare," Cerquetti, like Callas, is careful to refrain from sounding too threatening on "lei," reserving her full fury for the phrases directed at Pollione. The last flourish on "Ah trema" lands with an uneasy portamento, never quite getting to the high C, but "Oh di qual sei tu vittima" is delivered with real sorrow, while every note is articulated in the passagework for the concluding "Vanne sì." There is no interpolated high D.

The opening scene of Act II is not delivered with as much nuance as we have come to expect. There may be a sob at "I figli uccido," but "Teneri figli" is basically sung straight throughout. The grateful listener, however, relishes how gorgeous the voice is here, while the historian reluctantly notes how unvaried the color becomes. As for "Deh! con te," addressed to Adalgisa, the climactic flourish may be clumsy, but most of the notes are there — and every one is beautiful. In fact, it's uncanny how much the word "costanza" in her "Ah! perchè" recalls the Ponselle sound. Unfortunately, in delivering this haunting melody, only Cerquetti's concluding words seem truly soft enough. It is the duet's cabaletta that is a real *tour de force* for Cerquetti. Even the earthbound Santini gets caught up in the excitement, and the staccati runs come out with surprising crispness.

Cerquetti sweetens the tone superbly for the radiant cadenza opening the last scene. This is supplemented by an excellent high C in her subsequent call for vengeance. The initial exchange with Corelli's Pollione may, again, not have as much variety as we should expect, but, once the two are alone, matters improve. Not only is there good vocal command of the lower-lying phrases in the duet, there is excellent dramatic desperation at "Vedi, vedi." Again, there is the absence of a trill, but otherwise the flexibility is excellent. Cerquetti's "è tardi" is frightening and is followed by some baleful portamenti that are still musical. The intricate passagework at "farti alfin" is equally musical. She imposes an awakened authority in this scene with a sneering smile in her voice at the announcement that a faithless priestess must be punished. One senses reluctantly that, for the moving change of heart at "Son io," she intends to go for a real piano but doesn't quite make it. Regret over this is offset by a deftly shaped "Qual cor tradisti," ending with a lovely soft close. About to divulge the secret of her children, Cerquetti's voice is still quiet but troubled for "Oltre ogni umana idea!" Unfortunately, she breaks up the cadenza at "Un prego ancor," going a bit wild. But in "Deh! Non volerli vittime" she does not disappoint, softening nicely on "pietà" and bringing superb intensity to her final moments.

A well-engineered stereo set on Decca/London from 1964 boasts Joan Sutherland's Norma, John Alexander's Pollione and Marilyn Horne's Adalgisa, all in their prime. Richard Bonynge conducts.

This set is rare in that it comprises a) practically no cuts, b) everything sung in the original keys throughout, c) all three accomplished *bel canto* specialists in optimum voice, and d) excellent sonics. Despite these assets, it is not as exciting a performance as some others. Sutherland's chief distinction is her peerless control of the most vocally conspicuous moments of the work, not in the connective tissue of the dramatic narrative.

On its own terms, the "Casta Diva" is as perfectly vocalized as one could hope. The interpretive stance is that of a reverie. Sadly, Sutherland repeats the syncopations in the second statement, just like all the others. One would hope better from the textually conscientious Bonynges. Perfect vocalism still obtains in a perfect trill and a superb *messa di voce* capping the aria. The reverie that is adopted for this timeless piece is entirely appropriate and Sutherland projects it with sincere feeling. It's not lack of commitment that strikes one in her singing. Rather, it's a lack of expressive variety. The "Casta Diva" is perfect (especially in its original key rather than the traditional transposition downward). Sincere as Sutherland's commitment is in "Casta Diva," she does not successfully convey the change of vocal face in the *materia di mezzo* signaling the stern leader promising Rome's destruction. The intricacy of the passagework is honored here better than by anybody, but the mood is not. Even vocally, her low notes lack force, surprising in light of her having started out as a mezzo. The tender opening of the cabaletta is given as a soft, intimate statement. The lack of pressure in the tone helps her deliver the flourish concluding the first statement in a single astounding phrase. Bonynge does opt for a small cut at one point, but most of the *da capo* is retained and liberally embellished. The coda features an impeccable treatment of the passagework on "diedi."

Her second scene opens, enabling us to savor a rich, sonorous middle range. She discloses to Clotilde her ambivalence toward her children, and fear at Pollione's possibly leaving her is also conveyed effectively in the inflection she gives "tentasse," but there's gravel in the voice going down to an awkward low B flat at "dubbio." Her greeting to Adalgisa conveys a genuine concern calculated to calm her guest. But this is a Norma easily distracted, and her unselfconsciousness is surprisingly effective when Adalgisa's tale awakens her memories. Her "Segui" is dangerously immersed in those memories, but when she discovers that she and Adalgisa have been singing of the same man, her outrage is anemic. Sutherland does not have the incisiveness to convey how much Norma is seething inside. Her lack of crispness with words has a great deal to do with this. It is disorienting to hear a "Ben io compresi?" with such a lack of incredulity. Her "tu tremi" doesn't seem to carry enough import. While her reminder of Pollione's children is perfectly affecting, the iteration of the word "fellon" seems almost matter-of-fact. She is more credible when she manages to infuse "Oh di qual sei tu vittima" with an overwhelming sadness. The opening of "Vanne sì" finds her sounding almost matter-of-fact again, but at least one can hear every note of this frequently abridged finale sung with great ease, and the whole is crowned with an interpolated top note that is spectacular.

It's rare to savor a reminder of Sutherland's beginnings as a mezzo. However, we are thrillingly reminded of this in her appropriately shadowed delivery of Norma's opening words to Act II, "Dormono entrambi." It's also reassuring to hear the word "schiavi" emerging so strongly. She sobs at "son i miei figli," and her sobs enter the very tone of her voice in her command to Clotilde that Adalgisa revisit her. But it would be wrong to characterize her stance here as merely a grief-stricken symbol. Her "Va" is quite peremptory. She also goes surprisingly *hard* at "Ho risoluto." There is great urgency for "io gli perdono, e moro." She withdraws more into herself with a nice piano for "abbandonati." Her "Mira, o Norma" with Marilyn Horne is fully worthy of its reputation as an extraordinary vocal display for both artists. There may be uncommonly slow tempi here, and we may not get the sense of trauma that Cigna and Callas have conveyed, but Sutherland wistfully interprets Norma's "Ah! perchè." The sense of clouds lifted characterizes both the singers' approaches to an invigorating cabaletta.

The beauty of Sutherland's cadenza of hope imparts a sense of timelessness to Norma's entrance lines for the final scene. Certain words later fall victim to a limp delivery, but others like "presume" are projected with uncommon strength. After a superb high C in her call for vengeance, "torrenti" is effective. She still seems too calm in recognizing Pollione, but there is an expressive *decrescendo* on "Sì, Norma." It's surprising, however, to hear this impeccable musician give an aspirate to ... "riam" of "feriam." After finding herself unable to kill Pollione, her excuse to the multitude is resolute. One understands why her people feel no hesitation in leaving her alone with him. She conveys well a sense of finality at the outset of their bitter duet. Certain words like "Pel tuo Dio" are delivered with quiet authority. There is an apt tone of farewell at "Adalgisa fuggirai" when she asks Pollione to forswear Adalgisa for good. She even manages to make her ultimatum sound magnanimous, although the low notes sound odd as when she first feared that Pollione might desert her. When she admits to him that she almost killed their children, she presents it as a moment of sad contemplation that climaxes in a *decrescendo* at "dimenticar." Her threat that Adalgisa must be burned, even her impeccable trills at Adalgisa's name, are given an incongruous delivery. "Indegno," though, is more compelling as she infuses this with a dangerous smile at being too late. Unfortunately, "è tardi" is less effective, since it lies too low for her. She seems almost to italicize "ti" in "ti vo' ferire." There is no carry-through in what seems another sad reading, this time for "Già mi pasco," followed by a withdrawn "farti alfin." The ending of this duet is spectacular as Sutherland opts for a surging top note before rejoining John Alexander. Nothing is particularly inexpressive in her change of heart at "Son io" and her determination to end her life. It simply lacks individuality and does not deliver the play of light and shade desired. Amazingly beautiful, however. She returns to an interpretive stance marked by regret in "Qual cor tradisti." We would expect the flourish at "Un prego ancor" to be handled nicely, and it is, and there is an authentic surge of urgency to her final poignant plea, particularly when she reaches the words "di lor pietà." Sutherland concludes with some tasteful embellishments as she repeats her final words to her father.

Certain aspects of Sutherland's Norma come out crisper and more nuanced in a later recording made also for Decca/London with, for once, an authentically soprano Adalgisa in Montserrat Caballé. Luciano Pavarotti sings Pollione, Samuel Ramey an impeccably *bel canto* Oroveso, and, as usual, Richard Bonynge conducts. Bonynge's way with the score in this later recording is more imbued with a sense of theatre, but, despite the greater variety in his approach, Sutherland's easy and honest delivery of every note exactly as Bellini wrote it is best heard in the earlier set of 1964.

A strong contrast is provided in Leyla Gencer's Norma with a more profound reading of the title role, but with frequent vocal compromises. Even the earliest and freshest souvenir of Gencer's Norma, in 1965 at La Scala, already has the glottal attacks that were to become ubiquitous, but one can be thankful that the instrument itself retains most of its vibrancy and color. In fact, its amazing capacity to weather the most continual abuse heartens us, despite the paradox that lies in such keen musical insights being projected in such an unmusical way. This "live" performance is another case of a reading that has been available on one or two different labels, including Melodram, but where each issue has been of typically limited distribution. Gencer's La Scala colleagues include Bruno Prevedi as Pollione, Giulietta Simionato repeating her Adalgisa of 1955 and Nicola Zaccaria his Oroveso. Gianandrea Gavazzeni conducts.

Gencer is strongly disapproving in her opening "Sediziose voci," though the glottal attacks undermine her authority to a degree. The instrument's continued strength is reflected in an effective low B, emphatic and sure on "morrà," and in her still beautiful *pianissimo*, heard here on a haunting "mieto," heralding an equivocal "Casta Diva." The opening phrases are unsteady, and there is a labored turn on "queste." One is grateful for a properly smoky "vel" and rhythmically alert passagework leading into "Tempra, o Diva." As is too often the case, the syncopation is merely repeated in place of Bellini's original *crescendo*. But the second statement is enhanced by an evocative turn on "regnar tu fai" done piano, even though the piano on the final "ciel" loses focus. In the *materia di mezzo*, we have a reasonably assured *diminuendo* on "cor" of "il cor non sa," however stark the effect seems without the familiar chain of upward turns on "sa." There are no untoward slips in the passagework of "Ah! bello a me ritorna," but it's not ideally fluent. One has to admire, though, a nakedly defiant inflection on "il mondo intero." Gencer drops off for a few phrases to deliver the climactic top note.

Gencer is inspired in conveying her conflicting feelings over the children in the next scene, a special urgency in "Soffro in vederli," and in her electrifying intimation of Pollione's leaving her, the low B flat at "dubbio." Then, in her initial exchange with Adalgisa, there is a residue of haughtiness, with an effective softening at "rimembranza" and at "Così trovava," which becomes a single long phrase, capped by a lovely piano on "trovava." However, in "Ah! tergi il pianto," the top note is unsteady, while the long *diminuendo* on "Ah sì" starts weakly, only becoming steadier as it softens. One must admire the neat passagework in "Ah sì, fa' core" and a good climactic high C, even though there is an ungainly transit to the low at the conclusion of the downward scale. The score is followed at the end of the duet with no interruption for applause, thus generating a fine dramatic momentum for Norma's shock at recognizing that Adalgisa is Pollione's beloved. This registers strongly in a deeply astounded "Ei," compromised a moment later by her anticipating a beat on "Ben io compresi?" In addressing Pollione directly, Gencer is at first deeply hurt for "e per chi," then aflame with fury for the "Oh non tremare," where there are some pitch problems, especially at the crucial "figli tuoi." She rattles fearsomely through some of the passagework and still displays a good high C, but she runs short of breath whenever going down the scale toward "fellon," losing ... "lon" both times. Her anguished rage is surprisingly undifferentiated in "Oh di qual sei tu vittima," and even in the *materia di mezzo* there isn't much holding back for "Lo compi." "Vanne, sì" has just as much fury, and one "indegno" is even spoken! She climaxes the scene with a strong high D. It is clear in this scene that the voice itself is in fine shape. One could only wish she showed a keener discipline in the *bel canto* passages and in a more carefully calibrated rage, however heartfelt her involvement in Norma's anguish.

Norma's emotional trials in the opening scene of Act II are made vivid enough in Gencer's interpretation. But with all the intrinsic strength of her vocal resources, signs of sloughing off accumulate, perhaps due to fatigue. The dramatic engagement remains as compelling as ever. No attempt is made to accommodate an awkward register break across "supplizio assai," and "si solleva il crin" seems poorly supported. There is a horrifying rasp on "uccido," and in the "Teneri figli" solo, the "Delizia mia" starts unsteadily, becoming better as it softens toward the end. When Norma abruptly cuts off the wistful strains of "Teneri figli" on "E io li svenerò," Gencer again fails to sustain a level tone, and "morti" turns gravelly. Perhaps this reflects dramatic expression, but if that was what was intended, it is not clear enough. There is so much dramatic insight of another sort in the anguish that Gencer projects here that the vocal mishaps come off as accidental and distracting. They don't seem integrated with her vocal projection of character. She is certainly effective in her quick "Feriam," followed by a hair-raising *fermata* on a prolonged and utterly secure "Ah! no" giving the lie to any suspicion of vocal trouble. So it seems to be inattention that is at fault. Still, the registers continue unmalleable in her initial exchange with Adalgisa. One can salute a convincing cry of anguish for "gli perdono, e moro" and a lovely piano on "Pei figli suoi." In "Deh! con te," "serbati" is given a richly expressive portamento, "abbandonati" gets a *diminuendo*, and while there are aspirates in the closing phrases, the high C is attacked and sustained perfectly. Gencer seems to be gasping in sorrow for her "Ah! perchè" in response to Adalgisa's "Mira o Norma" while some tones seem unintentionally constricted to no apparent purpose. Dramatic purpose there is, however, once she accedes to Adalgisa's plea in the *materia di mezzo*. Her "Hai vinto" vividly conveys the point of no return and becomes the epitome of a new hope. Unfortunately, both Gencer and the usually spirited Simionato fail to capitalize on this and do not deliver the ascending staccati in the cabaletta crisply. These are not really staccati at all, and this lack makes much of the concluding *insieme* limp.

In Gencer's final scene, the high C in the opening flourish of hope is also compromised, attacked flat and not successfully sustained. Typically, the high C suddenly becomes fine in her call for vengeance, and her "Sterminio" is properly awesome as well, but the gravelly problems return as she confirms that it's war, once and for all. It's surprising that, once Pollione is caught, there is no attempt to make "Son vendicata adesso" an aside, and her "Sì, Norma" is also an entirely public pronouncement. There is a desperate urgency both to her astonishment at not having the heart to slay Pollione on the spot and to her hasty announcement to the multitude. Then, at the opening of Norma and Pollione's fateful duet, the unsteadiness returns, together with some aspirates. Her "Giura" is partly spoken, but this is effective in context, redeemed, in addition, by her sorrowful treatment of the confession of having nearly killed the children. This is one of the most compelling moments of Gencer's final scene. It is complemented by the admirable drive of her "Solo! Tutti/I Romani," culminating in a sure reading of its headlong passagework and a blazing "perirà." Then, we are thrown back to *parlando* for "è tardi," and she misjudges her breath in the "Già mi pasco." Gencer and Prevedi plunge immediately into the transitional sequence following the duet without waiting for applause. Here, we have one of Gencer's most telling inflections: her aside, "Io rea, L'innocente accusar del fallo mio?" is a brilliant moment of alarmed self-awareness, intimate in its delivery.

The key moment of Gencer's "Son io" has too marked a portamento, but a good *diminuendo* on "i" of "io," offset by a clumsy release. The effect of Norma's sacrifice is better heightened by Gencer's more elegant portamento on ... "ge" ... of "ergete." The "Qual cor tradisti" is enhanced by fine *decrescendi* at the end of the first three phrases but culminates in a slightly scooped final note, which only reaches true pitch when it becomes piano. What a pity that "Romano" goes flat and the word "con" founders on a nasty register break. In the final *materia di mezzo*, Gencer's "Oltre ogni umana idea" is an entirely public proclamation, while her "Son madre" is a hasty, muted admission for her father alone. The poignant flourish on "Un prego ancor" is attacked full voice and only becomes piano on the bridge note immediately before ... "go" of "prego." This is followed by a wrenching sob. The closing "Deh! non volerli" comes out as a devastating wail, with a choppy line at "abbi di lor pietà." This is a troubled reading by a singer with great insight, a fine instrument, but unsure technical control.

In assessing the next recorded interpretation, featuring Elena Souliotis, it has proved impossible to avoid a personal approach. For one thing, the critical brickbats thrown its way are startling: "much that is simply below standard";[45] "She [hasn't] the delicacy" ... "a lack of variety, and insistence — which sometimes amounts to vulgarity — on making effects by power rather than subtlety";[46] "the sort of release that can ruin a record company's reputation" ... "the opera is massacred" ... "It would be tedious to list [all Varviso's cuts]" ... "imitation Callas without the genius" ... "seems stiff and amateurish" ... "mezzo-like sound thins out drastically in the upper register."[47]

However, this Decca/London 1967 recording does not seem as uniformly awful as this reviewer had been led to expect. The cuts may be severe, but that doesn't necessarily make the performance worthless. Since both Souliotis and Anita Cerquetti were mainstays of the Decca/London catalogue and had similarly abbreviated careers, the tendency has been to pair them together as somehow comparable. I would submit that Souliotis may have been the more imaginative artist, however superior Cerquetti's basic instrument. Souliotis has clearly "connected" with Bellini's music. There is an affecting directness to much of her singing, and the voice is capable of sounding plangent and well-focused. I, for one, feel convinced by her reading. She offers a richer and more steady sound here than in her *Anna Bolena*. Interpretively, she doesn't match the subtlety of someone like Callas, particularly in the Margherita Wallmann broadcast of 1955. But then, who does? Souliotis still gives a vivid enough reading to transform the listener into a spectator — and there are some musical felicities as well. It's a rare musician who, in the frenzy of the "Vanne, sì" at the conclusion of the first act, can soften the "Figli oblia, promesse, onore" just enough to convey the nostalgia of what Pollione and Norma once had. This is imagination and alert technical delivery combined. Granted, Souliotis has no trill, but, after all, neither do some others. She occasionally exaggerates the contrasts already built into Bellini's own score, threatening "To gilde refined Gold, to paint the Lilly." She doesn't sound as opulent as a Milanov or a Sutherland — let alone a Cerquetti. But few do. Souliotis offers a creditable assumption, not merely better than her Bolena vocally, but a thoughtful, musical reading with individual touches that linger in the memory long after. Such insights suggest a stylistic acuity of a high order. She is not "stiff and amateurish"! Mario Del Monaco repeats his Pollione from 1955, and Fiorenza Cossotto is heard as Adalgisa, in a reading as vocally easy as any of the most sumptuous, but not as insightful as a Ludwig or a Simionato. She does deserve high marks for her impeccable *bel canto* style. Carlo Cava's Oroveso, however, is inadequate, and one doesn't regret this recording's largest cut: all of Act II, Scene 2, with its elaborate chorus for the Gauls and Oroveso's big moment, "Ah! del Tebro." The conductor, Silvio Varviso, parallels his lacklustre contribution in the Souliotis *Bolena*. As an overall presentation of Bellini's score, this is undeniably a flawed rendering, but I find it redeemed by the sheer heart of its moving protagonist.

Souliotis's opening *scena* establishes the character right away. Her "Sediziose voci" is a real rebuke, while her suggestive softening on "Leggo del cielo" immediately conveys her function as that law's devout priestess. The low B on "morrà" is excellent, as is the lyricism of "L'ora aspettate" and the telling change of vocal face for an imposing "L'ora fatal." But once peace is invoked, Souliotis sets one up for a prayer with an ethereal "mieto." She is utterly absorbed in the "Casta Diva" from its opening phrase, and the dominant impressions are of humility and simplicity. That straightforward quality is reflected in a slight *accelerando* for the passagework bridging the two statements, integrating the turns into the entire piece. Like everyone else so far, Souliotis and Varviso simply repeat the syncopation in "Tempra, o Diva" rather than performing Bellini's original *crescendo* for the second statement. One regrets the absence of the customary upward turns on "sa" leading into the cabaletta, which itself is beguiling. She conveys a picture of a woman somehow youthful in her love, although mature in her self-possession. There is good passagework here, including an accomplished "diedi," and she builds the entire closing bars as one gigantic phrase, eliding a climactic top note to the whole. Varviso does not opt for the *da capo*.

In the next scene, her conflicted feelings over the children draw out some qualities that certain critics might find crude. It's not that she conveys her feelings through sheer power, it's that her occasional habit of making built-in contrasts overt comes to the fore at "Amo in un punto ed odio I figli miei!" She makes the difference between a piano "Amo" and a peremptory full-voice "odio" too obvious. But she redeems it by softening suggestively further on at "Ei tace/Il suo pensiero" and rendering a gloomy low B flat on "dubbio." Her initial approach to Adalgisa is intriguing, but not at all sisterly. She is matter-of-fact, with a ready authority that is neither preening nor too easy. Even her "M'abbraccia" is ceremonial, neither womanly nor up close and personal. She permits herself some evocative simplicity for "rimembranza," but splits the difference on the "Segui" line: she leaves "Segui" abstracted, while "t'ascolto" is back to business, with her reflections put aside. She turns on the magic once more with a spine-tingling downward scale on the "Ah sì" that introduces the duet. Her delivery of the solo "Ah sì, fa' core" becomes gentle from "Al caro ogetto" on. The climactic C is secure enough, but does not maintain the gentleness of the phrases leading up to it. When Adalgisa first tells Norma where her suitor is from,

Souliotis's "Roma" is suddenly in the manner of a sharp interrogator. She is not shocked or angry yet, but she seems to be scrutinizing Adalgisa closely. When she realizes the suitor's identity, she then becomes clearly dangerous, sounding downright ugly on "Ei! Pollion!" In confronting Pollione with his treachery, Souliotis startles by softening at "tu tremi," making the moment intensely private. The passagework in "Oh non tremare" is fairly well-handled, with a deftly tender inflection on "figli tuoi." "Fellon," however, loses effectiveness because her low and her breath falter at the end of a downward scale. Her high C is still secure. The "Oh di qual sei tu vittima" suffers from curtness, lacking full sweep. Things look up once Souliotis is back to addressing Pollione directly: she sings "Lo compì" to him, and the utterance is baleful indeed! There is supreme indignation in the "Vanne, sì," although she uses less chest than one might expect. It is here that she gives the listener a poignant glimpse into the troubled couple's happier past with a nostalgic "Figli oblia, promesse, onore." Souliotis then opts for an effective high D to close the act.

The opening of the second act is almost as strong. She is clearly weary at the start of "Dormono entrambi," and the word "matrigna" drips with disgust. A peremptory "Muoiano" contrasts with a suddenly tender "Sì," letting the listener know, almost like a question mark, of oncoming doubts. "Un gel mi prende" offers an intimation of helplessness in the unusual coloring of her low in place of the customary baleful sound. "Teneri figli" conveys heartbreaking nostalgia, although her abrupt "Ah no," as her resolve cracks, offers urgency only, not genuine horror. Moreover, she seems too collected in her command to Clotilde that Adalgisa be summoned, with not much suggestion of trauma at having nearly slain her children. This lapse is partially redeemed by the proper chill of death at "e poi … si mora." But she is overly determined and collected with Adalgisa too. Maybe the tone softens later on in the exchange, but Norma's crucial vulnerability in this scene only becomes apparent with her pleading "Deh! con te, con te li prendi." Even here, she regains her "all-purpose" strength at "Basti a te." Then there is a surge of pride in her rejection of the notion that Pollione's old affection for Norma could be restored with pleading. But helplessness is dominant in a deeply affecting "Ah! perchè," and a suitably urgent "Hai vinto" leads into a tender "Trovo un'amica ancor." It is frustrating that Varviso's business-like reading of "Sì, fino all'ore estreme" disturbs the mood: the fine passagework from both Souliotis and Cossotto emerges devoid of dramatic specificity — a perfunctory conclusion to what could have been an insightful rendering.

At the opening of her last scene, there is a respectable delivery of Norma's tender cadenza of hope, even though she too soon telegraphs her nasty change of mood with an all-knowing "Favella!" There is no question, however, that her subsequent flourish of vengeance with its towering high C is nothing short of superb. Her muted asides, as soon as Pollione is apprehended, are just as good, and her "Sì, Norma" becomes intensely private. There is vivid despair in her "Poss'io sentir pietà," even though she then seems to announce without skipping a beat her blustering decision that Pollione first be interrogated. The opening of the "In mia man" also rings with authority, despite a disorienting tenderness—why?—for "fuggirai," awkwardly telegraphing a more apt softening of tone at "io ti perdono."

But from the moment Souliotis utters a hectoring "Giura," she is inspired for the balance of the scene. There is sadness and infinite weariness in her description of how close she came to dispatching her own children, and only on the word "dimenticar" are we back to the erstwhile threat in her voice. There is expressive passagework as she tears into "Solo? Tutti/I Romani," and while the absence of any trills here is regrettable, the musicality of much else is welcome. Dramatically and vocally, she seems utter mistress of the situation in the "Preghi alfine?" with her mind entirely made up. When faced by an expectant multitude, Souliotis delivers a heartbreaking "Io rea, l'innocente accusar del fallo mio?" No one else has conveyed such overwhelming pity for Adalgisa, and the "Son io" lingers in a haunting piano. She is still in a daze when declaring "Io stessa! Il rogo ergete," with "Norma non mente" utterly impassive. Then, as in her "Casta Diva," it is Souliotis's affecting simplicity in the "Qual cor tradisti" that dominates. The line "Tu sei con me" is the only moment where an intimation of destiny recalls the priestess. The magically soft dynamics for much of the rest, including the final tapered high note, set the inward tone for this ensemble. In the *materia di mezzo*, even her softened "umana idea" prepares us for a painful confession to a father, not a strong declaration by a public figure. Her "Son madre" is thus a sad, but hushed, interjection, and "un prego ancor," while not a full-fledged piano, has poignancy, which carries over into her "Deh! Non volerli vittime." Here, Varviso's perfunctory tempo does not affect Souliotis's expressive dynamics, culminating in a moving *decrescendo* on the "pietà" ending the solo. Souliotis then takes full advantage of the one *ritardando* Varviso affords her toward the conclusion of the final ensemble: her subtle lingering on the caressed phrase "Tu mel prometti," with its perfect balance of anguish at the farewell and of poignant relief at her father's promise, is more heartbreaking than ever. This Norma truly loved her children after all.

The next interpreter to record the role complete is Montserrat Caballé. Based on her studio effort made in 1972 for RCA, one would hardly guess that here is one of the finer interpreters of the role. She may not have the fertile imagination typical of a Callas, a Gencer or a Souliotis, but she is certainly capable of more inner feeling than we hear in this dubious set. Fatigue, evidenced in shortness of breath, unsteady tone, inattention to nuance — these are the problems that beset this studio reading. Moreover, despite her voice being more spinto than *drammatico*, she is usually capable of riding the grander phrases of the Druid priestess with greater aplomb than here. Usually, her phenomenal breath control and keenly focused tone can cut through any challenge Bellini offers. Placido Domingo contributes a musically impeccable but inexpressive Pollione and Fiorenza Cossotto an Adalgisa somewhat superior to the one in the flawed Varviso set. Carlo Felice Cillario's conducting is more attentive than

Varviso's, but not as probing as Votto or Gavazzeni, never mind Panizza or Serafin. Ruggero Raimondi's Oroveso is, however, luxury casting indeed, vocally and dramatically, but he alone cannot redeem a perfunctory offering.

To appreciate the true greatness of Montserrat Caballé's Norma, one must sample those "live" recordings that feature her in full glory when she is clearly "up" for the occasion. One such complete broadcast, recalling the classic Wallmann/Callas/La Scala of 1955, preserves a *Norma* where all three principals are thoroughly engaged dramatically and in strong voice: Giuseppe Patané leads an outdoor performance at the Festival d'Orange, 1974, vivid in its evocation of a mythic tale where passions are paradoxically at their rawest and also their most bottled-up. Montserrat Caballé, Jon Vickers and Josephine Veasey offer uniformly compelling performances. Neither Vickers nor Veasey may be the last word in *bel canto* elegance, but they are accomplished musicians who think dramatically when making music, and musically when making drama. Agostino Ferrin sings Oroveso.

This epochal performance has been released on CD by Serenissima and Opera D'Oro. Montserrat Caballé's voice is completely warmed up from the moment she first comes on. Despite only fair sound quality, one is immediately struck by both a richness and a steadiness in her mid-range that always mark those occasions when she is in top form. Her commanding accents to the Druids do not carry the kind of sharp disapproval heard from others, but she and Patané give a full measure of significance to her prophecy of the fall of Rome, capped by a strong low B. There is then a luminous top note on "mieto" to end the recitative. Her use of portamento in the "Casta Diva" brings solemnity to the entire ceremony. The syncopations are begun piano, swelling for their climactic note. As is customary, Caballé merely repeats the syncopations in the "Tempra," only this time they are not attacked piano. She crests the aria's concluding flourish on "fai" with an exquisite *pianissimo* and ends with a respectable stab at a trill (not always a Caballé trademark) and another *pianissimo* for "ciel." In the *materia di mezzo*, we hear crisp passagework with a sweeping delivery of "Dal druidico delubro/La mia voce tuonerà," becoming a single musical utterance. This is offset by no upward turns on "sa." In the cabaletta, we can sense Norma's heart quickening at the thought of reviving Pollione's love. There is good passagework throughout, and the divisions on "diede" are excellent. The whole ends with a ringing top note. She does not take the repeat. If one of spinto weight rather than *drammatico*, is obliged to do this, then one can't help feeling this is the way it should be done: disciplined access to a broad range, fluent phrasing, and prodigious breath control.

As the second scene opens, there is another ideally weightless *pianissimo* from Caballé on "Nol fossi," but she stumbles slightly in her lower middle at "tentasse." There is a respectable low B flat on "dubbio." In her audience with Adalgisa, Caballé is at first grave and concerned, turning dreamy on "rimembranza," then grave again on "Segui." "Così trovava del cor la via" is taken on one breath, with a piano of ineffable beauty on ... "vava" of "trovava." This is followed by a gentle, fluent reading of "Ah sì, fa' core, abbracciami," with an assured top note at its climax, but no piano. After the duet, she is immediately upset at Adalgisa's suitor being a Roman, despite her still being ignorant of his identity. When she finally realizes who he is, there is an emphatic glottal attack for "Pollion!" But her "E per chi" turns suddenly sad, changing to a softly biting inflection on "tu tremi?" She delivers the most fluent reading of the "non tremare" fireworks since Sutherland, and she is the first one since Callas to combine outrage with musicality. Her portamento on "per" of "per te" is both deft and clearly livid. In the "Oh, di qual sei tu vittima," she softens momentarily at "Fonte d'eterne lagrime," and one marvels at the keen focus of her full-voiced denunciation on "L'empio." In this trio, all three principals show themselves true musicians, and their conscientious reading opens a world of understanding of Bellini's vision. In the final ensemble, Caballé hurls out "sì" and "indegno" with startling violence, and Patané brings the act to a rousing conclusion.

Unfortunately, both the Opera D'Oro pressing and the Serenissima lack the entire opening of Caballé's crucial scene holding the knife over her children. The indexing may list this sequence as present and accounted for, but both CDs take up this scene at Adalgisa's entrance following Norma's solo. The sequence is intact on a Bel Canto Society video of the same performance, where Caballé delivers a thoughtful opening. She grows sterner at "matrigna," but her suffering is clearly revealed when she sobs on "un gel mi prende." There is a poignant caress for "delizia mia," overtaken by greater anger than ever as she delivers the "Di Pollion son figli." The horror she feels at herself is vivid as she suddenly decides not to kill her children. But she is in full command as she orders Clotilde to bring Adalgisa to her, and her "si mora," alone, conveys real determination. In the scene with Adalgisa, where both CD editions pick up the thread, Caballé produces a hint of hysteria on "contaminata," but she is more reconciled to her fate at "Deh! con te," with its easy delivery and an excellent top note. From a sense of resignation, she turns detached altogether as the "Ah! perche" unfolds with prodigious skeins of endless phrasing, seemingly without limit. There is incisive passagework in much of the duet, properly spellbinding as a once strong woman is now bewildered at altering her entire life. "Hai vinto" in the *materia di mezzo* conveys a new resolve in contrast to the withdrawn accents of the duet's first half. The cabaletta is distinguished by a piano *ritardando* for the flourish leading into the *da capo* of "Sì, fino allore." The sense of decision is enhanced by a long hold on the climactic high note at the close.

Norma's final scene opens with another languorous *ritardando*, "del primo amor ai dì," leading to a lovely high C, very different from her epic high C as she calls down vengeance a moment later. Despite an essentially spinto instrument, Caballé's adroit shaping of utterances like "Guerra" are of surprising grandeur, while her muted asides as the Druids usher in the apprehended Pollione are equally effective. Typical of the dramatic give-and-take throughout this reading is the artistic rapport shown in Caballé's response to a privately uttered "Norma" from Vickers. As she publicly confirms "Norma," she conveys the message that Pollione is facing the priestess now, not his beloved. Caballé also conveys her continued weakness for Pollione as she finds herself unable to strike him. There is some bluster in her rationalizing with her people that Pollione must first be "questioned," but it is suitably unconvincing. Left alone with Pollione, the "In mia man," whirls from a canniness in "M'odi," to a scornful "poi," to a threatening recall of her moment of truth with their children. Clearly, the implication here is that she could still bring herself to slay them, despite her soft rendering of "Mi poss'io dimenticar." Her attempted trills are not too clear in the "Adalgisa fia punita," but the solo leads effectively to an almost whispered "Preghi alfine" delivered after a pregnant pause. "È tardi" finds her the priestess again. As compensation for Caballé's blurred trills, "Posso alfarti alfin" boasts handsome passagework, and one wonders whether any two artists have surpassed the oneness of musical approach that Caballé and Vickers show in the duet's closing measures. The all-important "Son io" is sustained on a rapt *rallentando*. Surprisingly, effective as this is, Caballé, the mistress of the *pianissimo*, does not go all the way down, but she renders a haunting "Qual cor tradisti," distinguished by a true piano at "orrenda" and "con te." Likewise, a fitting *pianissimo* closes the ensemble. She has now become all intimacy and vulnerability: there is another softening in the voice when she decides to divulge the secret of her motherhood, leading to a hushed "Son madre" to her father Oroveso. The intimacy is sustained with him: she makes a magically extended utterance of "un prego ancor," "pre" ... cresting to the flourish followed by a suspended *pianissimo* on ... "go" and leisurely spinning out of the rest of the phrase. Her "Deh! non volerli vittime" may be as perfect as it's possible to be: an apt *ritardando* on "fiore," the rest infinitely inward and personal. There is then a grand surge of tone from both Caballé and Vickers bringing the opera to a close.

Something else comes to a close with this performance: *Norma* recordings that work as a totality. There are scenes yet to be heard in later sets where greatness can still be glimpsed, but the sovereign control over the full sweep of the title role and the shape of Bellini's opera proves elusive more often than not. One can hope that achievements like Caballé's, Vickers', and Patané's will come about again some time, but the glimmerings of an exceptional new generation today must first fullfil their potential before matching the peaks of earlier generations. It is instructive that, despite Cigna's inheritance of the García tradition from a Marchesi pupil, Emma Calvé, her genuine strengths did not extend to ideal control over the fioritura, making her Norma symptomatic of a slight falling-off in the tradition. Yet, despite this, the tradition grew stronger again in subsequent decades, first with the more fluent, if less imaginative, Milanov, and then with the more mercurial Callas, the more plush-sounding Cerquetti, the more vital Souliotis, and the more elegant Caballé. So there seems no reason to doubt that such abundance can come again, perhaps in ensembles as happy as Callas's with Wallmann and Votto in 1955, Cerquetti's with Santini in 1958, and Caballé's with Patané in 1974.

The occasional greatness of Beverly Sills in this role complements that of Gina Cigna. Like Cigna, Sills inherits the García tradition through another

Marchesi pupil, Estelle Liebling. But, where Cigna must defer to her juniors in matters of suppleness, Sills falls short in aptness of instrument. Made in 1973 for ABC, the Sills *Norma* has Enrico Di Giuseppe as an undersized Pollione, Shirley Verrett as a peerless Adalgisa, and Paul Plishka as a baritonal Oroveso. James Levine conducts a reading long on energy, short on elegance.

Sills' instrument, heard a year after her *Anna Bolena*, may, if anything, be slightly more frayed here than in that opera, but her actual singing seems more at ease with Bellini's shifts of tessitura than with the more volatile ones in *Bolena*. Problems still remain. Intrinsic to Sills' struggle for grandeur are her slender instrument, the occasional querulousness, and some flatting toward the top. One must accept these in order to savor certain shapely phrases and stylish flourishes whose fluency and elegance of dynamics recall a Félia Litvinne, an Adelina Patti, or a Giannina Russ. These are formidable assets, and combined with interpretive instincts that equal the best, Norma as a person emerges occasionally, thanks to Sills' alert music-making.

Aspects of the opening *scena* may mark some of her strongest moments: "Casta Diva," rendered quite slowly and in the original key, is suffused with a remarkably sylvan feeling, particularly in the passagework ending the first statement. The syncopations are nicely managed and, for a wonder, Sills follows the original long note in place of the syncopations for the *da capo*, even though she does not deliver it *crescendo* as written. There is an excellent trill in the cadenza. In the *materia di mezzo*, a haunting effect is the "audible-tears" inflection given the upward turns on "sa." In "Ah bello," the words dance, and one is forcefully reminded of the difference between lyric coloratura and heroic coloratura: this is clearly not the moment for the latter, being an inward sentiment recalling younger, happier days. Sills understands this. She is strictly the private and vulnerable woman only, for now. The passagework on "diedi" is good, all the embellishments in the uncut *da capo* inspired. Her reach for greatness in this first scene is not misplaced.

There is, though, not such an abundance of revelation in the second scene, chiefly because of its more heroic nature. Furthermore, Verrett's luscious sounds as Adalgisa, matched with a fine legato, tend to overshadow Sills' Norma. She is happiest in her tender delivery of "Te non lega eterno nodo all'ara," freeing Adalgisa from her vows. This is matched by a broadly phrased joint flourish as the two conclude the duet, "Ah sì, fa' core." Sills caps the flourish with a deft trill. Once she has expressed her fury at Pollione with accents that don't really match the heroic proportions Bellini gives it, she surprises with a depth of lament on "Fonte d'eterne lagrime." One must salute an indomitable musicianship that attacks the final "Vanne, sì" uncut. She conveys an implacable declaration of justice from on high, reserving a sense of personal hurt for one word, "indegno."

Possibly, one of the finest moments in her interpretation is her "Deh! con te, con te li prendi" in the next scene: she opens with a subtle sense of separation between "Deh" and "con te," sustaining the solo with breathless urgency, winding up with a fine high note, securely attacked and richly expressive. Her "Ah! perchè," rather than being drained or withdrawn, is anguished and deeply personal instead, a reading recalling another Marchesi inheritor, Gina Cigna. As a musical statement, Sills' and Verrett's uncut cabaletta is a remarkable achievement bringing a strong reading of their scene together to a fitting conclusion.

The last scene is not as consistently satisfying, given Di Giuseppe's discomfort with some of Pollione's requirements and Norma's return to a more heroic stance. Sills still makes a good distinction between a tender delivery for her opening flourish of hope with its caressing high C and a dynamic delivery for her vengeful utterances with a slashing high C. Once Pollione is captured, how remarkable to hear feverish, not muted, asides. Levine's quick tempi here enhance the effect. Sills is then completely unstrung at seeing herself falter before slaying Pollione, and she is brilliant in her painfully blustering and insincere excuses to the multitude, done with an almost total absence of portamento: an angular, *pro forma* delivery. Genius. Alone with Pollione, she offers a vivid reading of her near infanticide, clearly at the end of her rope. Aside from Callas, this is the most expressive reading of the trills describing Adalgisa's punishment. The "Già mi pasco" is grandly phrased, and an effective high note caps the duet. These remain assets in her handling of this confrontation, despite moments of strain that remind one how much Sills sacrificed in tackling this repertoire. Then, before the double ensemble, her floating "Son io" ranks with the most moving readings on disc: a deeply melancholy delivery, it achieves a graphic aural picture of simply letting go, shimmering into silence on ... "o" of "io." The inflection on "Norma non mente" seems to convey a newly found scorn for the easy way out, almost as if the last thing she would wish now were to be judged a coward. Memorable are the deft miniature *decrescendi* applied in the opening of "Qual cor tradisti." One regrets the loss of vocal focus as the solo grows to a climax, but the ensemble ends effectively with a *diminuendo* on the high G. The final "Deh! non volerli vittime" may go a bit unsteady in its last measures, but it makes a positive effect in general. As in Norma's last duet with Adalgisa, Sills is scrupulous here in maintaining a subtle separation between the word "Deh" and the words following it. Particularly happy is her first "Abbi di lor pietade," which emerges deeply moving and is complemented by a floated top note for the second "pietà." By curtain time, the sense of an undernourished instrument in this role may still linger, but Sills' security in Bellini's musical language remains welcome.

The next Norma, Cristina Deutekom ("live" at San Francisco, 1975) is available on the Gala label. Robleto Merolla, Tatiana Troyanos, and Clifford Grant sing Pollione, Adalgisa, and Oroveso. Carlo Felice Cillario (familiar from Caballé's disappointing studio recording) conducts.

Deutekom has a fuller sound than Sills, but still somewhat bright for the role and shaded with less imagination. She can convey authority, but without much individuality. She still shows some of the suppleness in coloratura that we remember from her *Armida* of 1970, and she knows how to project an imposing persona through the passagework. She does not have an ideal suavity in reflective moments like "Casta Diva": a hint of a squeeze on certain tones can sometimes induce a tight vibrato that is unappealing. The tinkling "marimba" effect, heard in her *Armida*, is not necessarily objectionable, but the clarity and articulation of her passagework suffer when the effect is not applied. This suggests a crutch, the only way she can maintain full accuracy. However, the "Ah! bello" at the end of the first scene is certainly made pretty exciting with this method.

As with Sills, occasionally overshadowed by Verrett's Adalgisa, Deutekom's Adalgisa, Tatiana Troyanos, also startles by a richer, more imposing tone coloring than the Norma. Deutekom can use a telling *pianissimo* in recalling her first days with Pollione, but it doesn't relate to any special tenderness. One has to concede, though, that the precision and velocity of her fioritura in the "Ah sì" retain their power to astound, and this solo features the most pleasing *pianissimo* so far. A good trill also distinguishes the concluding flourishes of the duet. Her deep-seated "Tremi tu" on discovering the truth is surprisingly effective, but the passagework in the "Oh non tremare" is pressed and awkward, the tone sometimes losing focus. The problems with the occasional squeezed tone grow more acute in the "Oh, di qual sei tu vittima." However, she is certainly livid enough for most of this scene. She ends the closing measures of the "Vanne, sì" with a grab at the high D that excites the audience, but that sounds slightly uncomfortable on the recording.

There are a few pitch problems at the opening of the second act and also some strain. Deutekom has trouble sustaining an easy line at a piano dynamic, which robs the struggle over her sleeping children of some of its poignancy. She has better control over her piano in "Deh! con te" to Adalgisa, and the polished fioritura serves to make one forget her problems in the previous scene. Troyanos' "Norma, ah Norma" represents some of her best singing in this performance. Deutekom then responds to Troyanos' "Mira, o Norma" with a beautifully shaped "Ah! perchè," showing her best control of dynamics yet. The "Sì, fino all'ore," while accomplished, is not entirely at the same lofty level.

In the final scene, Deutekom's control of dynamics is excellent as she spins out her hopeful phrases with a radiance that encompasses a soft high C, matched by a stentorian high C as she prepares for vengeance a moment later. Once Pollione is apprehended, though, the delivery tends to be crude. Only when Norma and Pollione are alone does Deutekom permit herself a little give in expressing the tumult Norma feels: "Mi poss'io dimenticar" emerges with a suggestion of a tear. The entire duet showcases her formidable energy in rattling through Bellini's passagework. Once the Druids are again assembled, she musters up a prolonged piano for "Son io." The "Qual cor tradisti" ends with an even finer piano on the closing high note. In the *materia di mezzo*, though, she fails to find the profound sorrow of the moment. The pleading flourish on "un prego ancor" is split in two: first, "un pre"... becomes a wordless vocalise of poignancy and sweetness, then, all of "un prego ancor" is sung in a gravelly manner to the second half of the flourish. Figuratively speaking, one might say both the Jekyll and the Hyde of Deutekom's Norma are encapsulated by this compromise. "Deh! Non volerli vittime" conveys extreme poignancy: even the deft figurations in Bellini's line become part of the expression of the whole. There is another accomplished piano, this time on "pietà." These creditable final moments do not entirely redeem a perfunctory last scene, but they suggest that, with a greater level of preparation, Deutekom could have found a more compelling interpretation throughout.

One artist who could never be called perfunctory is our next Norma, Renata Scotto. Like Beverly Sills, her lyric soprano counterpart in the *Norma* discography, she recorded the role with James Levine in 1978 for CBS. Her colleagues are Giuseppe Giacomini and Tatiana Troyanos as Pollione and Adalgisa. As in Levine's earlier recording, Paul Plishka once again sings Oroveso.

Perfunctory Scotto is not, but, as with Sills, her Norma poses fundamental questions concerning the type of vocal instrument required. Her eventual performance of it at the Metropolitan Opera's opening night in 1981 drew considerable criticism. Scotto canceled the Saturday afternoon broadcast, so there is no known document of her Norma at the Met. This 1978 recording, then, is recognizable as what New York heard. She seems beside herself with fury in her rebuke of the Druids at the opening. But she offers a *pianissimo* as she prepares the Druids for a prayer, the "Casta Diva." She sounds badly strained in the syncopations leading to high B flat (she sings this in the traditional key of F). The soft downward scales leading into "Tempra, o Diva" are, however, exquisite. Once in the "Tempra," not only does she follow Bellini and render the original single note in place of the syncopated ones of the first statement, she also follows the original *crescendo* marking and links the note to the high B flat at the crest of the passage as a single phrase, something nobody else has yet done. One regrets that the same strain evident in the syncopated notes can be heard as she swells the long note of the *da capo*. As if to compensate, the cadenza closing the aria is enhanced by another exquisite downward scale done in a haunting *mezza voce*. Alas, in the *materia di mezzo*, her voice does not "tuonerà," it splatters. There are, in addition, squally divisions in the cabaletta, although they emerge softer in the *da capo*. The voice goes off the rails again in the coda, and she opts out of the usual top note climaxing the *scena*. There is much here that is verbally perceptive, and one is reminded of what a fine poet Felice Romani really is. But the price the listener pays for this kind of poetic interpretation may seem too steep for many. Scotto's slender instrument is pressed to its limits—and beyond.

A sense of unease pervades the next scene as Scotto divulges her fears to Clotilde. More special is the way she renders her initial phrases to the troubled Adalgisa. These phrases are indicative of sympathetic memories long before her aside, "O rimembranza." Once this all-important phrase has been delivered, Scotto seems to be expressing pity for herself as much as for Adalgisa, and by the time Norma frees Adalgisa from her vows, Scotto's muted instrument is disembodied, a wraith suffused in bittersweet memories. Vulnerability dominates.

"Ah sì, fa' core" is given in the palest colors. At this point, one has no doubt that Norma is as helpless a creature as Adalgisa. One wishes the abrasive top note climaxing this solo didn't break the spell. Scotto's *pianissimo* is still in respectable shape here; one wonders why she didn't simply soften the top note the way several others have. If she seems overstretched here, that is doubly the case for her incensed solo on learning the truth of Pollione's infatuation for Adalgisa: "Oh non tremare" becomes painful in its lack of authority and stringy top notes. Even the passagework is clumsy, with almost half the figurations badly blurred. Her "Oh, di qual sei tu vittima" becomes easier, centered, as it is, in the midrange, with telling inflections for Romani's lines. One can only regret the way her voice continues to rebel in its upper reaches as we move toward the close. Painful loss works better than unmitigated fury in Scotto's "Vanne sì," making it more vocally persuasive in her case. One is grateful that she also eschews an interpolated top note at the curtain.

Emotional extremes at the opening of Act II are tellingly conveyed as Norma is wrenched by her conflicted feelings, gazing at her sleeping children. At the same time, vocal lurches distract too much from Scotto's mastery at fusing the poetic and the musical. With all her dramatic genius, only the bittersweet phrases of "Teneri figli" attain the greatness of other fine readings. Another moment of greatness is the opening half of "Deh! con te," where she is clearly a beaten woman. Then, taking the cue from the word "disprezzata," she raises the temperature, and her vocal control is altogether too undisciplined to ignore. "Ah! perchè" repeats the same pattern: great vividness in all her inward phrases of pain and regret, offset by vocal lunges and unsteady tone whenever a musical gesture becomes too outward.

The final scene does not break the pattern, but there is a striking *pianissimo* for the rapturous high C at "del primo amor ai di felici," however strained her approach up to it. Alone with Pollione, "Pe' figli tuoi" recalls the tenderness and anguish of "teneri figli," but the magic is momentary. She then conveys fear at herself on revealing her terrifying thoughts toward her children. Moments like a whispered "è tardi" evoke shivers. After the duet, her *pianissimo* comes to her aid more than once, partially redeeming vocal handicaps. It imparts deep expression to her "Son io"; "tradisti," "perdesti," "orrenda," and "con te" enhance her "Qual cor tradisti," however tenuous her final high G. Another fine *pianissimo*, deftly shaped, adorns the flourish at "un prego ancor." Her final "Deh! Non volerli" is heartbreaking in its shadowed coloring, sadly losing effectiveness as Scotto climbs up the scale. Her poetic insights throughout the role are certainly treasurable. Others with vocal lacunae have been able partially to overcome them with a musical assurance partly lacking in Scotto.

Like Scotto, Maria Bieshu, the next recorded Norma, will indulge in an occasional glottal attack, and similar vocal lunges. The difference is that Bieshu's instrument is authentically heroic. In fact, her fault, if anything, is a propensity to throw her brazen tone around too freely. The irony is that, after we've spent so much time at the opposite end of the spectrum, we suddenly have a

Norma who is too much Norma the warrior and too little Norma the mother. Recorded in 1986, this Melodiya recording is led by Mark Ermler. Bieshu's colleagues are Gegam Grigoryan as Pollione, Ludmila Nam as Adalgisa, and Georgi Seleznev as one of the finest Orovesos on disc, in a class with Pinza, Siepi, and Raimondi.

Bieshu applies an occasional piano at moments in the "Casta Diva," but her vocal face doesn't change significantly. Moreover, passagework can be ungainly. It's startling to hear her reverse the usual pattern: instead of repeating the syncopated notes, which is wrong, Bieshu sings the one note both times—equally wrong! Despite this and other eccentricities, including questionable Italian and scooped top notes with suspect pitch, the Milanov-like clarity of her upper register and her fearlessness can grow on one. There is an elemental excitement in her uncut cabaletta, clumsy divisions and all. She tackles this with a power not heard for a long time, projecting a distinct character here. It may not be the well-rounded persona we are accustomed to, but it is a vivid enough individual revealed with compelling candor.

In the next scene, Bieshu achieves nothing striking until the duet with Adalgisa. Not until then does she modify a hectoring delivery that threatens monotony. With Adalgisa, she treats us to a stunning piano on "nodo" as she frees Adalgisa from her vows, and her "Ah! sì, fa' core" features commendable shading, contrasted with what has gone before. Her most spectacular high notes come in the "Oh non tremare," where the high Cs ring out with a suggestion of more power in reserve. More emotion comes into play as she offers an "Oh, di qual sei tu vittima" on the verge of tears. A rousing "Vanne sì" may offer no new insights, but with some unfamiliar music restored, the full sweep of her rage makes its own excitement.

What a shame that, despite her abundance of tone, Bieshu's "Teneri figli" at the opening of Act II exposes one of her least attractive features: a shortness of breath. She simply does not have the requisite control for the Bellinian phrase. Still, one has to wonder whether anyone has shown more spaciousness of tone at "e poi … si mora." No question that hers is a major instrument. But the positive impressions of such a sound are undercut by a "Deh! con te" that strays frequently from pitch. The "Ah! perchè" is a distinct improvement: although having its share of glottal lunges, the line is not as seriously compromised, the musical authority is surer, and there is more chance for the voice to maintain the luminous quality so reminiscent of Milanov.

In the final scene, Bieshu delivers a rushed flourish and a rushed high C on "ai dì," compensating somewhat with, at least, an efficient high C for her cry of vengeance a moment later. There is no clear aside as she thunders indiscriminately, seeing Pollione led on as a captive. She even indulges an occasional extramusical exclamation mark to highlight phrase endings. There is, in addition, recurrent unsteadiness and gravelliness in the low. Not until the duet and Norma's recall of the moment she nearly killed her children is there a change. In warning Pollione that she almost forgot her very nature, Bieshu imparts a keen edge of lament to her confession. It is the most compelling moment in the duet. The menace in her threats against Adalgisa is also compelling up to a point, but blurred passagework detracts from the effect. The mood, though, is successfully sustained past the duet in her pulverizing "accorrete" summoning back the Druids. She then draws a convincing contrast with a genuinely troubled "Io rea,/L'innocente accusar del fallo mio?" and a piano on "Son io." Although she doesn't find the sense of renunciation in "Qual cor tradisti," "orrenda" is softened in a way suggesting a Milanov in its approach. She lofts a few haunting pianos in the closing measures. Ermler's lumbering tempi in the *materia di mezzo* compromise still further Bieshu's limited range of expression, but she musters a respectable flourish on "un prego ancor" with a genuine piano at its crest. Despite a generally unvaried "Deh! non volerli vittime," she sweetens beautifully on "Oh padre," and the ending is enhanced by the final phrases of Seleznev's imposing Oroveso. The story of Bieshu's Norma is one of refulgent means tied to spotty musicality.

Today's Norma, Jane Eaglen, was recorded for EMI, "live" at La Scala in 1994. Her colleagues are Vincenzo La Scola as Pollione, Eva Mei as Adalgisa and Dimitri Kavrakos as Oroveso. Riccardo Muti conducts.

Eaglen's is a fine instrument. She has the energy to convey the danger in the character. One wishes there were more elegance in her treatment of Bellini's sensitive shaping of Romani's lines. There is, in addition, not the full degree of dynamic variety one might expect from an instrument of such remarkable resources. Still, that might seem churlish after surveying a generation of Normas who have shown either musical assurance, vocal strength, or beauty of tone, but never all three. In Eaglen's case, a modicum of all three is welcome. Her command of intricate fioritura may not be ideal, but, again, it shows musical discipline, whatever its four-square quality.

There's a touching earnestness to Eaglen's entrance lines but they lack magnetism and sweep. Better is the "Casta Diva" with its murmured opening and caressed downward scales. Surprisingly, she chooses, like Bieshu, to opt for the single held tone both times rather than the syncopated notes. If the "Casta Diva" is gratifying, Eaglen's cabaletta is one of the most successful on disc. Her command of coloratura may lack fleetness and personality, but her "Ah! bello" is still special. Literally complete, it displays a basic facility that works well with an ambitiously ornamented *da capo*. Typical is the consistently unbroken shaping of "il cor ti diedi"—rare to hear every single note of this from a singer with flexibility and rich coloring throughout the range, ready to ornament where needed.

Eaglen's low notes ensure a strong exchange with Clotilde over Pollione and the children. Her agitation spills over into her interview with Adalgisa through abstracted remarks to an unexpected visitor. Adalgisa only has Norma's undivided attention at "O rimembranza," launching a sequence where Eaglen projects alternating feelings of nostalgia for herself and alarm for Adalgisa at the thought of another suffering the same pangs she has. Her singing in "Ah! sì, fa' core" is musically neat, if not particularly imaginative. Following their duet, there is complete transformation in "Roma!" where she clearly knows the truth at that very moment. It's as if the breath is knocked out of her. When she confronts Pollione, "Oh non tremare," Eaglen gets the big things right: tremendous high Cs, fluent delivery of the torrential downward scales, huge spans of breath, a strong finish. If anything were needed to confirm her title to this role, it is her handling of this passage. And she is splendidly furious. The mood is sustained into the "Oh, di qual sei tu vittima." She finishes up by making a nice distinction between repressed anger at "Lo compi" and an explosion for the "Vanne sì." Anguish may not be as evident in the sound of her voice as in others, but her splendid rage and musicality make for a stunning curtain.

The opening of Act II fails to find the heartbreak in "Teneri figli." Eaglen is efficient with the prodigious phrases and their high tessitura, but this doesn't project as an utterance of inadvertent love. She remains impeccably musical — and impersonal. In the rest of the scene, one is more aware than before of her dependence on a theatrical gasp after crucial utterances. It seems a substitute for the shading of the voice itself. The gasp is more apparent in transitional moments when Eaglen does not have a set solo to lean on. Thus, "Deh! con te" (opening the duet with Adalgisa) and "Ah! perchè" suffer far less. But all the same, "Ah! perchè," aside from a softened "molli affetti," still suffers from an earnestness that lacks specificity. This is one of Norma's most painfully vulnerable moments, something one wouldn't guess from the way it sounds here. Partly redeeming this impersonal quality is the bracing joint *da capo* of the duet's cabaletta, where ornamented sprints up the scale transform the scene's final moments into pure electricity.

As the final scene opens, there is good breath control for the piano cadenza with its soft high C, but it doesn't really float as cleanly as one would like. Better is Eaglen's clarion high C in her vow of vengeance, showing greater security as the warrior than as the beloved. Upon the Druids being summoned, we have an epic "Sterminio!" On Pollione's capture, she becomes subtler, with a sly smile on "Sì, Norma," and a convincing aside on "Poss'io sentir pietà!" She then pulls herself together for the multitude, as she announces the need for an interrogation. Once launched in the duet with Pollione, "E la vita io ti perdona" is downright conspiratorial, leading into a tense recounting of her near infanticide. Unfortunately, she attacks her threat against Adalgisa with trills that fizzle too soon, compromising the shape of the phrase. An intriguingly grave reading of the "Preghi alfine" is likewise offset by shortness of breath in the "Già mi pasco," but there is then excellent passagework at "Posso farti alfin" leading to the coda. A good touch is the way she breathes "Io rea,/L'innocente accusar del fallo mio," and her piano in "Son io" floats more successfully than elsewhere in this scene. In the "Qual cor tradisti," Eaglen adopts telling rests before the recurrent ... "ti" ending of the top two lines, "tradisti," "perdesti." This sets the tone for the sequence, as does the tender "Quest' ora orrenda" against the closing ensemble. A creditable *decrescendo* on the final G ends the number after a brief flicker of pitch insecurity. She is then breathless and intimate in her confession of motherhood to her father. It almost sounds like a conscious adoption of the interpretive approach first heard from Gina Cigna and Ezio Pinza. That stance is not maintained consistently, though, and even the fluency of her flourish at "un prego ancor" is offset by its not being as soft as it could be. A breathless sense of horror marks the "Deh! non volerli vittime." This is not as moving as some others but, instead, a strikingly desperate plea where Norma is lashing out at fate rather than accepting it.

A role like Norma, like the role of Hamlet, will continue to attract widely different interpreters. When we recall the apparent variety in Giuditta Pasta, its famed creator, one suspects that, though Ponselle and Cerquetti bring the most ease to the role, Maria Callas, Leyla Gencer, and Elena Souliotis come closest to matching Bellini's multi-faceted vision and the prototype of the *assoluta*.

9

Donizetti (1797–1848): *Gemma di Vergy*

It could be argued that even the most celebrated Norma interpreters in Bellini's and Donizetti's own time each had vocal hurdles. Wilhelmine Schroeder-Devrient's ease with it, for instance, was always suspect, however apt her vocal persona. So it seems uncertain whether or not she was ever a Giuditta Pasta or a Maria Malibran in the role. At the same time, though Bellini was a great admirer of Pasta's interpretation, even she only gave it full musical justice for a very short while. (It seems that very soon after *Norma*'s world premiere Pasta's sense of pitch became so seriously impaired it precipitated a rapid vocal decline.) Even Malibran had the role in her repertoire for a mere two years before her untimely death.

A conspicuous exception to all three was Giuseppina Ronzi–De Begnis, one of the few consistently satisfying Normas for much of the 1830s, which she sang with success for nine years from 1834 to 1843. Though both Pasta and Malibran have been well researched in modern scholarship, this has led to a relegation of Ronzi–De Begnis, a crucial figure in the history of *bel canto*. As a result of the scholarly lionization of Pasta and others, Ronzi–De Begnis has been neglected until the recent *bel canto* revivals.

This neglect is understandable because the greater difficulty of the two most significant roles Donizetti wrote for her, the title role in Donizetti's *Gemma di Vergy* (1834) and Queen Elizabeth in Donizetti's *Roberto Devereux* (1837), has militated against their having the kind of currency that Norma has achieved.

Thus Ronzi–De Begnis herself has been necessarily a shadowy figure. Going by these two very special roles that she created, however (they are the next two significant *assoluta* roles to follow Pasta's Bolena and Norma), Ronzi–De Begnis may possibly have been the most remarkable *assoluta* of them all. Lord Mount-Edgecumbe remarked on the skill with which she invariably controlled her instrument, and even Guillaume Cottrau, one of her few detractors, though a friend of Ronzi–De Begnis's admirer, Donizetti, admitted that, musically, she was superbly trained.[48]

Ronzi–De Begnis sang in public for a long time, making her debut in 1814 and retiring around 1845. In fact, the unusual length of her career for that era came about in spite of the difficult challenges she would sometimes accept. She sang Giulia in Spontini's *Vestale* at Florence when she was only 17 years old. Among her other roles, she took on Elena in Rossini's *Donna del lago*, a mezzo role, when she was 23 and eventually became a leading favorite in Naples by the time she was 31. As a regular star there at the Teatro San Carlo, she began her first Naples season with a rendition of the mezzo role of the Rossini Desdemona in which, Donizetti wrote, she "sang par excellence and also sustained well the dramatic side of her role."[49] The 1830s were to be her most remarkable years. Having already touched base, as it were, in both the mezzo and soprano repertoires, she essayed in 1834 many remarkable feats aside from the all-important premiere of Donizetti's *Gemma di Vergy*. During 1834, she sang not just her first Norma and Bolena in Rome cheek by jowl with, in Florence, the mezzo roles of the Bellini Romeo and her well-practiced Rossini Desdemona. And 1834 was also the year of a strange version of *Maria Stuarda* produced in October, a little over a year before the Malibran premiere proper, of which more presently. In general, with the many achievements during this decade, Ronzi–De Begnis's career was quite successful, but there were those who were not so enthralled by singing that seemed too self-conscious. For instance, even though Guillaume Cottrau, as already mentioned, acknowledged the worth of Ronzi–De Begnis 's training, he still wrote of her as follows:

> I don't know if I have yet spoken of Madame De Begnis, as I am scarcely one of her fans. I am therefore a lonely exception, not merely amidst her most avid admirers but amidst nearly the entire public at large, because her voice utterly displeases me and her expression always seems a bit far-fetched and, I would say at the same time, too differentiated (you understand?) on every word and practically every note. But I must admit that she is an admirably schooled musician, that she has some taste, and, above all, that she is a very striking figure.[50]

In reading Cottrau's description of Ronzi–De Begnis's "differentiating," one is forcibly reminded of the descriptions of Pasta's "encyclopedic" expressiveness whenever applying some special color to a musical phrase. As with Ronzi–De Begnis's innate instrument, Pasta's too was likewise described as not being intrinsically beautiful. Yet Lord Mount-Edgecumbe claimed that Ronzi's voice was capable of a certain "sweetness" alongside her "flexibility" and her "considerable … taste."[51]

As to the imaginative use to which such an instrument might be put, it seems actually to have been Ronzi–De Begnis's habit of "differentiating," so decried by Cottrau, that attracted Donizetti to her artistry in the first place.

If Ronzi–De Begnis did have good taste, such considerations will always remain among the most frustratingly subjective in the realms of opera and of song. One person's "scrupulous" will always be another observer's "precious," one person's "vulgar" another's "honest," and so on. Even Cottrau seems uncertain, since, while acknowledging Ronzi–De Begnis's taste, he, at the same time, complains of it as if it was already too much of a good thing. We can only believe, though, that excellent musicianship would have been essential for doing justice to the complex vocal writing Donizetti was eventually to compose for Ronzi–De Begnis, and that quality she certainly possessed. In fact, Donizetti is on record as having once written of Ronzi–De Begnis that, at the very least, she had "more going for her (because actually she has the bigger ass ...)" than did Malibran.[52] Finally, when one reads contemporary descriptions, there are always repeated references to the sheer presence, the theatrical flamboyance, that these artists had in person. Evidently, Ronzi–De Begnis, with her "striking figure," was no exception.

We are already indebted to William Ashbrook for attesting to Donizetti's admiration of Ronzi–De Begnis's habit, seemingly reminiscent of Pasta and, perhaps, of one or two others, of giving to "practically every note" a special expression. Ashbrook, in his *Donizetti and his Operas*, points to the unusual vocal writing for the final scene in Donizetti's *Fausta* (1831), the first of the five Ronzi–De Begnis vehicles Donizetti composed for her:

> ... in Fausta's aria-finale, 'Tu che volli già spirto beato'..., not only the sweep of the opening phrases ... but also the sixteenth-note figurations at the words "Te lo chiedo per quanto io t'amato" are accented to produce an alternating effect that fits Cottrau's word ["nuancée" translated as "differentiated"].[53]

The role of Fausta is actually a rather perfunctory role, vocally and musically, until this final scene. Not even these final moments made this opera in any way remarkable, nor did it turn the rather predictable Fausta into anything like an *assoluta* part. The importance of this scene lies rather in its position as the first experiment on Donizetti's part with Ronzi–De Begnis's expressive capabilities. It was a mere hint of things to come rather than a striking achievement in itself. The technical spectrum tapped in this scene stands out from the rest of the score, but it is not true *assoluta* material. Nor was Donizetti's second Ronzi–De Begnis vehicle of 1832, *Sancia di Castiglia*. One detail of some interest, though, was Donizetti's choosing to end this score with an *andante* cabaletta rather than the more traditional *vivace* or *allegro*. This meant ending the opera with an opportunity for Ronzi–De Begnis to spin out unusually long phrases and so to demonstrate her breathing capacity, a choice made again later on in the course of Donizetti's and Ronzi–De Begnis's seven-year collaboration. In addition, the distilled feelings for Sancia's final scene were both more vivid and, at the same time, more subtly worked out than was the case for the ending of *Fausta*.

A step closer toward Ronzi–De Begnis's first *assoluta* part was her participation in a strange and frustrating production in Naples of *Maria Stuarda*. Strictly speaking, it wasn't really *Maria Stuarda* at all. What it was was a premiere of a grotesque concoction mandated by the censors of Naples. This concoction was entitled *Buondelmonte*.

In a way, this may have been indirectly brought about because of the electricity that Ronzi–De Begnis was able to generate on stage. After *Maria Stuarda* as originally written had been in rehearsal a number of weeks, a nasty scene transpired while Ronzi–De Begnis, as Stuarda, and Anna del Sere, as Elisabetta, were running through the confrontation scene between the two queens at the end of the second act. At the point where Ronzi–De Begnis, with her habitually expressive declamation, called her tormentor a bastard child ("vil bastarda"), del Sere was so convinced that Ronzi–De Begnis was going beyond mere acting that she physically attacked her, who then defended herself with even greater ferocity than del Sere had first used. In the upshot, del Sere, and not Ronzi, ended up spending a few days confined to her bed. It is likely that, as a result of this row, the censors actually started getting nervous over the "sensationalism" of the libretto. Their meddling with the work certainly began just around this time (September 1834). At first, they started suggesting all sorts of alterations, and then King Ferdinand of Naples banned *Maria Stuarda* altogether after the dress rehearsal. Meanwhile, before that took place, opening-night nerves were stretched to the breaking point. "Donizetti always shields that common tramp of a del Sere," snapped Ronzi–De Begnis to no one in particular. Unfortunately for her, Donizetti heard. "I shield no one," he said to the startled Ronzi–De Begnis, "the British Queens in our opera were tramps and so are the pair of you." This seems to have shut Ronzi–De Begnis up.[54]

But as soon as the King made his pronouncement, bedlam ensued. In an attempt to salvage some of the music, and perhaps also because Donizetti did not look forward to his *prime donne*'s reactions at being deprived of an important premiere, some other plot/story/text was looked for that could use the *Stuarda* melodies. One was duly found: *Buondelmonte* concerning the feuds between the Guelphs and the Ghibellines. Donizetti, holding his nose and not wishing to trust anyone else, made the drastic rearrangements that were necessary, saw *Buondelmonte* through some pell-mell rehearsals, and, as soon as it was mounted, vowed that only the original *Stuarda* could henceforth be presented in Italy. To Donizetti's intense satisfaction, *Buondelmonte* never again saw the light of day.

As for *Maria Stuarda*, its true 1835 premiere at La Scala took place with Maria Malibran creating the title role. Pasta's great rival, Malibran had made her operatic debut in 1825, and her first and only *assoluta* role was Norma in 1834. Like Pasta, Schroeder-Devrient and Ronzi–De Begnis, Malibran too performed the Bellini Romeo and a number of other mezzo parts as well. She relished alternating high soprano and mezzo-soprano and contralto roles. At the time that she made her debut, she was actually described as a contralto. A singular example of Malibran's versatility was her successfully alternating, in

Rossini's *Semiramide*, the title role with the contralto role, Arsace. Her range of over three octaves seems to have extended from the low D below middle C to the soprano high E. It appears that her instrument did not consist of similarly colored tones throughout its compass. Thus, her upper register sounded very much like a soprano's and afforded a striking contrast to her lowest contralto register. In fact, occasional reference is made to the "dead" notes that she had squarely in the middle of her range, which did not resonate to the same degree as the rest of her voice, and which partook of neither her contralto nor her soprano timbre.[55] She would apparently disguise the insufficiency of these middle notes by embellishments juxtaposing her two "true" voices. Both of these true voices were exceptional, but there is, in a novel by Lady Blessington, a singularly evocative description of Malibran's low that helps explain the amazing effect she had on her hearers: "it arose from an inspired, passionate, and despairing heart, in an intensely profound consciousness of the insufficiency of mortal powers to satisfy the aspirations of an immortal spirit to a release from its earthly trammels."[56] Actually, in such a description, one can't help being reminded of the heartrending effect of Kathleen Ferrier's or Helga Dernesch's lower registers. It seems that it was the haunting, melancholy kind of quality we already associate with these two extraordinary divas of the twentieth century that was customarily expected from the *assoluta* of the 1830s. The shortness of Malibran's career (she died after a riding accident at the age of twenty-eight) precluded her eventually singing all the *assoluta* roles that might otherwise have been hers. But her *Norma* still established her as one of the elect.

In creating Maria Stuarda in 1835, Malibran introduced a role that features a number of the characteristics of an *assoluta*. Its range extends from the low A flat to the high B natural. While it does not have the same degree of recurrent heroic moments that are in the nine roles we are concentrating on, Stuarda does furnish opportunities for emotional communication through the fioritura and the extremes of vocal range that are typical of the true *assoluta* roles. Donizetti even altered some of the passagework for the flamboyant Malibran, allowing her exciting moments of contrast from register to register. These Malibran passages are adopted by Joan Sutherland in her complete recording, while Beverly Sills and the deeply stirring Janet Baker hew more to the original, penetrating more deeply into the character. Olivia Stapp, the only singer to have performed all six women in Donizetti's Tudor trilogy (Bolena, Stuarda, and the *Devereux* Elisabetta along with Giovanna, Elisabetta in *Stuarda*, and Sara), has pointed out that Donizetti, in *Maria Stuarda*, has given us for the two roles of the antagonistic queens, Mary Stuart and Queen Elizabeth, two halves of an *assoluta* role. On the one hand, Stuarda has distinct requirements for the two-octave-plus range of an *assoluta* and for the alternations in tessitura that go with it, though not having her full complement of heroic, declamatory phrases. On the other, Elisabetta requires not even a two-octave range (it only extends from the middle C to the high B), though that range is exploited through shifts in tessitura, along with heroic phrases that, unlike Stuarda's, are comparable to those of the

assoluta. It is in this way that these two roles complement each other in form-
ing an *assoluta* whole.[57]

In the 1834 premiere of Donizetti's improvised adaptation, *Buondelmonte*,
Ronzi–De Begnis had been given a chance for the first time to star in a Donizetti
opera whose music at least displayed the composer's gifts in near top form. As
such, it was clearly a greater challenge than either *Fausta* or *Sancia*. Donizetti
now realized that Ronzi–De Begnis, who would be appearing at La Scala that
December, was ready for a real *assoluta* part, and he immediately furnished her
with *Gemma di Vergy*.

In a *New York Times* interview in 1976, Montserrat Caballé made a crucial
comment that was eventually to launch this author on the present survey.
Caballé, having already sung Norma at the Metropolitan and elsewhere, and
recalling Lilli Lehmann's oft-quoted comment that one Norma was the equivalent of three Brünnhildes, made the fascinating statement that one Gemma was
equal to three Normas. Upon being asked why, she stated from her experience
singing the role that the *passaggio*, that tricky part of the voice where the mid-
range and the upper register meet, was much more ruthlessly exposed in
Gemma's music than in Norma's. She was not casting doubt on the vocal
supremacy of Bellini's *Norma* with respect to its position in today's operatic
repertoire. Rather, she was invoking the justly revered role of Norma precisely
in order to put the staggering vocal requirements of the rarely performed Gemma
into proper perspective.

Donizetti did not bring to *Gemma* the musical consistency he had brought
to *Maria Stuarda*, and to the opera that, however flawed, gave him his first taste
of Ronzi–De Begnis's full potential, *Buondelmonte*. His unevenness in *Gemma*
may have been partly due to its clumsy two-act libretto by Emanuele Bidera.
Thus, it is easy to understand why *Gemma* has not remained a staple of the
repertoire. The title role, with its by now customary *assoluta* range from low B
flat to high C, is full of incredibly difficult vocal and technical contrasts and
almost impossible to cast. The entire opera as a work does not really take off
until the second act. The characters, including Gemma herself, give one few surprises in either their basic actions or their emotional development.

One is still grateful for many of the peaks in Act II, particularly the affecting final scene. In sheer vocal terms, this sequence brings together many of the
assoluta characteristics separately displayed at other moments throughout the
opera. While some of Gemma's earlier scenes have occasional arbitrary or over-
repetitive contrasts, the final scene does not misfire, dramatically or musically.

Ronzi–De Begnis, in premiering *Gemma* in 1834, was given her first opportunity to capitalize on her full vocal potential. Thus, its title role had to be more
taxing than any other *assoluta* role yet composed, notwithstanding the extreme
difficulties in *Anna Bolena*'s final scene. In fact, Ronzi–De Begnis had just triumphed in a Rome *Bolena* earlier that year, but the staggering technical accomplishment embodied in Ronzi–De Begnis's creation of Gemma was unprecedented.
No diva ever before had sung music with such constant extremes, and she helped

launch *Gemma di Vergy* on a successful run of twenty-six performances during which she does not appear to have shown any signs of fatigue.

Gemma's final sequence contains a greater portion of the technical ingredients in the character's music than any other scene in the opera. It particularly depends, in the way it was written, on the vocal expression and staying power of an extraordinary singer. In the hands of a great interpreter, the finale can be quite effective.

Gemma, having failed to give her husband, the Conte di Vergy, any children, has had their marriage anulled by him behind her back so that he may marry Gemma's rival, Ida. Having tried by both gentle and extreme means to gain back her husband, including a thwarted attempt to kill Ida, Gemma, in the last scene, has come to the very church where her former husband is now marrying her rival.

Tamas, Gemma's unrequited suitor, has just left, secretly intending to kill the Count. Gemma, unaware of his plan, finds relief in being near the church and in being alone. In a passage beginning with the words, "Eccomi sola alfine," Gemma offers up a prayer. In sharp contrast to her previous agitated scene with Tamas, her vocal line here is sinuous and graceful and seems to express, in its lyrical use of the *passaggio*, a sense of repose lacking elsewhere. One can sense that her volatility up to now has exhausted her, almost as if her only chance to escape from herself is in escaping the company of others. The prayer, in its projection of sudden calm, requires not just a resilient upper register but an unusually long breath. When thoughts of what is going on inside that church overtake her, the nature of the vocal line is altered. In the passage, "Da quel tempio fuggite," she calls down a curse on the bride and groom in music that requires a darker, heavier tone than the prayer. Heroic flexibility, with an energetic instrumental accompaniment, marks this curse, as the vocalist must constantly dip down into her low register. Yet, long as some of these phrases are, there is a percussive element to individual notes that is nowhere hinted at in the prayer, causing their musical effect to be fragmented. As Gemma realizes she is having a dangerous burst of vituperation, her low B flat on "... bro" of "labbro" signals the horrified end of this mood. With the cavatina that follows, "Un altare ed una benda," her religious feelings are tied, for the first time, to a mood of regret and genuine forgiveness. Her character's total transformation is as compelling as it is startling: her singing adopts a lyrical use of the high and also the low register. This softer use of the low is as pervasive as her heroic use of the low in the curse. She wishes nothing for herself but a cloister in which to end her days. A quiet cadenza and low B flat on "pen ..." of "pensier" concludes this elaborate three-part sequence of prayer, curse, and cavatina.

At this point, Gemma's private thoughts are interrupted by a tumult coming from the church. Tamas rushes on to the stage, and, in front of all, he tells Gemma it was for her sake, to relieve her suffering, that he has just killed the Count! But Tamas suddenly realizes that Gemma does not see the murder as an act of love, and he kills himself.

Gemma, feeling the eyes of the world on her, and recalling the intemperate curse she laid on both her former husband and his new bride, tries to persuade herself in the concluding *da capo* aria, "Chi m'accusa," that she is free from guilt of her husband's murder. Featuring intricate flourishes at the conclusion of both sections, this aria exploits both the flexibility and the strength of the upper register as Gemma shows that her love even now for the murdered Count makes it impossible that she could in any way have condoned Tamas's action. Gemma's desperate longing for her own death concludes the opera.

Gemma di Vergy established itself immediately in its own time because its title role was such an inviting *tour de force* for exceptional *prime donne*. Some superb divas from the next generation as well, more associated with Verdi than Donizetti, also essayed the part, but by that time there had been significant changes in casting practices that will be dealt with in greater detail when we get to Verdi.

Gemma on disc

Montserrat Caballé is the only artist available in this role. Columbia issued her 1976 concert presentation commercially. This was at Carnegie Hall and featured Luis Lima as Tamas, Louis Quilico as the Count and Paul Plishka as Guido. Eve Queler conducts.

Caballé is often lax with words through much of this performance. Moreover, a sameness takes over the interpretation. Granted, this is partly because of Gemma as a character, but she develops in the last act from fury to despair to forgiveness, and this is not altogether reflected in Caballé's singing.

More engaged is Caballé's earlier "live" broadcast from the Teatro San Carlo in Naples. The other singers at Naples are superior, and perhaps more exciting principals sparked a greater involvement in its protagonist. Giorgio Lamberti is heard as Tamas, Renato Bruson as the Count and Mario Rinaudo as Guido. The conductor is Armando Gatto. This has been put out by Myto.

At the outset, we have a *pianissimo* flourish on "sonno" that is exquisite. This is one of those occasions when Caballé can offer a real trill. As icing on the cake, she gives another fine *pianissimo* flourish on "io mescerò" at the conclusion of the opening *scena*. She also knows when to project a heightened sense of urgency: "Oh che favelli tu?" at the start of her encounter with Guido bristles with impatience. With all her flamboyance, she is scrupulous with the agility in the music. The deft passagework at "della mia mente" is particularly effective. Unfortunately, her fury at being told of the Count's intentions to remarry causes an unsteady moment on "ah no," and she ends her first scene by dropping out for several notes to recoup for an effective climax.

Her next scene and the trio "Un suo sguardo" is marked by more expert passagework sung in her trademark *pianissimo*. She offers a fine *diminuendo* to introduce "Di ch'io vada," a solo which soars easily over the whole ensemble. She rings down the curtain with a superb delivery of the opening solo for the final ensemble, "La sposa, la sposa."

In Act II, one becomes aware of increasingly unclear sound quality in the recording. The overall ambience seems more distant than most of Act I. We can still appreciate what Caballé is doing, and the fainter sound does not preclude the listener's relishing her singing, since the general sound is more than adequate, even at the end. But the change in quality is puzzling.

In Act II, Scene 2, Caballé is entirely warmed up. Her voice's ease throughout its range is breathtaking. Her leaps down to the low register in a phrase like "ragion del forte," when holding her rival hostage at knife-point, seem effortless. Other typically wide-ranging moments like "L'indissolubil laccio" are also excellent. This scene climaxes on a ringing top note that fuses clarity and strength.

It is heartening to hear Caballé in her final scene impart similar strength to individual words, "mentisci" or "proferir": ... "io sarò morta" is rendered with a sob. And her vocalism hews to the same high standards of the previous scenes with no apparent fatigue. There is fine control over the passagework at "Quanto amor s'accese in me," for example. It is also startling to hear "Ah sii pietoso; Se non parto, se qui resto" rendered in one long breath. In her grand *scena* and prayer, the beauty of the falling words "dovrò" or "di Dio" linger long after. We sense her indignation when intimations of her curse on the wedding couple start to appear at "insieme." Once the curse does appear in its full force, the impact is overwhelming: whenever a word coincides with an emphatic chord in the orchestra, Caballé digs into its opening vowel with force, carrying her expansive tones right down to low B flat on "labbro." The orchestra is suddenly hushed at that point, when horror overcomes her at what she has just uttered. This is transformed into true remorse, with a "Gemma è di Dio" that is soft and moving. Her long breath does not desert her in the prayer as she links a previous phrase to "Non ti turbi." This prayer peaks with an elaborate cadenza launched piano and then swelled as she moves back down the scale. A minute of frenzied applause greets this *tour de force*, the finest moment in the opera. Serenity is abandoned when Caballé desperately sings the cabaletta after Tamas has killed her faithless husband and then stabbed himself. This feverish quality emerges effectively, although she seems to slack off in the concluding third of the first statement. The second time, however, she gives a more forceful delivery of "Moglie infame" and "Ma di me." Again she seems to coast right before the final notes, but the climax itself is excellent. The close ends up amazingly strong and helps put the seal on one of the most ambitious challenges of Caballé's career.

❧ 10 ❧

Donizetti
(1797–1848):
Roberto Devereux

If there is any such thing as the very peak of a genre, or if one subscribes to the notion that the development of an art form describes a parabola with its apex and its descent, then there is validity for claiming that Donizetti's *Roberto Devereux*, with its extraordinary writing for the role of Queen Elizabeth, comes at the very peak of the *assoluta* genre. It was the last role of this sort actually composed by one of the three main *bel canto* composers of the early nineteenth century (Rossini, Bellini, Donizetti), and it was Donizetti's last great success in Italy before establishing himself successfully in France and Vienna.

Introduced in Naples on October 28, 1837, the ingredients associated with *Roberto Devereux* augured well for the dramatic concision of Donizetti's music: notably, a libretto by Salvatore Cammarano, influenced partly by a Romani libretto for Mercadante; the assumption by Ronzi–De Begnis of the *assoluta* part in a Donizetti premiere, and the superior quality of the characterization on which the plot was based, the familiar story of Queen Elizabeth I and Robert Devereux, Earl of Essex. As for the music itself, the balance achieved here by Donizetti between the lyrical and declamatory singing required for Queen Elizabeth was an epitome of the ideal for an *assoluta*. The pacing of the emotional temperature in the Elizabeth scenes was marked by an artistically perfect equilibrium. In accomplishing this, the expressiveness and vivid nature of Donizetti's music stayed at an inspired level throughout the work. As with Gemma, Elisabetta also had some declamatory phrases placed squarely in the *passaggio*, which required the resiliency mandated in Gemma's music. Elisabetta was also the last role to contain the kind of concentrated scene that, like Bolena's last moments, included all the technical characteristics that made up the ingredients of the *assoluta* role.

Unlike Bolena, though, Queen Elizabeth's biggest scene falls exactly in the middle of her role and not at its conclusion. Also, this scene concentrates more on the heroic aspects than did Bolena's similar scene. Finally, all of Elisabetta's scenes require, in their unusual length and emotional concentration, the kind of vocal stamina that was ordinarily expected of the *assoluta* in only one or two scenes per opera — another distinguishing mark of this role that set it apart from all the others.

At Queen Elizabeth's, or Elisabetta's, entrance in the opera's opening scene, she is shown in an inwardly troubled mood. Since she is confiding to a very close friend, Sara, Duchess of Nottingham, her fondest hopes that Essex would renew his affection for her, the vocal stance here is not exactly heroic, but it is certainly wide-ranging. The Queen is momentarily expecting Essex's arrival for a special audience that she has granted him upon the persuasion of Sara's husband, Nottingham.

There is more than a suggestion in the Queen's opening recitative that she would gladly have granted Essex an audience, but was anxious not to appear too willing. She confesses her fears that Essex might now love another and tells Sara of the charge of treason brought against Essex. The cavatina, "L'amor suo," uses contrasting registers in a contained way. The Queen is first describing her contentment during her early days with Essex, and then reflects on what little meaning life holds for her without him. Intricate flourishes using the upper half of the voice and going up to high B flat, and a series of three trills in both the upper and lower half of the voice, the lowest trill being at A natural above middle C, mark the parameters of this aria. The phrase with the trills is on the words "Le delizie della vita" (The pleasures of life) where Elisabetta is describing how painful such things would be if Essex were to betray her. In encompassing more than one register of the voice, her trills may, in this context, express an ambiguity that epitomizes the gloom that is clouding over what was once a sense of hope and purpose. Whatever resiliency in her character is being expressed here, the implied hopefulness conveyed by using only the flexibility of a lower range evaporates, as we shall see, in the second act. (In place of the taxing trills, Donizetti offered a second option of three descending scales instead, one of which starts at high B flat.)

Though a deputation from the Lords following her opening aria establishes Essex's clear guilt, and their right as peers of the realm to pronounce final judgment on him, the Queen is adamant that not enough proof has been presented and is overjoyed when Essex's approach is announced.

On anticipating their first meeting in such a long time, Elisabetta, in a cabaletta reminiscent of Norma's first-act one, sings her own: "Ah! ritorna qual ti spero" (Ah! return as I hope), with the radiantly voiced wish that she and

Essex might once again be as they were. Elisabetta's aria here has an even higher tessitura than Norma's cabaletta to the "Casta Diva." Elisabetta now sings some intricate coloratura, reaching above high B flat for the first time to hit six high Cs. She will sing another high C later on in Act II, but the role never goes higher than that. Two of the high Cs in this Act I cabaletta climax a repeated series of eight syncopated high Bs, recalling those in "Casta Diva," though used here in an *allegro* to express Elisabetta's forgiveness of Essex if he is but willing to return to her now, "innocente sei per me" (for me you are innocent).

Upon Essex's arrival, Queen Elizabeth dismisses all the lords, ladies, attendants, etc., and learns that his "treason" has been the result of too much leniency with the already surrendered Irish rebels. The Queen assures Essex of her royal protection and reminds him of the ring he is wearing, which represented a token for him to send her any time he was in danger. She promises that presenting the ring at any time will still guarantee his deliverance from peril.

Elisabetta then launches into a duet with Essex with a lilting solo, "Un tenero core" (A tender heart). This solo uses the *passaggio* in much the same way that Gemma's prayer did in her last scene. It also heightens the impression that the Queen's sense of life and hope is bound up with the feelings that once existed between them. Vocally, a bright upper register is required here, as she sadly reminds Essex of their happy past and their vanished dream of love ("sogno d'amore").

In the duet's transitional section, Essex continues to talk vaguely of his duty to his sovereign. Elizabeth, exasperated now, traps him by talking of "a certain heart here at court that beats for you." When Essex accidentally blurts out a simple "Then you know," Elizabeth's worst suspicions are confirmed. The Queen demands, as his sovereign, that Essex reveal the name of the woman he loves. Immediately, Essex withdraws back into his shell, but, having let down his guard, it is too late.

His abrupt denial of any amorous intentions toward another woman, after having practically admitted her existence, goads Elisabetta into her first heroic coloratura music as she sings the solo "Un lampo, un lampo orribile" (A horrible glimpse) that opens the final *vivace* of Elisabetta's and Essex's duet. Frustrated, in an aside, over not knowing the name of her rival, the Queen realizes that, whoever the woman is, she will surely be punished if the faithless Essex is condemned to death. Gone are Elisabetta's magnanimous thoughts of "Ah ritorna." Now she longs only for revenge. Not only is this coloratura quite intricate, the instrumental accompaniment is, for the first time, emphatic as well. The tessitura of this solo once more entails much upper-register singing as the *passaggio* is now used heroically. A few more feeble protestations from Essex, and the duet ends with the Queen finally sweeping out. This last sequence made such an effect at Aix-en-Provence with Montserrat Caballé as Elisabetta that the applause was prolonged enough for Caballé to come back on stage and make a solo bow before the music could resume.

The second act, and Elisabetta's second scene, is the heart of the work. It is here that the final confrontation between the protagonists leading to Essex's royal condemnation takes place. Other crucial elements of the plot have already been made clear to the listener by the time the Queen's wrath is unleashed. Most important, the listener is now aware that the Queen's rival is actually Sara, the very Duchess of Nottingham whose husband assisted in bringing about a royal audience for Essex. That husband, the Duke of Nottingham, has been helping Essex out, clearly unaware of the latter's affection for his wife. Unfortunately, due to the Queen's compelling her, Sara has been constrained to marry Nottingham during Essex's absence in Ireland. It is obvious that Essex and Sara have been in love for a long time, before there were any thoughts of marriage with Nottingham. Yet, during Essex's time away, the only effective way open to Sara of preventing the Nottingham marriage was that of confessing her love for Essex — a course that would have had disastrous consequences for all concerned. Therefore, Sara has had to allow herself to go through with the Nottingham marriage. After his troubled audience with the Queen in Scene I, Essex has a sad reunion with Sara in Scene II. They both regret their lost happiness. As a last love token, Essex gives Sara the ring Elisabetta gave him and Sara gives Essex a special scarf that she has made for him. Nottingham has previously told Essex in all innocence that he was troubled to observe his wife quietly weeping alone while holding the scarf in her hands.

As the second act opens, we learn that the Queen, restless and silent, has been awaiting word on the trial. She receives Lord Cecil with the news that Essex has been given the death sentence. Nottingham, still Essex's friend, has been chosen to hand it to the Queen to sign. He is expected momentarily. Before Nottingham's arrival, Raleigh tells the Queen of having caught Essex returning to his palace at dawn. He also tells her of an attempt to search Essex's person for incriminating papers, but what has been found instead is a strange scarf that occasioned a struggle as Raleigh's men took it from Essex. He then hands the scarf to the Queen, and she immediately suspects the worst. "Ho mille furie in petto" (A thousand furies are within me), she sings, and Nottingham then sadly comes in with the unsigned death sentence.

All of the foregoing is recitative, but, upon Nottingham's entrance, a measured *larghetto* duet is struck and Nottingham asks that Elisabetta not sign the death warrant. He is answered, in Elisabetta's similarly measured reply, "In questo core" (in this heart), by a cold assurance that, as she has obtained incontrovertible evidence of Essex's betrayal, she shall now send him to his death. The portentous phrases sung here suggest the same dense vocal production in the low of Norma's recitative, "Sediziose voci," and her "In mia man." The apparently powerful sound Ronzi–De Begnis used in interpreting the lower-lying passages of the Bellini Romeo, for instance, was evidently meant to be used here as Elisabetta announces her conviction of Essex's faithlessness. Of course, Nottingham is horrified and attempts to dissuade Elisabetta from her course, insisting that she has heard unreliable stories put out by Essex's enemies. But the Queen only becomes more peremptory. The two halves of their duet serve to overlap Elisabetta's first use, in the *larghetto* section, of the full heaviness of her lower range with one of her last uses of its flexibility in the brisk conclusion. Her loss is thus prefigured in a heavy low before rallying to flexibility at the conclusion. Insisting that there can be no further discussion of the evidence she has received, Elisabetta then launches into the intricate vocal writing, "Taci: pietade o grazia" (Silence: pity or mercy), where she declares that it is pointless even to attempt Essex's defense. During this final section of their duet, Elisabetta must dip down to five middle Cs.

When Essex arrives for final sentencing, he is greeted by the Queen's sardonic recitative and an elaborate *terzetto*. Within this *terzetto*, Donizetti brilliantly delineates Elisabetta's feelings. The sequence is made up of some of the most vivid vocal pyrotechnics ever composed. It embraces all of Elisabetta's heroic requirements, featuring not just the most taxing but also the most inspired music in this rewarding *assoluta* role. From only the greatest operatic composers have come a select handful of happy inspirations that by their perfection serve to vindicate the all-too-frequently overblown art of opera itself. Such concentrated sequences would be the entire dawn scene involving Lensky's and Onegin's duel in Tchaikovsky's *Eugen Onegin*, the Siegmund/Sieglinde duet in Wagner's *Die Walküre*, or the dungeon scene in Beethoven's *Fidelio*. The list goes on, but the *terzetto* in the second act of *Roberto Devereux* clearly belongs with this special group. Donizetti, in an intangible way peculiar to genius, has managed, along with these other composers, to impart unusual concentration and focus, to make the emotional crises especially vivid and individualized rather than generalized and pretentious.

Elisabetta now taunts Essex with his cravenness in not telling her he loved another woman. This recitative is followed by a heroic coloratura solo, "Un perfido, un vile" (A traitor, a coward), in which the Queen completely loses control and calls Essex a worthless, dishonorable man whose treachery is plain to see, and she shows him the scarf given her by Raleigh. The instrumentation here is as insistent as at the conclusion of the first-act duet, while the coloratura writing is as intricate as it is heroic. It may even be possible that the wide-ranging passagework at the words "Del tuo mendacio/Il muto accusatore" (The silent accuser of your deceit) is an inspired variation on Armida's fioritura climaxing her fury at Rinaldo. Rossini's opera had, in fact, just been revived at La Scala the previous year (1836) after a long hiatus from the Italian stage. At any rate, "Un perfido" marks the last point in Elisabetta's role at which the full degree of florid intricacy is called for. Thus, from this point on, not merely is the low, following the Nottingham duet, no longer used for agility, but now the entire range, or whole vocal persona, becomes less resilient. When Elisabetta pulls out the scarf, she ends the solo with a series of sustained middle F sharps against the insistent instrumentation and against the exclamations of Essex and Nottingham. Again, this new strong lower register introduced at the beginning of the Nottingham duet is required.

Essex is startled by the scarf, but it is Nottingham who is more deeply hurt, since he recognizes it as the one Sara had been secretly holding when he glimpsed her weeping. He now realizes that its discovery on Essex's person, the man he thought his friend, can only mean that Sara has been unfaithful to him. Nottingham, though, cannot outwardly accuse Essex in front of the Queen for fear of what might happen to Sara for daring to be the Queen's successful rival.

Gathering herself together, Elisabetta solemnly tells Essex, in a powerful *largo*, "Alma infida" (Unfaithful soul), that he would have been more fortunate buried alive than facing the wrath of a child of Henry the Eighth. This is the lowest-lying moment of her entire role, and the one that seems to call for the darkest tone production of all. This twenty-one bar solo has two middle Cs, and, for the first and only time in the role, Elisabetta's vocal line here goes down to low B and low B flat. There are two low B flat's, the first of them in the phrase characterizing Henry the Eighth. When she sings "dal tremendo ottavo Enrico" (of the awesome Henry VIII), there is a properly awesome arpeggio at "… mendo" of "tremendo" going from high B flat to middle D on "… men …" and hitting low B flat on "… do." The second low B flat comes at the end of the solo when she sings its last two words, "O traditor." Here, the low B flat is on "O." As in *Médée*, *Bolena*, and *Norma*, the conspicuous use of the low B flat, the lowest note ever reached by Elisabetta, in such a context seems to function dramatically to highlight the point of no return.

In addition to the technical hurdles associated with this sudden use of the lowest register, Elisabetta must also sing one staggeringly drawn-out phrase in the *largo*'s second half running five measures.

When Essex and Nottingham join to turn this section into a full-fledged trio, Nottingham expresses horror at Essex's cuckolding him while Essex, seeing Nottingham's realization of the truth written on his face, expresses terror, not for himself but for Sara's safety.

For the coda to the trio, Elisabetta joins in, and she soars over the ever-swelling orchestral accompaniment and the combined voices of Essex and Nottingham to sustain her final high C of the entire role against this full ensemble. After this moment, Elisabetta never again touches the extreme top of her extensive range.

This concludes the most striking sequence in any *assoluta* role.

In the *materia di mezzo* preceding the second-act finale, Nottingham breaks out in a rage at Essex, but to shield Sara, he has to pretend his anger is purely directed at the insult Essex has given the Queen. Elizabeth, deeply impressed with Nottingham's zeal, realizes she is not ready to accept Essex's death. In a futile effort to recall Essex to her side, she tells him his life will be spared if he names her rival. Now it is Nottingham's turn to feel terror. But Essex, to Nottingham's relief, has no wish to involve Sara and defiantly bids the Queen sign the death sentence. Livid now, the Queen summons the entire court and, in full view of everyone, signs it with the announcement that the execution will take place at noon. The moment of death will be known by the cannon shot fired the second Essex is beheaded.

Then begins the *stretta* of the second-act finale, "Va, la morte." This consists of an overwhelming surge of rhythmic energy, launched by sweeping phrases from Elisabetta. The sheer vocal range these phrases require is considerable, though their overall tessitura is centered very much in the upper half of the voice, and the use of the *passaggio* here is easily as heroic as in the cabaletta to the first-act duet. The requirements for flexibility, though not so intricate as in "Un perfido, un vile," are just as heroic, and the phrases must be sustained against just as energetic an orchestra and ensemble.

In this ensemble, Nottingham, though relieved at Essex's refusal to name Sara, is by no means appeased and, in fact, finds the headsman's block all too inadequate as a personal revenge. Like the final ensemble of the first act of *Anna Bolena*, this *Devereux* finale consists of two statements of the same melody and a coda. When Joan Sutherland performed Bolena, she embellished the *da capo* of the Act I finale, and it brought down the house. It is probable that Ronzi–De Begnis too, famous for her roulades, made a strong effect with her ornamentation when she sang the *da capo* of the *Devereux* Act II finale at Naples in 1837. Finally, in the coda, Elisabetta must sing out, in full voice and above the entire ensemble, a succession of thirteen high As and two high B flats.

As the reader has perhaps noticed, not only is this act comprehensive in its embracing of every heroic vocal effect of Elisabetta's role, it also helps highlight a structural aspect of the role that Donizetti sculpted with incomparable skill: a meticulously constructed crossroads at which certain aspects of Elisabetta's character are laid to rest forever and certain others are developed to be further explored in the final act. There is the profound shift in the prevailing manner in which the lower range is used, epitomized in her last use of a flexible low in "Un perfido" and in her use of a heavy low when showing Essex the scarf in the phrases immediately following. There is also the final collapse of energy in Elisabetta's character that Donizetti conveyed musically through the agility epitomized for the last time in the fioritura for "Un perfido, un vile," and the last high C at the conclusion of the trio. For the reader, this transformation is quite evident in the chart provided in this chapter.

The question is sometimes asked, whenever a consistent structural aspect is seen in any dramatic masterpiece, whether or not the composer is conscious of it while creating. In this case, it would seem probable that Donizetti's awareness of the intricacies of the form actually made his structuring of the Queen's transformation a matter of deliberate artistic choice.

The last scene of the final act concerns the Queen's remorseful hope that Essex may yet send the ring that would be her warranty for excusing him from execution. She is even ready to allow Essex to live with someone else. For her, anything now is preferable to the thought of him being put to death. Cecil then brings word that Essex is being conducted to the place of execution and, furthermore, that Essex has not given him any special token to be passed on to the Queen. But the ring does eventually arrive. Sara brings it, confesses to being the unknown rival, and desperately implores Elisabetta to stop the execution. The Queen appears willing to ignore Sara's confession for the moment and, upon receipt of the ring, sends immediately to stop the execution. The cannon shot announces that she is too late. Nottingham then tells Elisabetta exultantly that he forcibly restrained Sara from approaching her in time with the ring so that he could have his own personal revenge. Elisabetta promptly places both Nottingham and Sara under arrest, and they are led away while the courtiers reproach Elisabetta for ruling for the sake of herself alone, rather than for the sake of the throne. To the accompaniment of the same reproaches, the opera concludes with Elisabetta's tormented, conscience-ridden hallucinations of Essex's ghost ranging about the court, and with her despairing wish that James VI of Scotland be made King of England.

This scene just described is, vocally, not quite as taxing as the second act, but there is still a requirement for vocal stamina and staying power. Her magnanimous hope that Essex can simply live in peace with someone else is expressed in a lyrical, poignant cavatina, "Vivi, ingrato" (Live, ungrateful one). Despite two unusual phrases here, where the vocal line extends first from high A down to middle D sharp and then from high A down to middle D natural, and even despite this aria's somber ending on still another middle D natural, the prevailing tessitura of this lyrical aria is nevertheless fairly high. Overall, the single most important requirement in the aria is very long breath control. Some of the phrases are upwards of four or five measures, and there is one, at the words, "m'abbando ..." (the aria's one high B natural is on "... do ...") "... na in eterno a sospirar" (let me be abandoned to sigh forever), that extends in an endless musical sigh for six measures.

When Nottingham has exulted in his vengeful restraint of Sara, we are ready for Elisabetta's final cabaletta, "Quel sangue versato" (That spilled blood). As in *Sancia di Castiglia*, Ronzi De-Begnis's last cabaletta here was not the traditional lively vocalise. Rather, "Quel sangue versato" is marked *maestoso* and features some extraordinarily long phrases. They are even more portentous than in the opening to the second-act duet with Nottingham, and here we see the fulfillment of the use of a heavy low. In fact, "Quel sangue versato" is as heroic and terrifying as its preceding cavatina is lyrical and hopeful. In this final *maestoso*, there are the most abrupt shifts imaginable from register to register. Twice, for instance, the singer must skip beyond an octave jump from the middle C sharp up to the E below high C. There are, also, heroic coloratura flourishes at the conclusion of both statements. Their degree of intricacy doesn't match that displayed, for the last time, in the second act. The energetic orchestral accompaniments, though, are fully the equal of those for the first-act duet and for "Un perfido, un vile." The first statement deals with Elisabetta's ruthless condemnation of Nottingham and Sara, the second with her sudden, conscience-stricken vision of Essex's ghost and of the disintegration of the throne. Since the same melody is sung in both main statements, the fact that it is sung to other words in the second statement necessarily entails the kind of "differentiating" Ronzi–De Begnis was known for. Not only is vocal shading of the most telling kind called for, different sentiments in the aria's second half demand that *da capo* ornamentation, of the type promulgated by the Bonynges, be strictly applied here as well. Only then can this "mad scene" for Elisabetta be tellingly contrasted, on a musical level, with her haughty sentencing of Nottingham and Sara. In the second statement, the words "Ov'era il mio trono s'innalza una tomba, in quella discendo, fu schiusa per me" (Where my throne once was there now rises a tomb; in that tomb I descend, it's been opened for me) are phrased in the score so as to be sung without breath for a staggering total of seven measures. On the final "me," Elisabetta sings a high B natural marked *ff*. For the coda, in which Elisabetta longs for the accession of the Scottish king, heroic phrases are sung against the full ensemble and the instrumental accompaniment. These closing measures contain six high As, one high B flat, and one high B natural.

So, in assessing these ingredients, we have in the *Devereux* Elisabetta that uncanny balance between the horrifying and the beautiful that was present in Médée's music; that well-wrought musical expressiveness which was in Reiza's; that dramatic concision which was in Bolena's, and even more constant demands for vocal stamina than were in Norma's. If summing up an art form means giving it its finest achievement, then Donizetti's *Roberto Devereux* must be regarded as the greatest dramatic music ever devised as a vehicle for an *assoluta*, displaying the ultimate potential of a classically trained diva's voice, musicianship, and technique.

At least one important Norma and Bolena of the past century, Beverly Sills, has stated that, despite a similar alternation between the upper and lower registers in *Anna Bolena*, *Norma*, and *Devereux*, Elisabetta has a more frequently heroic use of that upper half. With Sills having singled out *Devereux*, and Caballé having done the same for *Gemma*, we now have two conspicuous *bel canto* specialists remarking on the supreme difficulty of music originally written for Ronzi-De Begnis.

There is yet another aspect to the ferocity of Elisabetta's requirements: as in a geographic map, one is aware of sharply etched contours bracketing distinctive sections. Whether of lyric or heroic passagework, these contrasted sections do not resemble similar maps for other *assoluta* roles; there, we would see both lyric and heroic sections bracketed by less defined margins. They would tend to flow into each other more. For the vocalist, the implications of the sharply delineated structure in *Devereux* are considerable. Most divas cope with heroic sequences by seizing every fleeting opportunity to let up on the vocal pressure. Granted, such "staging areas" may be fleeting, but at least they sometimes are there. Not so in *Devereux*. Here, any heroic sequence can mean fifteen minutes or more of furious non-stop "action." There is less time to prepare the vocal cords, and it's harder for the singer to catch her breath.

Finally, *Roberto Devereux* as a whole is a work equally compelling throughout in that all the "secondary" characters are dramatically explored through music almost as expressive as that for the Queen.

At its 1837 premiere, the triumph this work enjoyed was overwhelming, and the work continued to be regularly featured throughout the remainder of the 1837–38 and subsequent San Carlo seasons. Not until Donizetti was well established in France, a number of years later, was he to savor again so sweet a victory on the lyric stage. *Roberto Devereux* was destined to be the last peak of his Italy years. The opera immediately began its progress through Europe and finally throughout the world. There were performances in Venice (1837–38, with Carolina Ungher), Lisbon (1838), Barcelona (1838), Paris (1838, with Giulia Grisi), Bologna (1838 and 1843, the latter with Giuseppina Strepponi), Havana (1839), The Hague (1840), Brussels (1840 and 1842), Pressburg (1840), Corfu (1840), Rouen (1841), Budapest(1841), Malta (1841), Odessa (1841), Berlin (1841), London (1841, with Grisi again), Lugano (1841), Copenhagen (1841), Mexico (1842), Athens (1842), St. Petersburg (1843 and 1845, the latter with Pauline Viardot-García), Smyrna (1843), Vienna (1844), Constantinople (1845), Corsica (1847), New York (1849), Agram (1852), Buenos Aires (1854), and so on. The last nineteenth-century revival was at Pavia in 1882.

It is always a risky proposition to draw biographically derived inferences from the emotional impact of a dramatic masterpiece. And yet, in the case of *Roberto Devereux*, there is such a vivid sense of trauma and loss in the music that the coincidence that Donizetti was experiencing the most tragic loss of his life inevitably invites some attention. This involved the double bereavement of the death of his newly-born child on June 13, 1837, and the illness and death of his wife of nine years, Virginia Vasselli, on July 30.

Unlike many other Donizetti operas, it is actually difficult to ascertain the exact weeks during which Donizetti was composing *Devereux*, for he abandoned his correspondence during Virginia Vasselli's final illness. We do know that *Devereux* was started no earlier than February 1837, and finished no later than September 1837. Thus, the work was brought into being during the very time that Donizetti saw his wife die. As he set about preparing *Devereux* for rehearsal, he was clearly referring to the loss of Vasselli when he wrote of the task in hand and of his new work, "this will be the opera of my emotions."[58]

His immediate response to her loss was so severe there was even fear of suicide on the part of others who persuaded him to move into a friend's house in order to "escape at least for a little from these scenes, from this furniture, from these stairs." At his friend's, he did not even move out of the bed provided him for about a week. When he eventually did, his friend Guillaume Cottrau kindly wrote his letters for him, to one of which Donizetti appended a short P.S. "I am a widower. Nothing more. Pray for her. Farewell. Donizetti." Back home, Donizetti always kept the door to Virginia's bedroom closed, and apparently it was never again opened during his lifetime.[59]

At the moment of crisis in Elisabetta's final cabaletta, as the cruel reality of a future without Essex has begun to sink in, she sings a somber series of middle F sharps to the words "non regno, non vivo" (I don't reign, I don't live). These two phrases are marked *maestoso* in the score and require the portentous sounds in the lower register associated with the second-act Nottingham duet, and also with their expression of hopelessness in any future existence. One may

ROBERTO DEVEREUX

ACT	SELECTION	1 FLEXIBLE LOW	2 INTRICATE COLORATURA	3A ABOVE HIGH B	OR 3B BELOW LOW B	4 LONG SEQUENCES	5 FLEXIBLE HIGH	6 HEROIC COLORATURA	7 HEROIC TONE	8 HEAVY LOW
I	Duchessa									
	L'amor suo	X	X			X	X			
	Nunzio son					X				
	Ah! ritorna		X	X		X	X			
	Donna reale					X				
	Un tenero core					X	X			
	Un lampo		X			X	X	X	X	
II	Ebben?					X				
	Non venni mai					X				
	In questo core		X			X			X	X
	Taci: pietade o grazia	X				X				
	Ecco l'indegno!					X				
	Un perfido	X	X			X	X	X	X	X
	Alma infida				X	X	X		X	X
	Scender vivo			X		X	X		X	
	Scellerato!					X				
	Va, la morte					X	X	X	X	
III	E Sara					X				
	Vivi, ingrato					X	X			
	Che m'apporti?					X				
	Quel sangue versato					X	X	X	X	X

Sequence where all assoluta elements are concentrated

choose to regard these sentiments as merely conventional within their context, yet it is possible they exerted a profound impact on Donizetti in connection with Virginia's final days. Not only is this moment an extraordinarily powerful one in the composer's musical setting, but Donizetti, in a bitter letter written later telling of his sense of loss, seems to be making reference to the words by Cammarano that he had set so tellingly. In November 1837, while composing *Maria de Rudenz*, he wrote to Virginia's grief-stricken brother of his feelings while bending over an unfinished score, "For whom do I work? Why? I am alone on earth. Can I live?"[60] This linking of an expression of bewilderment in the face of one's vocation, his "work" and Elisabetta's "reign," with one of desperation in the face of one's very existence, "Can I live" in the letter and "I don't live" in the aria, is uncanny at the very least, if not actually deliberate.

Donizetti never again would compose so energetic a vehicle for Ronzi–De Begnis's talents and, in fact, never again composed any music for the kind of defining *assoluta* roles that Elisabetta and Bolena are.

Of course, other masterpieces of a different kind were to follow. Donizetti's vocation was not destroyed, though it changed direction. After having used Naples as his artistic center for over a decade, he took the first opportunity following Virginia's death to settle in Paris (1838), to break his ties with Naples once and for all, and to absorb those French operatic traditions he was to master so brilliantly in works like *La Fille du Régiment* (1839) and *Dom Sébastien* (1843).

Though, in this fashion, Donizetti's creativity was eventually revived, his feelings of grief would always be acute, particularly in July. It seems as if this renewal of creative activity in France was a direct result of his bereavement — his way of preserving his sanity for as long as he could. At one point, he even wrote, when admitting that he still felt stricken by the loss, "I am working. ... Music has great power over me." "I would be dead [without it]."[61]

The Virgin Queen on disc

As the peak of the genre, *Roberto Devereux* is likewise the last *assoluta* vehicle to represent a composer at the height of his development. This will contrast sharply with both of Verdi's contributions, which show the younger man still in the process of finding himself, while Donizetti's most characteristic style fuses with the *assoluta* to produce in *Devereux* a masterpiece that can only be accorded its due if performed with implicit trust in the composer's intent: to project human character purely through the vocal line. His knack at this gives him the scope needed to develop certain characters in depth, though leaving others relatively sketchy, simplifying both context and situation. Donizetti depended less on the latter, using it when deemed essential. Character exploration is the essence of the *assoluta*, and why Donizetti is especially gifted at bringing her to life. His masterful experience in the form marks every bar of Elisabetta's music. This is what makes *Devereux* so special and why any valid performance must display the intimate feelings implicit in the music, not just its mechanical difficulties. This opera is the summation of an idea enshrined in a style: the idea that the female voice can express any emotion through a style entailing rigorous application of technical and musical discipline. If emotional communication can be enhanced through elaborate vocal gesture, Donizetti doesn't hesitate to supply it.

There is no doubt that Leyla Gencer "live" in 1964 and at Naples, where the opera was premiered over 125 years earlier, boasts the most appropriate vocal timbre for Elisabetta of all her interpreters on disc. But in addition, she's "top of the line" when it comes to conveying the final wrenching scene, vocally and emotionally.

Overall, I might still take Caballé for the role. She has more suave vocal control and, arguably, a more beautiful sound. In addition, Beverly Sills has the distinction of being the only one with an uncut first scene, every note of its intricate coloratura rendered with impeccable accuracy, where even Caballé and especially Gencer take conspicuous shortcuts.

Nevertheless, Gencer projects more of the Queen's persona than anyone. She may not fully match Sills's command of nuance, but the polarities of the character are clearer, and she conveys a genuine assumption of true royalty in conflict with simple humanity. Her conductor, the highly individual Mario Rossi, is a close collaborator. Although working with an inferior orchestra, the gravity of the drama comes through with him as with nobody else. He may occasionally indulge in unusually distended tempi, even as he will speed up on a possible whim. But there is usually a valid dramatic reason for these shifts. Perhaps, one may indulge the momentary suspicion that necessity, brought about by an inadequately rehearsed orchestra, is occasionally the mother of Rossi's invention. After all, this 1964 performance is the first twentieth-century production of entirely unfamiliar music. Still, such uncertain impressions are more the exception than the rule.

Of Gencer's colleagues, only Piero Cappuccilli's Nottingham is in any way distinguished. Anna Maria Rota's Sara is ungainly in places, while Ruggero Bondino's Devereux is clearly too weak. Like many such performances recorded "live," this one is only available on a variety of fairly obscure CD labels.

At Gencer's entrance, her dark vocal coloring instantly commands attention. Here is an artist able to use Elisabetta's occasional forays into chest voice to expressive advantage. Against that are Gencer's occasional troubles in getting there. Sometimes she is able to swoop down impressively, sometimes the gears fail to mesh and there is some gravel in the tone. In addition, she no longer has the fluency in coloratura of her Bolena six years earlier. None of the three trills are observed at the line "Le delizie della vita" in the opening cavatina, and the cabaletta is badly truncated in the *da capo*. There are some effective *pianissimi*, but the main impression is hit-and-miss. Poorly meshed registers result in some startling glottal attacks as well. The ensuing duet with Devereux shows her in better control, with the nuances better tied to genuine character development.

Gencer may not give the impression of careful preparation as much as deeply affecting sincerity. She allows a rich empathy with the character to carry her through. Her musical instincts are highly developed, making the momentary rough-and-tumble of her improvisatory approach seem a good price for such spontaneity. Unfortunately, the difficult passagework in the coda of the duet's cabaletta trips her up badly, and she drops out entirely for a few measures leaving the inadequate Bondino alone to "face the music."

Things improve by the opening of the second act, when the admirable Cappuccilli becomes Gencer's partner in Elisabetta's duet with Nottingham. Maestro Rossi indulges in some strange tempi here, but most of it makes sense when there are artists like these two demonstrating such conviction. The occasional distentions in tempi may partly be due to a need to accommodate Gencer's inability to navigate passagework beyond certain speeds—the highly ornamented repeat of the line "la sua perfidia e certa" for example. But Rossi balances that with the appropriate surge in tempo here and there, imparting real tension and bite to the sequence. One must be grateful that Gencer and Cappuccilli bring us face-to-face for the first time with the magnificence of Donizetti's rich gifts at vocal characterization. After this, Gencer must face Bondino's Devereux of Essex once more. Although one can't be certain, there is the suspicion that his presence occasionally throws her off. She does not convey the natural sweep so typical of her scene with Nottingham. Of course, the trio with Nottingham and Essex is the most difficult music in the entire role, so nerves may well be at fault here. Her struggles with "Un perfido, un vile" are not pleasant. Even though the downward scales are pretty much intact, the ensuing passagework at "mendacio" and "accusatore" is a mere blur. Even the non-florid "Alma infida," with its rich opportunities for chest voice and its two low B flats, does not match expectations as her registers seem more apart than ever. She recoups for a fair high C in the sweeping ensemble line that follows, but the effect still comes off a bit wild. The stirring finale shows her improved, and one savors the baleful inflections of words like "l'infamia discende." Rossi truncates the coda somewhat, but he brings a great rush of excitement to the concluding measures.

Anyone who has heard Gencer's recreation of Elisabetta's final moments, with librettist Cammarano's merely efficient presentation of the Queen's sense of guilt at having sent Essex to his death, knows how expressively concise and "true" Donizetti's heartfelt music can be.

Gencer vindicates Donizetti's genius in a reading that honors the music. The listener is left in no doubt that here is Donizetti's own outpouring of grief and guilt,[62] as searing as any scene of its kind. Gencer's achievement in this scene is a triumph of both expressive and technical resources. The restlessness she conveys as the final scene opens is transformed into a pitifully trapped desperation for the cavatina. Although there remain fleeting signs of the register breaks, she is in far better control here and rarely unmusical. Granted, the long phrase for "m'abbandono in eterno a sospirar" may not be shaped as indicated in the score. But this moment that seems so like the "endless sigh" it describes has not yet been performed in our time as the single six-measure phrase Donizetti evidently intended. Gencer snatches two extra breaths here while at least preserving the right feelings of anxiety and wistfulness throughout. Maestro Rossi helps by tightening the tempo a bit. Notable is the sudden change of coloring in Gencer's voice when she abruptly addresses Cecil after the cavatina. Once Sara's errand of mercy fails, one can almost taste the Queen's disgust as she attacks Sara with "Tu perversa." Although the final cabaletta is not as disciplined as the cavatina, one can't help feeling that Gencer has correctly judged this sequence in giving it a keening quality, preparing the listener for the desolation of her "Non regno" and "Non vivo" and the stark hallucinations of the final *da capo*. For the latter, Gencer's descents into chest voice rarely miss their mark and are usually molded firmly into the entire phrase. Throughout the *Devereux* discography, it is Gencer's final scene that brings us in closest touch with the greatness of this work.

Montserrat Caballé may not probe as deeply as Gencer, but she sings with more musical authority, although her voice does not bring with it the same innate command. In its way, Caballé's instrument is still imposing, registering most strongly through brilliance and strength. Gencer may come closer to the ambiguous mixture of timbres suggested in contemporary descriptions of Pasta, Ronzi–De Begnis and other *assolutas*, while Caballé's unambiguously soprano coloring combines a beauty and a sheen more associated with the traditional dramatic/heroic sound. Perhaps, if Gencer's timbral ambiguity ties in with what we suppose was the actual Ronzi sound, then Caballé's effortlessness ties in more closely with the easy delivery that Ronzi–De Begnis was so celebrated for in her Rossini roles.

Although Caballé's earliest *Devereux* is in 1965, only one year later than Gencer's, we hear her interpretation at its most developed in 1977 at Aix-en-Provence. Even here, she does not have the dramatic assurance of Gencer, but she sings with some feeling and her customary musicality. Featuring Julius Rudel conducting and José Carreras as a sterling Essex, this is a thoroughly professional mounting marked by greater ensemble efficiency than at Naples, albeit with less individuality and spark. Carreras, in his youthful prime, is matchless and makes one regret all the more his premature decline. Vicente Sardinero's Nottingham isn't a patch on Cappuccilli's, while Susanne Marsee's Sara shows a badly frayed voice woefully inadequate to the demands of her part. Nevertheless, as an overall reading of the score, this is arguably one's best introduction to the score. HRE released this performance first on LP, and they subsequently issued a CD edition on their Legato label, although by now there are a number of other small companies that have also published this broadcast. There is even a video edition.

While Caballé is an improvement on Gencer in the opening aria, her fluency is still not ideal. For the critical phrase "Le delizie della vita," we again do not get all three trills, although Caballé makes a respectable stab at one of them, "… li …" of "delizie." What distinguishes her opening cavatina are the amazing *pianissimi*, threads of sheer gossamer that threaten to break at any moment but never do. Here is where one senses that Caballé is investing the richest possible feeling in the music. Unfortunately, the cabaletta is again trimmed in the *da capo*, but not by as much as with Gencer, and some of Caballé's embellishments are certainly exciting. The Elisabetta/Essex duet renders a brilliant effect when two solid musicians are in their element. Here, we can't help feeling, is the scene of Donizetti's imagination. A sequence that ranges all the way from hesitant avowals of love to expressions of hate, the supple musicianship and heartfelt expression in the Caballé/Carreras partnership give it full justice. One can understand how the musical discipline needed in Donizetti becomes essential to conveying the dramatic message.

Nobody is in such sure command of the crucial second act as Caballé. She is, by turns, brooding, bitter, hectoring, pleading — and nearly always musical. The passagework in the Nottingham duet is far more fluent than in Gencer's throat, although not as strong a dramatic statement, perhaps partly because Sardinero is not the incisive partner that Cappuccilli is. When Carreras comes on for the trio, things really wake up. Caballé swings into her denunciation of Essex with a relish that is startling. The passagework at the words "mendacio" and "accusatore" may be somewhat modified, but Caballé shows more musical assurance than Gencer. Sung this way, the phrases just seem more plausible. Although Caballé's low is not as rich as Gencer's, it is heartening that, in "Alma infida," Caballé manages to take the lurches down to the low B flat with greater suavity. These low notes are, at least, present and accounted for, and the whole passage is negotiated with none of the gravelly tones that afflicted Gencer. There are again a few glottal attacks, but they don't seem out of place — and they don't compromise her musicality. The high C at the crest of the ensemble is massive and sure and brings a proper climax to the phrase. For the finale, Caballé's delivery may not be as baleful as Gencer's, but, again, she does not falter before its wide range and maintains clear, steady tone down to the middle C sharp. In addition, for once, we hear, courtesy of Maestro Rudel, the massive coda uncut.

Caballé's final scene is not quite at the same level, although still remarkably accomplished. There may be a fatigue factor here, as she sang so splendidly in Act II. Could it be that a surprising catch in her final *pianissimo* at the conclusion of the third scene's opening cavatina is the price she has to pay for singing so energetically in her previous scene? Even though the rest of "Vivi, ingrato" is perfectly fine, this flaw at its conclusion somehow detracts from the effect of the whole, which is a shame. Fatigue may also be the reason why even Caballé, legendary for her long breath, does not choose to follow Donizetti's original phrase-marking for the "endless sigh." Instead, she snatches two extra breaths. Still, Caballé's final cabaletta and its hallucinations come off very well, even though not with that irreplaceable keening quality that Gencer drew. Caballé is still tremendously effective, and her top notes soar over the whole ensemble, giving this sequence an elemental thrill different from the keening in Gencer, but perhaps equal in quality.

A role that would compel a spinto like Caballé to cut corners would surely give serious problems to a lyric like Beverly Sills. There are, however, several reasons why Sills' reading is important: She is the only *Devereux* Elisabetta extant on disc to have been trained in the Marchesi/García school; and her superb acting is grounded in masterly musicianship, rather than in an abundance of vocal color à la Gencer. In addition, while Caballé may give the most beautiful reading, it is also the most generalized, where Sills gives the most specific. One is reminded of the references to Ronzi–De Begnis's extremely nuanced style when listening to Sills. Last, but certainly not least, Sills is the only one with the technique to perform the role uncut. For once, we hear the first-act cabaletta complete, and what a treat! Sir Charles Mackerras is a sympathetic, elegant partner, although one might hanker for somewhat more brio in the later scenes. The main consideration here is Sills' imagination in reflecting Mackerras's generally contained approach and making it function effectively. Among Sills' colleagues, only Beverly Wolff, the Sara, is equally successful in thriving on Mackerras's musical discipline and in delivering a reading that combines scrupulous musicianship with heartfelt interpretation. Hers is the finest Sara on disc.

The closeness we feel to Elisabetta as a human being is palpable in Sills' hands. All one need do is sample a phrase in the opening scene like "E basta, o Sara" and the vulnerable woman stands before us. This is genius. The opening cavatina "L'amor suo" is dreamlike. The voice sprouts wings, floating with an unbearable poignancy. It is a cherished memory: a memory of youth. The easy flexibility becomes the acme of expression. Effortless, deftly communicative trills are sprinkled everywhere in a grasp at happiness, and Sills does all three written trills at "Le delizie della vita." She follows this by finishing the reverie with the full cadenza as written in the score, complete with the concluding B flat on the stave. The ensuing uncut cabaletta features a dazzlingly embellished *da capo*: even the opening flourish ushering in the reprise features not just the two high Cs indicated but additional ones in rapid alternation with the high B. Further on, one especially magical effect is an alternating warble of E and D sharp below high C on the word "amor." Once she and tenor Robert Ilosfalvy start their duet, we begin to hear the emphatic accents signaling the eventual emotional collapse of this Queen. Ilosfalvy has a rich and easy tone, but not the musical imagination needed for this part — nothing terribly wrong, but his reading is not memorable. As for Sills, it is in this duet that we first get a hint of the challenging game she was playing in taking on this role of roles. In order to compensate for the lack of an effective low register, she almost talks a few of the lower notes, giving, as some others have noted, an unsettling impression more of petulance than of grandeur. For all that, her brio more than makes up for what is lacking and pulls the listener into a world full of doubt and frustration. Effectively embellished phrases in the final moments of the duet are climaxed with an interpolated high D.

Unfortunately, in Act II Sills puts considerable pressure on her voice throughout, much more than in her first-act confrontation with Essex. Her partner in the opening duet with Nottingham surely doesn't help things: baritone Peter Glossop exercises minimal control over a fractious instrument. In addition, by now one cannot ignore a particularly troubling element in the Sills Elisabetta: the constant skirting around of low-lying phrases that typify this role and contribute to its being the special challenge it is. Sometimes Sills will simply transpose certain stressed words or phrases up an octave, or sometimes she will resort to *parlando* effects that relieve her of the need to sustain inordinately deep utterances. For added emphasis, she will sometimes attack certain low-lying words such as "alfine" with a heavily stressed apoggiatura (placed far higher than a mere tone or semitone above the subsequent unstressed syllable). Elsewhere in her range, the tremendous pressure she is exerting causes certain notes in the *passaggio* to go slightly flat, the G at the top of the stave on "... ga ..." at "irrefragabil prova" in the Nottingham duet and the E flats at "sen" and at "... des ..." of "accendesse" in the "Alma infida" being particularly uncomfortable. Most startling of all is her use of a baleful rasp for dramatic effect whenever the tessitura threatens to become too mezzo-ish. When taunting Essex with his craven denial of being in love with someone at court, Elisabetta's second "no" is delivered in this rasping way. The same is true for the words "tu pure" when she is touched by Nottingham's outrage, ostensibly on her behalf. The most unnerving use of this effect is at the word "Ostinato" when she is finally confronted by Essex's defiant call for death before revealing the name of the woman he loves. One can still be grateful for the unerring precision of her passagework for "Un perfido, un vile," the first truly accurate rendition we've heard. The final *stretta*, "Va, la morte," is characterized sharply enough, although it's plain that Sills has nothing in reserve. Mackerras does make one odd change: in the concluding measures of the *stretta*, instead of retaining the reiterated "sì" preceding the climactic notes, he simply has Sills (and the entire ensemble) sustain their tones of the preceding phrase through the ensuing measures, only picking up the thread at the final "Ah sì, sarà," which Sills caps with a prolonged high A.

Remarkably, the last scene of Act III was recorded in a single take, a tribute to Sills' superb dramatic skills. Again, as in Act I, we have in Sills' voice the remarkable alternation of the waspish Queen and the vulnerable woman in love. For "E basta, o Sara" in Act I, we have here a melting "Io sono donna alfine." The critical test of phrasing and musicality in the Act III cavatina, "Vivi, ingrato," is the endlessly "sighing" phrase, "m'abbandona in eterno a sospirar." Since Ronzi–De Begnis was such a phenomenal technician, we can guess that she sang all six measures as a single phrase; twentieth-century Elisabettas never do this. The best they can do is snatch a few extra breaths within those measures while maintaining an overall sense of continuous sighing. This is what Sills achieves in this take with Mackerras. She snatches two extra breaths (before "in" and "a") but still maintains the right feeling as she drifts slowly down a long scale. The disruptiveness of the two snatched breaths is thus kept to a minimum. Again, this is strictly a compromise, although an effective one. Then at the aria's conclusion, in the closing cadenza which Sills takes unchanged, she breathes before the second downward scale and before another iteration of "a sospirar." She ends on the aria's original middle D, on which Mackerras immediately steps to launch the middle section of this final *scena*. There is no pause here. For Elisabetta's final majestic cabaletta, "Quel sangue versato," she presses on the voice way too much, but her genius as a tragedian makes this extremely effective. Again, certain words like "rosseggia" become apt windows on her despair in a way that less imaginative artists could never achieve, and there is, finally, the stunning effect of an interpolated high D as her final cry.

Sills has evidently rethought certain things by the time we hear her "live" in 1970. Her colleagues at New York City Opera are for the most part superior to those in the recording studio. Domingo may not be the most heartfelt Essex, but he is more consistently musical than Ilosfalvy. Louis Quilico is not much more stylish at *bel canto* than Glossop, but he has the advantage of a plusher instrument. Only Susanne Marsee's Sara does not match Beverly Wolff's, but then nobody's does. As for Rudel, his contribution complements Mackerras's. Where Mackerras offers elegance and restraint, Rudel's relative brusqueness leaves less room for the inwardness so striking in Sills, while his energetic approach enhances her innate theatricality. However, all the expressive elements intrinsic to Sills are present and accounted for. There is more genius and inspiration from Sills at City Opera, but possibly more stylish music-making with Mackerras.

In Act I, it is surprising that at City Opera Sills does not do the written trill on "vita" the way she does with Mackerras since, at the same time, she still retains a number of other interpolated trills from the studio set. Unlike the Mackerras, this Rudel performance shows Sills ending the first cavatina with a high B flat instead of taking the lower alternate as written. In launching the *da capo* of the cabaletta, she only inserts one extra high C instead of the series offered with Mackerras. She has also modified somewhat her ornamented reading of the line "e cadranno i tuoi nemici."

In Act II, under "live" conditions, emphatic attacks like the apoggiatura on "alfine" come out so violently that they're marked by cracking under the heavy stress. It is notable, however, that the E flats in the *passaggio* at "sen" and "… desse" are better tuned here than in the recording studio, while the G in "irrefragabil prova" still goes flat. At the same time, despite her generally more vibrant approach "live," she is modifying still further some of the stress in the chest register in this scene: for instance, perhaps partly to avoid the emphasis on a final E flat above middle C at "… tor" of "traditor" (where the singer has already been required to produce a low B flat!)," she speaks "… tor" at a raised pitch instead of singing the E flat as she had in the recording studio. Later in the scene, while she does sing through the lines "e tu fremi, tu pure, dell'oltraggio che a me fu recato," unlike the baleful rasp that marked her "tu pure" with Mackerras, she also substitutes higher pitches for the Es above middle C at "pu …" of "pure" and "…ca …" of "recato." Later, for "Ostinato," the sung B on the stave simply gets submerged in the orchestral fabric. In strong contrast to this pattern is another rasp here that she now delivers "live": her spoken "Va" before launching the final *stretta*. Now, it's the Mackerras that has the less emphatic reading, although still spoken, not sung. At the conclusion of the *stretta*, while Rudel restores the reiterated "sì" before the final phrases, he does dispense with Elisabetta's final "Ah sì, sarà" by having Sills hold the high A for the previous "sarà" as her final note.

In Act III, we hear essentially the same "unstrung" interpretation we heard in the studio. Of course, the sheer effectiveness of this comes partly from the fact that, vocally, Sills herself is getting unstrung. To go by some of the remarks she has let drop in a number of interviews, she was apparently keenly aware that she was liquidating her vocal assets with this role. But she clearly uses that fatigue deliberately for dramatic effect. It is sobering to think how deliberate this exploitation of her conscious vocal abuse is. Her phrasing is not so broad as in the earlier recording. The "eternal sigh," instead of being negotiated with two extra breaths, now needs three. She ends the cavatina with another interpolated high note, similar to that in Act I, eschewing the original low ending on a D above middle C that was retained for Mackerras. Rudel also brings everything to a full stop at the cavatina's conclusion, instead of stepping on the final note to launch the middle section of this *scena* as Mackerras had done. The final cabaletta is much as in the Mackerras, the same heartbreaking inflection on "rosseggia," the same fevered approach to the flourishes at "conceder potrà" and "Sì, sì, per me," together with the final high D at the end.

While one is grateful to have such a document, the sonics here do leave a lot to be desired. One should be thankful for what one has, since there was no broadcast of this first run. But the pressing and the packaging of the GDS CD of this rare document might benefit from a more conscientious approach. The index points on this edition are simply grotesque. Yards and yards of set pieces will be ignored, followed by some arbitrary demarcation for a new section inside some ensemble number. Clearly, either all such sections should be indexed or only the initial entrance points of entire numbers should be. To offer neither in any consistent way makes GDS's indexing downright bizarre.

The last to record her stab at this Everest of a role is Edita Gruberova on Nightingale in 1994. Maestro Friedrich Haider honors the universality of Donizetti's genius more than anyone since Mario Rossi, and he can boast a more accomplished orchestra than Rossi's Neapolitans: the Orchèstre Philharmonique de Strasbourg. Ettore Kim's Nottingham doesn't live up to the promise of an attractive instrument, but at least he has one, whereas Don Bernardini's Devereux promises and gives nothing special. Delores Ziegler sings Sara. The performance lies heavily on the shoulders of its sterling conductor and its challenged prima donna. It is also the best-engineered set of this opera available.

Gruberova's opening scene in Act I is probably her most successful. Its tessitura suits her, allowing her to sound both her most comfortable and her most expressive. Some of the shading we hear is admirably telling, and there is an easy spontaneity to her singing that is not so apparent in later scenes. In these, the wild swings in tessitura are less congenial and the sledding gets harder. In her Act I recitative, there may already be signs of a wobble, but the vulnerability of the character is still paramount, keeping vocal pressure to a minimum. The recitative is enhanced with imaginative use of the appoggiatura. In the cavatina, she deftly inserts a few additional trills and accomplishes a gossamer "Le delizie della vita," written trills and all. She caps the aria with a true *messa di voce* in the cadenza. In the cabaletta, the high C is occasionally driven, occasionally clear and easy. Notable are the glittering embellishments in the *da capo*, particularly expressive for "amor ti guida," and lovely upward passagework on ... "cen" ... of "innocente." But the sequence of high Bs leading to yet another C is harsh and, after a small cut, she goes right for a wobbly climax. There is nice discrimination of "Roberto" and "Conte" once she greets Essex, and, as soon as she and Roberto are alone, Gruberova does much of the private exchange like a - "reseduction," with the odd moment of regally collecting herself as politics intrudes. This alternation of the regal and the intimate pulls the listener in, and we have a magical lilt on "i giorni miei" and a suggestive shiver of contentment for a soft "giorni avventurati." "Un tenero core" also starts strongly, capped by another *messa di voce*, this time on "disparve." But as soon as the Queen's impatience is aroused, Gruberova's discipline breaks down: a wobble on "pugnar" and "altar," an unfocused "splendea," and a flat ... "per" ... in "superba" and "sa" ... in "sarà." The wobble takes over again in the coda with another flapping climax.

Gruberova starts the second act lost in thought, giving an abstracted quality to her opening lines. As soon as she is alone with Nottingham, though, she is all emphatic protestation, and this compromises the line. She all but gasps the lowest notes in her peremptory denial of Nottingham's plea, even though the trickiest passagework higher up comes out well. When we reach the second-act trio, her gingerly approach to the coloratura, while precise, robs it of full expressivity, at the same time sparing us the vocal strain heard with Nottingham. There is still the occasional sour note here, but the overall effect is less unmusical. Considering the strain elsewhere, one can understand Gruberova's cautious choices, even approve them perhaps, while regretting their necessity. An all-purpose raptness is used at odd moments, robbing the trio of some of its urgency. "Alma infida" makes a fragmented effect sung this way, and "whisked" low B flats don't help. There's also an ungainly scoop to the high C in the coda. The pressure on her voice for her ultimatum to Essex in the *materia di mezzo* becomes altogether too pronounced for comfort. Startling in the midst of the vocal abuse is a whispered "Parla." For the stretta, "Va" is a disgusted cry, highly effective, but the "Va, la morte" turns into another gasp lower down. The *da capo* is embellished with some imagination, but this time the lowest note of "discende" isn't even sung: the voice simply peters out before she can reach ... "de." Top notes too continue sounding strained.

The recitative in the final scene shows what dividends Gruberova can reap when she uses her accomplished *pianissimo* and greater variety of coloring through less pressure. There are still some uncomfortably driven phrases, but the salutary mood at the opening is partially restored in her "Vivi, ingrato." Here, commendable phrasing and contained tone make their welcome effect, with phrasing that demonstrates Gruberova's superb breath control. Her hushed urgency at "Ho veduto" is a vivid sound picture of shame, and the "endless sigh," while again not executed as a single statement, has her snatching two discreet breaths, with a fleeting trill on ... "spi" ... of "sospirar." Some stridency in the final measures gives way to an affecting piano at the close. The *materia di mezzo* is marked by a blood-curdling scream at the enormous cannon boom confirming Essex's beheading, a rasped "perversa," and a sobbed "spingesti." At first, Gruberova goes for the spooky rather than the grief-stricken in "Quel sangue versato." This is effective enough until she tackles spun-out *crescendi*, like "v'aspetta;/Si vil," that ultimately lose real expressiveness from sheer tonal collapse, despite the impressive breath control. Her flexibility remains notable: the flourishes on "conceder potrà" and "Sì, sì, per me" are excellent, and the transition to the repeat is enhanced by a vivid "non regno, non vivo," spoken in accents of utmost despair. Compromises in the *da capo* also come too thick and fast for comfort: the all-important "rosseggia" is whispered at its low ... "sse" ... — adversely affecting the expression already there in Donizetti's musical setting — and the intense utterances as the repeat gathers steam falter. This makes it clear that Gruberova is in over her head, an excruciatingly wailed top D completing the picture of both a character and a singer *in extremis*!

One wishes there were a somewhat richer recorded legacy for this role of roles, but one remains grateful for Sills' first act, Caballé's second act, and Gencer's third. Perhaps, a totality will never be possible for such a daunting character!

❧ 11 ❧

Time of Transition

Other divas in the Ronzi–De Begnis/Pasta tradition were taking on some of these *assoluta* roles at the time that Donizetti was phasing out his Italian activities and Verdi first making his way. A celebrated mezzo-soprano, Carolina Sabatier Ungher, who had made her professional debut in 1821 singing in the premiere of Beethoven's *Ninth Symphony*, had already switched to higher soprano roles by the late 1820s. The nature of her upper tones was in sharp contrast to the rest of her voice, but she continued singing soprano roles till her retirement in 1840. She was a celebrated *Maria Stuarda* and was also one of the first divas following Ronzi–De Begnis to sing the *Devereux* Elisabetta when Venice staged Donizetti's new opera during the 1837–38 season. Donizetti wrote *Parisina d'Este*, *Belisario*, and *Maria de Rudenz* for Ungher.

One of the most important *Devereux* Elisabettas of all was Pauline Viardot-García, Malibran's sister. Viardot-García sang, along with certain mezzo roles such as the Bellini Romeo, a number of soprano roles and also a greater number of *assoluta* parts than Malibran ever did. In addition to performing Elisabetta in the St. Petersburg mounting of 1845, Viardot-García sang Norma and the Verdi Lady Macbeth. Actually described by Berlioz as having three voices, soprano, mezzo-soprano, and contralto, Viardot-García's vocal foundation at the time of her operatic debut in 1839 appears to have been the middle mezzo-soprano register, with two altogether different sounds grafted on to it at either end. Her three-octave range extended from low F to high F, and she could sometimes extend her middle register timbre within that range down to the low B flat and up to the high B flat. In recognition of her talents, Meyerbeer composed the role of Fidès in *Le Prophète* especially for her. When this opera premiered in 1849, Viardot-García was able to show off her enormous range and ability to use her agile instrument for emotional expression even in the fioritura. The only *assoluta* ingredient missing from this role is the degree of alternation of tessitura present in a Norma or an Elisabetta. While the vocal range of Fidès uses the full complement of an *assoluta*'s voice (from low G to high C, incidentally the same range as that for Rossini's *Armida*), Fidès's tessitura stays more in the middle register than would any defining *assoluta* part. In our time, Marilyn Horne has been an important exponent of the role. Viardot-García's decline started only a few years after the *Le Prophète* premiere, though her impersonation of Lady Macbeth in 1859 was already toward the end of her career. She prepared a much-adjusted version of the opera used in the Höngen recording reviewed in Chapter Thirteen. Viardot eventually retired in 1863 after having participated in a special series of Gluck revivals spearheaded by Berlioz. These culminated with *Alceste* in 1861 and with approximately 150 performances of *Orphée* between 1859 and 1863.[63]

Another diva from the time of Viardot-García who was part of this tradition was Marietta Gazzaniga Malaspina Albites, a mezzo-soprano who, like Ungher and Viardot-García, switched to certain higher roles following her debut in 1841. Among her mezzo roles was Eleonora in Donizetti's *Torquato Tasso*, but she was soon singing other Donizetti works as well requiring a much higher instrument — works such as *Lucrezia Borgia* and *Poliuto*. One *assoluta* part that she eventually sang was the title role in Bellini's *Norma*.[64] Verdi even wrote the taxing role of Lina in his *Stiffelio* for her, premiered in 1850. Lina requires an unusual range and the ability to color agile vocal writing in an expressive way. The intricacy of its fioritura is quite demanding, and many of its shifts in tessitura are not easy. However, it does not have that *assoluta* portion of heroic flexibility that a defining *assoluta* role should have. Instead, fioritura and heroics are each within their separate spheres. The role requires a secure low A and an easy high C. After quite a successful career, Gazzaniga Malaspina retired in 1862.

Clearly, there seems to be no question that, during the height of the 1830s, it was the deeper-voiced singer who participated in the *assoluta* premieres and in most of the other *assoluta* performances of that time as well. But this kind of technical variety, and the diva who, like Ungher, Viardot-García, or Gazzaniga Malaspina, would uphold this tradition, was no longer in the ascendancy for mastery of the *assoluta* repertoire after about the time of the *Devereux* premiere. Now, there was a significant change brought about in casting. This seems to have been largely due to the influence of two Divas especially who had their first successes in the early 1830s, but who were in no way typical of that period. They were Eugenia Tadolini and Giulia Grisi. Though these two singers were exceptions to the prevailing vocal tradition of their time, and though they were never given the opportunity by any composer of actually creating an *assoluta* role, they still managed, by their example, to effect a thorough change in the map of operatic casting for the ensuing decades.

Eugenia Tadolini made her operatic debut in 1828 as a high soprano. The lighter, juvenile leads were thus her first roles. She was one of the first singers to move into the heavier *assoluta* parts after starting out as the equivalent in opera of the ingenue. Unlike most of her contemporaries, therefore, she did not come to the *assoluta* repertoire through the mezzo *fach*, or even as a singer who, like Ronzi–De Begnis, was immediately proficient in both the soprano and mezzo repertoires. Tadolini began her career with Cimarosa's *Il Matrimonio Segreto*, Donizetti's *L'Elisir d'Amore*, Giovanna in *Anna Bolena*, the soprano version of Rossini's *Il Barbiere*, and other works requiring an essentially bright vocal persona. Then, in 1835, while she was already in the process of starting in on some of the heavier roles such as the Donizetti *Fausta*, she sang her first *Norma*. This was followed by a surprising revival a year later of a twenty-year-old Rossini opera whose greatest popularity had so far been won in Germany and Austria, none other than his *Armida*. This revival of Rossini's one *assoluta* vehicle took place at La Scala in 1836 and showed how far the acceptance of Romantic vocalism had come in Italy when an antiquated *opera seria*, that had been given a lukewarm reception at its Italian premiere, could yet be given a successful revival at Italy's foremost opera house. Tadolini does not appear to have sung either Armida or Norma again, but in 1842, in Vienna, she moved on from Giovanna in *Bolena* to the title role, and, in 1848, toward the end of her career, she sang Lady Macbeth at Naples, one year after *Macbeth*'s premiere and against, as we shall see, the composer's express wishes. Her first and only mezzo role, Leonora in Donizetti's *La Favorita*, came in the same year and at the same house. She retired very soon after that in 1851.[65]

Like Tadolini, Giulia Grisi also made her debut in 1828. Though she had already won for herself quite a reputation by 1835, singing both Bolena and Norma, she, like Tadolini, was not in the true *assoluta* mold of the early years of the nineteenth century. There are contemporary references to her range as being from high C to middle C only, and also that she started her career in the same *fach* as Tadolini. In fact, only a very few years after her creation of Adalgisa, her first Norma did not at all meet with Bellini's approval. He judged her imcomparable in the simple, pure sort of roles, but incapable of sustaining exalted personages in a noble, tragic style. Unfortunately, he was fighting against the tide — not against the prevailing preferences and traditions of his own time, but against the rise of the high soprano voice for the impersonation of strong women that was to overtake the operatic world after *Devereux*. What the future would hold is epitomized in Henry Chorley's approving attitude toward Grisi's "frantic charm," "which possibly belongs to the true character of the druid priestess."[66] To him, the very fact that, even at the height of Norma's rage, Grisi was unable to convey anything forbidding was actually her special asset in his eyes, despite the composer, rather than her main flaw. To him, therefore, the character, even in her reprehensible actions, was still to be regarded as more sinned against than sinning. She must be charming and appealing to insure the sympathy of the audience.

What Bellini himself, though, regarded as Grisi's genuine artistic strength is shown in the role of Elvira in his last opera, *I Puritani* (1835). Grisi rehearsed this role with Bellini for the world premiere at the Paris Opera, and the part is about as different from Norma as a part could be, while still being a true *bel canto* role. Here is the quintessential ingenue with a consistently high tessitura, and, while the orchestral fabric throughout the opera is somewhat more richly developed than in *Norma*, the use of the instrumental accompaniment in Elvira's scenes is always far less assertive than in Norma's music.

To give Chorley some credit, even he drew the line when hearing Jenny Lind attempt Norma with her amazingly high instrument going no lower than the middle D but capable of reaching up to the G above high C. The resulting distortion of the Druid priestess was, claimed Chorley, "as entire, as aimless as it is possible for so remarkable an artist to make. The actress and the play had no agreement."[67]

Donizetti had occasion to mount a slightly revised version of *Roberto Devereux* for Giulia Grisi and Giovanni Battista Rubini at Paris in 1838. He wrote Rubini an exciting new aria, composed an overture using the new melody, and gave him an altogether different melody from the prima donna's at the conclusion of the first-act duet for Elisabetta and Essex. In revising the first-act duet in this way, Elisabetta's music was slightly altered as well. Where before, Elisabetta's concluding music for this duet had extended down to middle D, her "harmonizing" music now only went down to middle F sharp. Though, in the overall scheme of Elisabetta's role, this does not alter the essential nature of her music, the fact that Donizetti rewrote these phrases so as not to extend them as low for Grisi as for Ronzi–De Begnis is suggestive of Grisi's weaker instrument. Grisi managed to pull *Devereux* through five performances at Paris over the course of two seasons, whereas Ronzi–De Begnis, in its first season, had played *Devereux* through regular weekly performances for nearly half a season and through a few more performances in later seasons. Grisi had no better luck with the role later on when she sang it in London in 1841.

Despite all this, Grisi also performed, in addition to the supreme role of the *Devereux* Elisabetta, Donizetti's other Ronzi–De Begnis *assoluta* part, *Gemma di Vergy*, in 1845. Less revision went into this 1845 *Gemma* than into the 1838 *Devereux*. Posterity, however, can be grateful to Grisi for having inspired the creation of Donizetti's most captivating comic heroine, Norina in *Don Pasquale* (1843). Regardless of the more enlightened attitude prevailing today toward the gripping drama found in the tragic Italian works from the age of *bel canto*, Donizetti's comic mastery is fully worthy of the popularity posterity has given it. What Donizetti has created in *Don Pasquale* is a magical combination of four musical characterizations that vividly recalls Beethoven's praise of the Italian comic spirit. Norina herself is a pert, irresistible embodiment of the best in *opera buffa*, one of the most radiant forms of theatrical art to emerge out of Western civilization. Her music has spirit, mockery, sparkle, wit. It is sculpted for a deft comedienne with a clear and resilient upper register capable of great flexibility and charm. Nothing in this fascinating package has anything to do with either Elisabetta, Bolena, or Norma. But it has everything to do with the tradition of the high soprano capable of great stamina, clean projection, with musical accuracy and homogeneous beauty. Only such a soprano can do proper justice to Norina's *lirico* music.

Finally, Grisi had her most conspicuous failure, and even her admirers had to acknowledge it, when she attempted toward the end of her career a rare and disastrous assumption of a mezzo-ish role, Fidès in *Le Prophète*. She finally retired in 1861.[68]

❦ 12 ❧

Giuseppe Verdi (1813–1901): *Nabucco*

It was, for better or worse, divas very much like Tadolini and Grisi who were to take over the *assoluta* vehicles more and more during the ascendancy of Verdi. After those two, many of the brighter-sounding divas who followed in their wake were to play a significant part in shaping the original and subsequent performing traditions for the two *assoluta* characters Verdi eventually concocted: Abigaille in *Nabucco* (1842) and Lady Macbeth in *Macbeth* (1847). As well as being Verdi's only *assoluta* creations, Abigaille and Lady Macbeth constitute the next *assoluta* roles central to this survey following Gemma and Elisabetta. As far as it is possible to know, they appear also to have been the last two defining *assoluta* roles ever composed to meet the criteria introduced in Chapter Three, and fully outlined in Chapter Four.

When Verdi was supervising La Scala's rehearsals for the premiere of his first opera, *Oberto* (1839), La Scala was in the midst of a run of thirty-eight *Devereux*s, which must have made an impression on the young composer. The kind of emotional energy up to then unique to passages such as the second-act finale of *Devereux* clearly influenced the vehement quality of the vocalism required for Abigaille in *Nabucco*.

Alongside this special quality, the moments of less vehement melody for Abigaille in the score seem arbitrary and uncertain. While all the technical and vocal contradictions intrinsic to an *assoluta* are exploited in Abigaille's music, such contradictions still fail to translate themselves into a vivid enough depiction of a character who might have as many different emotions as she has vocal capabilities. Abigaille is simply mean — and that's all! Her second-act cavatina of sudden susceptibility and nostalgia comes out of nowhere and goes nowhere. Her remorse and suicide at the end, "Su me ... morente," has all the conviction of the feeblest *deus ex macchina*. Verdi's unimaginative librettist, Temistocle Solera, may have been partly responsible.

This one-sidedness in Abigaille's musical characterization, though, is also due to her being unsuited, dramatically, to any vintage *assoluta* treatment at all. Up until now, the *assoluta* heroine could be a figure of admirable courage (Reiza), or she could be a supernatural figure capable of great tenderness (Armida), or she could be a leader of a community more sinned against than sinning (Norma, Bolena, Elisabetta). So, since dramatic justification is the lynchpin of the *assoluta* tradition, it is bewildering if a composer chooses the *assoluta* treatment for a character of unmitigated evil.

Even Médée, evil as her final course of action is, first sings to us as a wronged woman. If Lachner's recitatives for *Médée* are removed, then Médée emerges as being very far from the tiresome ogre that is Abigaille. Until one gets toward the end of Médée's second act, we do not hear from her musically what we hear from Abigaille almost all the time. But Abigaille is in no way a wronged woman. It is true she has been scorned by Ismaele, but even here there is no question of betrayal. We know that Ismaele has always been honest with her, making clear her fundamental unattractiveness for him, and, during the course of the opera, it does not take us very long to figure out just how unattractive she is. Her very nature remains forbidding, and the mainsprings of her evil actions involve much more than just her thwarted affection (she herself calls it "una furia") for Ismaele.

I am not implying that it is wrong to render in music a powerful characterization of a formidable, evil figure bent on destruction. It is simply that Verdi chooses to use the *assoluta* singer primarily to portray villainesses.

Verdi's music leaves the impression that, with the increased importance of high sopranos in heroic writing, the very notion of a woman singing in a somber way had become unnatural, inherently sinister, to Verdi's generation. Whether on the surface or not, was the young Verdi unsettled by the kind of character that had to be projected in shifting vocal moods? Is this why Verdi confined such shifts within a sinister context? As a corollary to this, since more conventional soprano voices were now singing *assoluta* roles, might extreme vocal writing have started to sound unnatural anyway? By now, extravagant vocalism was clearly emerging from higher voices than the deeper instruments originally chosen for a Norma or an Elisabetta.

Had the wide range of a Malibran, with her darker tone, become irrelevant, at least for Verdi? At the least, Verdi's reserved assessment of her, so unlike the unquestioning acceptance of Malibran's contemporaries, draws a stark contrast: "Very great, but not always. At times sublime, at other times eccentric. Her singing style was not of the purest."[69] One is dealing with a new era where naturally easy lower registers are no longer associated with defining *assoluta* parts, i.e., an era like Verdi's or our own where naturally deep female voices are already being widely used for altogether different repertoire.

Still, despite his own generation's upheavals, Verdi's early works retained their roots in much that went before, and the music for *Nabucco* was no exception.

In every single *assoluta* score, the orchestral accompaniment is unusually energetic and emphatic. And this is still the case with *Nabucco*. But the sheer density of Verdi's orchestral textures for Abigaille marks a new stage in this genre. Henry Wisneski, in his book on Callas, cites soprano Elena Souliotis who has said that "Abigaille has to shout."[70]

The two most crucial scenes in Abigaille's music are her *scena* in Act II and her confrontation with Nabucco in Act III. The recitative with which her second-act scene opens uses the middle range of the voice as an incidental bridge for the extensive phrases flamboyantly placed at the voice's two extremes. Abigaille is half triumphant, half incensed, having found written proof on her adoptive father's person, Nabucco, of her lowly parentage. Having been born a slave, she has been brought up in complete ignorance as Nabucco's royal daughter. Brandishing the stolen document, she resolves to take over the throne, thus placing her sister, Fenena, who has dared to win Ismaele for herself, her "father," Nabucco, and his entire realm under her tender mercies.

As her vocalism swings through the extremes of her instrument's range, this opening recitative ends on an extravagant two-octave interval from high C to middle C at the word "sdegno." Unlike the recitative, her ensuing cavatina, "Anch'io dischiuso," has a remarkably consistent tessitura throughout. As Abigaille suddenly admits that even she was once susceptible to love, fairly intricate phrases keep her in the upper middle register from which she occasionally floats even higher to the topmost reaches of her voice. This entire aria has, in its intricacy and high tessitura, an ethereal quality, thus drawing a contrast with the hard, peremptory nature of the phrases at her entrance.

Upon being told by the High Priest of Bel that Fenena has been discovered releasing some Hebrews, and that, in addition, rumors have been circulated of Nabucco's demise thus leaving the throne empty for Abigaille to claim, Abigaille then eagerly thanks the High Priest and promises herself, in the cabaletta, "Salgo già," a ruthless reign as Queen in which the full rigor of the law will be visited by her upon Fenena and upon anybody else who dares oppose her.

A full-fledged heroic agility marks this aria, as Abigaille sings against the full energy of the Verdian orchestra. In contrast to "Anch'io dischiuso," "Salgo già" has a lower tessitura where overall phrases hover around the lower middle range. High notes quite incidentally give way in the last line of her statement, "l'umil schiava a supplicar," to a series of repeat flourishes exploiting the entire compass of her voice. A traditional *da capo* of this statement followed by climactic phrases against the full chorus end the scene.

Grace Bumbry, in remarking on the somber vocal persona in most of Abigaille's music, has, nevertheless, stressed the requirement in this second-act *scena* for two different sounds, that for the cabaletta being the stern Abigaille persona we all love to hate, that for the cavatina being more floating and lyrical.[71]

In Abigaille's Act III confrontation with Nabucco, a wildly alternating tessitura reminiscent of her Act II opening recitative typifies Abigaille's music here as she implacably declares herself sovereign. Appealing to his worst instincts, she tricks the temporarily mollified Nabucco into signing a decree sentencing all the Hebrews to death. Only after handing the signed decree to the guards does Abigaille then exultantly tell her "father" he has also signed Fenena's death warrant as well. When Nabucco realizes Abigaille will not give Fenena a reprieve, he is determined to invalidate her claim to regal power by using the document proving her lowly birth. Of course, unbeknownst to him, Abigaille has the document herself, and she scornfully tears it up before his eyes.

In the cavatina of Nabucco's and Abigaille's duet, "Oh, di qual onta," Nabucco laments his helplessness in the face of his implacable "daughter." Unlike Abigaille's Act II *scena*, here Abigaille's solo continues the extreme alternation of tessitura present in her recitatives. There is some agility required here as well.

In the following *materia di mezzo*, Nabucco, in a desperate effort to halt the slaughter of the Hebrews and of Fenena, summons back the guards—only to be promptly arrested by them on Abigaille's orders.

Abjectly pleading with Abigaille to let Fenena go and Abigaille can remain Queen with his blessing, Nabucco launches the cabaletta "Deh perdona." Still unpitying and smarting under Nabucco's threat to reveal her lowly parentage, Abigaille responds with a high-lying solo expressing her determination not to be a merciful, "weak" sovereign of Assyria. Again, a certain amount of agility is required here. In fact, for this cabaletta, the agility required is of almost as heroic a quality as in her "Salgo già" from the second act, and the instrumentation is far more energetic here than it is in this duet's preceding section, the "Oh, di qual onta."

While neither Tadolini nor Grisi sang *Nabucco*, two of the most significant divas to follow as high sopranos in the *assoluta* repertoire, Giuseppina Strepponi and Teresa De Giuli Borsi, were very much involved with its earliest performances. Strepponi was the creator of Abigaille on the occasion of *Nabucco*'s premiere at Milan on March 9, 1842, having made her operatic debut as a high soprano in 1834 as Adina in Donizetti's *L'Elisir*. Similarly light roles like Adalgisa in *Norma* and Amina in *La Sonnambula* were to follow. From these parts, she moved into heavier ones like Lucia until, in 1838, she dropped Adalgisa from her repertoire and did her first Norma during an autumn engagement at Cremona. Her association with Verdi followed soon after, and she accepted the role of Abigaille from Verdi several years after the Cremona *Norma*. *Nabucco*'s 1842 world premiere was a total success and launched Verdi on his way, but even though Strepponi's accomplishment as Abigaille was theatrically exciting, she seriously affected her voice by singing the strenuous role. Apparently, the resultant vocal problems were only too evident. By this time, *Anna Bolena* was also in her repertoire, and a steady vocal decline only eight years after her operatic debut was under way. The straw that broke the camel's back was undoubtedly the *Devereux* at Bologna in 1843, effectively ending her active career as a regular company performer. For the next few years, she sang only in four isolated opera productions. They were a single *Lucrezia Borgia* and a single Elvira in *Ernani* in 1844, a single Giselda in *I Lombardi* in 1846, and, because her histrionic achievement in *Nabucco* had, at least, been so striking, two requested repeats of Abigaille in 1845 and 1846. But, in 1846, she had to call a halt. Over ten years later, Giuseppina Strepponi became Signora Verdi.[72]

Though Verdi's regard for Strepponi's artistry was deep and abiding, he may actually have preferred Teresa De Giuli Borsi for the role of Abigaille; accounts are unclear. She was one of the most successful early sopranos to venture into the *assoluta* repertoire. Giuli Borsi stands as one of the first sopranos to have been both a *drammatico* soprano and one conversant from the start with *assoluta* roles—and she lasted. She performed a number of Verdian dramatic soprano roles that partook of some of the *assoluta* characteristics. As one of the first to have this proficiency already developed at the time of her debut, in 1839, she immediately started singing both soprano and *assoluta* roles without any kind of gradual breaking in. She achieved this despite never having tested the ease of her lower register by actually sustaining a mezzo-tessitura part throughout a whole evening — or, conversely, the ease of her extreme high by starting, like Grisi or Tadolini, with high-lying roles such as Adina.

The success and the length of Giuli Borsi's career (1839–1866) strongly suggest an enviable ease in all three registers, but, since she maintained a consistently soprano repertory throughout those years, she was clearly not the kind of *assoluta* that Pasta, Ronzi, or Viardot were. It seems the lack of any timbral variety was a characteristic of Giuli Borsi. She assumed Norma almost immediately after her 1839 debut and there was no easing of the heroic nature of her roles at any time after that. In 1842, the very year of *Nabucco*'s premiere, Giuli Borsi was already taking on Abigaille's music in Milan (where Strepponi had created the role) and winning Verdi's strong approval. Evidently, she had none of the vocal difficulties with this monster that Strepponi encountered. Around this same time, she was one of the first divas of her generation to take on Ronzi's first *assoluta* vehicle, *Gemma di Vergy*. From 1843 on, she was given many world premieres and in 1850 assumed the role of Lady Macbeth. In the year of her retirement, 1866, she was given, for the first time, the role of Amelia in *Un Ballo in maschera* (premiered in 1859), one of the heaviest dramatic soprano roles that Verdi wrote.[73]

Abigaille on disc

It seems that the last *assoluta* role written with the expectation of perfect singing may be Abigaille. This in spite of the Verdi Lady Macbeth, which was the last with all the earmarks of this type on paper. As we shall see, a letter from Verdi will indicate a wish for Lady Macbeth "not to sing at all." No such latitude has surfaced regarding *Nabucco*. This may leave it in a unique historical position. But no one would claim it as a peak in Verdi's output like *Nabucco*'s predecessor *Roberto Devereux* in Donizetti's. Abigaille does not embrace the profundity and subtlety of Elisabetta. The brashness of Maria Callas's youthful Abigaille, extant in a "live" broadcast from Naples in 1949, fits better, where subtlety is not much in evidence. Only in Abigaille's occasional reminiscences of when she loved without bitterness, and in her dying words in the last scene, does Callas afford us a rare glimpse at a complexity not typical in Abigaille. With all the virtues of Callas's interpretation, though, this recording has one forbidding stumbling block impossible to ignore: the sound is so atrocious that it is almost unlistenable. While Callas is magnificent, much of the thrill in her mastery of this role ends in frustration because of the distortion every time the music rises slightly above *mezzo piano*. All the small labels that have released this broadcast, including Estro Armonico, Legendary Recordings, and a number of others, are clearly transferring from the identical faulty source. None is able to surmount it. Regrettable, too, that this performance features a much celebrated interpretation of the title role: Gino Bechi's Nabucco. Like Callas's Abigaille, no other recording preserves Bechi's Nabucco either. This double historical value makes the broadcast essential to the *Nabucco* discography. It is an inspired reading of the work as a whole, thanks to Vittorio Gui's baton. Luciano Neroni sings Zaccaria, and Gino Sinimberghi, Ismaele.

That the finest performance of *Nabucco* on disc should be the least listenable is a shame. Callas's low B launching "Prode" of "Prode guerrier" in her entrance recitative cannot really be heard. But we can savor the way she then tears through her flourish, threatening Ismaele with her vengeance at "sospeso," like some bird of prey, swooping down on an easy low B flat. As the trio starts, her "Io t'amava" is at first merely reproachful, but the bird of prey is heard again for "Una furia è quest'amore," then changing to a suggestion of regret tinged with nostalgia for "Ah! ... se m'ami." The ease with which she integrates both her personal sense of opportunities lost and her palpably dangerous bitterness, and the way she conveys these with scrupulous musicality and impeccable vocalism, sets this reading apart. In the *insieme* section, Callas successfully delivers, against the counterpoint of Ismaele and Fenena's vocal lines, a glistening downward scale, superbly articulated and resonated with authority.

She is even more fearless in her grand *scena* in the second act, and in her confrontation with her adoptive father in the third. In the opening of Act II, Callas justifies Verdi's lurches from register to register by successfully evoking the danger Abigaille poses to one and all. She is all tense determination on realizing that her adoptive father's stolen parchment tars her with illegitimacy. Her dive from a rock-solid high C to a precise middle C two octaves down is dizzying. For the cavatina, "Anch'io dischiuso un giorno," she adopts a musing delivery: her thoughtfulness and the way she shapes every phrase in this tricky aria is a wonder, although the usually sympathetic Gui hustles her along too much in the concluding phrases. She still manages a nice *diminuendo* on the final note.

In the cabaletta, "Salgo già del trono aurato," her decision to seize the throne by force is projected vividly with unerring control of pitch and endless reserves of breath: "Ben saprà la mia vendetta/Da quel seggio fulminar" is rendered as one sweeping phrase, and some of the trills make a bracing effect, although one can't hear every one of them, due to the wretched sound quality. The repeat is omitted and she concludes with a ringing high C.

In Act III, when the time comes to face down her father, the erstwhile King, it is readily apparent that Abigaille now has no heart at all. Implacable from the start, she offers a terrifying flourish at first as she shoves the warrant for the Jews' deaths into Nabucco's hands. Nabucco then twits her with her illegitimacy, the lineage of a slave, as he threatens her with the parchment he thinks he has. "Qui volli attenderti! Io schiava?" snaps Callas, and she rips the parchment to shreds. Her breathtaking passagework as she flings the torn pieces at Nabucco's feet culminates in a veritable snarl on "menzogner." In the cavatina of their duet together, "Oh, di qual' onta," there is another nasty snarl as Callas anticipates the populace bowing down before a mere slave in "Alfine cadranno i popoli/Di vile schiava al piè." In the cabaletta, "Deh perdona," both Gino Bechi and Maria Callas are electrifying. This is the high point of the entire performance. Callas is triumph incarnate, and Bechi's searing desperation matches her intensity. Here, Gui comes into his own as well. The scene climaxes on a secure high E flat from Callas and Bechi's high A flat. It is in sequences like these where one most regrets the recording's poor sonics.

In Abigaille's remorseful final moments, having swallowed poison, Callas manages to invest the "Su me … morente …" with a combination of the poignant and the eery. There are bewildering somersaults in dynamics for "Costor s'amavano …/Fidan lor speme in te" as her life ebbs, and the startling ease in her lowest register, for "pondo del mio delitto," seems to mirror abject despair. She concludes by punctuating the ends of certain phrases with a stabbing gasp before fading away in a haunting "Non maledire a me!"

The second recorded Abigaille, and the first commercially released one, is Caterina Mancini. A Cetra *Nabucco* from 1951, Mancini's colleagues include Paolo Silveri in the title role, Antonio Cassinelli as the Zaccaria, and Mario Binci, the Ismaele. Fernando Previtali conducts.

Mancini's entrance in the first scene is marked by an uncertain flourish at "sospeso": begun slightly flat, it's followed by a clumsy adjustment where she almost runs out of breath. Her lowest register is fine, although there are hollow tones in the lower middle. For the most part, hers is an angular delivery, even though she tries to impart an easier line for the atypical phrases of tender recall at "Io t'amava." Still, the persona behind the voice doesn't change much.

At first, the Act II *scena* finds Mancini uncertain: there is too much caution in her opening words until a vivid "schiavi." Her overall declamation remains robotoid, and one note squarely in her middle register cracks, "e" in "e più folli ancor." At the climax of the recitative, there is an intrusive breath before "sdegno" and the high C is barely sustained, though she gets the two-octave interval down to middle C right. The opening line of "Anch'io dischiuso" catches the shallowest part of Mancini's voice. There's some subsequent improvement in her control during the entire aria: she manages a flourish on the word "amore" nicely, while one regrets that "soffriva" goes flat on the … "fri." There are some other flat tones, but a real plangency is heard in a repetition of the words "un giorno sol." The concluding cadenza is rushed. Surprisingly, the cabaletta, "Salgo già," makes a better effect. Her control of Verdi's breakneck writing here is efficient. She doesn't really have a trill, but she feints at one. There is no *da capo* and she does not take a high note at the end.

Abigaille is at the crest of her fortunes in Act III, Scene 1, and Mancini's initial impact reflects that. The word "chiedete" emerges with a regality that is unmistakable. She is now a full queen. However, the word "suggello" lands right in a hole in her voice, while the passagework has her running short of breath. When offering the warrant for Nabucco to sign, there are also a few flat notes. In the crucial flourish on tearing up the proof of her illegitimacy, she drops a few notes while scurrying up the scale. Nevertheless, she and Previtali phrase the "Oh, dell' ambita gloria" magnificently, using a majestic tempo. There is no shortness of breath here. The problem returns, though, in the final "Esci! Invan mi chiedi," where reasonably accurate passagework is balanced against the awkward breath once more.

In the last scene, Mancini's "Su me … morente …" is generally moving, if not very individual. "Discenda" emerges gravelly, but this does not disrupt the dramatic effect of a remorseful human being during her last moments on earth, where even a hint of sharpness seems part of the expression. Her descent down to the low at "pondo del mio delitto" is extremely good. She also introduces a moving, but tightly controlled, vibrato on "maledire," to suggest life ebbing away.

In 1966, Elena Souliotis made a *Nabucco* recording for Decca/London. The combination of her Abigaille and Tito Gobbi's vivid Nabucco place this performance almost at the Callas/Bechi level. Since the engineering here also happens to be superb, this makes the overall set preferable, hence the best recording of *Nabucco* in the discography. One wishes Carlo Cava's inadequate Zaccaria were not on the Souliotis/Gobbi *Nabucco*, but there is simply no other well-recorded set that offers consistent excitement from both leads under an authentic Verdian, Lamberto Gardelli. Bruno Prevedi sings Ismaele.

Souliotis is particularly exciting in passages such as the Act II recitative and the Act III confrontation with her father, where she really sings up a storm. Her coloratura is not the finest (she has no trill), but the voice seems hale and hearty. We hear her first opposite Prevedi's Ismaele in the opening scene. Here, the character is established right away, very much in the Callas manner. No question here of a fearsomely solid low B on her entrance. Her flourish on "sospeso," while not the last word in fluency, is securely in place and utterly in character. Her "Io t'amava" opening the trio is marked by a lightened "Ah , se m'ami" and expert molding of the downward scale in the coda.

In the recitative opening the Act II *scena*, fearless vaults throughout her range climax in her spectacular leap on "sdegno" from the high to the middle C, setting the standard for all who follow her. Her ferocious recitative stands in proper contrast to the aching regret heard in the cavatina, "Anch'io dischiuso un giorno"; her "piangeva" is delivered with a tender *decrescendo*, and her voice softens further for that elusive "giorno." For the cabaletta, "Salgo già del trono aurato," we return to the stern face of the recitative, passagework hurled out with the same fearlessness as at her entrance. As we have come to expect, she does not offer any of the trills, making her achievement slightly less complete than the rest of the *scena*. Her combination of the same legato with stark verbal pointing fuses the formidable vocal and dramatic challenges as well as anyone: "schiava" tolls with its fearsome low notes. Then, an ironic sweetness takes over when the word is repeated, and there is an exciting downward scale at "supplicar." The *da capo* is included, although there is not much differentiation with the first statement, let alone any ornamentation. Of course, one is grateful that she takes no vocal shortcuts, aside from the absent trills. She even whips through every single note of the preparatory measures leading up to the traditional high C, which she nails.

One might wonder whether some of the spectacular ease she demonstrates at this time is a manufactured achievement of the recording studio. Fortunately, a "live" performance later the same year, broadcast from La Scala, can be used as a spot-check. Giangiacomo Guelfi sings the title role and Gianandrea Gavazzeni conducts. Since most of the published editions, including the Opera D'Oro, run fast, one must adjust the speed to savor keener descents into chest voice and the same spectacular leap from the high to the middle C. She has rethought the cavatina to an extent, but it emerges just as fluently: this time there is even more wistfulness, but less sheer ache, and "chi del perduto incanto" has gained a more distant quality. The cabaletta is just as fearless and precise. In addition, she rings more changes on "schiava": it still tolls just as fearsomely in her low, but later, she further calibrates its repetition, alternating ironic cringing with unmistakable defiance. Gavazzeni snips out the *da capo*, and Souliotis takes a breather for some of the closing measures, delivering an even more rousing high C at the curtain.

A distinct asset to the studio recording made earlier in the year is Souliotis's sterling collaboration with the Nabucco of Tito Gobbi. Act III is their finest moment. Souliotis offers Stygian darkness in "Custode/Del seggio tuo qui venni" and a creepy sweetness for "Un altra figlia." Her command of passagework remains assured enough, although there are slight aspirates to her "Porre il regal sugello/Al voto suo dêi tu!" A delightfully catty "Qui volli attenderti" heralds a flourish free of aspirates as she rips up the parchment before Nabucco's eyes. In the duet, "Oh, di qual'onta," there is surpassing grandeur in her "Oh, dell' ambita gloria," and when the sentiments are repeated in tandem with Nabucco's own vocal line, she oh-so-sweetly savors the notion of sovereignty. This is chilling. A high point, literally and figuratively, in the *materia di mezzo* is her reiteration of "Sì" to the stunned Nabucco as she orders him taken prisoner. She projects authority at first, then, in repeating it higher up the scale, she shows impatience at her "father" 's incredulity — "Don't you get it?" In the duet's cabaletta, "Deh perdona," there is a rhythmic spring to her singing, typical of her zest throughout the opera, but Gardelli does not have her interpolate an added top note at the conclusion.

As Souliotis dies in Act IV, she successfully imparts ebbing strength through an infinite range of dynamic nuance. There is genius in the way she suggests an uncanny sense of being freed of all weight with a piano right on the word "Solleva." And as she delivers her final measures, she shows she can use her dark low to suggest helplessness as well as brute strength.

Her Abigaille, excellent as it certainly is, may not have the same degree of individuality found in something like her Norma. She still invests heart and soul into the challenge of making the music dramatically terrifying, yet always musical. The singing itself is so sure, and the role itself may not call for the kind of probing needed for Norma anyway. She may not be as fully developed a musician here, but vocally, her Decca/London *Nabucco* is her surest accomplishment.

It is sobering to put the magnitude of this accomplishment alongside the next Abigaille, Renata Scotto. Here is an artist who is capable of so much, yet even her great gifts pall before Souliotis and the terrors in Abigaille's music. Released in 1978, this EMI recording features Matteo Manuguerra as Nabucco, Veriano Luchetti as Ismaele, Nicolai Ghiaurov as Zaccaria, and, in the supporting role of Fenena, Elena Obraztsova. Luxury casting is provided in the young Robert Lloyd as the High Priest of Baal. Riccardo Muti conducts.

Verbal highlighting remains Scotto's strongest asset as she spits out her scornful words at Ismaele in her first scene. This is offset by an inevitable wobble on "sospeso." There is, though, a true *pianissimo* for "Ah, se m'ami," and she negotiates the downward scale in the coda the same way.

In the recitative of her great Act II *scena*, Scotto is sharp on "fosse" in the low, rasps badly at the attack on certain words like "tale," talks the word "folli," and shrieks the high C, reaching the middle C two octaves down without much flair. The cavatina is somewhat more composed: a flourish on "intorno," for instance, is poignantly done, offset by edgy tone as she climbs the scale on "incanto," and a pinched and squeezed cadenza. There are clumsy lunges throughout the cabaletta, and while she makes some attempt at the trills, they're not too convincing. She does include the *da capo*, but simply screams the concluding measures. Muti, as is his wont, has his prima donna eschew the traditional high note at the end.

Her confrontation with Manuguerra's superb Nabucco in Act III opens auspiciously with some collected tone in the middle, but the flourish on "Al voto suo dêi tu" quickly turns edgy again. A conspiratorial quality takes over at "Perfida! Si diede al falso Dio," and there is tense indignation at "Io schiava?" In the duet, an initial attempt at grandeur founders on pressured tone, but the *materia di mezzo* yields a telling detail: keen satisfaction in a deadly quiet "Che disprezza il tuo poter!" Surprisingly, she starts out her "Esci! Invan mi chiedi pace" with respectable control of the passagework, but the climactic measures suffer from her customary problems, and a dire wobble ends the scene.

The final moments may be her finest singing on the recording. We hear mellow, heartbreaking tones for "Su me ... morente" and a tender piano on "Fidan" that is deeply affecting. Her low may show the usual signs of nasality, but it becomes effective on "del mio delitto," and, higher up, a hushed "Solleva" is almost as striking as Souliotis's. Her *pianissimo* on ... "ro" of "venero" is also good, but there is an abrasive climb up to it at full voice. A gasped "Non ma ..." in "Non maledire," and a rapt final "Non maledire a me" as the line is repeated, closes the most creditable stretch in her interpretation.

Ghena Dimitrova's Abigaille was well practiced by the time her DG recording was released in 1983. Apparently, though, she herself was aware of having gone through a bad patch around the time it was made. She had not been well. Her title to the role lay primarily in massive vocal power, so unlike her immediate predecessor. But she does not have the latter's musical or poetic imagination. That is supplied more in the occasionally wilful, occasionally inspired conducting of her *maestro*, the late Giuseppe Sinopoli. Piero Cappuccilli sings Nabucco, Placido Domingo, Ismaele, and Evgeny Nesterenko, Zaccaria.

Her entrance is compromised by a low B that is not secure, but she offers a naturally threatening "Talamo/La tomba a voi sarà," possible with a voice like hers. Unfortunately, she loses the low B flat in the flourish on "sospeso" and lacks the legato for the "Io t'amava!" She does soften the tone for "Ah, se m'ami," but, like Mancini, there isn't too much change in face. The downward scale in the coda is taken extremely softly, and Sinopoli ends the trio just as quietly.

The recitative to her Act II *scena* packs a certain punch, but moments of uncertainty, like ... "sse" of "fosse" that catches her at a gap in her middle, detract. Memorable is a snarly quality in "alla minor Fenena," and the run in "iniqui/Tutti" is good. A similar flourish at "il mio furore," though, is insecure, and she can barely finish the lower half of the two-octave leap on "sdegno," showing some insecurity in sustaining the middle C. This seems due more to misjudged breath and phrasing than to any inherent weakness in her low. The cavatina, while characterized by rich tone, has too much of a plummy quality, conveying more a sense of trudging from note to note than one of instinctive feeling. One might characterize such singing as "quoting" the music rather than expressing it. This language of dots seems more an occasion here for efficient sound-making than for communication. This reading doesn't lack dynamic variety; it's simply that the reason for the variety doesn't seem tied to innate expression. She's more expressive in the cabaletta where she seems less hemmed in. As with other interpreters, there are no trills, but her flexibility is expressive in its simple way. The *da capo* is included, although, as with most who include it, any differentiation with the first statement seems minimal. The high C is downright exciting, forcing acknowledgement of an imposing instrument, if not one of ideal musicality.

In Abigaille's Act III confrontation with the Nabucco of Piero Cappuccilli, one realizes how huge Dimitrova's voice is. Her idiosyncracies may be exaggerated by DG's close studio miking. In addition to a slight unsteadiness and lack of focus, there is some slurred passagework, but as the scene develops, her suppleness improves. The apparent choppiness of her line is a recurring problem, and it adds to a vaguely throaty quality that, again, may be unduly exaggerated by the close miking. There is an abundance of energy to much of the confrontation, although "Oh, dell'ambita gloria" seems perfunctory in expression. A galvanized "Esci! Invan mi chiedi pace" contrasts with Sinopoli's slow tempo for Nabucco's phrases. These suddenly require of Dimitrova a quiet dynamic for interjections like "Insano."

Dimitrova's final appearance in Act IV imparts a matter-of-fact quality to death, but a nondescript death is not what Verdi's music suggests. She improves with "Solleva Iddio" and even manages an atypical *pianissimo* on "venero," though not with a floating quality. There is an unruly delivery of the syncopated notes on "me" and a quiet desperation on the final "Non maledire." In the final analysis, Dimitrova's Abigaille lacks individuality, even though her vocal abundance, however unvaried, seems indispensable in this brutal role.

Koch/Schwann has released a "live" 1996 performance of the Arena di Verona production starring today's leading Verdi baritone, Paolo Gavanelli, in the title role. His portrayal is worthy of the finest on disc, however uneven his colleagues. The performance is led by Anton Guadagno, Gilberto Maffezzoni sings Ismaele, and Paata Burchuladze is Zaccaria. The Abigaille, Monica Pick-Hieronimi, makes an inauspicious entrance, but by the end of the evening she is intriguing and grows appealing in an odd way. Some well-defined tones in the middle high have a shine to them, although the low is weak, and, in addition, there are bad rasps in the register break. The entire voice takes its sweet time steadying down, there being acute examples of wobble throughout the range until the end of Act II! It is clearly not a lightweight instrument, despite its translucent coloring. Unfortunately, the lurches from register to register are particularly uncomfortable in her recitative "Prode guerrier," and the flourish on "sospeso" is pretty much a muddle. Then, in the "Io t'amava," a haunting "avrei" shows how comfortable her voice can be in spun-out lines where the vocal action is not too fast or furious. We have a soft downward scale in the coda in which the more appealing qualities of the instrument come through.

In her Act II recitative, there is a fine flourish on "iniqui tutti," offset by more rasping and register lurches. On "sdegno," she doesn't quite reach the high C and badly aspirates a mere approximation in her low register for the middle C. Impossible to avoid is her frustrating lack of any projection of authority at this point. Her wistful cavatina is a distinct improvement: a tender "altri al duol"; a fine legato for "mi torna un giorno sol"; a well-handled descent on a later "duol," plus a musical weeping inflection on a later "un giorno sol." There is occasional shortness of breath, but she ends with assurance on a lovely cadenza.

The cabaletta, while lacking optimum power, is precise enough, with a respectable try at all the trills. There is no *da capo*, and she ends on a solid high C.

Her Act III confrontation with Nabucco starts oddly with an almost yodeled delivery of the wide-ranging passagework on "al voto suo dêi tu," but her subsequent flourish on ripping up the parchment is more impressive, despite a sour finish. Alongside Gavanelli's "Oh, di qual'onta," which is perfection itself, Pick-Hieronimi's reasonably musical "Oh, dell'ambita gloria" somehow seems weak. There is no projection of an expressive sweep to the melody, precisely what her formidable partner shares with all great artists. This failing would matter less if Gavanelli weren't so overwhelming. She does end the first part of the duet with a nice cadenza on "al piè." Her most fluent singing is in "Oh, vedran se a questa schiava" in the coda.

Pick-Hieronimi's affecting vulnerability at her final appearance is vaguely reminiscent of Mirella Freni. There is that vivid sense of actually addressing someone directly in "Ah! tu dicesti," and she practically owns the *pianissimo* on "venero"—it feels absolutely right the way she floats it. The syncopations on "me" climax in another *pianissimo* that is even more mesmerizing. Pick-Hieronimi's credentials as a born Abigaille may remain in question, but this fine ending confirms her credentials as an accomplished musician.

More vocally suited to the role, but not such a musician, is today's Abigaille, Maria Guleghina. Her interpretation can be heard in a "live" recording on Valois from 1998. Daniel Oren conducts. Renato Bruson, sounding sadly frayed, sings Nabucco, Fabio Armiliato is Ismaele, and Ferruccio Furlanetto is Zaccaria.

Here is a singer with no weakness at the bottom of her voice. Her low B in "Prode" is strong. Her problem lies in a wild top register. It is evidently a powerful enough top, but it sounds undisciplined. The voice itself would appear not fully warmed up. "Sospeso" is delivered easily enough if not with ideal crispness. As soon as she launches into "Io t'amava," a lack of focus in the tone can no longer be ignored. In addition, the line breaks up badly at certain words like "potrei," while passagework is sometimes attacked flat.

Basic breath control problems dog her from the outset of her grand *scena* in Act II; the overall effect lacks authority as she drops the end of some phrases. The flourish on "furore," however, is good, while the high C for the daunting two-octave drop on "sdegno" is a bit screamy. Singing on an indistinct vowel, Guleghina then takes an extra breath in the middle to launch a repeated "sdegno" on a breathy middle C. The cavatina is a slight improvement. The opening is properly rapt, and "degli altri al duol/Ah! chi del perduto" makes an impressive effect, sung on one breath. Nevertheless, there are still enough moments of uncertain control to compromise the mood. Soft passagework is aspirated; for "Soffriva," the tone itself turns as wild and unfocused as in Act I; the line is fractured at "Piangeva all'altrui pianto," and a turn on "incanto" is badly mangled. In the cabaletta, she doesn't have the trills. But, more important, the strong low of the first act seems absent, as the word "schiava" is lost entirely. Throughout this bravura piece, passagework is also poorly articulated and a flat high note seals an uncertain first statement. In the *da capo*, she is somewhat more precise, presumably because she adopts a softer attack. In the coda, though, she drops out of the closing measures, preparing herself merely for another screamy high C. All in all, pretty discouraging.

The third act is a marked improvement, showing that she must have a severe warm-up problem. Suddenly, we have a good delivery of the climactic turn in the flourish on "suo," and she is more involved, with tense indignation at "Qui volli attenderti" uttered through clenched teeth. The passagework is cleaner in the *insieme* phrases with Bruson (awfully unsteady here). More magnificent yet is both the musical and dramatic effect of Guleghina's "Sì ... d'una schiava/Che disprezza il tuo poter," which ticks off perfection. The "Esci! Invan mi chiedi pace" is sung at a slower tempo than usual, but it is highly effective. Her delivery here marks a brilliant fusion of vocal and dramatic authority. It may be her best moment, with the voice finally showing what it can do when fully warmed up. She then softens at the close of the solo with a quietly biting "al disonor." In the coda, when she interjects another "Esci," it becomes a heartless dismissal, dripping with disgust.

In her final scene, Guleghina portrays an Abigaille almost too weak to get her words out. "Fenena" is desperate in its weakness. Some imagination is applied too with a "Punita o ben ne sono" that is delivered with a mini-*crescendo* on ... "ta" and a musical shudder. Her head tones are now in play, with an affecting piano on "s'amavano," an especially translucent tone on "Solleva Iddio," and a clean attack on "venero," even though the crest of the piano is a bit breathy. There is a beautiful *crescendo* on "a me," but, instead of delivering syncopated notes leading to its climax, Guleghina delivers one long sumptuous tone leading to the phrase's upward conclusion.

There is some fine singing from this Abigaille, but one is intrigued that it should be concentrated in the last two acts only.

✑ 13 ✐

Verdi
(1813–1901):
Macbeth

Though Giuli Borsi, being a special favorite of Verdi's, could have been expected eventually to take on the role of Lady Macbeth, the opera's actual premiere took place in 1847 with an altogether different diva, Marianna Barbieri-Nini, creating this last *assoluta* role. In Lady Macbeth's music, the aesthetic problems associated with applying the *assoluta* vocal traditions to a persona of pure evil are dealt with somewhat more imaginatively than in Abigaille's *Nabucco* role. Verdi still seems to eschew that peculiar nobility that is the hallmark of Donizetti's queens, for instance, or of Norma. Again, as in the case of Abigaille, this lack appears to be due to Verdi's regarding an *assoluta* characterization as the province only of the unnatural persona. Francesco Maria Piave's libretto for *Macbeth* did not salvage quite as much of the original Shakespearean texture as Boito's genius would in *Otello* and *Falstaff* at the end of Verdi's operatic career. But Verdi, nevertheless, always regarded *Macbeth* as one of his favorites. It premiered on March 14, 1847, at the Teatro della Pergola in Florence.

Lady Macbeth's vocal odyssey is effectively encapsulated in four specific arias, three of which have been frequently excerpted since the rescuscitation of this work during World War II. The arias are Lady Macbeth's "Vieni, t'affretta…. Or tutti sorgete" in Act I when she first learns of the witches' prophecy from Macbeth's letter; "La luce langue" in the first scene of Act II when she anticipates Banquo's murder; "Si colmi il calice" in the last scene of Act II when she

187

toasts the guests during Macbeth's hallucination of Banquo's ghost, and the Sleepwalking Scene, "Una macchia," in the last act.

The first of these, frequently referred to as the letter scene, has, in the "Vieni" cavatina, a mildly florid display of what seems to be deliberately opposed vocal registers. Another requirement in this section is the ability to spin out a pair of trills in the lower half of the voice at the words "Io ti darò valore." The "Or tutti" cabaletta is a *tour de force* of heroic coloratura and, unlike the climactic flourishes in Abigaille's cabaletta, constantly juxtaposes the different registers of the voice throughout the piece. The coloratura flourishes here are just as intricate as they are heroic, fully equalling the combination in Abigaille's "Salgo già," and easily surpassing the suppleness required in Lady Macbeth's "Vieni" cavatina. At one point, in a long somber phrase ending with the word "immota," the singer must go as low as Lady Macbeth's range ever takes her (a low B at "ta" of "immota"); then right after that the music swoops up to phrases lying almost as high as the role ever goes. This cabaletta has no real tessitura at all and is about as close as Verdi came to the extreme contrasts present in Queen Elizabeth's final aria at the conclusion of *Roberto Devereux*.

Originally, in the anticipation of Banquo's murder at the opening of Act II, Verdi had the Lady sing the aria "Trionfai." This was a somewhat perfunctory bravura piece that added nothing new or unexpected to the character. Its range is from middle D to high C. Nearly twenty years after *Macbeth*'s 1847 premiere, Verdi mounted a revised version for Paris with a considerably rewritten libretto by Charles-Louis-Etienne Truinet and Alexandre Beaune. Not much is known of the Lady Macbeth for this production, a Mme. Rey-Bolla, save that she was near the end of her career. She was the first performer to sing the new "La luce langue" in place of the old "Trionfai."

"La luce langue" is a thoroughly remarkable piece consisting of a continuous skein of melody going seamlessly from a cavatina structure for its opening moments to a kind of cabaletta for its rousing finish. As Martina Arroyo points out, there are a few phrases in the aria that stay high, requiring an easy high B. The prevailing tessitura is nevertheless much lower, and only a singer with a low register capable of sustaining Norma's "In mia man" or Elisabetta's "Alma infida" could hope to do full justice to this specially composed Verdi aria.[74]

The role of Lady Macbeth as created by Barbieri-Nini already required elsewhere in its music the kind of use of the lower register that made it a real *assoluta* part, but the exigencies of the new "La luce langue" now put it far closer to mezzo than Abigaille ever is.

Immediately preceding the final section of this new aria, there are two somber phrases lying completely in a contralto tessitura, "Ai trapassati regnar non cale" (the dead have no desire to rule) and "A loro un requiem, l'eternità!" (for them a lasting peace, eternity), and ending with another low B on "... tà" of "l'eternità."

By introducing a new aria at this point with its unusual use of the lowest register, Verdi may perhaps be honoring the tradition of invoking a role's lowest note to mark the falling action of the drama, thus following in the footsteps of Cherubini, Bellini, and Donizetti. This once again recalls Cherubini's way of using the *assoluta*'s lowest note to intimate the crucial nature of Creon's decision to let Médée stay one extra day; Bellini's way of intimating the shattering discovery on Norma's part of Pollione's betrayal with Adalgisa, or Donizetti's way of highlighting Bolena's arrest and Elisabetta's condemnation of Essex. Verdi may thus be giving the hearer a hint of the importance of Banquo's murder as the springboard for Macbeth's eventual decline and loss of credibility. It is hard to be absolutely certain of this, but it is an unusual coincidence that in five of the nine *assoluta* roles with which this survey is concerned — Médée, Bolena, Norma, Elisabetta, and Lady Macbeth — their respective lowest notes all become conspicuously used at that act or scene actually depicting or immediately preceding the point of no return.

In this special *scena* for Lady Macbeth, the closing cabaletta section ends with the last use of heroic coloratura in the score. The instrumental accompaniment is heavier than in any previous *assoluta* aria. A voice of Wagnerian weight is essential if the concluding phrases are to have an effect.

One Wagnerian diva who has performed this role, Birgit Nilsson, a singer whose lower range was never as strong as her upper, said of this entire act that, "without any time to shift gears, one must leap fearlessly from the profound 'La luce langue` to the merry coloratura of the banquet scene."[75] Lady Macbeth's "Brindisi" ("Si colmi il calice") to the assembled guests is the only aria of the four being scrutinized here that has not been regularly excerpted. One can see why. The same perfunctory quality that afflicted the eventually rejected "Trionfai" is also a characteristic of this drinking song. However, Verdi let the "Brindisi" stand in the 1865 Paris version.

Certainly, in the case of "Trionfai," its superficiality is all the more awkward since it concerns private thoughts that seem to pierce the heart of the character's obsessions. Yet, in the case of "Si colmi," the music is only concerned with a "merry" façade for her visitors, so it just barely passes muster. The nature of its intricate coloratura is strictly high-lying, bright, and unheroic in vocal weight. The Amazonian qualities of Lady Macbeth are clearly being soft-pedaled here. Within its context, as a projection of a lighter, less somber vocal persona, and as a polar opposite to the preceding aria of her innermost thoughts, "Si colmi" functions as a clever dramatic touch.

The iron will of the Lady is suggested by her determination to sing yet another verse of her "rallying" song after Macbeth's first Banquo hallucination. In this connection, critic John Ardoin has called attention to an extraordinary effect that Callas wrought for this reprise when singing the role at La Scala in 1952:

> The Macbeth "Brindisi" is presented first in sharp design, and Callas sings it with appropriate incisiveness and her usual care for detail.... When the aria reappears after Macbeth's first hallucination, Callas pointedly sings it in a heavier, more covered manner, as though trying by force of her will to gloss over Macbeth's outburst and command a reversion to gaiety at the banquet.[76]

Reference has already been made to the unconvincing ending of Abigaille's role, a moment of sudden personal remorse after such fury and determination. When it comes to *Macbeth*, rather than presenting remorse as a believable development on the part of a singularly unattractive character, Shakespeare showed Lady Macbeth's dissolution in the form of nightly restlessness and mental collapse. Piave wrote this out faithfully in his libretto and gave Verdi the opportunity of composing what was, in essence, a "mad scene" of singular originality, "Una macchia." The composer strongly believed that this scene and the Act I duet for the Macbeths following Duncan's murder were the two most effective sequences of the score.

When one observes how Verdi, musically, shaped the course of his villainous *assoluta* heroines, one realizes that a kind of reversal has taken place. The usual pattern for those *assoluta* heroines predating Verdi was to present them at the outset of the opera at a relatively secure point in their existence, and with serene, even music to match. The metamorphosis from this kind of self-control to great dramatic outbursts by the end of the opera was demonstrated in *Armida*, where we heard the sorceress's transformation from a limpid beloved of Rinaldo's to a vengeful harpy in her final scene; in *Anna Bolena*, where the heroine's sorrowful acceptance of her bleak existence with the King gave way to heroic utterances and scornful pyrotechnics in her final aria; in *Norma*, where the heroine went from "Casta Diva" in the first scene to chesty threatening trills to Pollione in the last, and in *Roberto Devereux*, where the Queen went from her lyric *scena* in the first act, "L'amor suo … Ah ritorna," to her thundering condemnation of Nottingham and Sara in the last, "Quel sangue."

Verdi turned this around. In *Nabucco*, the scheming warrior, Abigaille, used a chesty tessitura starting on a threatening low B with her opening recitative, "Prode guerrier." Her entire energies were at first bent on conquest and destruction, then ended in an almost too facile way with an aria of ethereal repentance. Now, in *Macbeth*, the Lady has begun with ambition and cruelty much like Abigaille's, changing to a flighty coloratura in the Banquet Scene and, finally, to seemingly disembodied phrases in the Sleepwalking Scene.

There are many shifts in vocal color required for "Una macchia," but the palette is less bold than Lady Macbeth's previous music. The aria ends on a notoriously difficult high D flat marked *pppp*. This is the highest that Lady Macbeth, or any other *assoluta* role, ever reaches. It seems only natural that, with the ascendancy of the straight soprano voice, the last *assoluta* part of this era should end with a technical feat solely within the capabilities of an easy high soprano.

By 1847, the tradition of the higher voice was everywhere. Verdi had originally expected his Lady Macbeth to be Johanna Sophie Loewe. She, like Verdi's other favorites at the time, was always a soprano. She debuted at Vienna in a revival of Donizetti's *Otto mesi in due ore*, the aborted Paris revision of which was discovered by Maestro Will Crutchfield in the 1980s. Adina and other light roles such as Amina in 1837 were to follow. Then, in 1838, in Frankfurt, Loewe sang her first Norma. Her career was now taking off. Though Verdi and Wagner are generally assumed to have been in fundamental disagreement regarding many aspects of opera, they shared a great enthusiasm for Loewe's artistry. When she made her concert debut in Paris in 1841, Wagner remarked on her

> ... triumphant success. She sang Adelaide as well as an Italian aria, thus showing us the difference between the German and Italian manner of singing.... On all sides it was acknowledged that she would prove a distinct asset here, since besides enormous vocal agility she possesses a beautiful voice, which is unfortunately not the case with the existing prima donnas, Dorus-Gras, Cinti-Damoreau and Persiani.[77]

Verdi went one step beyond Wagner. He gave her the roles of Elvira in *Ernani* and Odabella in *Attila*. Though the role of Elvira does not require the heroic flexibility of a defining *assoluta* part, the spinto agility needed for her main aria, "Ernani, involami," is, nevertheless, considerable. Rosa Ponselle spells out some of Elvira's difficulties in her autobiography:

> Here was a soprano role that had given nearly everyone else problems. The best-known piece of music in the score, "Ernani, involami," illustrates why: the vocal line lies extremely high one moment, then drops impossibly low the next. In between are passages that require total security of technique. Some consider it the most difficult soprano aria Verdi ever wrote. I found it less so.... For me it was a moment of victory because, after the "Ernani, involami," my hardest work in the score was done. From then on it was a pleasant downhill coast till the final curtain.[78]

Loewe's career was fairly short. After having been involved with the *Ernani* premiere in 1844 and the creation of Odabella in Verdi's *Attila* (1846), her intonation soon began to fail her. A performance of *Ernani* at Florence in the autumn of 1846 greatly upset Verdi; all of a sudden "It was impossible," Verdi commented, "to sing more out of tune than Loewe did." The eventual world premiere in 1847 of *Macbeth* was consequently given to Marianna Barbieri-Nini, and Loewe duly retired in 1848.[79]

It's ironic that certain mezzos like the superb Shirley Verrett have recorded Lady Macbeth, since the role happens to be one of the few *assoluta* roles created by a straight soprano. Perhaps it is this part's twentieth-century associations with mezzo that have fostered a few misleading descriptions of its creator as a mezzo as well. In fact, Marianna Barbieri-Nini was always a soprano like the other *assoluta*s of Verdi's generation. She made her debut as a soprano in 1840 and continued singing in that *fach* throughout her career. Soon after her debut, she was heard in such near-*assoluta* roles as Lucrezia Borgia and Semiramide. She already had the *assoluta* Anna Bolena under her belt by the time she created Lady Macbeth.

Preparations for *Macbeth* were unusually prolonged, and there was considerable tension throughout the rehearsal period. Though it is actually unclear whether Barbieri-Nini's voice was as gorgeous as Loewe's, her intense work apparently pleased Verdi. He had wanted something more than straight singing in many passages of the arduous role, due to the dramatic demands in projecting the nonhuman feelings and actions that characterize the Lady's personality. There may even be a possibility that he chose Barbieri-Nini for the role because of her unusually plain looks! The fact that consummate vocal artistry was required, though, seems obvious. By the time of her retirement in 1856, Barbieri-Nini, in addition to performing Bolena and Lady Macbeth, had also sung Gemma and Abigaille.[80]

Shortly after the *Macbeth* premiere, Eugenia Tadolini, in an 1848 production, sang the Lady at Naples. Though Verdi had already twice considered giving the role to a soprano, and had eventually gone beyond merely considering it when Barbieri-Nini became available, he protested at so radiant a vocal persona taking the role in a detailed letter sent to the Teatro San Carlo:

> Mme. Tadolini looks beautiful and good, and I should like Lady Macbeth to look ugly and evil. Mme. Tadolini sings to perfection, and I should like Lady Macbeth not to sing at all. Mme. Tadolini has a stupendous voice — clear, limpid, powerful: I should like in Lady Macbeth a voice rough, harsh, and gloomy. Mme. Tadolini's voice has angelic qualities: I should like the voice of Lady Macbeth to have something diabolical about it.[81]

However, the Teatro San Carlo stood by its prima donna!

At first sight, it is a puzzle what exactly was going on here. Verdi had already considered assigning the part to a beautiful voice in the person of Loewe before her sense of pitch went bad. So it cannot have been beauty *per se* that he was objecting to. Some impresarios, nevertheless, have taken this letter quite literally and have routinely concurred with the frequent casting of a lesser vocalist for Lady Macbeth — a vocalist who, in addition, might not even have the flexibility for Verdi's intricate vocal writing.

Others, like Leonie Rysanek, a sumptuously voiced Lady Macbeth if ever there was one, suggest that Eugenia Tadolini may have been a poor actress, and that therefore this was Verdi's tactful way of dealing with the fact that the histrionic demands of Shakespeare's villainess would have been beyond her capacities.[82]

For both these interpretations, there are decided problems. On the one hand, it seems unlikely that Verdi would bother to compose the last *assoluta* role of his era and then bend over backwards to insure that, not only would it not be given to a proper kind of singer, it would actually be given to a performer who was "not to sing at all." On the other, the explanation that Tadolini was a poor actress will not suffice. When Donizetti first experienced the soprano's artistry quite a number of years before *Macbeth*, his reaction was perhaps one of the most unequivocal ever recorded in the history of opera: "She is a singer, she is an actress, she is everything."[83] No, Tadolini was clearly one of those lucky artists who had it all.

It may be that tact was partly the reason why Verdi couched his objections as he did. But it seems on closer examination that a criticism of Tadolini's *fach* as a limited kind of soprano was what was really involved. Though Verdi still stuck to his artistic attitude that the *assoluta*'s music was suitable for female villainy only, and though he still, nominally, appears to have maintained his generation's acceptance of the straight soprano in the *assoluta* repertoire, he was beginning perhaps to see — as he had not in his initial casting of poor Strepponi as Abigaille — that a darker sound, call it dramatic soprano, call it mezzo, whatever, was essential. Though sopranos were still being used by him, Verdi was becoming more appreciative of singers who could darken the voice at will.

Tadolini did not have the ability to sound "gloomy" or "diabolical," which Verdi wanted. Thus, while we should take with a grain of salt his saying that Lady Macbeth should "not be sung at all," he must have meant it when he insisted that this *assoluta* role must not sound clear, limpid, or angelic.

Verdi's artistic development showing a gradual leaning toward the deeper female instrument manifested itself two years after the Tadolini *Macbeth* in his giving the role of Lina in *Stiffelio* (1850) to mezzo-turned-soprano Gazzaniga Malaspina, and this leaning reached its ultimate fruition in the decision to give Lady Macbeth what was, in effect, a mezzo aria, the "La luce langue," fifteen years later in Paris.

After the crudities of Abigaille, Verdi's imagination and deeper understanding of the expressive latitude of a multi-colored voice were shown in the greater subtlety of Lady Macbeth's music. The specter of caricature has been exorcised and true character emerges. This music may not have the artistic sureness of the greatest *assoluta* scores from Verdi's predecessors, who show a profounder understanding of what such vocal writing can contain. Still, Lady Macbeth offers unusual interpretive opportunities for a performer capable of doing full justice to a Norma or a Queen Elizabeth. Verdi, the last to compose *assoluta* operas, does reveal a more restless genius than his compatriots. *Macbeth* has isolated scenes where Verdi's narrative greatness emerges positively against the clichés of the time. But such scenes often demonstrate greater mastery over dramatic structure, and what Verdi himself termed "la parola scenica," than inner psychological exploration. Verdi would master the latter soon enough, and there are already hints of that in *Macbeth*, but the balance between the psychological and the narrational would remain different from Donizetti throughout Verdi's career. The *assoluta* idiom was not Verdi's true métier.

Shakespeare's Lady on disc

Since Verdi went to the lengths of saying "I should like Lady Macbeth not to sing at all," this shows us how far we've come from the heyday of Donizetti. Probably Verdi was suggesting nonsinging as a preferable alternative to homogeneous vocalism, which now struck him as inadequate. His varied texture is intricate enough in *Macbeth* to qualify the Lady's music as defining *assoluta* writing. Hence, thoroughly polished singing of a sort familiar to Donizetti must have been in Verdi's mind at some level. It was clearly a contradiction.

After his rather brash exercise of vocal expression in *Nabucco*, Verdi started bringing back in *Macbeth* an importance to the *word* that had not been current in Italy for decades, even though Bellini had been moving in that direction.

The caliber of recorded interpreters of Verdi's Lady can sometimes be pegged as much by their attentiveness to the word as by their discipline in musical values. Musical values do not carry the full expression of three-dimensional character in the Lady that they do in Donizetti's finest writing. Although the Lady's sheer music may carry more emanation of character than Abigaille's, verbal values are now more essential. If they aren't honored in performance, the Lady can seem crude alongside a Donizetti queen. This is not a qualitative judgment on Verdi, but it is a distinction in method, and betokens a final break with one aspect of the *assoluta* idiom that our early examination of Weber brought home: that the mere sounds of an inspired artist transforming the composer's dots into conveyed feelings could be self-sufficient in presenting a three-dimensional character. No longer. In Verdi's Lady, the inspired librettist is once again needed. The result heralds a whole range of pioneering Verdi works that are equally fine. The *assoluta* era closes.

Mezzo-soprano Elisabeth Höngen inaugurates the recorded legacy of complete *Macbeth*s. We hear her Lady in an entire radio performance from 1943 under conductor Karl Böhm. This also features baritone Mathieu Ahlersmeyer in the title role, tenor Josef Witt as Macduff and bass Herbert Alsen as Banquo. It was first released on a Urania LP. There are some rather startling Böhm cuts in this performance. Perhaps the most puzzling one goes right from the conclusion of the Lady's opening cabaletta to Macbeth all alone, thus snipping out the exchange where husband and wife plot the murder. We get no direct encounter between the two until right after the King has been killed!

While Höngen's reading is marked by a strong sense of dramatic commitment, it lacks the variety found in some of her successors. This may be due partly to her having performed the opera in German translation. For most interpreters, the key moments, in terms of character development and musical revelation, are the opening Letter *scena*, the duet "Fatal mia donna" after the regicide, the "La luce langue," the "Brindisi," and the Sleepwalking Scene. This is certainly true of Höngen. Like most interpreters, she appears to accept that the Macbeths' "Ora di morte" duet, added in Paris for the conclusion of Act III, is simply a moment of consolidation, rather than further development for the character.

Although one is intrigued by a mezzo in a complete *assoluta* role, the perils in *assoluta* singing are apparent in Höngen's adoption of Pauline Viardot-García's changes in 1859, when the latter was already in decline. Aspects of this version will be spotlighted as the individual changes are noted in the Höngen reading.

Throughout the performance, much of Höngen's singing is marked by a recurrence of quavery tone. In her entrance recitative, she adopts Viardot-García's decapitation of the highest note in its concluding flourish. These changes fit her voice well, as it is clear she is at her strongest in the middle high. There are, however, scant signs of *bel canto* schooling, while we know that was not true of Viardot-García. There are no trills for Höngen's entrance *scena*, and there is ungainly passagework throughout. It is heartening, however, to relish the imagination of a true actress. For instance, however clumsy the downward scale at the conclusion of the cadenza ending "Vieni! t'affretta," Höngen sees it as a faintly amused, faintly exasperated laugh, and delivers it that way. Maybe not too musical, but it honors the spirit of the role! A moment later, when the messenger informs her of the King's visit, the eery sweetness of Höngen's "Hier" is enough to curl one's hair. Too bad that, due to the German translation, the cabaletta's low B at "immota" does not make its full effect. Höngen must use the word "grauen" and lingers on the "n" consonant for the low B, robbing the moment of the ominous open vowel on "immota." The full effect of the cabaletta is also compromised by the omission of the *da capo*, and a severely truncated coda. In the regicide duet, "Fatal mia donna," there is an occasional cackling effect to her singing. Surprisingly, Höngen shows some real concern with Macbeth and his troubled feelings instead of the usual exasperation. Her vocal suppleness seems somewhat improved, albeit the passagework in the duet is not as demanding as in her entrance aria. Some staccati register well and there is a flow to her singing that is not apparent earlier. The grace notes for the phrases opening "Quell' animo trema" are also given special point. There is a problem here that typifies much of Böhm's entire reading: an over-deliberateness that robs the work of the spontaneity intrinsic to what Verdi was attempting. One can appreciate the furtiveness that Höngen injects into the introduction to the duet's cabaletta, but that admirably offhand touch is negated by Böhm's rigid treatment of the cabaletta. Höngen again surprises with even finer staccati at the end, but they lose focus after a few bars.

In Act II, Höngen's "La luce langue" boasts some nice soft effects here and there, and her low B, on "Ruh," is very strong. However, she becomes winded by the coda, and, even though the climactic top tones are strong enough, one notes that they are not sustained effectively — a sign of caution. The problems attendant on Höngen's occasional quavery tone persist in the "Brindisi." Compounding that, we miss out on any more trills, and the Viardot version lowers a few high notes. Höngen does the first statement of the "Brindisi" without the usual cut of the awkward phrases midway, but they are not delivered cleanly. For the climax, she offers an unmusical tremolo instead of a real trill. After delivering the uncut first statement, the reprise all but disappears, shrunk down to little more than the *insieme* phrases for the assembly.

The Sleepwalking Scene partially redeems this uneven reading. The actress is allowed some play here, and Höngen takes advantage of that. She adopts a stark *marcato* when thinking of the old King's blood. Then, in recalling the Macduff family, she suggests the sound of a small infant. An eery *ppp* is used to good effect as she wonders whether her hands will ever be clean. A sudden gasp is heard before the final phrases beckoning Macbeth to bed. These and an array of like touches bring this nighttime odyssey vividly to life. Against that is a badly blurred flourish when she urges Macbeth to compose himself. Well before the concluding phrase with its high D flat leading down to the D flat on the stave, all the preparatory lines are down an octave as well. This is then linked to a similar transposition of the final phrase with its high D flat. Here, however, rather than simply maintain the same intervals an octave down, Höngen is heard bringing the final lower D flat up to the score's original D flat on the stave, making both notes one and the same pitch — a disturbing effect.

Our next Lady, Margherita Grandi, provides the earliest recording we have in the original Italian. We are fortunate to have her in the entire role, since she never recorded it complete in the studio. Her interpretation survives thanks to a somewhat murky taped radio broadcast from 1947. Francesco Valentino sings the title role, Walter Midgley is Macduff, and Italo Tajo sings Banquo, an interpretation we hear again later. The conductor is Berthold Goldschmidt.

Grandi starts with somewhat unsteady tone in the opening *scena*. But in the cavatina "Vieni, t'affretta," there are two deft trills at "Io ti darò valore" by way of compensation: she softens for the first one on "ti" and comes out in full voice for "va" … of "valore." We hear another soft dynamic when she tackles the low B further on. It is perhaps surprising in the years B.S. (before Sutherland) to hear a *bel canto* performance taken with all repeats intact, but such is the case here. Grandi and Maestro Goldschmidt include the *da capo* of the cabaletta "Or tutti sorgete." It is here that Grandi's voice finally steadies down to disclose an expressiveness used with imagination. Her interpretation is always alert to the mercurial nature of the Lady's character as limned by Verdi. She can be forbidding one moment but almost playful the next: typical is the chillingly breezy — and reassuring — laugh when she tries to rally her husband in the duet following the regicide. Also telling are her clean upward staccati in the same duet.

Act II begins with a deeply considered "La luce langue." The inflection on "È necessario" makes it an angry rebuke to herself rather than the usual general pronouncement for all. A little further on, while she may make the low B at "eternità" very soft, it is still apparent from the way she shapes the entire phrase that she is perfectly comfortable with this tessitura. The final brisk coda is a musical and dramatic triumph. The *slancio* shown here is matched by Goldschmidt's sympathetic baton. He is right there with her all the way. Grandi is so caught up in the feelings of the coda that she sweeps right through the closing "chi fu predetto Re cadrà" as a single phrase, linking the top note on "Re" with the concluding climax on "… rà" of "cadrà" as part of a single musical thought! In the next scene, Grandi sings every note of the first statement of the "Brindisi" without cutting the middle section. She surpasses herself in the *da capo* when, midway through the repeat, she prolongs an utterly spectacular trill, sustaining it during a long *crescendo*.

But she eventually pays the price for all this derring-do: it is evident that, finally, vocal fatigue has set in, what with a number of severe pitch problems in the final Sleepwalking Scene. Her alertness to detail remains unimpaired. She is able to go from virtual sobbing at "balsami non può" to sharply reining in everything at "il sangue." Her high D flat at the end unfortunately disappears into the radio crackle, so it's hard to tell whether the note comes out right.

Intriguing it is to go from someone reasonably adept in the *bel canto* style to two dyed-in-the-wool Wagnerians, Martha Mödl and Astrid Varnay. It seems instructive to examine them side by side, since they complement each other in so many ways, each seeming to make up for the other's lapses. In any case, Lady Macbeth is one *assoluta* role much associated with Wagnerian voices. Let's take a look at these two divas in three excerpts: the Letter *scena*, the "La luce langue," and the Sleepwalking Scene.

Mödl's Lady is available on a Myto CD of a "live" performance, broadcast from Berlin in 1950. Joseph Keilberth conducts and Josef Metternich sings the title role. This performance is in German. Ironically, taking Verdi's written remarks too literally, there would seem to be an overwhelming feature to Martha Mödl's Lady that disqualifies her immediately: a sumptuous instrument. In the Letter Scene, the warmth and shine of the voice dominate one's first impressions. But, as Mödl proceeds through the opening recitative, it becomes obvious that here we have a great actress of the lyric stage as well, one who can make the voice fully as expressive as it is beautiful. The quickening of her blood in the wild abandon of her singing reflects a palpable relish for all the hurdles awaiting those seeking a throne. These terrors and other obsessions evoke a macabre joy from this Lady. The results are riveting. In combining a sumptuous tone with such commitment, is Mödl too good to be true? Well, her cavatina tells us something more: on the one hand, utter grandeur, a true legato, surging top notes, and a triumphantly assured close, but on the other, one blurred trill here, one not attempted there, and an occasional awkward breath. While the balance is clearly on the credit side, technical matters might stand some improvement. There is bizarre confusion in the *materia di mezzo*, with the Messenger failing to make an appearance! Without the Messenger announcing the King's visit, the embarrassed Mödl is deprived of her musical cue, and this throws her off until the orchestra helps her regain both her bearings and her dignity. The cabaletta betrays Mödl's ungainly passagework, and she drops out during the closing measures, gathering her forces for a final ringing top note. Even so, the variegated colors in her opulent sound and their rich drama galvanize the audience into a thundering ovation.

The Astrid Varnay broadcast is in the original Italian. First released on a Melodram LP, it comes from 1951 and is led by Vittorio Gui. Ivan Petrov is Macbeth. Varnay offers a stark reading of the spoken letter. Hers is a forbidding sound that is certainly imposing but anything but warm. Not a beautiful voice at all, there is still a surprisingly clean delivery of the flourish leading into the cavatina, in contrast to Mödl's less precise delivery. Balanced against Varnay's crispness is her tendency to lag behind the beat. In addition, unsteadiness and lack of legato intrude in the "Vieni! t'affretta!" But there is a respectable stab at all the trills, and she takes top notes without as much swooping as Mödl, though at some sacrifice of the latter's elemental surge. Varnay's guttural tone is sometimes a liability, but seems to work with the character. If only her control of pitch in the mid-range were more secure. One likewise regrets the absence of real color in the low. The cabaletta features more of her deftly articulated passagework and a sweeping delivery of the final measures in one breath!

In the "La luce langue," it's disconcerting to find Mödl this time showing uncertainties in pitch. There is still a rich gloom pervading her delivery, especially suited to this aria, and her "Noch ein Verbrechen" ("Nuovo delitto") gets a vivid whisper. Unfortunately, these pitch uncertainties vie with signs of fatigue in the coda: she is plainly short of breath, her top is not as full as earlier, and she screams the final high note.

Varnay supplies an alternative here with a cleaner top. However, there is exaggerated scooping, and she flats badly on ... "sar" ... of "necessario." But this is preceded by a nice snarl on the second "Nuovo delitto!" The coda is riddled with wobbly tones, becoming more so as it proceeds, but there is a fine high note at the climax.

In the Sleepwalking Scene, Mödl whispers the opening, then succumbs to wide-eyed terror. This manic delivery is more extroverted and maenadic in its desperation than usual. We can even hear her running around the stage at odd moments, and the "Will these hands ne'er be clean" (in German) becomes a musical cry of despair — unforgettable. There is a hair-raising piano for the blood on her hands. "Banco ist tod," however, shows a recurrence of the fatigue in her high, and some passagework is later blurred. She loses breath on the high note climaxing the first iteration of "Komm," and transposes down the entire final phrase with its fearsome *pianissimo* high D flat.

Varnay's interpretation is the more traditional one, still troubled but dreamier. Once again, key words like "vegliardo" and "mani" wobble badly. Oddly, she makes a slight cut toward the conclusion: snipping out the last "andiam andiam, Macbetto" with its downward lurch into the low. Alongside these lapses, there are deft details that contrast with the more impulsive reading from Mödl: an eery "Di Fiffe il Sire" and "non surse ancor"; a *diminuendo* on "può"; implacable tones for the "I panni indossa"; crisp handling for the intricacies of the "non t'accusi," and another accomplished *diminuendo* at the crest of an upward scale on "Macbetto." She also ascends softly on an altered final "Andiam," starting lower than in the score, cresting only on the last syllable, without following the original approach to the *pianissimo* high D flat. On balance, Mödl's Lady remains the more involving, but Varnay, despite her bleaker tones, is the solider musician.

The next significant figure in the *Macbeth* discography is Maria Callas. It's hard to imagine anyone more suited to the role. She sang in only one production of it throughout her career, although, in her case, it's hard to imagine any other role so strewn with might-have-beens: at one point, Toscanini could have done it with her, while later, the Metropolitan could have enjoyed her Lady opposite Leonard Warren's Macbeth. But in the end, all she did was this one production directed by Carl Ebert at La Scala in 1952 and conducted by Victor De Sabata. It was telecast and an audio aircheck survives on various labels. Sadly, no kinescope is extant. The most readily available CD is a pressing on EMI.

However, this does not have the superior sound of the BJR LP. If the Verona label continues reprocessing BJR material, that would be the edition to acquire. Unfortunately, Verona distribution is spotty in most places. Callas never sang the complete role in the recording studio, although she did record three excerpts on a recital disc. The Ebert production at La Scala features Enzo Mascherini as Macbeth, Gino Penno as Macduff and Italo Tajo reprising his Banquo of five years earlier. Victor De Sabata's inspired baton makes this performance a gem. Unfortunately, while De Sabata and most of the principals are perfectly fine, there is a severe stature gap in the title role. Mascherini is simply not adequate either to his colleagues or Verdi's demands. Consequently, for much of the performance, Callas interprets alone. But her brilliant collaboration with De Sabata pays rich dividends.

In Act I, Callas's opening "Vieni! t'affretta" is marked by a very measured tempo that turns this opening sequence into something utterly portentous. There are fine low trills here, but the ending of the cavatina, effective as it is, does have a momentary intonation problem on "… gnar" of "regnar." She recovers the pitch, and the moment is not seriously affected, but it's somewhat startling for her to show such problems at this early stage of her career. The cabaletta is a tour de force. Unfortunately, she does not do the *da capo*. Still, every note of her intricate passagework is in place and De Sabata infuses the whole with superb energy. She shows easy command of the full range required, from clarion top tones down to a properly mysterious low B. In the post-assassination duet, Callas stays very calm. She's even reasonable at the repeated "Follie," evidently assuming that Macbeth can listen to reason if she says it often enough…. She indulges a quiet chuckle at her husband's fright when she launches "Sei vano, o Macbetto." At the "Quell' animo" section, the grace notes, clearly etched, express a combination of both amusement and scorn. Impatience and anger first appear after Macbeth declines to go back into the guest chamber with the dagger. "Dammi il ferro" is snapped out sharply with some real annoyance, but she still maintains a contained and quiet air. She only loses her cool at her return from the chamber, when singing of the blood now on her hands as well. Maintaining her hushed approach, she manages to impart a breathless urgency in the duet's cabaletta, with its fine upward staccati. De Sabata ends this scene effectively by having both Mascherini and Callas exploit the rests provided by Verdi as they make each syllable essentially a gasp: "un" "vil" "ti"—"mor."

In Act II, there is a thoughtful opening for "La luce langue," making it very much a private statement. The second "Nuovo delitto" is practically whispered, with a suggestion of unease, before Callas rallies for "È necessario." The deep phrases starting "Ai trapassati" open somewhat nasally, going soft for the low B of "eternità." The brisk coda is evil triumph, with a snarl thrown in. There isn't deep contentment here, although she permits herself a tiny glimmer of a smile midway. It's only momentary, and the harsh stance returns immediately thereafter. There is more smile in the "Brindisi" in the Banquet Scene. She does not soft-pedal her essential strength when singing to her guests, but it's the strength of an exuberant hostess, not a ruthless queen. Her trills are meticulously in place, making it regrettable that De Sabata cuts the middle section in the first statement. This "Brindisi" is Callas's sunniest moment, but the mood doesn't last. "Voi siete demente?" Callas asks her husband through clenched teeth. Exasperation and scorn give way to a cold iron smile in the voice at "gioia" aimed at the guests. She is evidently seething in the reprise of the "Brindisi," which features an even better trill than before at the final phrase.

The Sleepwalking Scene shows a harrowed Lady at the outset, De Sabata giving a restless quality to these nocturnal ramblings. There is then disgust at "vergogna" and the suggestion of lament at "vegliardo." She becomes unglued, a quietly babbling whine for "Di Fiffe il Sire." Then we are confronted with the image of someone caught like a rat in a trap at "Di sangue umano." She rebukes Macbeth sternly with her "Banco e spenta," slamming down on a terrifying "fossa" deep in her chest voice. We have another striking *crescendo* as she moves up the scale on "Andiamo." For the final phrase, the *pianissimo* high D flat is attacked cleanly and softly enough, but then she swims a bit in finding the pitch for the descent back to the treble stave an octave down. This is still a spellbinding conclusion. After Callas's last note, the audience withholds its applause during part of the postlude until she leaves the stage. Then they finally let go and the roof caves in. Both Callas and De Sabata maintain a nervous and feverish quality throughout this scene, honoring not only the restless rhythms of Verdi but a similar tension from Shakespeare's original scene as well. Verdi clearly meant to parallel that, and De Sabata and Callas are to be commended for having brought it out.

For many, the three excerpts Callas made in the recording studio in 1958 with conductor Nicola Rescigno were fine achievements: the Letter *scena*, the "La luce langue" and the Sleepwalking Scene. They are effective, but not as compelling as her readings in the telecast. Personally, I own up to being in an apparent minority when it comes to the studio account of the Sleepwalking Scene. It may be one of her more celebrated recordings, but it's always been something of a contradiction for me. Somewhat over-deliberate and segmented conducting seems to make for almost as over-deliberate and segmented phrasing from Callas. The irony is that she happens to be in strikingly good voice here, and there are certainly some evocative moments, not all of which are highlighted in the same way on the telecast. But what is more in one instance makes for less as a whole. Performed this way, the studio account becomes almost a stately oration. It's hard to see the nervous Shakespeare here, let alone the real Verdi, particularly after the earlier revelatory treatment of De Sabata.

Carl Ebert was supposed to direct Callas in *Macbeth* again, this time at the Metropolitan Opera, in the 1958–59 season. However, Sir Rudolf Bing, engaged in a game of brinkmanship with Callas's husband, Meneghini, finally canceled her contract on the day of her Dallas *Médée*. Callas's replacement was Leonie Rysanek, an artist who brings more vocal abundance and spontaneity to the role than Callas does, but whose technical and musical gifts are better suited elsewhere. Rysanek still imparts a vivid vocal face to the role, even though her brave spontaneity is not, in the end, as fully effective as Callas's calculation. The Met production was recorded for commercial release by RCA. Rysanek's Macbeth is Leonard Warren in one of his finest roles, Macduff is newcomer Carlo Bergonzi and Banquo is Jerome Hines. Erich Leinsdorf conducts.

From the moment Leonie Rysanek first raises her voice in song, following her spoken reading of Macbeth's letter, we seem in the presence of something demonic, possessed to the point of frenzy — a quality Rysanek could summon up on stage. It's heartening that, in the proper role, this can come across on a recording. Verdi wished to hear "something diabolical" in the role and Rysanek manifestly obliges. The paradox is that the glowing beauty of her sounds are so brilliantly capable of evoking terror. We not only hear this quality in the wild vocalism of the opening "Vieni! t'affretta!"; we also are made aware of it in Rysanek's chilling *pianissimo* for the phrases in response to the tidings that the old King will be visiting that night: "Duncano sarà qui? qui? qui la notte?" Unfortunately, the cabaletta is less effective because it requires more flexibility and mandates that the singer reach down to the low B. Rysanek, with all the sumptuousness of her instrument, is not quite up to either the flexibility or the low-lying vocalism expected here. Even the opening "Vieni" finds her wanting for the low-lying trills. Her duet with Macbeth following the assassination also shows some gaps in her technique. Although the grace notes at "Quell' animo" come out crisper than some of her other "little notes," to use a Birgit Nilsson term, the passagework in the coda is pretty imprecise. Dramatically, she's inspired: she shows true alarm at Macbeth's carrying on so when she comes out with an urgent repetition of "Follie." Her anxiety and, finally, utter impatience with Macbeth is well charted: it climaxes in an exasperated reading of "Dammi il ferro": she actually adds an "O" at the start of the line ("O dammi il ferro"), stepping on Warren's previous note in the process, practically telling him "We have no time for such nonsense!" Brilliant.

In Act II, "La luce langue" is not as effective as her opening "Vieni" in Act I. This is due to the simple fact that this aria lies considerably lower than her entrance aria. She cannot connect the phrases going lower down with her glorious sounds further up since she is a quintessential dramatic soprano, not a true *assoluta*. The low B fails to make a strong effect. The mood of the aria, nevertheless, is well caught, and there is an exciting surge of demonic energy for the higher-lying coda. It's nice to hear higher singing in the "Brindisi." Still, Rysanek is not ideally precise here. Again, there is no trill. She may sing it uncut, but with a few ungainly lunges at the passagework in the tricky middle section. Before the reprise, there is a glimmering of smoldering fury at "Voi siete demente?" Then she attempts to soothe her husband before resuming her party song. The reprise comes out peremptory and harried. Again, a startling effect.

The Sleepwalking Scene is brooding from the start. But it seems relatively unnuanced as well, as if parallelling the detachment of a dream. The riddle is that the essential stance is impassive but also forthright: straight-ahead assertions, not wispy phrases suggesting "stream of consciousness." Things don't start changing until more anxiety and concern enter at the repetition of "io non saprò," where the tone becomes softened and the phrase ends with a stifled sob. Then her tone gets conspiratorial at "Di sangue umano." There is a spectacular *decrescendo* at "può" of "balsami non può." Her weakly sighing "Ohimè" is preceded by another more overt sob. She breaks the phrase after "Banco e spento" giving the following "e dalla fossa" greater emphasis, perhaps also to renew her breath for a precipitate dip into the low on "fossa," which, frankly, is not effective. This is offset by one of the eeriest — and softest — readings of "non surse ancor" anywhere. The flourish at "Non t'accusi" comes out perfectly, bound into the phrase. This is capped by some high spellbinding *pianissimi* for the last phrases that are as creepy as they are ravishing. Oddly enough, Rysanek does not make the final high D flat anywhere near that soft. It is a semi-strong note instead, taking us out of dreamland rather than pulling us further in. The motivation is not immediately clear. Her *pianissimi* leading up to this final moment have been so effortless it seems unlikely that a *pianissimo* was really beyond her at this point. So we are left with a question.

Nineteen sixty was a banner year for two important productions, one at Covent Garden with Tito Gobbi and Amy Shuard, and one at Palermo with Giuseppe Taddei and Leyla Gencer.

One can only wish that Gobbi had been paired with Gencer at Palermo. One doesn't often hear a true partnership in this work, and Gobbi and Gencer would have made sparks together. Taddei, Gencer's Palermo partner, is richly communicative, singing with great imagination, but he is caught in uneven voice, expressive and plangent sounds alternating with moments of unsteady tone, shortness of breath and gravelly attacks. Gobbi may not vie with a Leonard Warren, or even a Taddei, when it comes to sheer sumptuousness of sound, but he is in good command of his instrument at Covent Garden. It's frustrating that his partner, Amy Shuard, while showing an equally healthy instrument, has only intermittent technical control.

Gobbi's and Shuard's colleagues are André Turp as Macduff and Forbes Robinson as Banquo. Francesco Molinari-Pradelli conducts. This broadcast is available on a number of different labels of limited distribution. The Bellavoce issue does not have any severe flaws, but its general sound is constricted, with minimal resonance around the voices. The effect is shrill and cutting.

One has to give credit to the resiliency of Shuard's top. She appears untiring, and there is a brilliant, hard quality to an easy upper register that complements some aspects of the character: the Lady's essential heartlessness and determination. It is also evident that Molinari-Pradelli is "babying" her throughout the coloratura sections. Passagework is sometimes labored or blurred and there is no trill. Her Italian also leaves a lot to be desired. She has a problem projecting effectively in the middle low register and is occasionally flat, although her very lowest notes can be quite respectable. She does make a good stab at the low Bs in the opening cabaletta and the "La luce langue." Shuard's problems with passagework are not confined to the opening *scena*. Throughout, a strong sustained tone in the high for some declaimed passage can often be followed by badly winded singing where she'll simply run out of steam in the middle of a roulade. A typical example is the unabridged "Brindisi," which sorely taxes her breath control. In general, the entire interpretation is cruder than most others. She may be conscientious enough in imparting the commitment required for the role, but one rarely gains a sense of discovery. The vocal stance is neither striking enough nor sufficiently varied to hold the listener's imagination. Even the bright and effective top betrays her at the close of the Sleepwalking Scene, where she cracks on the high D flat. She then proceeds to sustain the note successfully, and on pitch, but the climax has been breached. A disappointing performance.

Leyla Gencer's 1960 broadcast with Giuseppe Taddei is the earlier of her two extant *Macbeth*s. As in the Varnay broadcast, Vittorio Gui is at the podium, and Gencer's colleagues include Mirto Picchi as Macduff and Ferruccio Mazzoli as Banquo. The CD pressing on the Living Stage label sounds as if the music is unfolding inside a metal tunnel. This is unfortunate, because the entire performance is one of the finest interpretations of Verdi's opera on disc. (There does exist an old LP edition on Rodolphe that is more listenable, although still identifiable as a primitive dub off an AM station.) Gencer's later *Macbeth* is a 1968 broadcast opposite Giangiacomo Guelfi, where she is heard in poorer voice.

In 1960, Gencer offers a potent, haunting interpretation fully as individual in its way as Callas or Rysanek. We seem to catch her at just the right moment here. There are few of the pitch problems encountered in the '58 Bolena, and, while register breaks are occasionally apparent, they have not yet led to the kind of gravelly attacks heard in *Roberto Devereux*. Too often, this artist has seemed just short of greatness. A telling phrase delivered with authority and imagination will be followed by something vaguely amateurish. Not here. For once, she stabs at greatness and achieves it. One can only regret that her *Devereux* was not sustained at such a high level. It may be possible that the staggering variety in Donizetti's Virgin Queen would still have proved too much for her even in 1960, but one would like to be sure, since her Lady Macbeth contains some of the finest *assoluta* singing on disc. In addition, she honors the dramatic persona Verdi wanted in a Lady Macbeth voice: here is a Lady who sounds both "gloomy" and "diabolical."

We are still aware of the occasionally "burpy" scoop in one or two glottal attacks during the opening *scena*, but they are rare enough thereafter not to impede musical flow. Her trills are in control, and she maintains good passagework in the following cabaletta, where the image of someone on the scent for blood is vividly conveyed. She maintains uncanny calm for most of Macbeth's expostulations after the murder, even for the repeated "Follie," which leads into some fine staccati. The grace notes are delivered clearly, matched to amusement at Macbeth's fears. Like Callas, she loses her cool momentarily for a genuinely angry "Dammi il ferro." She regains her composure, though, upon returning with blood on her hands, impassively observing that it's time to wash up. More urgency takes over for the brisk coda ordering Macbeth back to bed, but Gencer is still magnificently unruffled — and her deft staccati here are nothing short of astounding!

Gui takes the "La luce langue" at a brisk pace, making it less brooding than usual. Her "È necessario" is an extroverted way of saying "let's get busy." The greatest contrast is made when the "Ai trapassati" is started very soft, growing louder, but not by much, for a solid low B on "eternità." One is occasionally aware of Gencer's weakness in her middle low register. However, she stays true to pitch, however relatively weak the tone in spots, and her communicative flair is unimpaired. In the coda, she ends strongly, delivering the final line with its two top notes as a single sweeping musical thought, recalling Margherita Grandi's way with these closing words. Her "Brindisi" in the Banquet Scene is a *tour de force*. Unfortunately, the middle section of the first statement is cut, as so often during these years. What remains is still dazzling — the image of a queen who revels in her new position. There is deft passagework, trills, tripping staccati suggestive of a stone skipping across a still pond. This is followed by a supremely self-possessed reaction to Macbeth's vision of Banquo's ghost. There is icy calm for "Voi siete demente?" Then, after delivering words of reassurance to the guests, as if trying desperately to convince herself that all is yet well, she conveys barely corralled panic in a vivid second statement of the "Brindisi," distinguished by one of her finest trills ever, but not capped by the traditional top note at its close — Gui's choice?

The Sleepwalking Scene is mesmerizing from start to finish. She practically murmurs her opening words. They become, in the process, a muted cry of despair. From this, she proceeds to give the absent Macbeth an overt taunt with "non osi entrar." Signs of slight vocal fatigue overtake her at "vegliardo," where she emits an unfortunate scoop. Her concentration may be disrupted momentarily, for she follows that by anticipating "Di Fiffe il Sire," before repeating the phrase correctly further on. But her interpretation gets back on track with an effective "Banco e spento" leading to a forceful "fossa" as she plunges down into her low. This is capped by a suitably haunted "non surse ancor." She reverses "Batte alcuno!" and "andiam, Macbetto," but this doesn't disrupt. The flourish on "Non t'accusi" is impeccable, and she follows this up with superb *pianissimi* on a repeat "Macbetto" and "andiamo." At the last second, a prolonged scoop on the final high D flat almost prevents her from reaching the note, but she just manages to get there before moving back an octave down. The overall phrase is still suitably dreamy to exert its proper effect. That she delivers such a powerful impact in these final minutes despite some lapses here and there is no small tribute to her compelling artistry.

A more plush-voiced Lady recorded "live" in 1964 is Grace Bumbry, a mezzo with a remarkably resilient top. There are two Grace Bumbry *Macbeth*s, this 1964 broadcast from Salzburg on Frequenz and a 1975 performance from Bologna on Golden Age Of Opera. The Salzburg is led by Wolfgang Sawallisch and features Dietrich Fischer-Dieskau in the title role, with Ermanno Lorenzi as Macduff and Peter Lagger as Banquo. The Bologna is under Armando Gatto, with Renato Bruson as a fine Macbeth, Luciano Saldari as Macduff and Agostino Ferrin as Banquo.

The Salzburg reading is enhanced by Wolfgang Sawallisch's energized baton. He infuses all his colleagues with a freshness that is not so apparent under Maestro Gatto. Salzburg's Fischer-Dieskau may not be as satisfying a Macbeth as Bologna's Bruson, and Bumbry herself may not exude as much sheer authority under Sawallisch as she does under Gatto. But both Fischer-Dieskau and Bumbry convey such a sense of adventure, and Bumbry's earlier assumption carries such a thrill of discovery, that, in the end, the earlier performance is the more memorable. A description of it follows.

Bumbry is breathless with excitement in speaking her husband's letter, and her energy is successfully maintained right through the recitative. She rides the crest of "retrocede" with magnificent ease and supplies adept staccati for "compiere," and there are good trills. Softer dynamics are used imaginatively, both for "Che tardi" and an elegantly tapered … "gnar" on the final "regnar." The passagework in the cabaletta is efficient enough, and she sports a good low B. There is no *da capo*; she drops out for a few measures in the coda and surges back for a magnificent climax. In the regicide duet with her husband, Bumbry's precise staccati convey anxiety, and the grace notes at the "Quell'animo" are superbly integrated. She is notably tense for the request that Macbeth smear the blood from the daggers, and, when he shies away, he's greeted by a sharply snapped "Dammi il ferro." The Lady sounds urgent but still collected upon her return. Then "Vieni" marks a change to a hushed delivery with the same precise staccati as before.

Sawallisch adopts a brisk tempo for "La luce langue." There is still the traditional thoughtful start, but, at this pace, a line like "La man colpevole che ferirà" can be delivered with an excellent legato, and there is a nice tension to the whole. "Nuovo delitto" is whispered, and Bumbry pulls herself together efficiently for "È necessario." The deliberate way the words emerge in this aria allows one to be more aware of Bumbry's still-forming Italian, the "l" in "fatale" sounding like a double "l" instead. Her mastery in this respect is far crisper in 1975. But this earlier performance remains special, with its excellent low B, the way she seems to pick huge intervals out of the air, and the polished passagework. Bumbry renders the final words as a single phrase, capping the finest moment in her interpretation. In the "Brindisi" in the Banquet Scene, she sounds like an unassuming party girl. One could argue that a contrast here is needed, but the sudden lack of aura around her clashes a bit. Certainly, a few of her trills, like those at "ferita" and "al cor," are striking, even though she doesn't nail every one. We have an excellent ascending run for "Muoia il dolor." A tense, but unflappable, delivery of "Voi siete demente" leads to a calm return to the party mode, and the repeat of the drinking song shows no upset from Macbeth's hallucination. Oddly, there are no crisp trills this time, and she blows one flourish before the traditional interpolated top note. Her projection of the character throughout this scene was better integrated in the '75 reading, conveying a distinct authority figure at ease in her castle, but without the fluency of this earlier broadcast.

In the opening of the Sleepwalking Scene, "Una macchia" sounds partly aghast and partly sorrowful. And from there, she proceeds through a bewildering array of colors and moods. At first, she shows solicitous care for her traumatized spouse on "non osi entrar," offset by a manic about-face for "vergogna." She strays from pitch on "immaginar," but the word itself is highlighted with a vivid gasp of horror; "mani" too goes off pitch. "Io non saprò" is launched piano but ends as an abrupt exclamation. There is also a spooked piano on "balsami." "Non può" is rendered with a sob, yielding to an eery sweetness on "surse ancor." "La cosa fatta" comes out in an impeccable legato, with an eery quality on "fatta." She handles elegantly the turn at "Non t'accusi" and "andiam, Macbetto." Then suddenly she is weary and resigned on her last "Macbetto." After showing such a wealth of imagination, the final phrase, with its *pianissimo* high D flat, catches her short: coming in late, this emerges full-voice, with a mere peck at the D flat. From gasps in the postlude, it is evident that the stage director here has her dying on stage at the conclusion of the scene. We don't seem to have that in 1975, where one can appreciate her launching the last phrase in time and attempting more of a piano on the D flat, even though it's once again rushed.

Birgit Nilsson's is possibly the most powerful voice ever to take on this role. Surprisingly enough, despite the haughty quality of her sound, she does not suggest the demonic as readily as Rysanek does. Everything in her interpretation seems geared toward the practical. Hers is emphatically the take-charge interpretation. We never forget who's boss— up until the Banquet Scene anyway. She recorded the Lady with Thomas Schippers. Her Macbeth is Giuseppe Taddei, Macduff is taken by Bruno Prevedi and the Banquo is Giovanni Foiani. It was released in 1964 by Decca/London.

At her entrance, Nilsson all but whispers the letter's conclusion. In the recitative following, it's rather hard to be sure whether or not the flourish at "retrocede" is really as blurred as it sounds. This set has very reverberant sonics. Unfortunately, during the "Vieni! t'affretta" it becomes clear that she has no discernible trill, and the passagework in the cabaletta is decidedly heavy-footed. When she reaches the phrase with the low B, there is even the suggestion of a slight tremolo. In the duet following the regicide, Nilsson alternates legato and staccato in the quick flourishes rather than doing them all staccato. With all these compromises, there is a fundamental angularity to her singing that somehow fits the character. Furthermore, the grace notes are exceedingly well handled, and she adopts an effective conspiratorial stance for much of the duet. This is clearly not a rattled Lady, but an eminently practical one with nerves of steel. After she returns from the chamber herself, she even imbues the thought that her hands are now as bloody as Macbeth's with a vague suggestion of amusement! With all the effectiveness of such touches, it's still troubling how the closing upward runs here again sound blurred, in contrast to the momentarily crisp grace notes of the duet's first half.

In Act II, her "La luce langue" comes out very matter-of-fact, not unduly assertive or diabolically triumphant. There's little energy spent on the phrase "È necessario." It's just a fact of life. An easy low B at "l'eternità" heralds the launching of the final coda, "O voluttà del soglio." This comes out as a luxuriant description of something startlingly cheerful and pleasant. This certainly matches the librettist's macabre imagery: "ecstasy of royal glory." Surprisingly, the top note on "Re" (King), while as easy as any Nilsson *acuti*, is not sustained, another example of Nilsson's matter-of-fact stance throughout the aria. While Nilsson's top shines brilliantly in the "Brindisi" in the Banquet Scene, she also comes up against the most problems here. The absence of a trill becomes especially awkward, and, while grateful that the middle section is retained in its entirety, one can't help noting how deliberate and over-careful Nilsson is in all the passagework. The effect becomes cumbersome. Still, she appears to achieve an interesting character transformation here, repressing a sob at "Voi siete demente?"

The Sleepwalking Scene starts in an absolute trance. "Tremi tu" is the height of serenity. Then "Orsù" betrays the first sign of agitation, with greater intensity reserved for "non può" and "Ohimè," which are rendered like musical sobs. The quaveriness resurfaces at "non surse ancor" as she dips into her lower register. It's hard to say how much of that is expression. Her alarm grows palpably at "Batte alcuno" and then she caps the scene with two striking *decrescendi* at "Macbetto" and "andiamo." Her final *pianissimo* D flat is duly soft, but it comes out a mite "whistly"—so mechanical, it might be the engineering.

One thing's for sure: the Nilsson Lady is in no way gloomy or diabolical. She is too sensible for that. She is, though, definitely heartless, then unstrung at the end. All of that is effective in a legitimately dramatic way. But if gloomy and diabolical is really what Verdi wanted, and he says it was, then Nilsson might have left him nonplussed. There is no gainsaying her vocal authority whenever the intricate passagework is neither too hot nor too heavy. Furthermore, the implacable security of many of the sounds she utters already carries its own forbidding persona. So perhaps Verdi would have been less concerned over the lack of complexity in the Nilsson sound. On the other hand, considering his last thoughts on this character in the low-lying "La luce langue," and in his own words regarding Tadolini on the "night figure" sound he wanted, my hunch is he would have found the Nilsson Lady much too "daytime" and straightforward.

Possibly, the ultimate in gloomy tone, together with vocal inconsistency the opposite of Nilsson's, is Elena Souliotis. One is never sure what resonance each word will have from note to note. One suspects that this is partly interpretation and partly making do vocally. In a way, her Lady Macbeth works well with some of her other colleagues on the recording. This set was made in 1970 under Lamberto Gardelli and features Dietrich Fischer-Dieskau's Macbeth, Luciano Pavarotti's Macduff and Nicolai Ghiaurov's Banquo. It, too, was a Decca/London release. Basically, what Souliotis and Fischer-Dieskau provide here is a story

of two ghouls. It is hard to imagine the Macbeths so much at one and so unre-
lievedly spooky. They seem to wear their spookiness like the proudest armor.
Souliotis's occluded diction only abets these Gothic impressions. The value of
dwelling at length here on her interpretation is both positive and negative. She
brings an abundance of imagination to her reading, while, at the same time, it
is salutary to be reminded just how difficult the Lady's music is.

Souliotis's reading of the letter drips with hardness and weary distrust.
Then her following recitative discloses much vocal uncertainty. The lows are
very strong, and very gloomy, but the top is uncomfortably driven and unfocused and her middle is almost nowhere — occasionally, it is inaudible. There
are no trills in her "Vieni! t'affretta." With all this, however, there is something
ear-catching about Souliotis's projection of mood and character that attracts
attention in a way that Nilsson never quite does. Little moments like her *subito
pianos* at "Ascendi, ascendi" lodge gratefully in the memory. The rhythmic fading of these trisyllabic utterances seems to suggest the image of someone who is
quite capable of shouting Macbeth into submission if she wished, but who is
anxious to appear reasonable and not blow her cover. "Ascen" ... may be assertive
but ..." "di" is almost cooed, as if to check herself. A whole character is brought
before our ears in this way. Still, the musical compromises start mounting up.
She startles by constantly indulging in slurpy portamentos and ungainly lunges
up to the high. She almost redeems herself with an effective *decrescendo* on the
final "regnar" closing the opening cavatina. This stance of private reverie is
effectively maintained with the messenger and beyond. Suddenly, Souliotis is
surprisingly withdrawn here. Soft and creepy tones are used for the recitative
leading into the cabaletta, and this stance is not dropped for the opening phrases
of "Or tutti sorgete." Then, cumbersome passagework undermines much of what
she is trying to achieve.

The result is that much of Nilsson now seems fluent indeed! It is no surprise, that, contrary to Nilsson in the first cabaletta, Souliotis's low B at "immota"
is tremendously powerful. Souliotis has that chest-heavy quality that Verdi seems
to have wanted for the Lady. Unfortunately, all the middle-low passagework is
rendered soft and fuzzy from her severe register problems. There is simply no
strength behind her projection of any of these notes. The conclusion of the first
statement of the cabaletta goes completely blurry. In the *da capo*, there is a surprising touch: the word "mortali" is rendered downright sweet, an especially
eery effect, and, to her credit, Souliotis does every note of the concluding measures. There is no "taking a breather" before the climactic top notes in the style
of so many others. Unfortunately, one's momentary admiration for her musicianship is dissipated by her vocal infirmities in the brief exchange with Fischer-
Dieskau, where husband and wife plan Duncan's murder. Especially at the
concluding phrase, where the Lady gives a grand flourish on the point of wel-
coming the King, Souliotis's delivery of the cadenza makes the occasional caution of Nilsson seem positively benign. We return to the stance of militant
spookiness in the duet following the assassination. In fact, both principals here

diligently remind their listeners how "scary" this is. To compound the hair-raising approach, the Lady's disorientation at her husband's troubled thoughts is signaled far earlier than in most sets: Souliotis renders her "Il regal figlio" in utter amazement at her husband's demeanor. She appears to catch his spirit of alarm at "Follie," and this reinforces the conspiratorial quality of Fischer-Dieskau's and her singing. Fortunately, unlike Nilsson, Souliotis manages the staccati handily.

On the other hand, the elusive grace notes suggest not much more than an emphatic shake of the head. Being musicians of a sort, both leads manage to conclude the first half of the duet with a real *decrescendo* that is both technically adept and truly expressive. There is nothing either practical or take-charge in the Lady's decision to go back into the guest chamber herself. Instead, she is exasperated, impatient, and more. Ultimately, the main impression is utter fury with her husband. Fevered as she is, this skittishness carries over into the coda where the articulation of the passagework is again compromised.

Act II features a "La luce langue" that is marked by shortness of phrasing, much of which is compounded by dropped syllables as she runs out of tone. As elsewhere, the phrases that lie right in the middle are what give her the greatest trouble. However, the occasional vividness of her reading cannot be gainsaid. "È necessario" emerges as an eminently practical "One's got to do what one's got to do." The all-important "l'eternità" and its low B are both highly effective and vocally assured. She concludes with a properly vindictive and triumphant coda in the grandest manner. The top may seem slightly raw but it is not unmusical. Compromises are made in the "Brindisi." At one point, having no trill, she substitutes a prolonged and quite effective *decrescendo* instead. Although one is glad to hear it done uncut, the register breaks become more pronounced than ever.

The "Ora di morte" duet in Act III is especially notable in this recording. This is not to say that Fischer-Dieskau and Souliotis have found an ideal way of performing this. In fact, their way flirts with parody. But what makes it unique in a morbid sort of way is their oneness of approach. If it can be said that this recording as a whole is the *locus classicus* of the "ghoul" approach, then clearly this duet is the epitome for both Fischer-Dieskau and Souliotis. Gardelli and his principals conceive this piece as an arch going from furtive, moustache-twirling conspiracy to unbridled blood-lust to furtive conspiracy again. It is certainly that, and one has to give this reading due respect for communicating its essence so unflinchingly. The moment when the mood of furtiveness is recovered is pinpointed by a joint and highly expert *decrescendo* on the word "vendetta." Still, one wonders what has happened to the rare deadliness of understatement elsewhere. That has its virtues too, lost in all this hamminess. Also lost along the way are key words in the Lady's music since much of this duet lies directly in Souliotis's crippled middle register. "Banco" of "Di Banco il figlio" becomes almost inaudible.

The Sleepwalking Scene may be one of the more highly wrought renditions out there. Not only do we have an effective piano at "immaginar," it may even be possible that Souliotis has read her Shakespeare for the words "mani io non saprò": in the original, when Lady Macbeth first speaks of cleaning her hands, she applies the term "sweeten." Souliotis does precisely that on the word "mani," sweetening the tone as if in veritable homage to the Bard. Another striking *decrescendo* on "non può," however deftly finished, is marred by its shaky attack in full voice. This is redeemed partially by another eery effect, a fluty voicing of "Sfar non puoi la cosa fatta." One wishes, in the face of such imagination, that there weren't so many acute vocal problems. However, almost at the outset of this scene, we are faced with a wobbly "tremi tu," and the wobble resurfaces a number of times thereafter at moments like "Banco e spento." She is even incapable of softening properly for the climactic high D flat, emitting a sort of wail instead.

It is hard to imagine any other recording where the perhaps unclear wishes of Verdi himself haunt us so: to wit, would he have recognized his own creation in this highly charged reading, or would the many musical compromises have struck him as simply beyond the pale? Unanswerable as that question may be, it behooves us at least to bear it in mind as we weigh the importance of the letter versus the spirit at the twilight of the *assoluta* era.

There is no conflict between the vocal persona and the musical discipline in Souliotis's Letter Scene under Oliviero de Fabritiis on her Decca/London recital disc of 1966. She seems faintly amused as she speaks the letter. There is even a sardonic quality at "serto," as if to say "Sure, the crown could be yours, but you wouldn't have it, knowing you." In the recitative, her concluding flourish on "retrocede" ranks with the best, and the cavatina starts with an alluring lilt, turning imperial on "accendere." Again, there are no trills, but what grandeur for the repeated "Io ti darò valore," where the skies seem to open! She is being sweet again on "Di Scozia," and "Che tardi" gets first a smile, then imperiousness. She is then swooning with enticement at "dono" and again at another "Che tardi," swinging into the final cadenza with utter panache. The exchange with the messenger is cut, and the opening of the cabaletta becomes determination incarnate, with accomplished passagework and a superb low B. Creepy sweetness returns at "pugnale," and we have bloodcurdling cheerfulness for the passagework on the repeated "petto percota." In the *da capo*, she sails right through the climactic passagework on "pugnal."

In tackling roles that bridge the divide between soprano and mezzo, Christa Ludwig brings out the temptress in many of them. She has called such roles "sexy" in characterizing their mix of "dark soprano and high mezzo." To give such roles an enticing quality, prior experience with lyrical passages is judged important.[84]

The key to Ludwig's Lady is her abiding love for her husband. To a degree, this may make her a less forbidding character than usual. Yet it also makes her more obsessive. Her dream is not just sovereignty, it's sovereignty with *him*, in whom she has greater faith than he does. In her eyes, her husband's self-doubts are not intrinsic to his character and have nothing to do with the *real* Macbeth she knows, gloriously capable of anything — and therefore her lodestar.

All this comes through in her singing. The conductor Karl Böhm is with her every step of the way in this 1970 broadcast, marked by far greater responsiveness to the ebb and flow of Verdi's writing than he showed twenty-seven years earlier with Höngen. Ludwig's colleagues are Sherrill Milnes as Macbeth, Carlo Cossutta as Macduff and Karl Ridderbusch as Banquo. This has been available on Legato and Foyer.

It's hard to imagine a more vivid reading of Macbeth's letter. The full import of "predissero un serto" almost stops Ludwig in her tracks. Her excitement is caught right at that moment. She maintains that excitement by evoking infinite possibilities in her recitative warning against indecision. Her warning doesn't come across as scornful upbraiding of her husband's customary caution. Rather, she is calling attention to the grandeur of which she knows he's capable. She launches the "Vieni! t'affretta" with a charge of rapture. Her trill on "accendere" is especially strong, imparting a delicious tingle of anticipation to the idea of sovereignty. She can taste the throne already, and, in her brief exchange with the messenger announcing the King's visit, her expansive delivery of "quale un Re si merta" shows us she is now a queen in all but name. The cabaletta continues strong with a confident low B, although one can sense Böhm slowing down for some of the passagework. The *scena* is crowned by two or three of the most opulent notes Ludwig ever sang. When, after the King is killed, Macbeth does not relish the murder as much as his wife, Ludwig's initial response is loving concern. But, after the repeated "Follie," her impatience grows. Still, her slight laugh at "Sei vano, o Macbetto" comes off more as reassurance than as the usual hard-edged amusement at his expense. The passagework here is strong and, later, the grace notes are cleanly struck in the "Quell' animo trema." Here is where the most distinctive aspect of Ludwig's interpretation first makes itself felt: there is a slight suggestion of growing disillusionment in Ludwig's description *a se* of her harrowed partner, and it is tinged with sadness. It's as if her vision of her husband as the glorious, uncomplicated tyrant at her side is momentarily clouded. There is little of scorn here, more of bewilderment. This is the touchstone of her interpretation. She finally snaps at him with "Dammi il ferro," but her return to a cowering spouse and the sudden awareness of blood on her own hands makes her begin to feel lonely. There is a distinct edge of fear in her urging that they make themselves scarce. The passagework is not as deft as previously either: the staccati are now more legato than detached.

Böhm takes the "La luce langue" quite slowly, and Ludwig responds by making it sound wary and serpentine through a liberal application of *glissando*. At this pace, the reiteration of "È necessario" becomes an arduous and deliberate statement, as if hammering something home that's now unavoidable, yet hurtful. The "Ai trapassati" here is baleful, while its concluding word, "eternità," though capped with a strong enough low B, is not sustained at the length of some others, obviating the kind of mini-*crescendo* familiar here. In the coda, the repeat of "O voluttà del soglio" brings a sensual caress on the words. The sybaritic feelings, arising from both sovereignty and from savoring it alongside her warrior husband, come to the fore. Her implicit dream of loving her husband on a bed made by violence now reaches its apotheosis. The image she creates is both alluring and repellent. Unfortunately, she is one Lady Macbeth who chooses to drop two or three notes preceding the climax on "Re" (King). Done this way, the "Re" certainly hits home, but one regrets the subterfuge. She is again savoring the luxury of shared power with her ruthless mate for the "Brindisi" in the Banquet Scene. She is blissfully enjoying the social whirl of this occasion. The trill is respectable enough, although not as crisp as that of other singers. The middle section of the first statement is cut, and she lunges a bit at some of the remaining passagework. The "Brindisi" is her most rapturous moment, while Macbeth's vision of Banquo's ghost at his place at table is her most painful. "Voi siete demente?" is uttered with abject disillusionment. She realizes now that his harrowed feelings are not momentary social pangs that can be readily overcome. They are intrinsic to his nature. She is not married to a ruthless tyrant. She is married to a haunted specter. Her dream of intoxicating power with a strongman is shattered. When she re-invites everyone to bring back the "gioia" of the happy feast, she sings this almost poignantly in an attempt to recover the intoxicated world of sovereignty in the previous scene. The shadowed reprise of the "Brindisi" is more clipped; there's less delicious languor and more precision. As a result, we have clearer trills and passagework here. But they are properly joyless. There is no top note added on for the conclusion of this reprise.

Ludwig's "Ora di morte" becomes an integral part of her interpretation. It is not the usual plotting duet. Rather, Ludwig makes of it a rapturous reconciliation with her husband. She is not so much caught up in the identity of their next victim. She is simply overjoyed that they are together and committing mayhem and horror once more. One can almost visualize her momentarily closing her eyes with a sense of relief and joy at "il tuo coraggio antico." She brackets "antico" by placing an infinitesimal *caesura* before the word and inflecting it with a keen caress. Her lurid dream is back.

In a way, this insight into "Ora di morte" makes the motivation behind her Sleepwalking Scene trickier. Her greatest joy must now turn into the image of a haunted, disillusioned soul. Granted, in showing her prickings of conscience as a sudden eruption, Verdi may be no more startling than Shakespeare. However, Shakespeare, it could be argued, provides her a more natural "lead-in" to her final scene through the upset that Macbeth causes her and their guests at the banquet. This, after all, is the original sequence of Verdi's 1847 version. Thus, the Lady's discomfort with her husband's disruption at the feast can be used as a more immediate bridge to her nightly dementia. The Paris version doesn't have this luxury, since the "Ora di morte" intervenes. Ludwig's night-time ramblings open with a stark, staccato articulation for each syllable, suggestive of a vivid nightmare world. She starts everything deadly quietly, becoming ever softer as the phrases unfold, culminating in a whispered "maladetta." She comes forth in a sad, disillusioned "Tremi tu" and then taunts her partner at "non osi entrar." She does confuse words at one point: instead of "Chi poteva in quel vegliardo," she substitutes vague sounds until she gets to "quel." She then recovers for an effective "tanto sangue immaginar." Here, the phrase first comes out as an hysterical cry, then an awed hush takes over for the repeated "immaginar." The Thane of Fife phrases start out catatonic and end with a suggestion of a repressed sob. The tone of lament is then reinforced on her final iteration of the word "saprò." She evokes pity for the poor "piccol mano," and "Ohimè" becomes a shudder. She becomes imposing, terrifying us with her "non surse ancor," like some emissary from the beyond. We then have an icy legato for "sfar non puoi," then a shift to stark, staccato articulation for "cosa fatta." The flourish on "Non t'accusi" is impeccable. The concluding measures are marked by one "andiam" in particular that's brought to an abrupt cutoff with an emphatic "...iam" like a whiplash, as if absorbing for the first time the full shock of what she's done. It hits home. Unfortunately, instead of doing the final phrase with its high D flat in key, she brings it all down an octave. Regrettable as this is, it seems preferable to what we hear from Höngen with the younger Böhm. There, in transposing down, Höngen, we may recall, changes the arch of the phrase by making the last two notes one and the same pitch. Here, with the Ludwig reading, the relationships at least stay the same.

In 1976, EMI released its *Macbeth*, featuring Sherrill Milnes in the title role, Fiorenza Cossotto as Lady Macbeth, José Carreras as Macduff and Ruggero Raimondi as a peerless Banquo. Riccardo Muti conducts.

Cossotto's opening reading of Macbeth's letter is not simply whispered at the close, but throughout, with convincing inflections of surprise, a contrast to the traditional oratorical approach. In the cavatina, we have real trills and fine control over passagework. Cossotto's singing in this opening *scena* is thoroughly engaged and communicative. To an extent, it lacks the individuality and the variety of nuance brought to this piece by others, though it is still an accomplished dramatic statement. The music is honored sufficiently enough both in the letter and the spirit. Others, like Amy Shuard, for instance, are certainly far plainer dramatically. It could even be argued that a more straightforward interpretation like Cossotto's has its place as an occasional corrective to some of the more meddlesome readings. Much of the impetus for this directness with the music — and the tremendous application of discipline from Cossotto — may be due to Maestro Muti, who presents an uncut performance of the final Paris version. The cabaletta "Or tutti sorgete," preceded by a quietly intense "Duncano sarà qui ... qui?" that gets softer and softer until the explosion at "Qui la notte," is heard with its *da capo* intact. Cossotto starts the cabaletta itself conspiratorially, biding her time for the grand outbursts. At "immota," the low B is quite soft, in both statements, while all the stops are finally pulled out in the concluding passagework — every note is delivered with scrupulous accuracy. It is surprising that, in the 1970s, we don't have at least some modest ornamentation for the *da capo*. Again, that could be due to Muti's literal approach. In the duet following the murder, Cossotto is breathless, a woman in a hurry, at the repeated "Follie," even though, harking back to Ludwig, she tries to comfort her husband rather than being cold and distant like Callas, or exasperated like Rysanek. The "Sei vano, o Macbetto" seeks to soothe. Later, the grace notes in the "Quell'animo" section are a bit breathy but effective. Then, on ordering her husband back into the guest chamber, the word "pugnal" is hard and implacable. Utter disgust oozes from her "Dammi il ferro," to be transformed into a harried, breathy persona once she comes out again, now remarking on her own bloodied hands. Good staccati end an effective scene.

In Act II, Cossotto immediately makes a striking impression in her reading of the recitative line "Immoto sarai tu nel tuo disegno?" Here, she adopts a cooed legato that sends shivers up the spine. In "La luce langue" itself, she opens the aria with the broadest kind of phrasing, maintaining an impeccable icy legato. The "Ai trapassati" passage is taken softly, even though she does expand the tone slightly for the concluding low B. Like Margherita Grandi and Leyla Gencer, Cossotto gives the entire last line as a single phrase, tying the top note to the final "Cadrà." The "Brindisi" in the Banquet Scene features some of the best trills in the *Macbeth* discography. It is rare to hear the middle section in the first statement sung at all, let alone sung with such accuracy. Every once in a while, there are a few slight aspirates, but they are not disfiguring — and there are those trills! Macbeth's disruption of the banquet is greeted with a quiet, impassive inflection on the word "demente." Then she adopts the iron smile of Callas for the word "gioia." She shows us, however, that the Lady is not imperturbable in a fidgety reading of the reprise for the "Brindisi." Again, she sounds a little breathless here.

The Sleepwalking Scene does not show much individuality. There are strong touches here and there, and the singing is not inexpressive, but the dramatic interpretation is not distinctive. One can certainly relish the mood Verdi creates with his music when everything is executed with as much honesty as it is here. The word "maladetta" is sung strongly. "Orsù" emerges sudden, startled. Further on, the "io non saprò" is an effective contrast: totally abstracted. Naturally, the flourish on "Non t'accusi" is flawless. Oddly enough, even though Cossotto goes quite soft for the final "Macbetto," the closing phrase and its high D flat is taken practically at full voice. Expectations are set up for the listener and then dashed. This is especially startling, since Muti is known for being a stickler with the score, and doing the high D flat other than soft is to ignore Verdi's own marking. One can only conclude that performing this note at any other level than full voice was beyond Cossotto's powers. Surprising in light of her facility in so many other respects.

This set closes with an intriguing bonus: rejected arias from the 1847 version, including the Lady's "Trionfai." It's amazing to hear the flourish on "rovesciar" go flat, especially since the passagework elsewhere is so secure. At least, one is grateful for the chance to hear this rare piece at all, if inferior, yet sung with such aplomb for the most part.

DG's entry from the same year as the Muti features one of the most satisfying Ladies on disc, Shirley Verrett. The recording itself is uncut, so one hears every note as in the Cossotto. The DG recording features Piero Cappuccilli as Macbeth, Placido Domingo as Macduff and Nicolai Ghiaurov as Banquo. Claudio Abbado conducts. Verrett later made another recording opposite Leo Nucci, conducted by Riccardo Chailly. But it shows her in less solid command of the music.

In this earlier Abbado recording, Verrett opens Macbeth's letter with a beatific smile in her voice and ends it in a whisper. There are respectable trills in the "Vieni! t'affretta." More especially, the coloratura is delivered entirely in character. One sees an individual through Verrett's use of her voice in a way that only the finest artists evoke. Her ending of the "Vieni" is somewhat startling, however. Instead of binding the final line together as the single traditional phrase we are used to, she pauses before the last "a regnar." Everything goes soft and pensive for the recitative line with its hushed "Qui," only to expand with a thrilling sense of purpose for the *crescendo* at "la notte." The cabaletta is grandly phrased with all the passagework in place, a fine low B and the *da capo* intact. Her Lady is an intelligent woman, fully aware of the stakes involved, communicated by dramatic musicianship. Her very sound carries that combination of gloom and the diabolical that Verdi wanted. In the duet following the murder, she charts the Lady's growing awareness of her husband's psychological torment with a master hand. There is just the smallest hint of vehemence on "ciglio" to be followed by a sense of wariness at what might be in her husband's head. The wariness is reflected in an uneasy inflection on her staccati. At "Sei vano, o Macbetto," she tries to give him courage, and the phrasing becomes expansive like a generous clap on the shoulder. At Abbado's measured tempi, the grace notes become thoughtful, reflective. Only when she reminds the two of them of their obligations to smear the guards with blood does she realize that she's been just as distracted as he has: the dagger *must* be returned to the chamber. When Macbeth shudders at the thought of going back in, Verrett flares up on the spot. Her "Dammi il ferro" is livid. Her effective projection of the conspiratorial and the surreptitious returns in her hushed, but matter-of-fact, remark that there is also blood on her own hands now. She attempts to calm him down, to get him focused. The actual notes in the staccati are again articulated fairly well, but they become almost legato in this coda. Frankly, it's hard to tell whether there is an artistic reason for this, or whether it is an indication of greater difficulty in this passage.

There is a slow, hushed approach taken for the opening of the "La luce langue." "Desiata" is marked by a slow, but effective, scoop. All here is portentous, and the second "Nuovo delitto" is whispered. For the "Ai trapassati," the quiet dynamic is well maintained, with, however, a slight *crescendo* on a good low B. The intimate feelings of the opening measures are not entirely shed, even in the triumphant coda. Verrett still projects this as a private thought, however spirited. For the final line, she chooses to breathe before the climactic top note rather than after. This allows her to link the top note over to the closing words as a single phrase. Her "Brindisi" features fine staccati and a frequent softening of the tone, almost a caress. A few of the trills turn slightly breathy, and the ending of the first uncut statement also has an occasionally explosive release or two. She is back into the wary mode of the Act I duet for her response to Macbeth's vision of the dead Banquo. There is icy calm at "demente" and her invitation for the return of "gioia" at the feast is deadly quiet, as if calmly saying "Why nothing's wrong!" One can only rattle this Lady at one's own peril! The sense of danger coming from her here is unique. She starts the reprise in the same quiet, seemingly deflated, way, but with the same tingle of danger underneath. She then warms to the toast in the concluding measures.

For the Sleepwalking Scene, she is effective at projecting the haunting image of someone with barely the strength to drag herself around. Her conscience has finally exhausted her. She moves inexorably from the portentous to the conspiratorial and back again. We have a hint of lament in "cosi codardo," leading to the utmost despair at "vergogna." She builds an arch of hysteria for the iteration on "tanto sangue immaginar," only to draw back in sudden horror for a final hushed "immaginar." We have another strikingly soft tone for "mani." She becomes all feline at "Di sangue umano," and adopts a consoling manner for the "piccol mano." Her "Batte alcuno" carries an unmistakable message: "*Nobody* should hear us!" From this cowed stance, her "andiam, Macbetto" develops into a soft invitation to bed. Her High D flat is also soft and well sustained, but, like some others, she swims a bit in coming down for the lower D flat on the treble stave.

Back to a Wagnerian now for the first recording ever of the original 1847 version. Rita Hunter was the mainstay of the celebrated English-language *Ring des Nibelungen* performances led by Sir Reginald Goodall, for many the leading Wagnerian of his time. Her repertoire extended considerably beyond Wagner, but it was as Brünnhilde that she reaped her greatest fame. Her *Macbeth* comes from a BBC broadcast of 1978, released on a Voce LP. Her colleagues are Peter Glossop as Macbeth, Kenneth Collins as Macduff, and John Tomlinson as Banquo. John Matheson conducts.

Hunter's entrance *scena* offers indifferent Italian and recurrent unsteadiness, with a smudged flourish on "retrocede." Her trills are not the crispest. Top notes become steadier for the cadenza and a hard, gleaming persona emerges. The warmed-up voice gets suppler in time for the cabaletta, although a few flourishes are still smudged and the low B is sharp. The *da capo* is included, and this time there is a fine low B. A superb top note climaxes the aria. It is now clear that the character being projected is simpler and less varied than from others. In the duet following the regicide, her singing is not sufficiently hushed, but one can appreciate the superb staccati. Nevertheless, she fails to differentiate the phrases showing confidence and those reflecting frustration. The ending is better, with a snapped "Dammi il ferro" and excellent flexibility in the coda.

Act II opens with the replaced "Trionfai" of Verdi's original version. Hunter's completely warmed-up instrument boasts a diamond-hard top and respectable flexibility. She may misjudge her breath for one flourish and slur the final one, but, on the whole, there is a certain excitement from her clarion tones, with a solid top note at the conclusion. The peak of Hunter's interpretation is her wonderful "Brindisi" in the Banquet Scene, one of the finest first statements that we have vocally, with an agility not customary for a Wagnerian. In the reprise, though, she does not adopt the traditional top note and doesn't register her consternation at Macbeth's hallucination.

The Sleepwalking Scene is inexpressive: some sadness at the "Oh vergogna," a soft shudder at "immaginar" and "non può," and that's about it. Strangely, some unsteadiness starts to return at odd moments like "mani." But there are still easy transits from top register to low in sweeping utterances like "Banco è spento, e dalla fossa." Measured against an alluring *diminuendo* on "Macbetto" is a blurred "Non t'accusi." A fine *messa di voce* on the "Andiamo" preceding the high D flat is offset by a final high note that is not soft at all.

One singer who has made a specialty of Verdi's *assoluta* roles, Ghena Dimitrova, was captured on tape "live" in an outdoor performance of *Macbeth*, 1982. Nello Santi is the conductor. Dimitrova's colleagues are Renato Bruson in the title role, Ernesto Veronelli as Macduff, and Bonaldo Giaiotti as Banquo. This was released on LP on the HRE label. Microphone placement is an issue with this release: from inside the audience, much rustling, shifting around, coughing, and so on, to distract from what's going on. One can at least be grateful that the mike was very close to the stage, making the singers less distant than on most such recordings.

On this tape, Dimitrova's entrance is truly bizarre: there is a vehement altercation going on in the audience, and it almost obliterates the Lady's spoken letter. What is apparent, though, from where she starts singing is that her voice is launched with a bit of a wobble. In the cavatina, she only attempts one of the trills, and it is not a success. She offers crude excitement in full-voice top tones that, while pressured, give off a roar that suits the character. She seems more nuanced when the messenger arrives. "Macbetto è seco?" is delivered softly with bated breath, and, since this phrase is *a capella*, she even slows the tempo. Her second "qui?" gets the same treatment. Once into the cabaletta, her passagework is clumsy, and there is an undisciplined quality in the *passaggio*. The *da capo* is omitted, and Santi goes straight for the coda, where Dimitrova drops out for a few measures, roaring back for a climactic top note. In general, there is not much word painting in this *scena*. In the regicide duet with Renato Bruson (who does not sound himself in this performance), Dimitrova launches the staccati as a murmur, increasing the indistinctness, not helped by only one grace note articulated in the "Quell'animo." But she has a solid grasp of the hushed feeling Verdi intended here. The vocal action in the closing "Vieni altrove" is sluggish, staccati included, but there is an apt frenzy to the conclusion.

The opening of the "La luce langue" in Act II has severe problems: Dimitrova cannot sustain a proper line at so low a tessitura. Even though the tone itself is authoritative, she isn't able to shape it musically. But more individuality in the words emerges on the second "Nuovo delitto" with its gasped ... "to."

Still, the vocal moments predominate: a startling *diminuendo* on "fatale," and in the coda, despite a wobbly start, a grand surge on "s'acqueta." In addition, strong, if not ideally focused, top notes mark the conclusion. In some ways, the "Brindisi" in the Banquet Scene is an improvement. She may not have ready trills, but she offers a good substitute *diminuendo* launching "Gustiamo," and the tone is kept forward and bright throughout the aria, complementing the greater cohesion with the conductor. Since nearby church bells are heard right during "Voi siete demente," it's hard to gauge her inflection for the line. After Macbeth has responded, she tries to soothe him, an effect compromised by a wobble on "Svegliate." In the reprise, she removes the customary pressure on her voice even further, trying gallantly for a simultaneous *diminuendo* plus a trill before "Gustiamo." Again, the *diminuendo* is fine, but the trill is not convincing. Suddenly, however, her trill does become convincing as the voice gets set for the concluding high note. Launched before that top note, it is articulated impeccably and truly sustained.

It is evident that the most vocal preparation and interpretive exploration have gone into the Sleepwalking Scene. "Maladetta" becomes a despairing sigh, "non osi entrar" starts forbiddingly and ends with a taunt. The voice flows evenly, and there is keener head resonance where needed. "In quel vegliardo/Tanto sangue immaginar," sung as a single phrase, crests with a *crescendo* on "vegliardo/Tanto sangue" and ends with a whimper for "immaginar." Too bad that the distinct sounds of a walkie-talkie intrude at one point, and, actually, there is considerable disturbance from all sorts of peripheral activities right through the middle section of the scene. But the listener can still appreciate a hushed "Rimondar sì piccol mano" and a piano "balsami." A good turn on the "Non t'accusi il tuo pallor" is matched by a *diminuendo* on "Macbetto" and a solid piano on an "andiamo." She finishes with an astounding *pianissimo* high D flat.

In 1983, Mara Zampieri, one of the more eccentric Ladies, recorded this opera. Her colleagues were Renato Bruson as Macbeth, Neil Shicoff as Macduff, and Robert Lloyd as Banquo. Giuseppe Sinopoli conducted, and the recording was made for Philips.

Certain subtle inflections suggest that Zampieri is rereading a letter she cannot tear herself away from, as though it's not the first time she has seen it. Once she starts singing the recitative, she offers eery, penetrating tones. There are respectable trills in the cavatina, and the whole is presented as a private thought: a rapt and conspiratorial "Che tardi?" reflects her entire approach. In the *materia di mezzo*, her "Trovi accoglienza, quale un Re si merta" is full of mystery and inner excitement. There is a long pause before a sudden loud "qui la notte," but the cabaletta starts quietly, like the cavatina. There are some aspirates in the passagework, and Zampieri delivers a weak low B. The *da capo* is present and accounted for, but there is a whined coda. In the duet for the Macbeths following the King's murder, Zampieri offers respectable staccati. "'Sei vano, o Macbetto" emerges with falling accents on individual syllables— a limp, monotonous effect. There is then an impassive "Dammi il ferro."

In Act II, Zampieri's handling of the recitative preceding "La luce langue" first suggests alarm at "Dove? Quando," when she realizes more blood must be shed, and then hushed eagerness for "Immoto sarai tu nel tuo disegno?" The logic of this reading is not clear. In the "La luce langue," alarm returns for the first "Nuovo delitto," but the second one shrinks into a whisper. She is back to impassivity for "È necessario" and then has some trouble finding the low B. The "O voluttà del soglio" seems too introverted. There is no glee. When it comes time for the Banquet Scene, we hear a surprisingly demure approach. Her neat trills in the "Brindisi" are crisp enough, particularly at "al cor," and one appreciates such precision. She is bewildered at Macbeth's hallucination, whispering a drawn-out "Voi siete demente" through clenched teeth. The reprise of the "Brindisi" reflects hushed terror; she barely pecks at the notes.

In Act IV, the Sleepwalking Scene has her murmuring the opening, although "ti dica" is suddenly vehement. This opening then leads into the same falling accents of her first-act duet, as she sings "Tanto sangue immaginar?" This touch is more suited to this scene, but ultimately loses effectiveness, because she has performed so much else of the music in this way. Better is her projection of a real lament at "Banco è spento," and "la cosa fatta" boasts imaginative use of the double "t" for emphasis. The turn at "Non t'accusi" is also well-handled. Unfortunately, she aspirates the supposedly *pianissimo* high D flat, sustaining it too loudly.

In our next recording, Sylvia Sass sings Lady Macbeth and Piero Cappuccilli is featured in the title role. Peter Kelen is heard as Macduff and Kolos Kovats is Banquo. Lamberto Gardelli conducts. This set was released by Hungaroton in 1986.

Sass opts for whispering the opening letter, clear diction contrasting with occluded vowels in her singing. She is not an inexpressive artist, but her singing seems to come from some other "place," disorienting the listener. Coming off the top note of the flourish on "retrocede," there is a distinct rasp, and she has recurrent problems with a wobbly top throughout. In the cavatina, her trills prove imprecise as well. An imaginative use of dynamics, as in her piano on "a regnar," is offset by a rickety cadenza. Her passagework in the cabaletta, if not a paragon of musicality, is precise enough, and she displays a strong low B. The *da capo* is included, and there is a good downward flourish leading to the final measures. She is overtaxed again in the climax to the aria. Her duet with Macbeth opens with the initial exchanges whispered, and she offers respectable staccati. An imaginative touch is her smile on the "Ma dimmi, altra voce." She ends the duet's first half with a haunting piano. In the coda, we have the same telling approach, with passagework that is both slinking and precise.

Occluded diction and unsteady tone detract from the opening phrases of "La luce langue." Sass does, however, honor the projection of gloom that Verdi clearly required. She cowers on "delitto" and is then decisive on "fatale," which, however, wobbles. A sly smile characterizes the "Ai trapassati," ending on a convincing low B. In the coda, she emits "soglio" with a suggestion of a whine, but it works as a projection of the newly made Queen preening at her luxuriant estate. A delicate "Brindisi" greets the guests in the Banquet Scene, and Sass stabs at a few of the trills, sometimes successfully, but one upward run is badly smudged. Her best top note on this recording closes its first statement. After her husband makes a scene, "Voi siete demente" projects contempt, but a steely smile takes over as she invites everyone to resume the party. There is now, however, an edge of unease in the repeat, which she climaxes with the traditional high note.

She is too deliberate for the opening of the Sleepwalking Scene, further offset by a wobbly "Tremi tu?" Her voice drips with disgust at Macbeth's cowardice on "non osi entrar," and "vergogna" is exasperated. She indulges in a few two-dimensional would-be Callas effects here, but "saprò" is a convincing sigh of despair, as is "Di sangue umano." "Può" gets its *diminuendo*, and "Banco è spento, e dalla fossa" is excellent, with a superb contrast from "spento" to "fossa," richly intoned. She is suddenly wide-eyed and vulnerable for a soft "non surse ancor," and there is a haunting *rallentando* on the turn at "Non t'accusi." Sadly, an upward ascent on "Macbetto" goes badly off the rails, and the final D flat is neither very soft nor very steady.

The last set brings us back once more to Verdi's 1847 original. Iano Tamar, already familiar as the original French Médée, is Lady Macbeth. Evgenij Demerdjev sings the title role, Andrea La Rosa is Macduff, and Andrea Papi sings Banquo. Marco Guidarini conducts. This set on Dynamic comes from a "live" performance in 1997.

In the spoken letter, one is aware of Tamar's tentative Italian. But her reading is effective, showing amazement at "serto." Her flexibility seems unsure in the flourish on "retrocede," but the trills in the cavatina are accomplished, and we have sweeping phrasing for "Ascendivi a regnar." The cadenza is shaped with imagination, expressing urgency at first, then quiet assurance. The cabaletta is heralded with a soft "qui," then an explosion of energy for "qui la notte." But she pulls back suggestively for the start of the cabaletta, making it conspiratorial, only opening up later on. An adroit low B stays expertly in line with the entire phrase, and there is buoyant passagework here. The *da capo* is included, but the passagework is not so sure the second time around, where she loses breath and drops a few notes. Despite such momentary lapses, both line and voice still seem better knit than in her Médée. In the regicide duet, she is properly jittery, and there are good staccati, although the grace notes in the "Quell'animo" are smudged. There is impatience in "Dammi il ferro," and she is still exasperated on her return from the bedchamber.

The rarely heard "Trionfai" at the opening of Act II shows sure control of the passagework, despite a moment of wildness. This is redeemed with greater accuracy in the repeat, even though she occasionally loses the last note from lack of breath. Still notable, however, is the way Tamar nails the final ascending flourish, lingering securely on the top note. The "Brindisi" is given a slower tempo than usual, perhaps to accommodate tricky passagework, rendered accurately enough here, though not as fluently as one might wish. Most of the trills are clear enough, but she can't seem to sustain prolonged ones like the trill launching "Gustiamo il balsamo." Her top here is at its best, with a rousing close. Once her spouse's hallucination lifts, her "Voi siete demente" emerges through clenched teeth, and there is icy quiet for the "Sedete, mio sposo." The repeat of the "Brindisi" is more abruptly rendered the second time, with less line but greater precision. For one thing, her trill before "Gustiamo il balsamo" is better sustained this time, though the interpolated top note at the close is a mere exclamatory peck.

"Tuttora," rendered dreamy and gloomy, epitomizes Tamar's delivery at the outset of the Sleepwalking Scene, while "Non osi entrar" is sung with a scornful smile. Possibly for dramatic emphasis, "codardo" veers slightly sharp, but the keenness of Tamar's dramatic shifts from phrase to phrase stays on track with a cowering "Chi poteva in quel vegliardo." The incredulousness on "immaginar" is compelling, as is a sighing "Queste mani io non saprò," softening for "E mai pulire io non saprò." Her breath is now surer, and "Arabia intera/Rimmondar sì piccol mano" becomes a single phrase, deftly shaped. Now we have Tamar applying her *diminuendo* on "può," and there is continued broad phrasing almost to the end of this scene. She persuasively climbs the crest of an ascending "andiam" through another haunting *diminuendo*. She continues expressively to the conclusion, although, vocally, "Non t'accusi" is aspirated and there is no softening for the *pianissimo* high D flat.

❧ 14 ❧

Assoluta Manquée (II)

Three categories that almost approach the *assoluta* model in complexity were inaugurated during the **A,i** era.

To begin with, the title role in Beethoven's early *Leonore* (1805), the original version of *Fidelio*, boasts taxing fluctuations in tessitura that afford the singer certain vocal opportunities very much akin to those of an *assoluta* vehicle. Here is a role that requires fully as heroic a tone as the *assoluta* together with as proficient a capacity in intricate and heavy fioritura, and almost as much command of both the lower and higher registers—almost, but not quite. Her full range, from middle C to high C, never quite reaches the lowest extension of an **A,i** role, and it is this restriction that makes *Leonore* the first **A,v** work. The only other part that follows the **A,v** model is Imogene in Bellini's *Il Pirata* (1827).

Two years later, in 1807, Spontini introduced *La Vestale*, where the leading role of Julia, which combines most of the qualities of an **A,i** role, including varied tessitura, still lacked the fullest extension at either end of her range. This **A,vii** of group comprises:

A,vii of Group

1807 Spontini: *La Vestale* (Julia)
1814 Beethoven: *Fidelio* (Leonore)
1835 Donizetti: *Maria Stuarda* (Elisabetta), described, *Gemma* section

The **A,iii** category was pioneered by Rossini in *Ermione*, premiered in 1819. Even though, as with an *assoluta*, the title role has a wide range and truly heroic agility throughout, its tessitura lies more consistently in the upper half of the voice than does the usual *manquée* score. Were it not for the heroic style that characterizes Ermione's rare use of the lower register, this role would scarcely be *manquée* at all. As it is, though, this work inaugurated the **A,iii** category, which consists of:

A,iii Group

1819 Rossini: *Ermione*
1843 Verdi: *I Lombardi* (Giselda)
1846 Verdi: *Attila* (Odabella), referred to, *Macbeth* section
1876 Wagner: *Siegfried* (Brünnhilde)

The 1840s, the last **A,i** decade, ushered in two new *manquée* models: the **A,vi** and the **A,iv**. Adriano in Wagner's *Rienzi* for Dresden (1842) introduced the **A,vi** model. This part, created by Wilhelmine Schröder-Devrient, differed from the **A,i** group in ways already described at the conclusion of the *Norma* chapter. It had no descendants, and it alone constitutes the **A,vi** category.

Fidès in Meyerbeer's *Le Prophète* for Paris (1849) introduced the **A,iv** model. Fidès is already described at the opening of the Transition chapter, in the section covering Pauline Viardot-García, who created the role. Fidès also set the pattern for Azucena in Verdi's *Il Trovatore* (1853).

The last division of the *manquée* repertory, the **B,ii** category, was also inaugurated by Viardot-García: the title role in Gounod's *Sapho* (1851). Here, the vocal and technical requirements of Gluck's *Alceste* and the **B,iii** model, involving comparatively modest, though still difficult, flexibility and great heroic strength, were wedded to an unusually volatile tessitura hitherto unassociated with the **B,iii** repertory. This *Sapho*/**B,ii** pattern is present in eight roles. They are:

B,ii Group

1851 Gounod: *Sapho*
1859 Berlioz: *Les Troyens* (Cassandre/Didon)
1861 Wagner: *Tannhäuser* ("Paris Venus")
1864 Meyerbeer: *L'Africaine* (Selika)
1867 Verdi: *Don Carlos* (Eboli)
1871 *Aida* (Amneris)
1882 Wagner: *Parsifal* (Kundry), described, Voices from the Past
1907 Dukas: *Ariane et Barbe-Bleue* (Ariane)

A diva who is a defining *assoluta* is not essential for all *manquée* writing. One assumes that representations of these *manquée* scores will be enhanced by gifted *assolutas* capable of performing *Norma* or *Roberto Devereux*. Given the taxing nature of the *assoluta* repertory, though, it is perhaps too much to expect, from such a frantically busy singer in our time, mastery of all the *manquée* roles connected with the *assoluta* tradition. But it is also unrealistic to expect a performer to base a career on only the nine primary *assoluta* operas, half of which are hardly ever performed.

What seems wisest and most realistic, both from the original composers' and from the singers' points of view, is the rigorous assessment of *manquée* roles according to each individual singer's particular strengths. It is conceivable that, despite a sufficient mastery of a number of *assoluta* roles, a truly endowed performer might still find certain **A,i** parts harder than others. Thus, though the *Devereux* Elisabetta would by its very nature stymie a greater number of divas than would any other *assoluta* role, one can understand why a gifted artist like Lauren Flanigan might find Lady Macbeth more taxing than Elisabetta, despite a prevailing sentiment among most *assoluta*s in the other direction.[85]

Taking this as a starting point, one might then apply such individual differences in capacity to each diva's repertoire choices among *manquée* roles. For instance, if Lady Macbeth seems more taxing to one than the Rossini Armida, then forego the **A,iv** category in favor of the **B,i** category; but if Armida seems more taxing than Lady Macbeth, then choose the **A,iv** category over the **B,i** category, and so on. These considerations would make the choices clearer and more practical. Of course, all of this is based on an assumption that one is dealing with a vocal phenomenon to begin with. An ability merely to make it through a performance of either role without dropping dead is beside the point. Rather, what is at stake is the ability to project easily the varied kinds of dramatic, musical, and vocal authority that this book celebrates. This must be the first prerequisite before a fair number of either *manquée* or *assoluta* scores can be attempted. Even if a striking level of mastery is apparent, only a restricted number of *manquée* categories is still feasible. Beyond that, many *manquée* roles should be conquered before exploring the defining *assoluta* repertoire.

Finally, in fulfilling the criteria for defining *assoluta* supremacy, an aspiring artist will have already shown signs of extraordinary vocal endowment early on; she will have attained professional vocal and technical experience in both high soprano and straight mezzo repertoire, and she will already have explored certain reaches of the *manquée* world. Only then can she possibly tackle and conquer two or three different *assoluta* roles. Should she do so, then and only then will she be an *assoluta* herself.

From the foregoing, it should be clear that mastery of certain *manquée* roles does not in itself guarantee ease with the *assoluta* repertoire. Likewise, authoritative renditions of certain *manquée* parts are not out of the question for divas who would never consider *assoluta* repertoire at all. For instance, Zerbinetta in *Ariadne auf Naxos* is not customary in a *manquée*'s repertoire, but that would not necessarily preclude an excellent Zerbinetta from being an entirely satisfactory Queen Marguerite (*Les Huguenots*), a *manquée* role. Or, similarly, the role of Erda might not be in a *manquée*'s repertoire, yet that would not preclude an excellent Erda from being an exciting interpreter of Fidès, another *manquée* role.

Even here there is a caveat, since it would still be harder, though not impossible, for a limited *manquée* to specialize in the A sub-groups than for an *assoluta* to master them. Only when it comes to the demands of the B sub-groups would claims to potential vocal fitness be more equally balanced between limited voices and *assoluta*s.

In conclusion, the *assoluta*'s performance of a *manquée* role is an enhancement, not a requirement. Only the defining *assoluta* role itself must be sung exclusively by the *assoluta*.

❧ 15 ❧

Voices from the Past

Who, then, counts as an *assoluta*? On the one hand, certain sopranos of the Gilded Age would be properly grounded for the occasional *Norma* or *Oberon* (today it would be the occasional *Norma*, *Nabucco*, or *Macbeth*). On the other, some of their contemporaries who shared the huge range of a Malibran or a Viardot-García, but were pegged as mezzos, never performed the *assoluta* repertoire. I would maintain it is this latter group who epitomize the true *assoluta* sound.

For example, the extraordinary Marianne Brandt (a pupil of the retired Pauline Viardot-García) flourished from 1867 to 1890. She tried as a mezzo-soprano to carry on the traditions of her revered teacher. Like Viardot-García, Malibran, Ronzi–De Begnis, and the others, Brandt did not just sing mezzo roles; some of her higher roles included a triumphant Beethoven Leonore, Selika in *L'Africaine*, and Donna Elvira in *Don Giovanni*. She had an unusually wide range from G below middle C to high D. But, despite her amazing capacities, Brandt was born a generation too late. The period in which she was active no longer associated defining *assoluta* vocalism with a phenomenon like Brandt, so she was only given the chance to master a few parts with mere connections to *assoluta* traditions— some of the *manquée* roles outlined in chapters 5 and 14 — rather than those of the Pasta or Ronzi–De Begnis repertoire.

Another example: Wagner, in 1882, appears to have conceived the role of Kundry in *Parsifal* as a memorial to the startling qualities he remembered in Schröder-Devrient, and felt he had come closest to the image he had in mind when he chose Brandt for a Kundry in *Parsifal*'s first run at Bayreuth. Like Adriano in *Rienzi*, Kundry does not have all the characteristics of a defining *assoluta* role. But she does have such an extraordinary number of the requisite shifts in tessitura that, in one production, Herbert von Karajan allocated different sequences in Kundry's part to two different singers.

Brandt's repertoire never went beyond such partially *assoluta* scores, which she always interpreted with intense dramatic excitement. However, her suitability for the real defining roles was not lost on one Cherubini devotee, Professor Ebenezer Prout, who was convinced Brandt would have made an ideal Médée.[86] The closest she came to such a part was the **A,ii** role of Rachel in Halévy's *La Juive*.

For our purposes, her career is of incalculable value[87] because she is the diva closest to the original *assoluta* tradition to have left audible examples of her artistry for posterity. They may be primitive acoustical recordings made in 1905, fifteen years after her retirement, but they still tell us a lot. True, Brandt's sixty-two years are readily apparent in her recording of the "Brindisi" from *Lucrezia Borgia*. But the most indicative selection is a German-language "Ah, mon fils" from Meyerbeer's near-*assoluta* warhorse, *Le Prophète*. Here, a voluminous quality in the instrument, a sweeping phrase, or a marked jump between two different registers become very evident. One recognizes a direct line not just to Viardot-García but to her great predecessors, Malibran, Pasta, Ronzi–De Begnis, and a handful of others who inspired the core *assoluta* repertoire. Every diva who would master the stylistic nuances of Norma, of Elisabetta, or of any of the **A,i** roles, owes it to herself to become acquainted with Brandt's recorded legacy, slim as it may be. It is our most immediate link to the original *assoluta* traditions.

The only adequately documented career of comparable authenticity is Félia Litvinne's. Like Brandt, Litvinne was a gifted Viardot-García pupil. But she emerged nearly twenty years later. Her voice was more brightly colored than Brandt's and may perhaps be less authentic as an example of the *assoluta* type. Nevertheless, Litvinne alternated mezzo and soprano parts with equal authority. Successful appearances in the mezzo roles of Leonora in Donizetti's *La Favorite*, Gertrude in Thomas' *Hamlet*, and Dalila in Saint-Saëns' *Samson et Dalila* did not in any way diminish her standing as one of the finest Wagner sopranos of her generation, as well as its leading interpreter of Gluck's *Alceste*. As a nominal soprano, she was permitted to venture closer to the *assoluta* repertoire than Brandt had. Thus, although still denied the **A,i** operas, Litvinne trumped Brandt's mastery of **A,ii** repertoire: Brandt had only done Rachel in *La Juive*, but Litvinne performed two Verdi **A,ii** parts, Elvira in *Ernani* and the *Trovatore* Leonora.[88]

Unlike the slender Brandt legacy, the Litvinne recordings in the early twentieth century for G&T, Pathé, Fonotipia, and Odéon are generous examples of an artist still engaged in an active career. While Brandt may be of greater historic importance, Litvinne may have more practical value for the vocal historian because of the wider window her many recordings offer on an equally extensive repertoire. Caught in her prime, Litvinne, whatever Brandt's historical precedence, may be the more indicative of the Pasta or Ronzi–De Begnis sound. She emerges as a deeply affecting artist, and she was the leading exponent of a soprano/mezzo tradition that was then fading. It's a pity her recorded examples from Viardot-García specialties are relatively sparse: missing are Fidès in *Le Prophète* and Azucena in *Il Trovatore*. As a Viardot-García pupil, a student of the very artist whose achievement as Fidès had inspired Verdi's own Azucena, it would be priceless to hear Litvinne in music from either. Of course, we can be grateful for the little we have of Brandt's Fidès, but it could have been illuminating to have heard an example of Litvinne's alongside it, let alone a few phrases from Azucena's second act, which neither recorded. Litvinne appears not to have performed Verdi's gypsy at all, although her Dalila recordings suggest she would have met the challenge as handily as Viardot-García had decades earlier. She can, though, be heard in an excerpt from another Viardot-García triumph: Litvinne's G&T of "O ma lyre immortelle" from the Gounod *Sapho* conveys a lofty sweep in its despair suggestive of various descriptions of the role's impassioned creator.

Fortunately, Litvinne left us two *Trovatore* excerpts from her celebrated Leonora: "Tacea la notte" and "D'amor sull' ali rosee," both in French, during recording sessions with Odeon in late 1907–early 1908. Perhaps, after all, it's only poetic justice that the most telling excerpts we have from Litvinne are these two arias. *Trovatore* is the very last work to embrace all the characteristics of *assoluta* writing, albeit not in one and the same role, Azucena and Leonora sharing the full gamut of *assoluta* writing between them — and how inevitable that Viardot-García made a specialty of alternating the two!

Trovatore's other claim to distinction is its resiliency in the face of changing operatic taste. Even the most durable of the full-fledged *assoluta* vehicles— *Oberon, Norma, Nabucco, Macbeth*— have flickered in and out of the international repertoire. Verdi's *Trovatore*'s foothold is sure, and thus every impresario's nightmare. Leonora remains arguably the most difficult heroine in the standard repertoire to cast, at least ideally.[89] Maybe Azucena was first intended as the more important character, but Leonora, because of the sheer variety in her music, is more of a challenge to the casting director. Perhaps this daunting factor, along with the tradition of making the love interest the chief concern of any opera, has helped turn Leonora into the *de facto* prima donna of the work, despite Verdi's instinct to give Azucena primacy. (The one time that I recall the Azucena getting a bow after the Leonora was during Fiorenza Cossotto's last performances of this role at the Met. Of course, those were special occasions.)

Hearing a diva like Litvinne opens our ears to the traditions that lay behind Leonora's music. Litvinne's "Tacea" recording is characterized by an easy projection of lovely tone, not uniformly colored, and the more fascinating for that. Maybe others have phrased both this and the "D'amor" more broadly. Certainly, the cramped French translation plays its part in this. But few have brought to the "D'amor" such a variety of inflections and shading. Litvinne's fearlessness in playing off different registers enhances the conflicted feelings in this piece. One can easily forget that this aria is not just a wish to comfort Manrico; as we move into its final section, Leonora hopes to guide her thoughts to Manrico without revealing her torment. It is in this inner conflict that Litvinne shows herself an interpretive master. Without compromising the ethereal quality of Leonora's music, she still manages to convey her heightened desperation through varying dynamics in the closing moments. All this is accomplished with due regard for exquisite trills, well-tuned scales, and a clean legato. At the conclusion, she offers a cadenza and a final descent into low chest voice instead of the "proper" ending on a high note. We can take exception to what may well be a dodge, but the directness and imagination of so much else in her singing reward continued study. If Litvinne helps remind us that Verdi was haunted by the traditions that nursed Viardot-García, then we today are haunted as much by these tantalizing phrases from a Viardot-García pupil of a bygone age.

To get beyond *manquée* recordings and hear early cuts of defining *assoluta* repertoire, one has to go further afield than Viardot-García's studio: Emma Calvé alternated mezzo and soprano roles with exhilarating ease, but her inheritance of the Viardot-García tradition came about indirectly through Mathilde Marchesi, not through direct training with Viardot-García or her brother Manuel, Marchesi's mentor and as celebrated a teacher as his sister Pauline. Still, Calvé's repertoire encompassed only the extremes of mezzo and soprano, not the meeting ground of the A group at all. In fact, the closest she appears to have come to the *manquée* repertoire of Brandt and Litvinne, let alone the defining **A,i** group that they all shunned, is the **B,i** part of Lucia.

Calvé did, however, leave us an important souvenir of her artistry in **A,i** repertoire during her concert tours in semi-retirement. At age 61, she recorded "Casta Diva" from Bellini's *Norma* for Pathé. Though musically sloppy, the aria is marked by a commanding rather than a traditionally rapt interpretation. Embellishments feature startling key modulations and an excursion into unabashed chest voice. Like Brandt's "Ah, mon fils," this is clearly a record of a singer past her prime, though still sounding remarkable enough for her age.[90]

At the other end of the spectrum, Adelina Patti, a quintessential lyric soprano who never attempted Norma and was entirely unsuited to it, recorded a "Casta Diva" at the end of her career that employed Pasta's original embellishments in the *da capo*. Ever precocious, Patti had learned them at the age of seven, directly from Maurice Strakosch, Pasta's accompanist.[91] By the time Patti made her record, age had robbed her of the breath control needed to sustain the aria's brutal phrasing, but her rendition is more stylish and elegant than Calvé's.

Ironically, soprano Lilli Lehmann's more celebrated "Casta Diva" from the same period sums up an entirely different tradition, having little in common with the practices of either Brandt or Litvinne. Lehmann's vocal beginnings as a high soubrette shaped much of her subsequent development as a dramatic soprano. Thus, even though her registers are as distinct in their way as those of her more authentic colleagues, there is relatively little of the alto to her, and that includes her low. This places her firmly among the well-grounded sopranos at the opening of this chapter who habitually took on *Oberon* and *Norma*, not among those who epitomized the *assoluta* and were restricted by the times in which they lived.

In the end, even Brandt, Litvinne, and Calvé, in their long careers, genuinely endowed *assoluta*s as they were, never performed an *assoluta* role. These three singers remain far removed from the era of Bellini and Donizetti, whose operas are a world away from Brandt and Litvinne's work with Wagner and Calvé's close identification with the French school. Still, their achievements and their fragmentary legacies may be all we have to indicate the variety of sounds that the pioneering *assoluta* composers held in their imagination.

❧ 16 ❧

Conclusion

What the nine **A,i** roles have in common is a set of specific moods unique to each opera's music and exclusive of the other eight. On the one hand, it may be correct to say that the *Devereux* Elisabetta, with the largest array of vocal and technical requirements, going from lyric soprano to dramatic mezzo and back, must be the most demanding *assoluta* role of them all, and the most difficult to cast. Yet, on the other hand, Lady Macbeth's singing to more energetic orchestration, and her frequently combative vocalism, may prove more tiring for certain divas than would Elisabetta's music, however volatile the latter.

Yes, *Roberto Devereux*, at the end of the day, would stymie a greater number of mezzos or sopranos than would any of the other eight operas, *Macbeth* included. But if, out of that already small élite capable of *assoluta* singing, an even smaller minority might still take Lady Macbeth as the more challenging, that fact only serves to highlight the striking individuality of the nine *assoluta* parts. Since most of these roles were tailored to a specific, phenomenal voice, we should therefore expect that each of these nine heroines would display highly individual patterns of contrast. All that they retain in common is their infinite variety.

These roles were never meant for any generally recognized vocal category of today — never exclusively for the pure, high soprano. Furthermore, a diva such as a Viardot-García or a Malibran, the type for whom most of these roles were intended, is more mezzo-soprano than soprano or contralto — however easily she may embrace these two extremes. It is arguable that it's more natural for a young, resilient mezzo to develop an easy high under a good teacher's guidance than for a young soprano to develop an easy resonant low.

The history of the *assoluta* repertoire began with Gluck nudging the world of opera away from the superhuman castrato sound to a vocal persona more recognizably human. Similarly, for the *assoluta* roles, their composers chose to avoid

both the rarefied high soprano sound of a Beverly Sills and the forbidding contralto sound of a Schumann-Heink. Both the simplicity of the high soprano and
the gravity of the deep contralto seemed too impersonal for the human frailties
and contradictions of an *assoluta* role. They would not do for capricious Druid
priestesses and willful British monarchs.

To make a tragic lead truly affecting, the *assoluta* composers started with
a beautiful mezzo sound, expanding the range and flexibility of such roles beyond
the normal mezzo's capacities. Thus, while renouncing the castrato freak show,
the composers did not renounce the superhuman vocalism that went along with
it. The unbroken tradition of astounding vocalism within this new context rendered such singing even more startling by generating a tension between the recognizably human and the superhuman.

There is the need for rigorous training today, and for restricting this repertoire to resilient vocal prodigies already showing an aptitude for both soprano
and mezzo writing early in their careers. Only then can we comprehend what
Bellini meant when he wrote of Pasta's vocalism that it was "encyclopedic"—
hence, the vocalism of the *assoluta*.

Appendix A

Chronology of 65 *Assoluta* Roles

In this chronology, those operas that have the defining *assoluta* roles are marked **A,i**. For easy visual identification, the year of premiere for each defining (**A,i**) *assoluta* role is printed **boldface** and preceded by a bullet •.

Those marked **A,ii–vii** are so marked in descending order of casting difficulty, "ii" being more difficult to cast, "iii" marginally less difficult, and so on. These still require a proficient *assoluta* but lack one or two attributes associated with **A,i** roles.

Roles marked **B,i–iii**, in descending order of difficulty, do not necessarily require a proficient *assoluta* diva but have, as a group, some stylistic attributes in common with **A,i-vii** and therefore may benefit from *assoluta* casting.

At the end of each entry, its sub-group marking is followed in parentheses by: (a) a number representing the number of roles in that sub-group; (b) a number representing the role's chronological numbering by premiere date* within its sub-group; and (c) a number representing the level of casting difficulty for that role within its sub-group, No. 1 being the least difficult and the highest number the most.

Where appropriate, an indication of a role's historic importance in the development of vocal type is included in brackets.

1767 Gluck: *Alceste*—**B,iii** (8,1,6)
[broke new ground, introduced a new vocal type—the easiest of those itemized]
1781 Mozart: *Idomeneo* (Elettra)—**A,ii** (12,1,1)
[an even more taxing role, introducing a newer, harder sub-group; easiest role in this new sub-group]

1782 Mozart: *Die Entführung aus dem Serail* (Konstanze)—**B,i** (16,1, 5)
[another new sub-group, not so taxing as **A,ii**]
1787 Mozart: *Don Giovanni* (Donna Elvira)—**B,i** (16,2,1)
[the easiest role in this sub-group; standard repertoire]

*When the premiere was posthumous, the date given is that of the composer's death.

1790 Mozart: *Così fan tutte* (Fiordiligi)—B,i (16,3,6)
[most difficult role yet in this sub-
group]
1791 Mozart: *La Clemenza di Tito*
(Vitellia)—A,ii (12,2,2)
[most difficult role yet in this sub-
group]
1791 Mozart: *Die Zauberflöte* (Königen)—B,i (16,4,4)
[standard repertoire]
•1797 Cherubini: *Médée*—A,i (9,1,
2)
[introduces the main group, and the
toughest]
1805 Beethoven: *Leonore*—A,v (2,1,1)
[a new sub-group]
1807 Spontini: *La Vestale* (Julia)—
A,vii (3,1,1)
[introduces a new sub-group]
1808 Haydn: *L'Anima del filosofo*
(Euridice)—B,i (16,5,3)
Haydn: *L'Anima del filosofo*
(Genio)—B,i (16,6,7)
[most taxing role in this sub-group
so far]
1814 Beethoven: *Fidelio* (Leonore)—
A,vii (3,2,2)
[most difficult role yet in this sub-
group; standard repertoire]
1815 Rossini: *Elisabetta, Regina
d'Inghilterra*—B,i (16,7,14)
[most taxing role in this sub-group
so far]
•1817 Rossini: *Armida*—A,i (9,2,1)
1819 Rossini: *Ermione*—A,iii (4,1,3)
[introduces a new sub-group]
1823 Rossini: *Semiramide*—B,i (16,8,
13)
•1826 Weber: *Oberon* (Reiza)—A,i
(9,3,3)
1827 Bellini: *Il Pirata* (Imogene)—
A,v (2,2,2)
[most difficult role in this sub-
group and the last]
•1830 Donizetti: *Anna Bolena*—A,i
(9,4,7)
[most difficult role so far in this
group]

1831 Meyerbeer: *Robert le Diable*
(Alice)—B,i (16,9,11)
•1831 Bellini: *Norma*—A,i (9,5,4)
[one of the more frequently done in
this group]
1833 Bellini: *Beatrice di Tenda*—B,i
(16,10,15)
[most difficult role in this sub-
group so far]
1833 Donizetti: *Lucrezia Borgia*—A,ii
(12,3,12)
[most difficult role ever for this sub-
group]
•1834 Donizetti: *Gemma di Vergy*—
A,i (9,6,8)
[most difficult role so far in this
group]
1835 Halévy: *La Juive* (Rachel)—A,ii
(12,4,4)
Halévy: *La Juive* (Eudoxie)—B,i
(16,11,12)
1835 Donizetti: *Lucia di Lammermoor*—B,i (16,12,8)
[standard repertoire]
1835 Donizetti: *Maria Stuarda*—B,i
(16,13,16)
[most difficult role ever for this sub-
group]
Donizetti: *Maria Stuarda* (Elisabetta)—A,vii (3,3,3)
[most difficult role ever for this sub-
group and the last]
1836 Meyerbeer: *Les Huguenots*
(Valentine)—A,ii (12,5,3)
Meyerbeer: *Les Huguenots* (Marguerite)—B,i (16,14,10)
•1837 Donizetti: *Roberto Devereux*
(Elisabetta)—A,i (9,7,9)
[most difficult role ever in this top
group]
•1842 Verdi: *Nabucco* (Abigaille)—A,i
(9,8,5)
[one of the more frequently done in
this group; the last role of this
degree of difficulty]
1842 Wagner: *Rienzi* (Adriano)—A,vi
(1,1,1)
[new sub-group, unique to this
role]

1843 Wagner: *Der Fliegende Holländer* (Senta)—B,iii (8,2,7)
[most difficult role so far in this least difficult sub-group]

1843 Verdi: *I Lombardi* (Giselda)—A,iii (4,2,2)

1844 Verdi: *Ernani* (Elvira)—A,ii (12,6,8)

1845 Wagner: *Tannhäuser* (Dresden Venus)—B,iii (8,3,3)
[standard repertoire]

1846 Verdi: *Attila* (Odabella)—A,iii (4,3,4)
[most difficult role ever in this sub-group]

•1847 Verdi: *Macbeth* (Lady Macbeth)—A,i (9,9,6)
[last role ever in this top group; one of the more frequently done]

1849 Meyerbeer: *Le Prophète* (Fidès)—A,iv (2,1,2)
[introduces a new sub-group, the most difficult role in it]

1850 Verdi: *Stiffelio* (Lina)—A,ii (12,7,10)

1851 Verdi: *Rigoletto* (Gilda)—B,i (16,15,2)

1851 Gounod: *Sapho*—B,ii (8,1,3)
[a new sub-group]

1853 Verdi: *Il Trovatore* (Azucena)—A,iv (2,2,1)
[last of this sub-group; standard repertoire]

Verdi: *Il Trovatore* (Leonora)—A,ii (12,8,9)

Verdi: *Il Trovatore* (Leonora)—without the fourth-act cabaletta—A,ii (12,8,5.5)
[the most difficult role in the standard repertoire]

1853 Verdi: *La Traviata* (Violetta)—B,i (16,16,9)
[last role in this sub-group; standard repertoire]

1855 Verdi: *Les Vêpres siciliennes* (Hélène)—A,ii (12,9,5)

1857 Verdi: *Aroldo* (Mina)—A,ii (12,10,11)
[last role of this degree of difficulty]

1859 Verdi: *Un Ballo in maschera* (Amelia)—B,iii (8,4,8)
[most difficult role in this sub-group]

1859 Berlioz: *Les Troyens* (Cassandre/Didon)—B,ii (8,2,2)

1861 Wagner: *Tannhäuser* (Paris Venus)—B,ii (8,3,4)
[most difficult role in this sub-group so far; standard repertoire]

1864 Meyerbeer: *L'Africaine* (Selika)—B,ii (8,4,6)
[most difficult role yet in this sub-group]

1867 Verdi: *Don Carlos* (Eboli)—B,ii (8,5,8)
[most difficult role ever in this sub-group]

1870 Wagner: *Die Walküre* (Brünnhilde)—B,iii (8,5,2)
[the least difficult of the standard-repertoire roles covered here]

1871 Verdi: *Aida* (Amneris)—B,ii (8,6,7)
[standard repertoire]

1876 Ponchielli: *La Gioconda*—B,iii (8,6,4)

1876 Wagner: *Siegfried* (Brünnhilde)—A,iii (4,4,1)
[last role and the least difficult in this sub-group; standard repertoire]
Wagner: *Götterdämmerung* (Brünnhilde)—B,iii (8,7,5)
[standard repertoire]

1880 Offenbach: *Les Contes d'Hoffmann* ("maîtresses")—A,ii (12,11,7)
[last role of this degree of difficulty]

1882 Wagner: *Parsifal* (Kundry)—B,ii (8,7,5)
[standard repertoire]

1907 Dukas: *Ariane*—B,ii (8,8,1)
[last role and the least difficult in this sub-group]

1927 Prokofiev: *The Fiery Angel* (Renata)—B,iii (8,8,1)
[last role and the least difficult in this least difficult sub-group]

1937 Berg: *Lulu*—A,ii (12,12,6)
[a tradition ends]

Appendix B

Sub-groups of *Assoluta*

The following is intended as a guide to the reader. All sub-groups itemized below are presented in descending order of casting difficulty: **A,i** at the top, **A,ii** next, and so on. The same applies to the descending order of individual roles listed within each sub-group.

The defining *assoluta* roles are in list **A,i**. These are followed by roles listed in **A,ii–vii** that lack one or two attributes associated with **A,i** roles but still require a diva proficient in *assoluta* repertoire.

Roles listed in **B,i–iii** do not necessarily require an *assoluta* diva but have, as a group, some stylistic attributes in common with **A,i–vii** and therefore may benefit from *assoluta* casting.

The numbers in parentheses indicate chronological order within each group.

A,i

Defining *assoluta* roles with extremely intricate and fully heroic fioritura, widely varied tessitura, a range extending up to at least high B natural and down to at least low B natural with at least one semitone beyond that in either direction, and a frequently emotive and energetic orchestra accompanying a dynamic vocal line necessitating a completely heroic vocal tone; premiered 1797–1847 (9)

1837 Donizetti: *Roberto Devereux* (Elisabetta) (7)
1834 Donizetti: *Gemma di Vergy* (6)
1830 Donizetti: *Anna Bolena* (4)
1847 Verdi: *Macbeth* (Lady Macbeth) (9)
1842 Verdi: *Nabucco* (Abigaille) (8)
1831 Bellini: *Norma* (5)

1826 Weber: *Oberon* (Reiza) (3)
1797 Cherubini: *Médée* (1)
1817 Rossini: *Armida* (2)

A,ii

The same widely varied tessitura and generally weighty vocal tone, but not quite such heroic agility; premiered 1781–1937 (12; the variant *Il Trovatore* Leonora, though listed twice, counts as one role)

1833 Donizetti: *Lucrezia Borgia* (3)
1857 Verdi: *Aroldo* (Mina) (10)
1850 Verdi: *Stiffelio* (Lina) (7)
1853 Verdi: *Il Trovatore* (Leonora [complete]) (8)
1844 Verdi: *Ernani* (Elvira) (6)
1880 Offenbach: *Les Contes d'Hoffmann* ("maîtresses") (11)
1937 Berg: *Lulu* (12)
1853 Verdi: *Il Trovatore* (Leonora [without fourth-act cabaletta]) (8)
1855 Verdi: *Les Vêpres siciliennes* (Hélène) (9)
1835 Halévy: *La Juive* (Rachel) (4)
1836 Meyerbeer: *Les Huguenots* (Valentine) (5)
1791 Mozart: *La Clemenza di Tito* (Vitellia) (2)
1781 Mozart: *Idomeneo* (Elettra) (1)

A,iii

The same difficult and heroic agility and formidable range, but with a prevailingly high tessitura; premiered 1819–1876 (4)

1846 Verdi: *Attila* (Odabella) (3)
1819 Rossini: *Ermione* (1)
1843 Verdi: *Lombardi* (Giselda) (2)
1876 Wagner: *Siegfried* (Brünnhilde) (4)

A,iv

The same kind of agility and range, but with a prevailingly middle tessitura; premiered 1849–1853 (2)

1849 Meyerbeer: *Le Prophète* (Fidès) (1)
1853 Verdi: *Il Trovatore* (Azucena) (2)

A,v

Varied tessitura and the same agility, but lacking the lowest extension of the *assoluta* range; premiered 1805–1827 (2)

1827 Bellini: *Il Pirata* (Imogene) (2)
1805 Beethoven: *Leonore* (1)

A,vi

Varied tessitura and the same agility, but lacking the highest extension of the *assoluta* range; premiered 1842 (1)

1842 Wagner: *Rienzi* (Adriano) (1)

A,vii

Varied tessitura and agility, but lacking the fullest extension at both extremes; premiered 1807–1835 (3)

1835 Donizetti: *Maria Stuarda* (Elisabetta) (3)
1814 Beethoven: *Fidelio* (2)
1807 Spontini: *La Vestale* (Julia) (1)

B,i

Varied tessitura; agility; not as weighty vocal tone; 1782–1853 (16)

1835 Donizetti: *Maria Stuarda* (13)
1833 Bellini: *Beatrice di Tenda* (10)
1815 Rossini: *Elisabetta, Regina d'Inghilterra* (7)
1823 Rossini: *Semiramide* (8)
1835 Halévy: *La Juive* (Eudoxie) (11)
1831 Meyerbeer: *Robert le Diable* (Alice) (9)
1836 Meyerbeer: *Les Huguenots* (Marguerite) (14)
1853 Verdi: *La Traviata* (Violetta) (16)
1835 Donizetti: *Lucia di Lammermoor* (12)
1808 Haydn: *L'Anima del filosofo* (Genio) (6)
1790 Mozart: *Così fan tutte* (Fiordiligi) (3)
1782 Mozart: *Die Entführung aus dem Serail* (Konstanze) (1)
1791 Mozart: *Die Zauberflöte* (Königen) (4)
1808 Haydn: *L'Anima del filosofo* (Euridice) (5)
1851 Verdi: *Rigoletto* (Gilda) (15)
1787 Mozart: *Don Giovanni* (Donna Elvira) (2)

B,ii

Moderately intricate, fully heroic style; varied tessitura; 1851–1907 (8)

1867 Verdi: *Don Carlos* (Eboli) (5)
1871 Verdi: *Aida* (Amneris) (6)
1864 Meyerbeer: *L'Africaine* (Selika) (4)

1882 Wagner: *Parsifal* (Kundry) (7)
1861 Wagner: *Tannhäuser* (Paris Venus) (3)
1851 Gounod: *Sapho* (1)
1859 Berlioz: *Les Troyens* (Cassandre/Didon) (2)
1907 Dukas: *Ariane et Barbe-Bleue* (8)

B,iii

Moderately intricate, fully heroic style; unvaried tessitura; 1767–1927 (8)

1859 Verdi: *Un Ballo in maschera* (Amelia) (4)
1843 Wagner: *Der Fliegende Holländer* (Senta) (2)
1767 Gluck: *Alceste* (1)
1876 Wagner: *Götterdämmerung* (Brünnhilde) (6)
1876 Ponchielli: *La Gioconda* (7)
1845 Wagner: *Tannhäuser* (Dresden Venus) (3)
1870 Wagner: *Die Walküre* (Brünnhilde) (5)
1927 Prokofiev: *The Fiery Angel* (Renata) (8)

Chapter Notes

Chapter 1

1. Henry Pleasants, *The Great Singers: From the Dawn of Opera to Our Own Time* (New York, 1966), p. 51.

2. Johann Joachim Quantz, Frederick the Great's flute master, describing "Farinello" [*sic*] and his extensive instrument, noted that in "later years it was extended several tones below without the loss of the high notes. The result was that in many operas there would usually be an adagio for him in the contralto range, and another in the soprano." *Ibid.*, p. 73.

3. In Lord Mount-Edgcumbe's *Musical Reminiscences*, Pacchierotti's voice is termed "an extensive soprano," yet the British music historian Charles Burney writes of his having sung tenor arias in their original pitch! Henry Pleasants concludes that Pacchierotti's range must have been at least three octaves. *Ibid.*, p. 85.

Chapter 2

4. *Enciclopedia dello Spettacolo*, vol. 8, cols. 1193–94.

5. *Ibid*, vol.7, cols. 1757–59. *New Grove's Dictionary of Music and Musicians*, vol. 14, pp. 286–87.

6. *Enciclopedia dello Spettacolo*, vol. 3, cols. 1053–55.

Chapter 3

7. George Jellinek, *Callas: Portrait of a Prima Donna* (New York, 1960), p. 104.

8. In Edward Bellasis, *Cherubini: Memorials Illustrative of His Life and Work* (London, 1912), p. 67.

9. Lanfranco Rasponi, *The Last Prima Donnas* (New York, 1982), p. 194.

10. *Enciclopedia della Musica* (1960), vol. 4, p. 186.

11. Arthur Pougin, *Cherubini: His Life, His Works, and the Part Played by Him in Art*, trnsltd. in *Musical World* (28 Jan. 1882–15 Mar. 1884), 1882, p. 621.

12. In Harold Lawrence, Introductory Notes and Synopsis for Mercury Living Presence LP recording OL-3-104 (Milan, 1957), pp. 4–5.

13. Wallace Brockway and Herbert Weinstock, *The World of Opera: The Story of Its Development and the Lore of Its Performance* (Random House, 1941, rev. 1966), p. 492.

14. Edward Bellasis, *Cherubini: Memorials Illustrative of his Life and Work* (London, 1912), p. 70.

15. Henry F. Chorley, *Thirty Years' Musical Recollections*, Edited with an Introduction by Ernest Newman (New York, 1926), p. 301.

16. Olivia Stapp in taped interview with the author.

17. Alan Blyth, ed., *Opera on Record* (London, 1979), Andrew Porter, "Norma," p. 155.

18. John Ardoin, *The Callas Legacy* (New York, 1991), p. 67.

Chapter 4

19. Francis Toye, *Rossini: A Study in Tragi-Comedy* (New York, 1963), p. 77.

20. *New Grove's Dictionary of Music and Musicians*, vol. 4, p. 524. *La Musica Dizionario*, p. 420. *Enciclopedia dello spettacolo*, vol. 3, cols. 1053–55.

21. Frederica von Stade in taped interview with the author. With disarming candor, she freely named one role she has sung as too uncomfortably soprano: Iphise in Rameau's *Dardanus*.

22. *New Grove's Dictionary of Music and Musicians*, vol. 4, p. 524.

Chapter 5

23. Henry Pleasants, *The Great Singers: From the Dawn of Opera to Our Own Time* (New York, 1966), p. 113.

24. Lanfranco Rasponi, *The Last Prima Donnas* (New York, 1982), p. 113

25. Soprano Martina Arroyo in taped interview with the author.

Chapter 6

26. Oscar Thompson, *International Cyclopedia of Music and Musicians* (London, 1975), p. 1635. *New Grove's Dictionary of Music and Musicians* (London, 1980), vol. 14, p. 301. Wallace Brockway and Herbert Weinstock, *The World of Opera: The Story of Its Development and the Lore of Its Performance* (Random House, 1941, rev. 1966), pp. 454, 501, 591.

27. Leider's ambitious debut session starts with Elisabeth's "Dich, teure Halle" (Wagner's *Tannhäuser*). This is followed by Leonore's "Abscheulicher" (Beethoven's *Fidelio*), Isolde's "Mild und leise" (Wagner's *Tristan und Isolde*), Aida's "O Vaterland" (Verdi's *Aida*), and the Countess's "Heil'ge Quelle" and "Nur zu flüchtig" (Mozart's *Nozze di Figaro*). She then ends with Rezia's "Ozean! Du Ungeheuer!" (Weber's *Oberon*) and Tosca's "Nur der Schönheit" (Puccini's *Tosca*).

Chapter 7

28. Henry Pleasants, *The Great Singers: From the Dawn of Opera to Our Own Time* (New York, 1966), p. 144 [italics added].

29. William Ashbrook, *Donizetti and His Operas* (Cambridge, 1982), p. 624.

30. *La Musica: Dizionario* (Turin, 1968), vol. 2, p. 577. *New Grove's Dictionary of Music and Musicians* (London, 1980), vol. 14, pp. 286–87. *Enciclopedia della Musica* (Milan, 1963), vol. 3, p. 390 (entry by Giacomo Lauri-Volpi). *Enciclopedia della Musica* (Milan, 1972), vol. 4, pp. 459–60. *Enciclopedia dello Spettacolo* (Rome, 1954), vol. 7, cols. 1757–59. Oscar Thompson, *International Cyclopedia of Music and Musicians* (London, 1975), p. 1634.

31. *Enciclopedia della Musica* (Milan, 1963), vol. 3, p. 390

32. *Enciclopedia dello Spettacolo* (Rome, 1954), vol. 7, cols. 1757–59.

33. Stendhal, *Life of Rossini* (Criterion Books, 1957)

Chapter 8

34. Geoffrey Skelton, trnsltd, *Cosima Wagner's Diaries* (New York, 1980), p. 35 (entry of March 7, 1878).

35. *La Musica: Dizionario* (Turin, 1968), vol. 1, p. 854. *New Grove's Dictionary of Music and Musicians* (London, 1980), vol. 7, pp. 737–38. *Enciclopedia della Musica* (Milan, 1963), vol. 2, p. 364 (entry by Giacomo Lauri-Volpi). *Enciclopedia della Musica* (Milan, 1972), vol. 3, pp. 213–14. *Enciclopedia dello Spettacolo* (Rome, 1954), vol. 5, cols. 1787–90 (entry by Rodolfo Celletti). Oscar Thompson, *International Cyclopedia of Music and Musicians* (London, 1975), p. 875.

36. Alan Blyth, ed., *Opera on Record* (London, 1979), p. 164 (Andrew Porter, "Norma").

37. Henry Pleasants, *The Great Singers: From the Dawn of Opera to Our Own Time* (New York, 1966), p. 155.

38. *Ibid.*, pp. 155–56.

39. Hector Berlioz, *Memoirs*, trnsltd. Ernest Newman (New York, 1932), pp. 315–17.

40. Alan Blyth, ed., *Opera on Record* (London, 1979), p. 160 (Andrew Porter, "Norma").

41. John Ardoin, *The Callas Legacy* (London, 1977), pp. 78–9.

42. *Ibid.*, pp. 203–4.

43. John B. Steane, *Voices: Singers & Critics* (London, 1992), p. 156.

44. In this GOP pressing, it's startling to hear Callas's "Ei!" in place of Cerquetti's. Was there damage to the original tape?

45. John B. Steane, *The Grand Tradition: Seventy Years of Singing on Record* (London, 1974), p. 550.

46. Alan Blyth, ed., *Opera on Record* (London, 1979), Andrew Porter, "Norma," p. 169.

47. Paul Gruber, ed., *The Metropolitan Opera Guide to Recorded Opera* (New York, 1993), Roland Graeme, "Vincenzo Bellini: *Norma* (1831)," p. 24.

Chapter 9

48. Guillaume Cottrau, *Lettres d'un Mélomane* (Naples, 1885), p. 16.

49. William Ashbrook, *Donizetti and His Operas* (Cambridge, 1982), p. 598.

50. Guillaume Cottrau, *Lettres d'un Mélomane* (Naples, 1885), p. 16.

51. *La Musica: Dizionario* (Turin, 1968), vol. 2, pp. 878–9. *New Grove's Dictionary of Music and Musicians* (London, 1980), vol. 16, p. 181–2. *Enciclopedia della Musica* (Milan, 1963), vol. 4, p. 51. *Enciclopedia della Musica* (Milan, 1972), vol. 5, p. 262. *Enciclopedia dello Spettacolo* (Rome, 1954), vol. 8, cols. 1193–4. Oscar Thompson, *International Cyclopedia of Music and Musicians* (London, 1975), p. 184.

52. William Ashbrook, *Donizetti and His Operas* (Cambridge, 1982), p. 627.

53. *Ibid.*, p. 325.

54. *Ibid.*, p. 85.

55. *La Musica: Dizionario* (Turin, 1968), vol. 2, p. 196. *New Grove's Dictionary of Music and Musicians* (London, 1980), vol. 11, p. 577. *Enciclopedia della Musica* (Milan, 1963), vol. 3, p. 80. *Enciclopedia della Musica* (Milan, 1972), vol. 4, pp. 99–100. *Enciclopedia dello Spettacolo* (Rome, 1954), vol. 7, cols. 8–12. Oscar Thompson, *International Cyclopedia of Music and Musicians* (London, 1975), pp. 1314–15.

56. Cited in booklet for *Marilyn Horne: Souvenir of a Golden Era* (London, 1966), p. 5, Christopher Raeburn, "Maria Felicita Malibran."

57. Olivia Stapp in a taped interview with the author.

Chapter 10

58. William Ashbrook, *Donizetti and His Operas* (Cambridge, 1892), p. 122.

59. *Ibid.*, p. 128, 122.

60. *Ibid.*, p. 126.

61. *Ibid.*

62. That guilt was mixed with grief has been strongly inferred by some recent scholarship: it now seems likely that Virginia Donizetti's death could have been brought on by exposure to the first stages of the syphilis that eventually destroyed her husband.

63. *La Musica: Dizionario* (Turin, 1968), vol. 2, p. 1414. *New Grove's Dictionary of Music and Musicians* (London, 1980), vol. 19, p. 694–5. *Enciclopedia della Musica* (Milan, 1963), vol. 4, p. 495. *Enciclopedia della Musica* (Milan, 1972), vol. 6, p. 316. *Enciclopedia dello Spettacolo* (Rome, 1954), vol. 9, cols. 1632–3. Oscar Thompson, *International Cyclopedia of Music and Musicians* (London, 1975), p. 2363.

64. *La Musica: Dizionario* (Turin, 1968), vol. 1, p. 762. *Enciclopedia della Musica* (Milan, 1963), vol. 2, p. 286–7. *Enciclopedia della Musica* (Milan, 1972), vol. 3, p. 100.

65. *New Grove's Dictionary of Music and Musicians* (London, 1980), vol. 18, p. 519. *Enciclopedia della Musica* (Milan, 1963), vol. 4, p. 342. *Enciclopedia della Musica* (Milan, 1972), vol. 6, p. 119. *Enciclopedia dello Spettacolo* (Rome, 1954), vol. 9, cols. 624–5.

66. Henry F. Chorley, *Thirty Years' Musical Recollections*, Edited with an Introduction by Ernest Newman (New York, 1926), p. 78.

67. *Ibid.*

68. *La Musica: Dizionario* (Turin, 1968), vol. 1, p. 854. *New Grove's Dictionary of Music and Musicians* (London, 1980), vol. 7, pp. 737–8. *Enciclopedia della*

Musica (Milan, 1963), vol. 2, p. 364 (entry by Giacomo Lauri-Volpi). *Enciclopedia della Musica* (Milan, 1972), vol. 3, pp. 213–4. *Enciclopedia dello Spettacolo* (Rome, 1954), vol. 5, cols. 1787–90. Oscar Thompson, *International Cyclopedia of Music and Musicians* (London, 1975), p. 875.

Chapter 12

69. George Jellinek, *Callas: Portrait of a Prima Donna* (New York, 1960), p. 320.

70. Henry Wisneski, *Maria Callas: The Art Behind the Legend* (New York, 1975), p. 61.

71. Taped interview with the author.

72. *La Musica: Dizionario* (Turin, 1968), vol. 2, p. 1233. *New Grove's Dictionary of Music and Musicians* (London, 1980), vol. 18, pp. 268–9. *Enciclopedia della Musica* (Milan, 1963), vol. 4, p. 312. *Enciclopedia dello Spettacolo* (Rome, 1954), vol. 9, cols. 488–9. Oscar Thompson, *International Cyclopedia of Music and Musicians* (London, 1975), p. 2195.

73. *La Musica: Dizionario* (Turin, 1968), vol. 1, p. 498. *Enciclopedia della Musica* (Milan, 1963), vol. 2, p. 28. *Enciclopedia della Musica* (Milan, 1972), vol. 2, p. 260. *Enciclopedia dello Spettacolo* (Rome, 1954), vol. 4, cols. 338–40.

Chapter 13

74. Taped interview with the author.

75. Birgit Nilsson, *My Memoirs in Pictures* (New York, 1981), p. 99.

76. John Ardoin, *The Callas Legacy* (London, 1977), p. 61.

77. *Wagner Writes from Paris*, transl. Robert Jacobs, Geoffrey Skelton (London, 1973), p. 113.

78. Rosa Ponselle & James Drake, *Ponselle: A Singer's Life* (New York, 1982), p. 83.

79. *La Musica: Dizionario* (Turin, 1968), vol. 2, p. 133. *Enciclopedia dello Spettacolo* (Rome, 1954), vol. 6, cols. 1593–4. Oscar Thompson, *International Cyclopedia of Music and Musicians* (London, 1975), p. 1273.

80. *La Musica: Dizionario* (Turin, 1968), vol. 1, p. 136. *New Grove's Dictionary of Music and Musicians* (London, 1980), vol. 2, p. 140. *Enciclopedia della Musica* (Milan, 1963), vol. 1, p. 184. *Enciclopedia della Musica* (Milan, 1972), vol. 1, p. 236. *Enciclopedia dello Spettacolo* (Rome, 1954), vol. 1, cols. 1482–3.

81. Henry W. Simon, "...Something Rich and Strange," Notes for RCA recording LM/LSC-6147 (New York, 1959), p. 6.

82. *Ibid.*

83. William Ashbrook, *Donizetti and His Operas* (Cambridge, 1982), p. 169.

84. Christa Ludwig in correspondence with the author.

Chapter 14

85. Lauren Flanigan in conversation with the author.

Chapter 15

86. In Edward Bellasis, *Cherubini: Memorials Illustrative of his Life and Work* (London, 1912), p. 70.

87. *New Grove's Dictionary of Music and Musicians* (London, 1980), vol. 3, pp. 199–200. *Enciclopedia dello Spettacolo* (Rome, 1954), vol. 2, cols. 1005–6. Oscar Thompson, *International Cyclopedia of Music and Musicians* (London, 1975), p. 283.

88. Wallace Brockway and Herbert Weinstock, *The World of Opera: The Story of Its Development and the Lore of Its Performance* (Random House, 1941, rev. 1966), *passim*. Michael Scott, *The Record of Singing* (Boston, 1977*)*, vol. 1, pp. 91–2. Oscar Thompson, *International Cyclopedia of Music and Musicians* (London, 1975), pp. 1268–9. *Enciclopedia della musica* (1960), vol. 3, p. 25. *La Musica Dizionario*, pp. 121–2.

89. Some may insist that Violetta in *La Traviata* is at least as difficult to cast. Yet Violetta is a **B,i** role, since her declamatory phrases don't require quite so much heft as Leonora's. Her range does not extend as low either. The heroine's partner is a factor here as well. Clearly, the two should be matched. It is very evident that Alfredo does not require the vocal weight of Manrico, making Violetta's confrontations with him less heroic than the equivalent sequences for Leonora.

90. Michael Scott, *The Record of Singing* (Boston, 1977*)*, vol. 1, pp. 88–91. Wallace Brockway and Herbert Weinstock, *The World of Opera: The Story of Its Development and the Lore of Its Performance* (Random House, 1941, rev. 1966), *passim*. Henry Pleasants, *The Great Singers: From the Dawn of Opera to Our Own Time* (New York, 1966), pp. 301–8.

91. Michael Scott, *The Record of Singing* (Boston, 1977), vol. 1, pp. 21–4.

Bibliography

Ardoin, John. *The Callas Legacy.* London, 1977, rev. New York, 1991.

Ashbrook, William. *Donizetti and His Operas.* Cambridge, 1982.

Bellasis, Edward. *Cherubini: Memorials Illustrative of His Life and Work.* London, 1912.

Berlioz, Hector. *Memoirs,* transl. Ernest Newman. New York, 1932.

Blyth, Alan. ed., *Opera on Record.* London 1979.

Brockway, Wallace, and Herbert Weinstock. *The World of Opera: The Story of Its Development and the Lore of Its Performance.* Random House, 1941, rev. 1966.

Chorley, Henry F. *Thirty Years' Musical Recollections,* Edited with an Introduction by Ernest Newman. New York, 1926.

Cosima Wagner's Diaries, transl. Geoffrey Skelton. New York, 1980, 2 vols.

Cottrau, Guillaume. *Lettres d'un Mélomane.* Naples, 1885.

Enciclopedia della Musica. Milan, 1963.

Enciclopedia della Musica. Milan, 1972.

Enciclopedia dello Spettacolo. Rome, 1954.

Gruber, Paul., ed. *The Metropolitan Opera Guide to Recorded Opera.* New York, 1993.

Booklet for *Marilyn Horne: Souvenir of a Golden Era.* London, 1966.

Jellinek, George. *Callas: Portrait of a Prima Donna.* New York, 1960.

La Musica: Dizionario. Turin, 1968.

Lawrence, Harold. Introductory Notes and Synopsis for Mercury Living Presence LP recording of Cherubini's *Medea,* OL-3-104. Milan, 1957.

New Grove's Dictionary of Music and Musicians. London, 1980.

Nilsson, Birgit. *My Memoirs in Pictures.* New York, 1981.

Pleasants, Henry. *The Great Singers: From the Dawn of Opera to Our Own Time.* New York, 1966.

Ponselle, Rosa, and James Drake. *Ponselle: A Singer's Life.* New York, 1982.

Pougin, Arthur. *Cherubini: His Life, His Works, and the Part Played by Him in Art,* transl. in *Musical World.* (28 Jan. 1882–15 Mar. 1884), 1882.

Rasponi, Lanfranco. *The Last Prima Donnas.* New York, 1982.

Robbins Landon, H. C. *Haydn: Chronicle and Works.* Vol. III: *Haydn in England.*
   London, 1976.
Scott, Michael. *The Record of Singing.* Boston, 1977, vol. 1.
Simon, Henry W. "…Something Rich and Strange." Notes for RCA recording of
   Verdi's *Macbeth*, LM/LSC-6147. New York, 1959.
Stendhal. *Life of Rossini.* Criterion Books, 1957.
Thompson, Oscar. *International Cyclopedia of Music and Musicians.* London, 1975.
Toye, Francis. *Rossini: A Study in Tragi-Comedy.* New York, 1963.
Steane, John B. *The Grand Tradition: Seventy Years of Singing on Record.* London,
   1974.
_____. *Voices: Singers and Critics.* London, 1992.
Wagner Writes from Paris, transl. Robert Jacobs, Geoffrey Skelton. London, 1973.
Wendschuh, Ludwig. *Über Joseph Haydn's Opern.* Coblenz, 1896.
Wisneski, Henry. *Maria Callas: The Art Behind the Legend.* New York, 1975.

Index